The Cambridge Companion to Canadian Literature

This book offers a comprehensive and lively introduction to major writers, genres, and topics in Canadian literature. Addressing traditional assumptions and current issues, contributors pay attention to the social, political, and economic developments that have informed literary events. Broad surveys of fiction, drama, and poetry are complemented by chapters on Aboriginal writing, autobiography, literary criticism, writing by women, and the emergence of urban writing in a country historically defined by its regions. Also discussed are genres that have a special place in Canadian literature, such as nature-writing, exploration- and travel-writing, and short fiction. Although the emphasis is on literature in English, a substantial chapter on francophone writing is included.

Eva-Marie Kröller is Professor at the Department of English, University of British Columbia, Vancouver. Her books include *Canadian Travellers in Europe* (1987), *George Bowering: Bright Circles of Colour* (1992), the only book on Canada's first poet laureate currently available, and *Pacific Encounters: The Production of Self and Other* (coedited, 1997).

D0209840

THE CAMBRIDGE
COMPANION TO
CANADIAN
LITERATURE

EDITED BY
EVA-MARIE KRÖLLER
University of British Columbia, Vancouver

CAMBRIDGE
UNIVERSITY PRESS

PUBLISHED BY THE PRESS SYNDICATE OF THE UNIVERSITY OF CAMBRIDGE
The Pitt Building, Trumpington Street, Cambridge, United Kingdom

CAMBRIDGE UNIVERSITY PRESS
The Edinburgh Building, Cambridge CB2 2RU, UK
40 West 20th Street, New York NY 10011-4211, USA
477 Williamstown Road, Port Melbourne, VIC 3207, Australia
Ruiz de Alarcón 13, 28014 Madrid, Spain
Dock House, The Waterfront, Cape Town 8001, South Africa

http://www.cambridge.org

First published 2004

Printed in the United Kingdom at the University Press, Cambridge

Typeface Sabon 10/13 pt   *System* LATEX 2ε   [TB]

A catalogue record for this book is available from the British Library

Library of Congress Cataloguing in Publication data

The Cambridge Companion to Canadian literature / edited by Eva-Marie Kröller.
p. cm. – (Cambridge companions to literature)
Includes bibliographical references and index.
ISBN 0 521 81441 3 – ISBN 0 521 89131 0 (pbk.)
1. Canadian literature – History and criticism – Handbooks, manuals, etc. I. Kröller,
Eva-Marie. II. Series.
PR9184.3.C34 2003
810.9′971–dc21   2003055128

ISBN 0 521 81441 3 hardback
ISBN 0 521 89131 0 paperback

CONTENTS

PLATES

MAPS

NOTES ON CONTRIBUTORS

E. D. BLODGETT is University Professor Emeritus of Comparative Literature at the University of Alberta. He has published widely on comparative
Canadian literature. He received the 1996 Governor-General's Award and
the 1997 Canadian Authors' Association Award for *Apostrophes*, a volume
of poetry. A renga with Jacques Brault entitled *Transfiguration* (1998) also
received the Governor-General's Award. Recent publications include *Five-
Part Invention: A History of Literary History in Canada* (2003).

MARTA DVORAK is a professor of Canadian and Commonwealth literatures
at the Sorbonne Nouvelle. She is the author of *Ernest Buckler: Rediscovery
and Reassessment* (2001) and has edited numerous books on Canadian writing and culture; three of her articles have received international awards. A
book on Nancy Huston is forthcoming. She is currently an associate editor
of the *International Journal of Canadian Studie*s.

SUSANNA EGAN and GABRIELE HELMS teach in the Department of
English at the University of British Columbia. Egan and Helms have collaborated as editors on the special issue of *biography*, "Autobiography and
Changing Identities" (2001) and on the special issue of *Canadian Literature*, "Auto/biography" (2002). Egan's books include *Mirror Talk: Genres
of Crisis in Contemporary Autobiography* (1999) and Helms is the author
of *Challenging Canada: Dialogism and Narrative Techniques in Canadian
Novels* (2003).

JANICE FIAMENGO, after spending a number of years at the University
of Saskatchewan, teaches in the Department of English at the University of
Ottawa. She has broad interests in Canadian literature and feminist the-
ory, with publications on Margaret Atwood, Sara Jeannette Duncan,
Linda Svendsen, and Nellie McClung. Recently published work on L. M.
Montgomery examines the politics of the regional landscape. Fiamengo is

completing a book on early Canadian women's strategies of rhetoric and self-presentation.

CORAL ANN HOWELLS is a professor of English and Canadian Literature at the University of Reading. She has been associate editor of the *International Journal of Canadian Studies*. Her publications include *Private and Fictional Worlds: Canadian Women Novelists of the 1970s and 80s* (1987), *Margaret Atwood* (1996, Margaret Atwood Society Best Book Award), *Alice Munro* (1998), and *Contemporary Canadian Women's Fiction: Refiguring Identities* (2003).

CHRISTOPH IRMSCHER teaches in the Department of English at the University of Maryland Baltimore County. He is the author of *The Poetics of Natural History* (1999; 1999 Language and Literature Award of the Association of American Publishers, Scholarly Division; 2000 American Studies Network Prize) and the editor of *John James Audobon, Writings and Drawings* (1999). His work on early Canadian nature-writing includes an essay on Philip Henry Gosse's *The Canadian Naturalist*.

RIC KNOWLES teaches drama at the University of Guelph. He is the editor of *Modern Drama*, an editor of the *Canadian Theatre Review*, and author of *The Theatre of Form and the Production of Meaning: Contemporary Canadian Dramaturgy* (1999, 2001 Ann Saddlemyer Prize for Outstanding Book on Canadian Drama and Theatre).

EVA-MARIE KRÖLLER teaches in the Department of English and the Programme in Comparative Literature at the University of British Columbia. She was the editor of *Canadian Literature* from 1995 to 2003. Her publications include *Canadian Travellers in Europe, 1851–1900* (1987), *George Bowering: Bright Circles of Colour* (1992), and the coedited *Pacific Encounters: The Production of Self and Other* (1997).

MAGDALENE REDEKOP teaches at Victoria College, University of Toronto. She is the author of *Mothers and Other Clowns: The Stories of Alice Munro* (1992) and is currently completing a book on Mennonite writing in Canada, as well as beginning a book on comedy in Canadian literature.

DAVID STAINES is Professor of English at the University of Ottawa. He is the editor of the *Journal of Canadian Poetry* and of the New Canadian Library. His books include *The Forty-Ninth and Other Parallels: Contemporary Canadian Perspectives* (1986), *Beyond the Provinces: Literary Canada at Century's End* (1995), *Northrop Frye on Canada* (with Jean O'Grady, 2003) and *Marshall McLuhan: Understanding Me* (with Stephanie

McLuhan, 2003). In 1998, he received the Lorne Pierce Medal for distinguished service to Canadian literature from the Royal Society of Canada.

ROBERT THACKER is Professor of Canadian Studies and English at St. Lawrence University. He is the author of *The Great Prairie Fact and Literary Imagination* (1989) and was the Director of Canadian Studies at St. Lawrence as well as the editor of the *American Review of Canadian Studies*. He edited *The Rest of the Story: Critical Essays on Alice Munro* (1999) and is working on a critical biography of Munro.

PENNY VAN TOORN is a lecturer in Australian Literature and Australian Studies at the University of Sydney. She is the author of *Rudy Wiebe and the Historicity of the Word* (1995), and coeditor of *Speaking Positions: Aboriginality, Gender and Ethnicity in Australian Cultural Studies* (1995) and *Stories without End* (2002). She has published extensively on postcolonial literatures and theory, focusing particularly on writings by and about Indigenous peoples of Australia and Canada.

ACKNOWLEDGMENTS

My thanks to the contributors to this volume for their professionalism and collegiality, to Donna Chin, Jennifer Yong, and Russell Aquino for expert technical assistance and research, to Susan Fisher, Alain-Michel Rocheleau, Allan Smith, Kevin McNeilly, and Glenn Deer for editorial and bibliographical advice, to Caroline Howlett for meticulous copy-editing, and to Sarah Stanton at Cambridge University Press for her efficiency and wisdom.

Margaret Atwood, "Progressive Insanities of a Pioneer," reprinted by permission of the author. George Bowering, "For WCW," reprinted by permission of the author. Robert Kroetsch, "Stone Hammer Poem," reprinted by permission of the author. Al Purdy, "The Country North of Belleville," reprinted by permission of Harbour Publishing.

NOTE ON POETRY

Quotations in the text from the following poems are drawn from the sources indicated:

Atwood, Margaret. "A Bus along St Clair: December." Atwood, *The Journals of Susanna Moodie*. Toronto: Oxford University Press, 1970. pp. 60–1.
—. "Progressive Insanities of a Pioneer." Atwood, *The Animals in That Country*. Toronto: Oxford University Press, 1968. pp. 36–9.
Birney, Earle. "Bushed" (1951). *The Collected Poems*. Vol. I. Toronto: McClelland and Stewart, 1975. p. 160.
Bowering, George. "For WCW" (1965). *Touch: Selected Poems 1960–1970*. Toronto/Montreal: McClelland and Stewart, 1971. pp. 24–7.
Klein, A. M. "Soirée of Velvel Kleinburger" (1928/31). *Complete Poems. Part I: Original Poems, 1926–1934*. Ed. Zailig Pollock. Toronto: University of Toronto Press, 1990. pp. 183–6.
Kroetsch, Robert. "Seed Catalogue." *Completed Field Notes: The Long Poems of Robert Kroetsch*. Toronto: McClelland and Stewart, 1989. pp. 32–51.
—. "Stone Hammer Poem." *The Stone Hammer Poems 1960–1975*. Lantzville, British Columbia: Oolichan Books, 1975. p. 54.
Page, P. K. "As Ten, as Twenty." *The Hidden Room: Collected Poems*. Vol. II. Erin: Porcupine's Quill, 1997. p. 23.
Pratt, E. J. "The Titanic" (1935). *Complete Poems. Part 1*. Ed. Sandra Djwa and R. G. Moyles. Toronto: University of Toronto Press, 1989. pp. 302–38.
Purdy, Al. "The Country North of Belleville" (1965). *Beyond Remembering: The Collected Poems of Al Purdy*. Selected and edited by Al Purdy and Sam Solecki. Madeira Park: Harbour Publishing, 2000. pp. 79–81.
Roberts, Charles G. D. "The Potato Harvest" (1886). *The Collected Poems of Sir Charles G. D. Roberts*. Ed. Desmond Pacey. Wolfville: Wombat Press, 1985. p. 91.

Scott, F. R. "The Canadian Authors Meet" (1936). *The Collected Poems of F. R. Scott*. Toronto: McClelland and Stewart, 1981. p. 248.

Smith, A. J. M. "To a Young Poet" (1934), "The Lonely Land" (1936). Smith, *Poems New and Collected*. Toronto: Oxford University Press, 1967. pp. 21, 50.

CHRONOLOGY

11,000 BC	Earliest records of human habitation (Bluefish Cave people)
985/986	First European sighting of Baffin Island ("Helluland"), Labrador ("Markland"), and the Gulf of St. Lawrence ("Vinland"), as recounted in Bjarno Harjulfsen's *Graenlendinga Saga*
1390–1450	Iroquois Confederacy
1497	John Cabot sails to Newfoundland
1534	Jacques Cartier sails to the Gulf of St. Lawrence
1556	First map of New France, by Giacomo Gastaldi, published in Giovanni Battista Ramusio's *Navigationi et viaggi*, an account of Cartier's 1534 voyage
1576, 1577, 1578	Martin Frobisher's Arctic expeditions
1605	Founding of Port Royal
1606	Marc Lescarbot's *Le théâtre de Neptune* performed in Port Royal harbor
1608	Quebec founded by Samuel de Champlain
1610	Henry Hudson sails to Hudson Bay; *Jesuit Relations* (publ. 1632–73) begin with Pierre Biard's letters from Acadia
1613	*Les voyages du Sieur de Champlain Xaintongeois*
1624	First written treaty (Algonkian-French-Mohawk Peace)
1639	Marie de l'Incarnation sails for Quebec
1659	Pierre-Esprit Radisson and Médard Chouart de Groseilliers travel to Lake Superior and Michigan
1664	François du Creux, in *Historiae canadensis, seu Nova-Franciae*, describes an "immensity of woods and prairies"
1670	Hudson's Bay Company begins operation

1697	Louis Hennepin's *Nouvelle découverte d'un très grand pays* features the first published illustration of Niagara Falls
1744	Pierre-François Xavier de Charlevoix, *Histoire et description générale de Nouvelle France*
1748	Marie-Élisabeth Bégon (1696–1755) writes letters to her son-in-law, published as *Lettres au cher fils* (ed. Nicole Deschamps) in 1972.
1751	First printing press in Nova Scotia
1753	Peter Kalm's *Travels* published in Sweden (English version: 1770)
1755	Deportation of the Acadians
1759	Battle on the Plains of Abraham
1764	First printing press in Quebec; *La Gazette de Québec* begins publication
1769	Frances Brooke, *The History of Emily Montague*
1774	Quebec Act
1778	James Cook in Nootka Sound
1783	An estimated 40,000 Loyalists emigrate from United States to Maritimes and Canada
1789	Alexander Mackenzie travels to Beaufort Sea (1793 expedition from Canada to Pacific, arriving at the Bella Coola River)
1812	War of 1812
1819–22	First Franklin overland expedition
1821	Thomas McCulloch, *Letters of Mephibosheth Stepsure*
1824	Completion of Lachine Canal; Julia Hart, *St. Ursula's Convent; or, The Nun of Canada*
1825	Oliver Goldsmith, *The Rising Village*
1829	Shanawdithit (known as Nancy or Nance April), the last known Beothuk, dies
1832	John Richardson, *Wacousta; or, The Prophecy*
1833	First Canadian steamship, the *Royal William*, crosses the Atlantic
1836	Catharine Parr Traill, *The Backwoods of Canada*; Thomas Chandler Haliburton, *The Clockmaker, or The Sayings and Doings of Samuel Slick of Slickville*
1837	Rebellion, Upper Canada, Lower Canada; Aubert de Gaspé fils, *L'influence d'un livre*
1838	*Literary Garland* (1838–51); Anna Jameson, *Winter Studies and Summer Rambles in Canada*

1839	Lord Durham's Report
1841	Act of Union (Upper and Lower Canada)
1844	Institut canadien founded; Toronto *Globe* established
1845–8	François-Xavier Garneau, *Histoire du Canada depuis sa découverte jusqu'à nos jours*
1845	Last sighting, in July, of Sir John Franklin's second overland expedition in Baffin Bay; Franklin's disappearance triggers some forty-two expeditions into the Arctic North between 1847 and 1879
1846	Patrice Lacombe, *La terre paternelle*
1847	Henry Wadsworth Longfellow, *Evangeline, a Tale of Acadie*
1852	Susanna Moodie, *Roughing It in the Bush*
1853	Moodie, *Life in the Clearings*
1854	Seigneurial system abolished; Reciprocity Treaty between Canada and the United States (the first international free trade agreement)
1856	Charles Sangster, *The St. Lawrence and the Saguenay*
1857	Ottawa named capital of Canada; Palliser and Hind-Dawson expeditions to Northwest
1863	Aubert de Gaspé père, *Les anciens Canadiens* (trans. by Ch. G. D. Roberts as *The Canadians of Old*, 1890); Goldwin Smith, *The Empire*
1864	Rosanna Leprohon, *Antoinette de Mirecourt*
1866	Napoléon Bourassa, *Jacques et Marie*
1867	British North America Act; Confederation; Constitution Act recognizes English and French as official languages in Parliament and Canadian courts; Sir John MacDonald Prime Minister 1867–73, 1878–91
1868	Canada First Movement founded; Catharine Parr Traill and Agnes Moodie Fitzgibbon, *Canadian Wild Flowers*
1870	Manitoba and North-West Territories join Confederation
1871	British Columbia joins Confederation
1872	Creation of the Public Archives of Canada (now the National Archives)
1873	Prince Edward Island joins Confederation
1876	Indian Act
1877	William Kirby, *The Golden Dog: A Legend of Quebec*

1880	Calixa Lavallée composes "O Canada" (words Adolphe-Basile Routhier); Ch. G. D. Roberts, *Orion and Other Poems*
1882	Royal Society of Canada founded by the Marquis de Lorne, Governor-General
1884	Standard Time Zone system; potlatch ceremony prohibited; Riel Rebellion 1884–5; Laure Conan, *Angéline de Montbrun*; Isabella Valancy Crawford, *Old Spookses' Pass, Malcolm's Katie and Other Poems*
1885	Canadian Pacific Railway completed; Chinese Immigration Act
1887–2001	*Saturday Night* magazine
1888	Archibald Lampman, *Among the Millet*; James de Mille, *A Strange Manuscript Found in a Copper Cylinder*; *Week* 1888–95
1889	William D. Lighthall, *Songs of the Great Dominion*
1893–1937	*Canadian Magazine* (combined earlier *Massey's Magazine* and *Canadian Magazine of Politics, Science, Art and Literature*)
1896	Sir Wilfrid Laurier Prime Minister 1896–1911; Gilbert Parker, *The Seats of the Mighty*; Ch. G. D. Roberts, *Earth's Enigmas*; *Maclean's Magazine* begins publication
1897	Women's Institute established
1898	Yukon Territory formed; Ernest Thompson Seton, *Wild Animals I Have Known*
1899–1902	Boer War causes divisiveness between English and French Canadians
1901	Ralph Connor, *The Man from Glengarry*
1904	Sara Jeannette Duncan, *The Imperialist*; *Emile Nelligan et son oeuvre*, ed. Louis Dantin
1905	Saskatchewan and Alberta become provinces
1907	Robert Service, *Songs of a Sourdough*
1908	L. M. Montgomery, *Anne of Green Gables*; Nellie McClung, *Sowing Seeds in Danny*; Martin Allerdale Grainger, *Woodsmen of the West*
1909	Canadian Commission of Conservation established
1911	Pauline Johnson, *Legends of Vancouver*
1912	Public Archives Act; Stephen Leacock, *Sunshine Sketches of a Little Town*

1913	National Gallery of Canada Act; Marjorie Pickthall, *The Drift of Pinions*
1914	Komagata Maru Incident; War Measures Act; Adjutor Rivard, *Chez nous*
1915	John McCrae's "In Flanders Fields" published in *Punch* magazine
1916	Voting rights to women in Manitoba, Saskatchewan, Alberta; Louis Hémon, *Maria Chapdelaine* (serialized in *Le Temps* [France], 1914)
1917	Halifax Explosion; Conscription Crisis; Battle of Vimy Ridge
1918	Albert Laberge, *La Scouine*
1919	Winnipeg General Strike; Immigration Amendment Act
1920	Group of Seven founded; Ray Palmer Baker, *A History of English Canadian Literature to Confederation*
1921	Mackenzie King Prime Minister 1921–6, 1926–30, 1935–48; Canadian Authors' Association founded
1923	Chinese Exclusion Act
1925	Frederick Philip Grove, *Settlers of the Marsh*; Martha Ostenso, *Wild Geese*; *McGill Fortnightly Review* (1925–7)
1927	Old Age Pensions Act; Grove, *A Search for America*; Mazo de la Roche, *Jalna*
1929	Persons Case
1931	Statute of Westminster
1933	Claude-Henri Grignon, *Un homme et son péché* (adapted for radio 1939; for television 2002); Charles G. D. Roberts, *Eyes of the Wilderness*
1934	Morley Callaghan, *Such Is My Beloved*; Jean-Charles Harvey, *Les demi-civilisés*
1935–40	John Buchan (Lord Tweedsmuir) Governor-General
1936	Canadian Broadcasting Corporation established as independent Crown corporation; Trans-Canada Airlines (changed to Air Canada 1965); First Governor-General's Literary Awards; Callaghan, *Now That April's Here and Other Stories*; A. J. M. Smith et al., *New Provinces*
1937	Donald Creighton, *The Commercial Empire of the St. Lawrence, 1760–1850*; Hector de Saint-Denys Garneau, *Regards et jeux dans l'espace*; Félix-Antoine Savard, *Menaud, maître-draveur*

1938	Ringuet, *Trente arpents*
1939	National Film Board; Howard O'Hagan, *Tay John*; Anne Marriott, *The Wind Our Enemy*
1940	Unemployment Insurance Act; voting rights granted to women in Quebec (the last province to do so); A. M. Klein, *Hath Not a Jew*; E. J. Pratt, *Brébeuf and His Brethren*
1941	Emily Carr, *Klee Wyck*; Sinclair Ross, *As for Me and My House*; Hugh MacLennan, *Barometer Rising*
1942	Dominion Plebiscite Act; Conscription Crisis; Internment of Japanese Canadians; Earle Birney, *David and Other Poems*
1943	A. J. M. Smith, *News of the Phoenix*; Smith, *Book of Canadian Poetry: A Critical and Historical Anthology*; E. K. Brown, *On Canadian Poetry: Essays on Canada*
1944	Creighton, *Dominion of the North*
1945	Gabrielle Roy, *Bonheur d'occasion* (1947 Prix Fémina); Hector de Saint-Denys Garneau, *Journal*; MacLennan, *Two Solitudes*; Elizabeth Smart, *By Grand Central Station I Sat Down and Wept*
1946	Canadian Citizenship Act
1947	Chinese Exclusion Act revoked; GATT (General Agreement on Tariffs and Trade); John Sutherland, *Other Canadians*; Malcolm Lowry, *Under the Volcano*; W. O. Mitchell, *Who Has Seen the Wind*
1948	Paul-Emile Borduas *et al.*, *Refus global*; Japanese Canadians (as last Asian Canadians) acquire the right to vote; Gratien Gélinas, *Tit-Coq*; Roger Lemelin, *Les Plouffe* (adapted for television 1953)
1949	Asbestos Strike in Quebec; Newfoundland enters Confederation
1950	Anne Hébert, *Le torrent*; Harold Innis, *Empire and Communications*; Dorothy Livesay, *Call My People Home*; John Coulter, *Riel* (stage; radio 1951, TV 1961)
1951	Indian Act; Massey Report; A. M. Klein, *The Second Scroll*; Marshall McLuhan, *The Mechanical Bride*
1952	Vincent Massey first Canadian Governor-General; National Library Act; Universal Copyright Act; Ernest Buckler, *The Mountain and the Valley*; E. J. Pratt, *Towards the Last Spike*

1953	Historic Sites and Monuments Act; Anne Hébert, *Le tombeau des rois*
1954	Ethel Wilson, *Swamp Angel*
1954–75	Vietnam War; Canada receives more than 125,000 draft evaders from the US
1955	Glenn Gould records Bach's *Goldberg Variations*
1956	Avro Arrow production canceled; Leonard Cohen, *Let Us Compare Mythologies*; Adele Wiseman, *The Sacrifice*; Sam Selvon, *The Lonely Londoners*
1957	Lester Pearson receives Nobel Peace Prize; Canada Council Act; New Canadian Library begins publication; Northrop Frye, *Anatomy of Criticism*; John Marlyn, *Under the Ribs of Death*
1958	Norman Levine, *Canada Made Me*; Yves Thériault, *Agaguk*
1959	Maurice Duplessis, premier of Quebec, dies; St. Lawrence Seaway completed; *Canadian Literature* begins publication under the editorship of George Woodcock; *Liberté* established; Mordecai Richler, *The Apprenticeship of Duddy Kravitz*; Sheila Watson, *The Double Hook*; Marie-Claire Blais, *La belle bête*; Irving Layton, *A Red Carpet for the Sun*; MacLennan, *The Watch That Ends the Night*
1960	Quiet Revolution 1960–6; Status Indians acquire the right to vote; regular jet service, Toronto–Vancouver; Margaret Avison, *Winter Sun*; Jean-Paul Desbiens, *Les insolences d'un frère untel*; Brian Moore, *The Luck of Ginger Coffey*; Gérard Bessette, *Le libraire*
1961	Margaret Atwood, *Double Persephone*; *Tish* 1961–9
1962	Trans-Canada Highway completed; Marshall McLuhan, *The Gutenberg Galaxy*; Earle Birney, *Ice Cod Bell or Stone*; Rudy Wiebe, *Peace Shall Destroy Many*
1963	Lester Pearson Prime Minister 1963–8; Solange Chaput-Rolland and Gwethalyn Graham, *Chers ennemis/Dear Enemies*; *Parti-pris* 1963–8; Farley Mowat, *Never Cry Wolf*
1964	McLuhan, *Understanding Media*; Margaret Laurence, *The Stone Angel*; Jane Rule, *Desert of the Heart*; Birney, *Near False Creek Mouth*; Paul Chamberland,

L'afficheur hurle; Claude Jasmin, *Ethel et le terroriste*; Jacques Renaud, *Le cassé*

1965   Canada adopts Maple Leaf flag; George Grant, *Lament for a Nation*; Northrop Frye, "Conclusion to The Literary History of Canada"; Hubert Aquin, *Prochain épisode*; Blais, *Une saison dans la vie d'Emmanuel*; Claire Martin, *Dans un gant de fer*; Edmund Wilson, *O Canada: An American's Note on Canadian Culture*; Roland Giguère, *L'âge de la parole: poèmes inédits 1949–1960*

1966   Medical Care Act; Cohen, *Beautiful Losers*; Réjean Ducharme, *L'avalée des avalés*

1967   Expo '67 in Montreal; House of Anansi founded by Dennis Lee and Dave Godfrey; McLuhan, *The Medium is the Massage*; George Ryga, *The Ecstasy of Rita Joe*; John Herbert, *Fortune and Men's Eyes*; P. K. Page, *Cry Ararat!*; Scott Symons, *Place d'armes*; Jacques Godbout, *Salut Galarneau*; Glenn Gould, *The Idea of North*; Yves Préfontaine, *Pays sans parole*

1968   Pierre Trudeau Prime Minister 1968–79; 1980–4; Dennis Lee, *Civil Elegies*; Aquin, *Trou de mémoire* (refuses Governor-General's Award); Pierre Vallières, *Nègres blancs de l'Amérique*; Michel Tremblay, *Les belles-soeurs*; Roch Carrier, *La guerre yes sir!*; Atwood, *The Animals in That Country*; bill bissett, *awake in the red desert*; Victor-Lévy Beaulieu begins *La vraie saga des Beauchemin*; Alice Munro, *Dance of the Happy Shades*

1969   Official Languages Act passed; Harold Cardinal, *The Unjust Society: The Tragedy of Canada's Indians*; Cardinal and Duke Redbird begin work on "Red Paper" (publ. 1970), in response to the Canadian government's White Paper proposing removal of special status for Native people; George Grant, *Technology and Empire*; Jacques Ferron, *Le ciel de Québec*; Robert Kroetsch, *The Studhorse Man*; Milton Acorn, *I've Tasted My Blood*; Atwood, *The Edible Woman*

1970   October Crisis; Royal Commission on Status of Women reports; Nuit de la poésie; Michèle Lalonde, "Speak White"; Gaston Miron, *L'homme rapaillé*; Atwood, *The Journals of Susanna Moodie*; Michael

Ondaatje, *The Collected Works of Billy the Kid*; Susan Musgrave, *Songs of the Sea Witch*; Robertson Davies, *Fifth Business*; John Glassco, *Memoirs of Montparnasse*; Margaret Laurence, *A Bird in the House*; Dave Godfrey, *The New Ancestors*; Audrey Thomas, *Mrs. Blood*; Antonine Maillet, *La Sagouine* (publ. 1971); Anne Hébert, *Kamouraska*; Rudy Wiebe, *The Blue Mountains of China*

1971   Alice Munro, *Lives of Girls and Women*; George Ryga, *Captives of a Faceless Drummer*; Paul-Marie Lapointe, *Le réel absolu: poèmes 1948–1965*

1971–4   Peter Gzowski hosts the CBC's *This Country in the Morning* (followed by *Morningside*, 1982–97)

1972   Atwood, *Survival: A Thematic Guide to Canadian Literature*; *Surfacing*; bp nichol, *The Martyrology*; Carol Bolt, *Buffalo Jump*; Ann Henry, *Lulu Street*; Fernand Ouellette, *Poésie: poèmes 1953–1971*

1973   Maria Campbell, *Halfbreed*; Dennis Lee, "Cadence, Country, Silence: Writing in Colonial Space"; Rudy Wiebe, *The Temptations of Big Bear*; Michel Tremblay, *Hosanna*; Rick Salutin/ Théâtre Passe Muraille, *1837: The Farmers' Revolt*; James Reaney, *Sticks and Stones* (first play of the Donnelly trilogy, publ. 1975); Herschel Hardin, *Esker Mike and His Wife, Agiluk*; David Freeman, *Of the Fields, Lately*; Calder case decided by the Supreme Court, leading to Nisga'a treaty in 1996

1974   Laurence, *The Diviners*; Aquin, *Neige noire*; Chief Dan George, *My Heart Soars*; Michael Cook, *Jacob's Wake* (publ. 1975)

1975   Cultural Property Export and Import Act; Lee Maracle, *Bobbi Lee: Indian Rebel*

1976   Quebec referendum on sovereignty defeated; Sharon Pollock, *The Komagata Maru Incident*; Marian Engel, *Bear*; Jack Hodgins, *Spit Delaney's Island*; Louky Bersianik, *L'Euguélionne*

1977   Berger Commission, *Northern Frontier, Northern Homeland*; Charter of the French Language adopted in Quebec; F. R. Scott, *Essays on the Constitution*; Timothy Findley, *The Wars*; Hodgins, *The Invention of the World*; Dennis Lee, *Savage Fields: An Essay in Literature and Cosmology*; Bharati Mukherjee, Clark

	Blaise, *Days and Nights in Calcutta*; Josef Skvorecky, *The Engineer of Human Souls*; George Walker, *Zastrozzi*; Rudy Wiebe, *The Scorched-Wood People*
1978	Munro, *Who Do You Think You Are?*; Aritha van Herk, *Judith*; Tremblay, *La grosse femme d'à côté est enceinte* (first volume of *Chroniques du Plateau Mont-Royal*); 25th Street Theatre, *Paper Wheat*; Immigration Act
1979	Antonine Maillet, *Pélagie-la-Charrette* (Prix Goncourt); Denise Boucher, *Les fées ont soif*; Mavis Gallant, *From the Fifteenth District*
1980	"O Canada" officially adopted as national anthem; George Bowering, *Burning Water*; Nicole Brossard, *Amantes*; Jovette Marchessault, *Tryptique lesbien*; Robert Kroetsch, *The Crow Journals*; Judith Thompson, *The Crackwalker*; David Fennario, *Balconville*
1981	Joy Kogawa, *Obasan*; Findley, *Famous Last Words*; Gallant, *Home Truths*; F. R. Scott, *Collected Poems*; John Gray, *Billy Bishop Goes to War*
1982	Patriation of Constitution, Charter of Rights; Michael Ondaatje, *Running in the Family*; Hébert, *Les fous de Bassan*; Munro, *The Moons of Jupiter*
1983	Beatrice Culleton Mosonier, *In Search of April Raintree*; Penny Petrone, ed., *First People, First Voices*; Régine Robin, *La Québécoite*; Sam Selvon, *Moses Migrating*; Makeda Silvera, *Silenced*; Susan Swan, *The Biggest Modern Woman of the World*
1984	Findley, *Not Wanted on the Voyage*
1985	Jeannette Armstrong, *Slash*; Fred Wah, *Waiting for Saskatchewan*; Atwood, *The Handmaid's Tale*; Dany Laferrière, *Comment faire l'amour avec un nègre sans se fatiguer*; Mukherjee, Blaise, *The Sorrow and the Terror*
1986	Robert Lepage, *Vinci*; Munro, *The Progress of Love*; Jane Urquhart, *The Whirlpool*
1987	Michael Ondaatje, *In the Skin of a Lion*; Rohinton Mistry, *Tales from Firozsha Baag*; Michel Marc Bouchard, *Les feluettes*; Michael Ignatieff, *The Russian Album*; Carol Shields, *Swann*

1988   Canadian Multiculturalism Act; Free Trade Agreement;
         Prime Minister Mulroney officially apologizes to
         Japanese Canadians for WWII internment; Tomson
         Highway, *The Rez Sisters*; Daphne Marlatt, *Ana
         Historic*; Lee Maracle, *I Am Woman: A Native
         Perspective on Sociology and Feminism*; Paul Yee,
         Saltwater City: The Chinese in Vancouver

1989   Highway, *Dry Lips Oughta Move to Kapuskasing*;
         Maria Campbell and Linda Griffiths, *Jessica*; Harry
         Robinson, *Write It on Your Heart*; Mordecai Richler,
         Solomon Gursky Was Here

1990   Meech Lake Accord fails; Oka Crisis; Maracle,
         Oratory: Coming to Theory; Thomas King, ed., *All My
         Relations: An Anthology of Contemporary Canadian
         Native Fiction*; Nino Ricci, *Lives of the Saints*; Munro,
         Friend of My Youth; George Elliott Clarke, *Whylah
         Falls*; Sky Lee, *Disappearing Moon Cafe*; Dionne
         Brand, *No Language Is Neutral*; Aritha van Herk,
         Places Far from Ellesmere; Réjean Ducharme, *Dévadé*

1991   M. Nourbese Philip, *Looking for Livingstone*;
         Monique Mojica, *Princess Pocahontas and the Blue
         Spots*; Bennett Lee, Jim Wong-Chu, *Many-Mouthed
         Birds: Contemporary Writing by Chinese Canadians*;
         Rohinton Mistry, *Such a Long Journey*; Douglas
         Coupland, *Generation X: Tales for an Accelerated
         Culture*

1992   Ondaatje, *The English Patient* (Booker Prize); Daniel
         David Moses and Terry Goldie, eds., *An Anthology of
         Canadian Native Literature in English*; Harry
         Robinson, *Nature Power*

1993   Thomas King, *Green Grass, Running Water*; King, *One
         Good Story, That One*; Jeannette Armstrong, *Looking
         at the Words of Our People: An Anthology of First
         Nations Literary Criticism*; Pierre Trudeau, *Mémoires
         politiques*; Jane Urquhart, *Away*; Carol Shields, *The
         Stone Diaries* (1995 Pulitzer Prize); Guillermo
         Verdecchia, *Fronteras Americanas/ American Borders*;
         Findley, *Headhunter*; Jacques Poulin, *La tournée
         d'automne*; Fernand Dumont, *Genèse de la société
         québécoise*; Paul Chanel Malenfant, *Le verbe être*

1994	Charlottetown Accord fails; M. G. Vassanji, *The Book of Secrets* (first Giller Prize); Shyam Selvadurai, *Funny Boy*; Hiromi Goto, *Chorus of Mushrooms*; Louise Halfe, *Bear Bones and Feathers*; Neil Bissoondath, *Selling Illusions: The Cult of Multiculturalism in Canada*; Munro, *Open Secrets*; Anne-Marie Alonzo, *Lettres à Cassandre*
1995	Quebec referendum on sovereignty narrowly defeated; Wayson Choy, *The Jade Peony*; Rohinton Mistry, *A Fine Balance*
1996	Nisga'a treaty; Atwood, *Alias Grace*; Anne Michaels, *Fugitive Pieces*; Anita Rau-Badami, *Tamarind Mem*; Gail Anderson-Dargatz, *The Cure for Death by Lightning*; Guy Vanderhaeghe, *The Englishman's Boy*; Ann-Marie MacDonald, *Fall on Your Knees*; Larissa Lai, *When Fox Is a Thousand*; Shani Mootoo, *Cereus Blooms at Night*
1997	Mordecai Richler, *Barney's Version*; Dionne Brand, *Land to Light On*; P. K. Page, *The Hidden Room*; Urquhart, *The Underpainter*; David Adams Richards, *Lines on the Water: A Fisherman's Life on the Miramichi*; Daphne Marlatt, *Mothertalk: Life Stories of Mary Kiyoshi Kiyooka*
1998	Munro, *The Love of a Good Woman*; Anne Carson, *Autobiography of Red: A Novel in Verse*; Hodgins, *Broken Ground*; Wayne Johnston, *The Colony of Unrequited Dreams*; Barbara Gowdy, *The White Bone*; Shields, *Larry's Party* (Orange Prize)
1999	Nunavut established; Adrienne Clarkson becomes Governor-General; Gregory Scofield, *Thunder through My Veins*; Alistair MacLeod, *No Great Mischief* (2001 IMPAC Dublin Literary Award); Caroline Adderson, *A History of Forgetting*; Bonnie Burnard, *A Good House*; Johnston, *Baltimore's Mansion* (2000, first Charles Taylor Prize); Robert Bringhurst, *A Story as Sharp as a Knife: The Classical Haida Mythtellers and Their World*; Claude Beausoleil, *Exilé*; Gaétan Soucy, *La petite fille qui aimait trop les allumettes*
2000	Ondaatje, *Anil's Ghost*; Atwood, *The Blind Assassin* (Booker Prize); David Adams Richards, *Mercy among the Children*; Elizabeth Hay, *A Student of Weather*;

Nega Mezlekia, *Notes from the Hyena's Belly*; Findley, *Elizabeth Rex*; Marie Laberge, *Le gout du bonheur: Adelaïde/Annabelle/Florent* (trilogy)

2001   World Trade Center attacked, Canada shelters thousands of stranded passengers; *Canada: A People's History* (CBC-SRC); Urquhart, *The Stone Carvers*; Richard Wright, *Clara Callan*; Yann Martel, *Life of Pi* (2002 Booker); Munro, *Hateship, Friendship, Courtship, Loveship, Marriage*

2002   George Bowering becomes Canada's first poet laureate; Austin Clarke, *The Polished Hoe*; Johnston, *The Navigator of New York*; Carol Shields, *Unless*; Mistry, *Family Matters*; Vanderhaeghe, *Last Crossing*; Michael Redhill, *Martin Sloane*; Michel Tremblay, *Bonbons assortis*

2003   Atwood, *Oryx and Crake*; Gowdy, *The Romantic*; Richards, *River of the Brokenhearted*; Michel Basilières, *Black Bird*; David Odhiambo, *Kipligat's Chance*; Frances Itani, *Deafening*; Ann-Marie MacDonald, *The Way the Crow Flies*; Jack Hodgins, *Distance*; M. G. Vassanji, *The In-Between World of Vikram Lall*; Elizabeth Hay, *Garbo Laughs*; Denys Arcand, *Les invasions barbares*

Map 1: Canada

Introduction

EVA-MARIE KRÖLLER

Life of Pi: Reception of a Canadian novel

The nominees for the 2002 Booker Prize included three Canadian books: Carol Shields's *Unless*, Rohinton Mistry's *Family Matters*, and Yann Martel's *Life of Pi*. The news was welcomed in Canada with great satisfaction, but because none of the authors was born in the country, media at home and abroad launched an intense investigation of how to determine the "Canadianness" of a writer. Depending on the nationality of the commentator, these reflections ranged from the congratulatory and envious to the suspicious and defiant. The *South China Morning Post* described Mistry as "born in Mumbai but liv[ing] in Canada" and Martel as a "Spanish-born writer living in Canada," although it did identify the American-born Shields as Canadian. Responding in the Toronto *Globe and Mail*, Charles Foran insisted that national labels must yield to creative identities because "their presence *is* the country" and "Choose Canada, and you are Canadian."[1] American and British papers alike ascribed these and other writers' remarkable success to the Canadian government's active deployment of literature as part of its Foreign Affairs portfolio and they praised its protectionist attitude towards the publishing industry. One expatriate Canadian journalist chimed in, declaring that the country's standards of living and personal liberty provided the "prerequisites for fine writing,"[2] a conclusion that may well come as news to writers from countries where literature has flourished despite (or, as some might argue, because of) adverse conditions. In contrast to commentators who drew a direct link between Canada's specific situation and its cultural boom, a long-time British observer of the Booker Prize concluded that the Canadians' success was not so much a national achievement as it was part and parcel of the Commonwealth's triumph over British metropolitan culture. Confirming Graham Huggan's and Luke Strongman's suspicions about the imperial legacy of the Prize,[3] this commentator went so far as to compare winner Yann Martel's "punching and high-fiving" with the excitement generated by "the gorgeous troupe of Maori dancers" on the occasion of Keri Hulme's win in 1985 for *The Bone People*, and he suggested that the Canadians' ascendancy was a logical sequel to the time when "the Antipodean literary tradition was all the rage."[4]

This description suggests that Martel is an "exotic" writer and therefore a natural Booker winner, but subsequent events also reminded observers that Canada occupies an ambivalent position between colonized and colonizer. Days after Martel had won the award, a controversy erupted over his use of the work of Jewish Brazilian author Moacyr Scliar. Accusations of plagiarism raged for a week over the worldwide web, with textual evidence examined by literary reporters from one end of the globe to the other, and Martel responding to the charges in interviews and chatroom-style conversations with his readers until the matter had been cleared up and had exhausted its usefulness as a news item. In Scliar's view and that of his supporters, Martel's alleged theft of ideas merely confirmed the insouciance with which western authors have long appropriated for their own success the work of writers from developing countries, and Brazilian newspapers were quick to produce lists of previous such cases. There was no question here of approvingly celebrating Canada's "coming of age," but rather the assumption that it had long taken its place among the established nations and adopted their paternalist attitude towards less privileged cultures.[5] Together with the discovery that the Booker-winning British edition of *Life of Pi* contained revisions (extensive or not depending on who was consulted) that did not appear in the original Canadian version, the discussions surrounding Martel's book are worth dwelling on in some detail, because they usefully illustrate some of the practical and philosophical complexities attending the study of Canadian literature. Other contemporary literatures, British writing included, also feature authors that are difficult to classify, Zadie Smith, Kazuo Ishiguro, and W. G. Sebald among them. In addition, there are characteristics, such as its position between colonizer and colonized subject, that Canada shares with other settler nations like Australia. Indeed, government reports on the situation of Canadian culture such as that of the Royal Commission on Bilingualism and Biculturalism (1963–9) have habitually drawn comparisons with South Africa, Belgium, Switzerland, Finland, and Norway to highlight areas of common concern with other nations. But its official bilingualism combined with the exceptional multicultural demographics that have been emerging since the 1978 Immigration Act also place Canadian culture in a situation of its own.

As the winner, Martel underwent special scrutiny for his Canadian credentials, although he has no doubts about these himself and responded to an interviewer's question "I assume you consider yourself a citizen of the world?" with an unequivocal "No. I'm Canadian."[6] Born in Salamanca, Spain to Québécois parents who moved their family to wherever their diplomatic postings subsequently took them, Martel was variously referred to by the press as "Spanish," "Canadian," "Montréalais," and "Québécois." His French Canadian pedigree was examined painstakingly because he writes in English and, although it was nominated for the Governor-General's Award in 2001, *Life of Pi* was virtually unknown in francophone Quebec when the Booker was announced, with the translation not scheduled to appear before 2003.[7] His father, Emile Martel, won the Governor-General's Award for his collection of poetry *Pour orchestre et poète seul* (1995), and his uncle, Réginald Martel, is a distinguished literary critic long associated with Montreal's *La Presse*, but Yann Martel's own preference for English proved to *indépendantiste* author Claude Jasmin that he was a "Québécois 'assimilé'," one who "refuse sa réalité."[8] RadioFrance by contrast insisted that Martel had been prevented only by his family's circumstances from acquiring the necessary proficiency to write in French. To forestall any criticism of the linguistic preferences of someone they were eager to "repatriate" into international francophone literature, the French media explained that schools in France had refused to accept him after he had received his early schooling in English during his father's posting in Costa Rica. They also cited the testimony of his parents, now retired and both working as translators (including translating their son's award-winning novel), as proof that Martel's French is beyond reproach. Meanwhile the English Canadian media were interested in using his French Canadian background to prove his *Canadian* credentials. To do so, they appropriated the insistence, frequent among Quebec's *indépendantistes*, that a family must document its extended presence in the province, preferably from a period pre-dating the Conquest, in order to prove that its genealogy is legitimate or *de souche* (or *pure laine*). Tellingly, the "here" in the *Globe and Mail*'s Sandra Martin's spirited defense of the author's passport credentials is Canada, not Quebec, when she points out that his father's family has lived in the country since the seventeenth century and his mother "is descended from settlers who came here in the 19th century."[9]

French and English

Martel's cool reception at the hands of Quebec critics and the need both in Canada and abroad to establish a genealogy for him arise from a number of historical complications. France was Canada's first colonial power, beginning in the sixteenth century with Jacques Cartier who claimed the territory along the Saint Lawrence River between the Gaspé Peninsula and

Hochelaga (now Montreal) in the name of François I and who returned to France accompanied by the captured Iroquois leader Donnacona and his sons. Hopes of finding rich deposits of minerals and a Northwest Passage to the Indies were, however, not realized, a disappointment that quelled official interest in the colony for the next fifty years or so and one that lingers on in the mocking name "Lachine" (a city now incorporated in Montreal and the place from where Cavalier de la Salle set forth in 1669 to find a direct route to China). Samuel de Champlain established a settlement in 1608 that allowed him to consolidate the kinds of commercial contact with the Indigenous population required to ensure the necessary supplies for the fur trade. Activities were soon extensive enough to justify the formation of trade companies like the Compagnie des cent-associés, but administration of the colony only became a success under Louis XIV, when its management was tightly organized to mimic that of France and the Intendant Talon oversaw vigorous developments in agriculture and local industries. Expansionism propelled exploration in the Great Lakes and Mississippi regions, often against the forceful opposition of the Indian nations who also kept a close eye on French settlements.

At the beginning of the eighteenth century, New France extended from Newfoundland and Acadia (now Nova Scotia and parts of New Brunswick), along the Saint Lawrence and Saguenay Rivers and into the area of the Great Lakes and the mouth of the Mississippi, with trading posts and scattered settlements in the West extending all the way to the foothills of the Rockies. In the Treaty of Utrecht of 1713, however, New France had to make extensive territorial and other concessions to the English, who by then had also established substantial trade interests in North America. The Acadians – farmers, fishermen, and trappers of French origin settled in parts of what are now the provinces of Nova Scotia and New Brunswick – were one casualty of the Treaty of Utrecht. Their territory was ceded to Great Britain, but they refused to swear an oath of allegiance to the new authorities, agreeing to an oath of neutrality instead. After they repeated their refusal in 1755, an estimated three-quarters of the 13,000 Acadians were deported to parts of what are now the United States and elsewhere, with families separated deliberately to undermine attempts to reconstitute themselves as a community, although substantial numbers later managed to return to their former settlements. Despite a remarkable flourishing of commerce and trade during the years of peace that followed the Treaty, New France ("quelques arpents de neige," to cite Voltaire's dismissive description) did not receive the attention from France, financial or otherwise, that was required to address its specific needs. Conflicting interests between the English and French came to the fore again during the Seven Years' War, often referred to as the first global war because it involved large parts of both the new and old worlds. Its decisive event for New France was the Battle of the Plains of Abraham in 1759, the "Conquest," when the English under James Wolfe defeated the French under the Marquis de Montcalm. The Treaty of Paris in 1763 ceded the colony to England.

Following the resurgence of French Canadian nationalism during the Rebellions of 1837, brought on by widespread dissatisfaction with British leadership, Lord Durham's Report on the Affairs of British North America (1839) declared that he found "two nations warring in the bosom of a single state" and that, as French Canadians were "a people with no literature and no history,"[10] it would be best to assimilate them. The Report led to the Act of Union (1841), bringing Upper and Lower Canada (the predecessors of modern Ontario and Quebec) together under one government. Its anti-French legislation, affecting the use of the French language, education, and civil law, together with the Report's insulting dismissal of their culture, spurred French Canadian intellectuals into action, so that by the time of Confederation in 1867, when the British North American colonies of New Brunswick, Nova Scotia, and Canada (that is, the earlier union of Upper and Lower Canada) were joined in a Dominion, francophone authors were engaged in extensive historical and cultural recovery work. Although the Constitution Act of 1867 recognized English and French as official languages in Parliament and Canadian courts, there was legislation in the late nineteenth and early twentieth centuries which seriously restricted the official use of French outside Quebec.

As outlined in greater detail in E. D. Blodgett's chapter on francophone writing, concerns about the survival of French culture continued to rankle, however, until the Royal Commission on Bilingualism and Biculturalism undertook to study the question systematically, recommending that the 28.1% of Canadians who cited French as their mother tongue in the 1961 census (the figure dropped to 22.9% by 2001) be assured public service in their language and that government business be generally conducted, and documents made available, in both English and French. For some Quebeckers, these recommendations and their implementation in the 1969 Official Languages Act were too little too late. Activities of the separatist *Front de libération du Québec* (FLQ) culminated in the events of 1970, the so-called October Crisis, when the FLQ kidnapped British trade commissioner James Cross and Liberal politician Pierre Laporte, and executed Laporte. Prime Minister Pierre Trudeau invoked the War Measures Act, under which more than 450 people were arrested, many of them prominent members of Quebec's cultural community. A vivid, although often overlooked, introduction to the tensions simmering between English and French at the beginning of the sixties, as well as to the ways in which historical events apparently long past continue to affect the relationship of the two language groups, is provided in *Chers ennemis/Dear Enemies* (1963). This is a dialogue between journalist Solange Chaput-Rolland and novelist Gwethalyn Graham, which includes impassioned exchanges over the Deportation of the Acadians in 1755 and the Conscription Crisis of 1942 (when the government reversed its pledge to avoid conscription, following a plebiscite during which Quebec voted strongly against the reversal). Chaput-Rolland provides numerous dramatic examples of the ways in which she and her language become invisible as soon as she leaves her province, and sometimes even within it. Indeed, when she writes about the predominance of "speaking white" – that is, English – her language often rises to the level of poetic manifesto, making it reminiscent of the famous poem "Speak White" recited by Michèle Lalonde during the *Nuit de la poésie* held in support of those arrested under the 1970 War Measures Act. In a more recent example of how history continues to haunt relationships between English and French, Michel Basilières's novel *Black Bird* (2003) features the eccentric "Desouche" family at the time of the October Crisis in Montreal. The book is all the more remarkable as the author, bilingual like Yann Martel, writes in English and comments throughout on the cultural baggage and creative potential of both languages.

Although the Bilingualism and Biculturalism Report underlined "the undisputed role played by Canadians of French and British origin in 1867,"[11] it also performed important groundwork in assessing "The Cultural Contribution of the Other Ethnic Groups," to cite the title of the relevant volume. It was these "other ethnic groups" that were to create the distinctive demographics that characterize the Canada of today and that make it increasingly daunting to maintain the earlier demarcations along "racial" (a term which, the Report hastened to point out, "carries no biological significance"[12]) and linguistic lines. The difficulty of slotting Martel into clear national or linguistic categories "tickled" fellow-writer Ken Wiwa's "transnational, translocated, postcolonial bones,"[13] as he was making one of his own regular journeys back to Nigeria, and it would have confirmed travel-writer Pico Iyer's often-repeated impressions of Canadian literature and the society it represents as perfect expressions of contemporary "multiculture."[14] The figures certainly bear out Iyer's observations. According to the 2001 census released in January 2003, 18.4% of all persons living in Canada are foreign-born, up from 17.4% in 1996, and 16.1% in 1991. While European immigration topped the list before 1961, it has now dropped to 20%, compared to over 50% from Asia, including the Middle East. Toronto in particular features ethnic diversity unparalleled by any other large city in North America or Australia, with 44% of its population born outside of Canada and with China, India, the Philippines, and Hong Kong at the top of the source countries, but "multiculture" is also high in Vancouver (37.5% foreign-born) and Montreal (18.4%). As a 2001 special issue of the *Canadian Geographic*, entitled "The New Canada," pointed out, the distribution of ethnicities in Canada mirrors closely the composition of the world's population, a phenomenon apparently not duplicated in quite this way in any other nation.

In the media, these developments tend to be described as recent and rather sudden, but it is an illuminating exercise to read through the essays collected in historian William Kilbourn's classic *Canada: A Guide to the Peaceable Kingdom* (1970) – published, ironically, in the year of the October Crisis – and to realize just how closely their national and international assessments of Canada's potential as "model-builder" overlap with the current enthusiasm. *The Economist's* Barbara Ward published her essay "The First International Nation" in the *Canadian Forum* in 1968, shortly after the release of the first two volumes of the Report prepared by the Royal Commission on Bilingualism and Biculturalism. She writes that the country might, "with lucidity and daring," "show . . . a way forward to the score of states . . . who harbour a number of 'nations.'" The Report pointed out that even at the time of the 1961 census almost 41% of Toronto's population were foreign-born, and that the percentage of Canadians who were of neither British nor French extraction had risen from 11% in 1881 to 26% in 1961. However, as noted above, the great majority of these were still European, and Canadian literature continued to be dominated by these origins throughout the seventies and eighties, even while the composition of the Canadian population was undergoing radical changes. Thus, teachers encouraging their students to research their ethnic backgrounds through the country's literature were able to refer them to works by and about Scandinavian, German, Austrian, Italian, Ukrainian, and Hungarian immigrants, but it was not until the watershed publication of Joy Kogawa's *Obasan* (1981) that students of non-European immigrant origin were beginning to have a choice of appropriate books to turn to. Even so, it took almost another decade for the explosive appearance of internationally acclaimed works from a wide range of cultural backgrounds to provide Canadian literature with its current diversity. Works by writers of European origin also underwent profound changes. Nino Ricci's bestseller *Lives of the Saints* (1990) set the signal by spending as much space on describing the Italian location of the hero's origins as it did on his Canadian destination. In its assertiveness, this was a significant departure from the amnesia (or retreat into folklore) that, for many legitimate reasons, characterized much earlier "ethnic" writing. Myrna Kostash's ongoing investigation, in *All of Baba's Children* (1977) and elsewhere, of the shifting meaning of "Ukrainian" in Canadian society provides an excellent illustration of the factors that influence immigrants' denial of, or pride in, their culture of origin.

Both multicultural demographics and the international success of Canadian culture have been linked to legislation under Prime Minister Pierre Trudeau (1968–79, 1980–4), and the two are closely interrelated. A signpost for the former was the Immigration Act proclaimed in 1978, which formulated a broad political, cultural, and humanitarian mandate, and asserted nondiscrimination as one of its fundamental principles. In its turn, official sponsorship of Canadian culture received a strong impetus earlier in the decade when President Richard Nixon's government imposed a 10% tax on imports into the United States, and Canada began to look for alternative trade partners in Europe, Asia, and South America. For the Department of Foreign Affairs and International Trade (DFAIT), culture and tourism became important tools in boosting interest in Canada. Generous programs in translation, book promotion, and teaching were put in place, and embassies like Etienne-Joseph Gaboury's Chancery in Mexico City (1982) were designed as showcases of Canadian culture and scenery, with auditoriums, libraries, and galleries to provide further information.

In its activities, DFAIT was able to draw on the ground-breaking work of the Royal Commission on National Development in the Arts, Letters and Sciences (more commonly known after one of its chairmen, Vincent Massey, as the "Massey Commission"), in the course of which Prime Minister Louis St. Laurent suggested that the Commissioners also concern themselves with the question of "[m]ethods for the purpose of making available to the people of foreign countries adequate information concerning Canada."[15] Clearly guided in their concerns by the recent war, the Commissioners looked at how Winston Churchill's invocation of "the traditions of his country" provided powerful ammunition in rallying "the British people in their supreme effort" (*Report of the Royal Commission*, p. 4). By contrast, the 1951 Report painted an alarming picture of the state of Canadian cultural industries as offering no such focal point in times of emergency and proposed a wide-ranging program of initiatives to improve the situation, resulting in the establishment of the National Library in 1952 and of the Canada Council, a funding body with the purpose of fostering work in the humanities, arts, and social sciences, in 1957. Although the definition of culture used by the Commissioners was sometimes backward-glancing in its elitism, the Report raised fundamental questions about the nature and business of homegrown culture, many of which came to the fore in the following decades: the role of Canada's dual colonial heritage, the pervasive influence of American culture, and the crucial significance of communication in a country vast enough to have six different time zones. At some of its most poignant moments, the

Report leaves the lofty stance of an official document and simply lists, in apparent awe at the magnitude of the required effort, the thousands of miles of landlines and axial cable required to enable communication and thus hold the nation together. The conclusion was, however, that no matter what the complications might be, Canada required a confident culture of its own not only to ensure self-sufficiency but also to make it a strong and desirable ally. A recent exemplary investigation of Canadian cultural politics, including its roots in the Massey Report, is Katarina Leandoer's *From Colonial Expression to Export Commodity: English-Canadian Literature in Canada and Sweden, 1945–1999* (2002), a study that is also alert to the problems of government sponsorship which may not place creativity at the top of its priorities. Leandoer's focus, as the title says, is Sweden, but many of the author's observations have broader application as well.

The Multiculturalism Act of 1988 may be seen as a sequel to the Immigration Act, ensuring the rights of new Canadians "to preserve, enhance and share their cultural heritage."[16] Some commentators, however, dismissed this policy as an ill-considered ploy in domestic and international politics which would only serve to add further divisions to existing ones. One of the most vocal critics was Trinidad-born Neil Bissoondath whose highly controversial *Selling Illusions: The Cult of Multiculturalism in Canada*, originally published in 1994, generated enough debate to require a revised and updated version in 2002. By contrast, other observers surmise that Trudeau's policies were a shrewd act of *realpolitik* to challenge Quebec separatism, both by creating a multicultural population little interested in the traditional disagreements of the two "founding nations," and by using foreign cultural policy as a showcase for federalism, thus counteracting Quebec's efforts to establish its own international network. The outcome, needless to say, is perceived as either positive or lamentable depending on the observer's background.[17] While the Commission on Bilingualism and Biculturalism found that citizens "in the 'others' category"[18] had little interest in, or were reluctant to express views about, the relationship between anglophone and francophone Canadians or its effect on Confederation, it is true that Canadian unity has since received emphatic support from recent immigrants, leading to Parti Québécois leader Jacques Parizeau's infamous suggestion, causing much embarrassment to his party, that the 1995 referendum on Quebec sovereignty was narrowly defeated by "money and the ethnic vote."[19] Support for national unity ranges from the complex civic work of organizations like the privately run Laurier Institute, which was instrumental in defusing the racial tension that threatened to erupt in the wake of large-scale immigration preceding the return of Hong Kong to China,[20] to some new citizens' enthusiasm for the country's much-debated national symbols. This was a remarkable departure from the findings of the Bilingualism and Biculturalism Commission, which found that few "others" had an "opinion on the issues of a new national flag and a national anthem for Canada."[21] The Maple Leaf flag was adopted after acrimonious parliamentary debate (among other things over the allusion to the French fleur-de-lys in the shape of the maple leaf) in 1965 and "O Canada," periodically questioned for its lack of inclusiveness even now, did not become the national anthem until 1980, but Hong Kong immigrant Bun Law's Canadian Flags Campaign has distributed hundreds of thousands of flags across the country for free. The family of Governor-General Adrienne Clarkson, a distinguished journalist, writer, and publisher, left Hong Kong after the Japanese invasion in 1941 and its members are therefore by no means recent arrivals; indeed, when she was first appointed to Rideau Hall, Clarkson was bitterly criticized for allegedly denying her Chinese roots. Since then, however, she has been called "simply the best" because, among other accomplishments, she has made herself into a model for immigrants' aspirations while expressing an unconditional allegiance to Canada.[22]

Native writing and internationalism

Although Penny van Toorn's chapter on Aboriginal writing will discuss these topics in detail (as well as surveying the relative implications of "Aboriginal," "Native," "First Nations," "Indian," and "Métis"), it is important to underline at this stage that the internationalization of Canadian literature goes hand in hand with, and derives impetus from, an increase in publication by Native writers. The 2001 census noted a 22 percent rise since 1996 in the number of people who identified themselves as Aboriginal, the result of both strong birth rates and greater assertiveness. These figures coincide with a remarkable ascendancy in literary activity and the political activism to which it is linked. The only texts by a Native author in a late 1970s anthology much used in university courses were a handful of poems by Pauline Johnson, complemented by excerpts from several explorers' reports describing massacres of missionaries, traders, and enemy tribes by Native people, causing one of my own students, a Haida, to leave the classroom in protest. Here too the availability of texts and the educational work they make possible lagged behind political events, also initiated under Trudeau. There had been no Native representation on the Massey Commission, and Native people were mentioned only in passing (and then with sometimes ill-concealed condescension), including one "Nootka Indian [who] traveled 125 miles to tell us about the vanishing art of his race and how in his view it might be saved" (p. 10). Some of the Native actors in George Ryga's controversial

Centennial play *The Ecstasy of Rita Joe* (1967) were arrested on the streets of Vancouver (thus providing realistic proof of the social problems depicted on stage), but at Expo '67 in Montreal the Indian pavilion made a strong and independent showing, and the presence of numerous Indigenous groups from other countries at the Fair provided solidarity and contacts. Because the border arbitrarily bisects ancient tribal lands, Native leaders have generally resisted the sharp distinction that Canadian nationalists tend to draw between the United States and Canada, and throughout the sixties and beyond, US civil rights movements, especially the American Indian Movement, furnished inspiration.

The decisive event was the 1969 White Paper on Indian policy that proposed the termination of special status for Native people, presumably on grounds similar to the ones on which the Trudeau government opposed Quebec separatism. The effect of the White Paper was to galvanize Native leaders and writers into opposition: Harold Cardinal published *The Unjust Society: The Tragedy of Canada's Indians* the same year and began work with Duke Redbird on the "Red Paper" in response to the government document. Maria Campbell's *Halfbreed* followed in 1973, Lee Maracle's *Bobbi Lee: Indian Rebel* in 1975, Beatrice Culleton Mosonier's *In Search of April Raintree* and Penny Petrone's anthology *First People, First Voices* in 1983, and Jeannette Armstrong's *Slash* in 1985. The year 1989 saw works by Tomson Highway, Maria Campbell (in collaboration with Linda Griffiths), and Harry Robinson, with steady publication every year since in all genres and several important anthologies, as well as international acclaim especially for the work of Thomas King. In 1990, Lee Maracle's *Oratory: Coming to Theory* and Thomas King's *All My Relations: An Anthology of Contemporary Canadian Native Fiction* were published; this was the same year that the Meech Lake Accord (which would have given Quebec special status under the Charter of the Canadian Constitution) failed, in part because of opposition from Native people, and that the Oka crisis erupted in which Mohawk Indians confronted federal troops when a proposed golf course threatened desecration of Native burial grounds. Also published in 1990 were Nino Ricci's *Lives of the Saints*, Alice Munro's *Friend of My Youth*, George Elliott Clarke's *Whylah Falls*, Sky Lee's *Disappearing Moon Cafe*, Dionne Brand's *No Language Is Neutral*, and Aritha van Herk's *Places Far from Ellesmere*, thus providing a remarkable array of established and emerging authors from a broad spectrum of very different backgrounds.

Some of Canada's public intellectuals have undertaken to mediate between English, French, Native, and multicultural interests and to interpret their relationships with each other for an international readership. The results can be to create even more divisiveness. In *Oh Canada! Oh Quebec!: Requiem*

for a Divided Country (1992), an extended essay based on a widely disseminated piece first published in the *New Yorker*, Mordecai Richler irreparably
angered Quebeckers with his observations on the province's language laws,
its alleged history of anti-Semitism, and its conduct toward Native people
during the Oka crisis. The resulting rift was so deep that novelist and filmmaker Jacques Godbout, introducing the festival *Quebec/New York 2001* in
the *New York Times* (five days after the attack on the World Trade Center,
no less), suggested that Richler, who had just passed away, "could...have
kicked off the New York festivities with a blast and could perhaps even have
finally apologized...for having described his French-speaking compatriots
as raving fanatics."[23] Not quite so drastic were the results of a 1995 conversation between Margaret Atwood and Victor-Lévy Beaulieu, broadcast
on Radio-Canada shortly after the failed referendum on Quebec sovereignty
and later published in both French and English as *Deux sollicitudes* (1996)
and *Two Solicitudes* (1998) respectively. Their dialogue is affable enough
while the authors talk about the business of being writers in anglophone
and francophone Canada, with Atwood playing pursed-mouthed Puritan
to Beaulieu's frivolous Frenchman. A tense moment occurs, however, when
Atwood insists, without much success, that Beaulieu address the role of Aboriginal people and their land claims should the province decide to secede, and
it becomes suddenly clear that no Native author has been invited to intervene
in their conversation.

Histories

A review of novels published in 2003, including Basilières's *Black Bird*, comes
to the conclusion that "[a]n obsession with history...has become the dominant mode of CanLit – the common *Canadian* link among this multicultural
country's wide diversity of writers."[24] The study group for the Royal Commission on Bilingualism and Biculturalism comparing Canadian history textbooks published 1954–64 for use in anglophone and francophone schools
would not have agreed. Instead they concluded with some exasperation that,
with respect to certain events and periods, "the two sets of authors are not
even writing the history of the same country."[25] As a particularly offen-
sive example, the authors cited Marjorie Hamilton's *Pirates and Pathfinders*
(1963) which "devotes 60 per cent of its text to the achievements of British
explorers alone and completely ignores the French" (p. 15). Notwithstanding
the extensive recommendations of the Commission for improvements in this
state of affairs, this view was echoed with some éclat in the reception of
the 2000/2001 television series *Canada: A People's History/Le Canada: une
histoire populaire*, co-produced by the Canadian Broadcasting Corporation

and the Société Radio-Canada. The viewer ratings for the show, modeled on Peter Watkins's *Culloden* (1964) for the BBC and Ken Burns's *The Civil War* (1990) for PBS, made history, but the reception of the series was sharply divided between anglophone and francophone viewers. Some Quebec commentators suspected that the project was a piece of federalist propaganda, whereas federalist politicians worried that it was motivated by separatism. One historian came to the conclusion "that the only real way to do a history of Canada would be to do three histories – written in three parallel columns on the page – one of the aboriginal experience, one of the French, another of the English," only to have the producer counter that the series was doing just that, as well as adding several other perspectives (immigrants, women, labor movements) and interrelating all of them.[26]

The producer's protestations notwithstanding, the series highlighted the problem of translating the idiom of one history into that of another when, in the English version, the anglophone narrator relentlessly anglicized the pronunciation of the numerous French words without which early Canadian history cannot be told (*voyageur*, *coureur de bois*, and so on), and when the francophone actors, using a French accent, spoke in English about the history of their own ancestors. Throughout the history of Canadian literature, translation has been used to bridge differences within the nation, and it has sometimes been necessary to falsify the original to obtain the desired result. Aubert de Gaspé's historical novel *Les anciens Canadiens* was published in 1863, four years before Confederation. Describing the effects of the Battle of the Plains of Abraham through the fortunes of the d'Haberville family and their friend, a Jacobite Scot by the name of Archibald de Locheill, the author still manages a conciliatory tone. The book was translated by Charles G. D. Roberts originally under the title of *The Canadians of Old* (1890), but renamed *Cameron of Locheil* in 1905, thus shifting the emphasis of the narrative from the d'Haberville family to the Scotsman who first befriends them and then, as a member of the British army, destroys their home. The report on Canadian history textbooks cited above locates a similar problem, but in reverse, in a translated textbook. The original *The Story of Canada* (1950) becomes *Notre histoire*, clearly having a more specific referent for the possessive pronoun in mind, and the authors note that there are subtle adjustments in the text to mute any interpretation that might be unfavorable to the French. Illustrations favoring an anglophile interpretation in the English version are replaced. For example, "an illustration [which] shows an English soldier rejoicing at the arrival of the British fleet" gives way to "a picture of [General] Murray setting fire to the farms of the St. Lawrence." With a tartness that distinguishes the tone of this study, making it a more emotional counterpoint to the determinedly objective Report on Bilingualism and Biculturalism, the authors add that "the soldier's smile [in the original illustration] would seem sarcastic to French Canadians" (Trudel and Jain, *Canadian History Textbooks*, p. 22). The most extensively discussed and manipulated image relating to the Battle of the Plains of Abraham is Benjamin West's painting *The Death of General Wolfe*. Drawing on Christian iconography to heighten the status of its subject, it appears in numerous literary texts in both English and French, but its mysticism was dismantled once and for all in the parodic speech-bubble version featured in Léandre Bergeron and Robert Lavaill's comic book *L'histoire du Québec* (1971).

The Canadian critic Linda Hutcheon has used the term "historiographic metafiction"[27] to describe such contemporary works as George Bowering's postmodern reading, in *Burning Water* (1980), of Captain George Vancouver's exploration of the Pacific Northwest, but the historical fiction published in English and French after Confederation and well into the 1920s also deserves to be studied for the numerous manipulative ways in which one set of books modifies versions of history presented in another. Of particular interest in this context are characters whose complex background challenges the very concept of nationality but makes them useful to several different parties. Among these characters are the French-speaking and Roman Catholic Jacobite Scots – like Archibald de Locheill – who startled French Canadian soldiers on the Plains of Abraham and, as mediating figures, make their appearance in both English and French Canadian historical fiction.[28] There is also Pierre-Esprit Radisson, a Provençal who shifted allegiance between the French and English several times, whose linguistic abilities continue to puzzle researchers to this day, whose expeditions with Groseilliers were instrumental in bringing about the Hudson's Bay charter in 1670, and whose swashbuckling has inspired numerous adventure novels in both English and French. Politicians interested in using Canadian history for propagandistic aims sometimes simply ignored the obstinate facts; thus, at the pageant celebrating the tercentenary of the arrival of Samuel de Champlain in Quebec (1908), Montcalm and Wolfe were seen leading their armies in fraternal harmony to ensure that festivities were ended on a positive note.

Book publishing and colonialism

In Michel Tremblay's novel *La grosse femme d'à côté est enceinte* (1978), set in 1942, the fat woman's husband, a printer, supplies his bed-ridden wife with books, several of them – as her scandalized sister-in-law observes – on the *Index* of books forbidden by the Roman Catholic Church. The episode illustrates a remarkable blossoming of book publishing in World War II

Quebec when French writers fled the Vichy government, and publishers in South America, New York, and especially Montreal took over the publication of their works, as well as reprinting a wide range of books that could no longer be imported from France. Dominated until then by religious and nationalist publications, the Montreal publishing industry suddenly found itself catering to an international market of no fewer than fifty-two countries, a process which greatly stimulated the publication of French Canadian literary works as well. Although business dropped off once the war ended, the episode produced lasting results for Quebec's intellectual life, providing emancipation both from conservatism at home and from colonial tutelage by France. For the fat woman, the greatest revelation comes not from the forbidden French books, important as they are as an escape from her suffocating domestic world, but from Gabrielle Roy's *Bonheur d'occasion* (1945), a novel describing Montreal working-class life during World War II. Tremblay's *Chroniques du Plateau Mont-Royal*, of which *La grosse femme d'à côté est enceinte* is the first volume, acknowledge a broad array of influences, ranging from the Greek classics to radio soap-opera, but they are also a major exercise in anti-colonialism: this is signaled not only by the central importance of Roy's book, which serves as a kind of blueprint for Tremblay's own, but also by one character's ritual journey to France, cut short because he realizes the latter is no longer necessary to his understanding of his identity.

The Massey Report pointed out with some envy that there was no comparable phenomenon in the English Canadian publishing industry during World War II, but there were some common concerns nevertheless. The inseparable interaction of the practical and the philosophical in questions of cultural identity has also long been a concern in English-speaking Canada, but because of the shared language the situation is sharpened by the dual presence of British colonial heritage and American cultural influence. Robert Thacker's chapter on short fiction in this volume illustrates the complications that arose when Canadian short-story writers routinely turned to British and American periodicals for publication because there was a lack of Canadian venues. Numerous Canadian authors first established themselves in the United States and Great Britain, sometimes altering their settings to suit their readers' tastes. The reverse, namely the use of Canadian settings by non-Canadian authors, is still considered unusual enough to have earned Carol Shields praise for "adopt[ing] Canada as her own, even using Canadian locales in her writing,"[29] while some of the need to adjust Canadian books to British and US markets lingers on in Canongate's revisions to the original Canadian version of *Life of Pi* for an edition that was also distributed in the United States.

Anglophone book publishing has been buffeted back and forth between colonial and independent markets for much of its history, with complicated navigations between Great Britain and the United States. In *The Beginnings of the Book Trade in Canada* (1985) and in his essay on the "Publishing Industry" in *Encyclopedia of Literature in Canada* (2002), George L. Parker describes a plethora of statutes and conventions affecting Canadian book publishing. These include the Imperial Copyright Act in 1842, the amendment five years later legalizing import of American pirated editions into British North America, the 1885 Berne Copyright Convention which shifted the attention from the place of publication to the book itself, and the 1891 agreement (in which Canada was included) between the United States and Great Britain to end the practice of book piracy. Between 1889 and 1894, Ottawa's Copyright Act was regularly vetoed by the British Parliament. An amended version passed in 1900 still failed to provide the necessary support to local publishing. Both the Canadian Society of Authors and the Canadian Authors Association were founded in part to challenge unfavorable copyright laws, but it was not until 1962 that serious progress was made when the O'Leary Royal Commission on Publications recommended that Canada sign the Universal Copyright Act. In a recurrent pattern this legislation solved some problems and created others, among them the influx of remaindered copies of foreign editions of Canadian books. Following the Massey Report, there were initiatives by the Foreign Investment Review Agency to protect the local publishing industry from foreign takeover, activities further strengthened through the Book Publishing Industry Development Programme.

The Massey Commission gratefully acknowledged US sponsorship of Canadian culture by the Carnegie, Rockefeller, and Guggenheim foundations and it tried to remain aloof from expressions of strident anti-Americanism resulting from a massive influx of American publications and television programs, but there were rumblings nevertheless. Although its representatives added that "[t]he fault is not America's but ours," the Canadian Writers' Committee declared in its presentation to the Commission that "[w]e would like to see the development of a little Canadian independence, some say in who we are, and what we think, and how we feel and what we do," while another commentator on the state of Canadian letters even spoke of "a crisis of orientation" (p. 225). National endeavor, rejection of American influence, and book publishing all came together in the cult that sprang up during the 1970s around John Richardson's historical novel *Wacousta; or, The Prophecy: A Tale of the Canadas* (1832). Pirated by Adam Waldie of Philadelphia four months after its publication by T. Caddell in London, Richardson's novel underwent extensive revision to alter the subtitle ("A

Tale of the Canadas" became "A Tale of Detroit and Michillimackinac"), to adjust punctuation and spelling to American usage, expunge dialect, and soften the lurid eroticism of the novel. Geographical and historical details were also adjusted: the *accent aigu* in Détroit disappeared, and details regarding alliances between Aboriginal people and the British were suppressed. In this mutilated edition Douglas Cronk perceived a malicious falsification of Richardson's supposedly patriotic intention to write a book for British and Canadian readers and "to persuade [them] to view Canada's heroic past with a more kindly and interested eye." As the Waldie edition was the most widely known, Cronk argued, "Canadians are... in real danger of having a distorted, erroneous view of Canadian literature."[30] Cronk's own contribution to solving the problem was an annotated edition, in 1987, of Caddell's original *Wacousta* published in a series prepared by the Centre for the Editing of Early Canadian Texts. Richardson surely also became a focus of Canadian nationalism because, in the sequel to *Wacousta*, *The Canadian Brothers; or, The Prophecy Fulfilled* (1840), he wrote about the War of 1812 during which Canada successfully rebuffed American aggression.

There was protest as well when the Ryerson Press was sold to McGraw-Hill in 1970, a transaction which the provincial government of Ontario did nothing to stop. In the years after World War I, which, in many ways and for similar reasons, anticipated the assertion of Canadian culture after World War II, the Ryerson Press under Lorne Pierce had undertaken a large program promoting modernist writers, publishing series of biographical and interpretive works (most notably the "Makers of Canadian Literature"), and commissioning a team of well-known authors to research travelogues about each province. Pierce's *An Outline of Canadian Literature* (1927) briskly enumerates the chief developments in French and English, adopting a no-nonsense approach to the assumed coexistence of the two literatures and to literacy as the means to national harmony and maturity. Using a trope widely employed to describe Canada's potential, he affirms that the country is a vigorous youth striding confidently towards greatness, and he sweeps aside stereotypes associated with Canada as contemptible efforts to stifle its self-confidence, revealing a few prejudices of his own in the process: "Mounties, bushmen, whiskey-runners, cow-punchers, Indians and pretty Pierres are not the collective logos of the Canadian spirit." He also anticipates the concerns of the Massey Commission and of the 1970s nationalists by requesting "that the only civilized country in the world, which does not make the study of its native literature obligatory in all its schools and colleges, will remove this unenviable distinction."[31] The cultural climate of the 1970s may be miles away from that which produced Lorne Pierce, but their faith in literature as creator of national identity made the editors of *Read Canadian: A Book about Canadian Books* (1972) his intellectual heirs nevertheless. The work, edited by a formidable trio consisting of Dave Godfrey (House of Anansi), Robert Fulford (*Saturday Night*), and Abraham Rotstein (*Canadian Forum*), was published in direct response to the sale of Ryerson Press.

As is frequently the case in Canadian culture, however, the allegiances in this nationalist phase are far from clear-cut. During the years of the Vietnam War, Canada received a large number of American draft evaders, many of them highly educated and therefore sometimes referred to as successors to the numerous university graduates among the eighteenth-century Loyalists who escaped the American Revolution and settled in Canada. Several of these draft evaders became influential participants in the cultural industries of their adopted country, as well as offering vocal criticism of the one they left behind. Doug Fetherling's memoir *Travels by Night: A Memoir of the Sixties* (1994), for example, uses the narratives of slave fugitives as a model to describe his own "escape" from the United States, although the *Manual for Draft-Age Immigrants to Canada* (1969), edited by Mark Satin, adopted a rather condescending tone in describing the country's resources – and this despite its publication by the House of Anansi, one of English Canada's most important nationalist presses. In an additional complication, efforts to differentiate Canadian culture from its American counterpart generated a renewed rapprochement with British culture which, according to the work of philosopher George Grant, provided a heritage of "civility" and con-servatism by choice that made Canada fundamentally different from the tradition of individualism and liberalism characterizing the United States. Elaborating on Grant's ideas, the poet Dennis Lee produced the manifesto "Cadence, Country, Silence: Writing in Colonial Space" (1973) about writ-ing in a language already inhabited and owned by others. Together with Lee's *Civil Elegies* (1968), this was perhaps the most complex and moving docu-ments to emerge out of 1970s nationalism. One of the few English Canadian authors ever to speak at one of these events, Lee first presented this piece in 1972, in French, at a *Rencontre québécoise internationale des écrivains*. Entitled "L'écriture et l'errance," this was one of a series of conferences that have regularly brought together impressive assemblies of contemporary writers, especially (but not exclusively) from francophone and Latin back-grounds. For both anglophone and francophone authors, the Free Trade Agreement between Canada, the United States, and Mexico (1988) renewed many of the earlier fears that Canadian culture was in danger of being swal-lowed up by its powerful neighbor. Some of the concerns were articulated in Laurier LaPierre's *If You Love This Country: Facts and Feelings on Free Trade* (1987).

A recurrent symbol to capture Canadian aspirations being brought down by American interests is the demise of the Avro Arrow, a Canadian-designed interceptor scrapped in 1956, allegedly to make way for US-built missiles. A 1997 CBC film on this episode provoked a commentary in the *Globe and Mail* acknowledging, in yet another allusion to Canada as vigorous youth, that "it was a spectacular plane, ahead of its time – sleek, fast and muscular." However, in a shift that echoes Grant and Lee, the author also reminds the myth-makers that the Avro was an instrument of destruction and that more lasting accomplishments are to be found in economic, scientific, and artistic accomplishments, as well as social security.[32]

The *Companion* and its chapters

In drafting the chapters for this *Companion*, we have had to make several important decisions about the best ways in which to deal with the diversity of Canadian literature within the restrictions of the series. The most significant of these was probably that relating to the question of francophone writing in Canada. To include a full account of it in each chapter would have expanded the volume well beyond its projected length. Instead, in addition to sketching out in the introduction some research questions that involve writing in French, we have opted for a comprehensive chapter outlining developments in francophone writing, with links to subjects in some of the other chapters. While this may be a cursory way of dealing with a literature the discussion of which could easily fill a *Companion* of its own, we felt that the other possibility – leaving it out altogether – was out of the question. Related to this decision is our handling of accents. In general, we use the English version of names that appear with accents in French but without in English (for instance, Quebec/Québec, Montreal/Montréal), except of course when they are part of a quotation in French. This means that, in the chapter on francophone writing, it has sometimes been necessary to use both versions side by side. The second organizational problem arose from the embarrassment of riches Canadian literature presents to the contemporary researcher. Virtually all of the chapters have had to be shortened to conform with space restrictions, but we have tried to make up for some of the resulting brevities by distributing topics across a range of chapters, each offering a different perspective. The chapter on fiction in particular provides something of an anchor for the discussions of short fiction, writing by women, and regionalism and urbanism, and coverage is coordinated between all four chapters to avoid redundancy. The chapter on regionalism and urbanism also includes drama and poetry and thus intersects with the chapters devoted to these genres as well. We decided to include a chapter specifically devoted to women writers because, among several other things, it permitted us to highlight specific questions arising from gender and sexuality. The heading is not the only way in which the topic could have been introduced, but given the prominence of Canadian women writers it is an appropriate one. The chapters on life writing, nature-writing, and exploration and travel are also in close communion. Introduction and final chapter work in counterpoint, the former reviewing some of the historical questions involved in the study of Canadian literature, the latter offering a reflection on its most influential theories. Finally, in keeping with the presence of Native people long before the arrival of explorers, traders, and settlers, the opening chapter discusses Aboriginal writing, but the topic is introduced throughout the *Companion* wherever appropriate. "Native" and "Indigenous" are spelled with capitals when they refer to "Aboriginal." Some sources we cite use the lower case, but in each instance the context is clear enough to distinguish the meaning from "native" and "indigenous" as in the more general "homegrown."

NOTES

My thanks to Dennis Lee for answering my questions.

1. Charles Foran, "As Canadian as...," *Globe and Mail* 19 Oct. 2002: pp. D5–6.
2. Aida Edemariam, "Us? Boring? Ha!" *Guardian* 27 Sept. 2002: n. pag., online, *Guardian Unlimited*, Internet.
3. Graham Huggan, *The Postcolonial Exotic: Marketing the Margins* (London: Routledge, 2001); Luke Strongman, *The Booker Prize and the Legacy of Empire* (Amsterdam: Rodopi, 2002).
4. Robert McCrum, "The Booker Revolution," *Observer* 27 Oct. 2002: n. pag., online, *Guardian Unlimited*, Internet.
5. Larry Rohter, "Canadian's Book Raises Hackles in Brazil," *New York Times* 9 Nov. 2002: n. pag., online, *IHT Online*, Internet.
6. Sabine Sielke, "'The Empathetic Imagination': An Interview with Yann Martel," *Canadian Literature* 177 (Summer 2003): p. 30.
7. "Littérature," *Le Devoir* 23 Oct. 2002: n. pag., online, <http://LeDevoir.com>, Internet.
8. Claude Jasmin, "Journal," 24 Oct. 2002, online, Internet. Jasmin posts a daily journal on the Internet under <http://claude-jasmin.com/journees>. The quotations are taken from one of these postings. Two volumes of his diaries have been published, *A coeur de jour* (2002) and *Ecrivain chassant aussi le bébé écureil* (2003).
9. Sandra Martin, "Canada Takes the Prize at Squashing Excellence," *Globe and Mail* 3 Dec. 2002: p. A23, online, <http://TheGlobeandMail.com>, Internet.
10. Lord Durham, *Lord Durham's Report: An Abridgement of Report on the Affairs of British North America*, ed. G. M. Craig (Toronto: McClelland, 1963) pp. 23, 150. The Durham Report was originally published in 1839.
11. General Introduction, *Report of the Royal Commission on Bilingualism and Biculturalism*, vol. I (Ottawa: Queen's Printer, 1967) p. xxii.

12. *Report of the Royal Commission on Bilingualism and Biculturalism*, vol. I, p. xxii.

13. Ken Wiwa, "The Square Root of Pi, Plus the Sum of Canadian Narratives," *Globe and Mail* 9 Nov. 2002: p. A15.

14. See Pico Iyer, "The Multiculture," *The Global Soul: Jet Lag, Shopping Malls, and the Search for Home* (New York: Knopf, 2000) pp. 116–71.

15. Louis S. St. Laurent, letter to Vincent Massey, *Report of the Royal Commission on National Development in the Arts, Letters and Sciences 1949–1951* (Ottawa: Edmond Cloutier, 1951) p. xxi.

16. "Canadian Multiculturalism Act," *Documenting Canada: A History of Modern Canada in Documents*, ed. Dave de Brou and Bill Waiser (Saskatoon: Fifth House, 1992) p. 657.

17. Gwynne Dyer, "Visible Majorities," *Canadian Geographic* (Jan./Feb. 2001): p. 50.

18. *Report of the Royal Commission on Bilingualism and Biculturalism*, vol. IV: *The Cultural Contribution of the Other Ethnic Groups* (Ottawa: Queen's Printer, 1969) p. 73.

19. Tu Thanh Ha, "The PQ's Narrow Ethnic Vision," *Globe and Mail* 11 Nov. 1995: p. D1.

20. Named after Prime Minister Wilfrid Laurier (1841–1919) who envisioned unity among Canada's founding peoples, the Laurier Institute is an organization whose mandate is to inform the public about the social and economic effects of Canadian diversity. See also the work of the Dominion Institute, a group founded to promote greater knowledge and appreciation of Canadian history.

21. *Report of the Royal Commission on Bilingualism and Biculturalism*, vol. IV, p. 73.

22. Julian Beltrame, "Simply the Best: Gov. Gen. Adrienne Clarkson Will Be Tough to Follow," *Maclean's* 24 March 2003: pp. 19–24.

23. Jacques Godbout, "In Quebec Culture, a Deep Skepticism of Tradition," *New York Times* 16 September 2001: section 2, p. 6.

24. Brian Bethune, "From Memory to Meaning," *Maclean's* 24 March 2003: p. 52.

25. Marcel Trudel and Geneviève Jain, *Canadian History Textbooks: A Comparative Study* (Ottawa: Queen's Printer, 1970) p. 14.

26. Jacques Lacoursière, cited in Mark Starowicz's *Making History: The Remarkable Story behind* Canada: A People's History (Toronto: McClelland, 2003) p. 314.

27. Linda Hutcheon, "Canadian Historiographic Metafiction," *Essays on Canadian Writing* 30 (1984–5): pp. 228–38.

28. See Andrea Cabajsky, "'Transcolonial Circuits': Historical Fiction and National Identities in Ireland, Scotland, and Canada," diss., University of British Columbia, 2002.

29. Douglas Cornish, "Letter to the Editor," *Globe and Mail* 19 July 2003: p. A16.

30. Douglas Cronk, "The Americanization of *Wacousta*," *Recovering Canada's First Novelist: Proceedings from the John Richardson Conference*, ed. Catherine Sheldrick Ross (Erin: Porcupine's Quill, 1984) p. 47.

31. Lorne Pierce, *An Outline of Canadian Literature (English and French)* (Toronto: Ryerson, 1927) pp. 240, 244.

32. "The Legacy of the Avro Arrow," *Globe and Mail* 18 Jan. 1997: p. D8.

I

Aboriginal writing

PENNY VAN TOORN[1]

Transformations of oral traditions

In September 1838, Peter Jones (Kahkewaquonaby), an ordained Ojibway Methodist minister, presented a petition to Queen Victoria from chiefs of the Mississauga Ojibway community at Credit River, where he had lived with his mother for the first fourteen years of his life. The petition asked that the Credit River community be granted the title deeds that would ensure their lands could never be taken away.[2] Kahkewaquonaby had written the chiefs' message in the roman alphabet, and they had signed it pictographically with their clan emblems. Attached to the document were some strings of wampum that Kahkewaquonaby read for the queen, as well as delivering his own oral supplication in support of the chiefs' request. Consisting of three forms of writing, and two kinds of oral utterance, the petition was a multimedia event, not merely a written text that could be trusted to speak for itself. Kahkewaquonaby's bodily presence, dressed in buckskin and moccasins, was necessary to authenticate and authorize the petition, to witness that it had been received, and to guide the queen's interpretation of the document in a manner most likely to ensure a favorable outcome for the Credit River Ojibway community. To work effectively, the written petition had to be delivered *as though it were an oral message*. Power and meaning did not reside in the alphabetically written document itself, but were activated through the ceremonial process of its face-to-face delivery, framing, and re-voicing by Kahkewaquonaby.

Over the centuries, cultures of the voice and the written word have become entangled in complex ways, both within and between Aboriginal and European societies. Far from automatically extinguishing oral traditions, writing can potentially sit beside them, and be integrated into the social etiquette of oral communication by means such as Kahkewaquonaby used when presenting the Ojibway petition to Queen Victoria. In recognition of the possibility that writing can be used to preserve and disseminate aspects

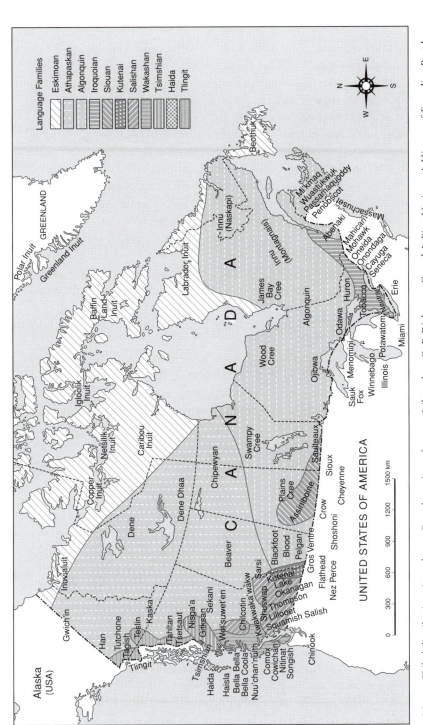

Map 2: Tribal distributions in and near Canada at time of contact[a] (based on O. P. Dickason, *Canada's First Nations: A History of Founding Peoples from Earliest Times*, 3rd edn. [Oxford: Oxford University Press, 2002] p. 47)

a   Various different spellings of Native tribal groups and place-names are currently in use.

of oral culture, Theytus Books, the first Native-owned publishing house in Canada, takes its name from a Salishian word meaning "preserving for the sake of handing down."[3]

Until relatively recently, however, the predominant belief among anthropologists, mission societies, media theorists, and government policy makers was that oral and literate cultures are successive, mutually exclusive stages in a single, unavoidable path of cultural evolution. This belief justified assimilation policies, which were considered merely a means of hastening the inevitable "progress" of "primitive" Aboriginal peoples into the "modern" world. Today, such ideas are discredited as relics of a colonialist ideology that justified European cultural domination by picturing Aboriginal peoples as Europe's primitive ancestors. Aboriginal peoples in Canada today are nonetheless living with the legacies of such ideas, having seen their cultures threatened or destroyed by missionaries who prohibited traditional languages and ceremonies, and by welfare and residential school systems that obstructed cultural transmission by separating children from their families. Erroneous as it was, the idea that cultures evolved from orality to literacy became a self-fulfilling prophecy because it was enforced through government policies.

Today's Aboriginal writers emphasize the importance of their oral cultural heritage both as a source of meaning in their lives and as a resource for their writing. While direct involvement in family and community life remains the primary means of oral cultural transmission, Aboriginal cultures are now passed down through a variety of additional means such as books, magazines, dramatic and musical performances, films, television, radio, and the Internet. Risks arise, however, when oral texts are disseminated through mass media into non-Aboriginal cultural domains where there may not be a Kahkewaquonaby to control what such texts "say" and how they might legitimately be used. In the absence of information about the functions it serves in its culture of origin, Aboriginal orature has often been misunderstood and evaluated inappropriately in terms of Eurocentric aesthetic criteria. ("Orature" is a term widely used to refer to forms of oral discourse such as stories, songs, and various kinds of ritual utterance. The word was coined because "oral literature" was a contradiction in terms.)

Anishinabe poet and cultural worker Marie Annharte Baker likens written records of Aboriginal orature to the fixative used by entomologists to preserve the bodies of insect specimens that typify their species.[4] Such petrification is a concern because Indigenous cultures have never been static in time, nor uniform across the country that is now Canada. The peoples of the Eastern Woodlands, Plains, Plateau, sub-Arctic and Arctic North, and West Coast speak around fifty different languages.[5] In diverse ecological contexts,

Aboriginal societies developed distinct economies, diets, technologies, and patterns of sociopolitical interaction, both with each other and, from the sixteenth century onwards, with Europeans. Each society has its own stories, songs, orations, and prayers. Some were kept secret within closed circles of initiates, others were known widely but performed only on special ceremonial occasions, while many circulated freely as an integral part of daily life. These oral genres express spiritual beliefs, encode moral and social values, preserve knowledge of history and culture, and provide frameworks for understanding how to live in accord with particular ecological environments. Stories, songs, orations, and prayers weave the universe into a coherent reality that remains, to varying degrees and through diverse combinations of channels, accessible to Aboriginal peoples in Canada today.

Diverse and mutable as they are, oral narratives from different parts of Canada share some common motifs such as creation events, sentient animals, birds and sea creatures, dreams and vision quests, songs and ceremonies, models of proper and improper behavior, and transformations back and forth between human and animal forms. Trickster figures feature in stories from all regions of Canada. While Coyote is perhaps the best-known and most wide-ranging Trickster in literary texts, s/he has various regional manifestations such as Raven in British Columbia, Old Man on the plains, Wisakedjak among the Saulteaux and Cree, Nanabozho among the Ojibway, and Glooscap among the Micmac.[6] For contemporary Aboriginal writers, the Trickster is at once a spiritual entity and a literary device for introducing narrative twists, jokes, and word games. Daniel David Moses sees the Trickster as crucial to "our attitude that things are funny even though horrible things happen."[7] Tomson Highway says the Trickster "straddles the consciousness of man and that of God, the Great Spirit."[8] Lenore Keeshig-Tobias, editor of *The Magazine to Re-Establish the Trickster*, emphasizes that "We learn through the Teacher's mistakes as well as the Teacher's virtues."[9]

Broadly speaking, traditional Aboriginal oral stories have their own conventions of expression and structure. Describing such conventions in terms of their difference from European literary norms is risky, however, because it can easily lead to sweeping generalizations about both cultures. It is probably safe to say, though, that (like Defoe but not Proust) traditional Aboriginal oral narratives are not usually concerned with deep psychological intricacies of individual characterization, although Inuit "mood songs" concisely capture moments of intense emotion and perception.[10] Like Laurence Sterne's novels but unlike popular detective fiction, some Aboriginal oral narratives may seem rambling and episodic because they do not build from the outset towards a single, revelatory climax. Like Shakespeare's problem plays, some traditional Aboriginal stories can also prove difficult to pigeon-hole in European genre categories because they combine farce, tragedy, religious allegory, secular history, didactic messages, and elements borrowed from foreign cultures. The language of Aboriginal orators and storytellers could be ornate, archaic, and figurative to the point of obscurity, like that of Europe's Renaissance sonneteers. Words serve in both cultures as instruments of power and social management, particularly in ceremonial and rhetorical contexts where it is desirable to frame arguments in oblique, circuitous ways in order to avoid direct confrontation or coercion. Today's Aboriginal writers adopt various orientations towards both Aboriginal oral and European literary modes, but all articulate an awareness of the power of words and stories, and of the different kinds of potency exercised by speech and writing.

What counts as writing?

While it is universally accepted that the Aboriginal peoples of North America have long practiced the oral arts of narrative, song, oratory, and prayer, the question of when they began to write elicits a range of possible answers. Depending on how authorship and writing are defined, Aboriginal writing has several alternative beginnings. If "writing" is taken to mean the act of individual physical composition of texts in alphabetic script, Native writing began at different times in different parts of Canada when missionaries taught literacy skills to Native children, and with the arrival of literate adults such as Mohawk Loyalist Joseph Brant (Thayendanegea), who moved to Lower Canada from the United States in the 1780s. However, if "writing" includes collaborative text-making processes such as transcription and dictation, in which the roles of author and scribe are performed by separate individuals, it is valid to say that some Native people were knowingly participating in the creation of alphabetically written texts during the early seventeenth century when Jesuit missionaries began transcribing their stories, songs, speeches, and messages to distant friends. Montagnais chief Noël Negabamat (Tekouerimat), for example, appears to have known exactly what he was doing when he dictated the following letter in 1652: "Father Paul LeJeune: I seem to see thee, when thy letter is read to me; and I seem to be with thee, when I speak to thee by the mouth, or the pen, of Father de Quen."[11] When Ottawa war chief Pontiac dictated his letters to British and French officials, was he any less an author than Joseph Brant who composed his military missives by hand,[12] or than Milton, Joyce, and other canonical English authors who used an amanuensis?

The question of when Aboriginal writing began hinges also on whether "writing" is defined narrowly as a graphic code for spoken language, or more broadly to include non-phonographic scripts such as pictographs and ideographs. If "writing" means alphabetic script, Native writing began in colonial institutions such as mission schools in the early nineteenth century. However, if like 'Nlaka'pamux elder Annie York we consider the petroglyphs and pictographs created by the people of the Stein River Valley in British Columbia to be "rock writings,"[13] then Native writing has been practiced for thousands of years. Petrone (*Native Literature*, p. 10) and others have referred to non-alphabetic texts such as the wampum of the Iroquois and the birch-bark scrolls of the Ojibway Midéwewin as mere aids to memory. The Ojibway, however, use the same word, "masinaigun" (derived from the verb "nin masinaige," meaning "I make signs") to refer both to the birch-bark scrolls and to paper and books.[14] Micmac poet Rita Joe calls Micmac hieroglyphics "the written word of the Indian / That the world chooses to deny."[15] By quoting (in translation) the Jesuit missionary Le Clercq's written record of the Micmac characters – "'I noticed children / Making marks with charcoal on ground,' / Said LeClercq" ("Micmac Hieroglyphics," p. 114) – Rita Joe places readers in a position where, if they trust the alphabetically written record, they must logically also recognize the Micmacs' non-alphabetic script as a functional writing system.

The existence of these scripts suggests that the history of writing does not follow a single evolutionary path leading to the roman alphabet, but rather an array of co-evolutionary lines of development in which diverse writing systems were devised in different places.[16] Just as literacy does not necessarily extinguish oral cultures, the alphabet does not inevitably supplant all other scripts. The Nunavut Territory, established in 1999, has two official writing systems, the roman alphabet and a version of the Cree syllabics. Nor have the Micmac hieroglyphics been extinguished by the roman alphabet. Although augmented by non-Native missionaries, the Micmac hieroglyphics have been considered an important symbol of Micmac identity and aid to language preservation since at least 1843, when Indian Commissioner Joseph Howe planned to set up Native schools in Nova Scotia, but found that Micmac parents resisted the idea of their children learning to read any script but the hieroglyphs. Micmac book culture also differed from European norms because it was practiced in accordance with traditional Micmac social etiquette. Where an elder and his/her pupil read from a single copy of a book, for example, the danger of the pupil accidentally violating the traditional Micmac sanction against making contact with an elder's leg was averted by printing each page of the book twice, head-to-toe on facing pages, so that teacher and pupil could both read the same page of text right-side-up, while sitting opposite each other with the book between them.[17]

Many European accounts of Native amazement at the "miracles" of writing and reading are a projection of the European observer's sense of their own cultural superiority, rather than a historical reflection of Native awe at the self-evident virtues of alphabetic script.[18] Aboriginal peoples' responses to books and writing varied in accordance with the circumstances in which they encountered them. While some saw books as powerful sacred objects, others dismissed them as irrelevant because of their manifest impotence against problems such as hunger and disease (Wogan, "Perceptions of European Literacy," pp. 407, 415). As well as evaluating books and alphabetic writing in terms of their own needs, Aboriginal peoples understood their workings in terms of their own existing categories of objects and activities. The Algonquian, for example, referred to the powers of alphabetic writing as "wussuck wheke," a cognate of the term for their own deerskin paintings (Wogan, "Perceptions of European Literacy," p. 413). The Huron, by contrast, understood written inscription in terms of an analogy between the snowshoe and the pen, both of which leave a trail or print on a white surface (Wogan, "Perceptions of European Literacy," p. 414). In recent times, the titles of two documents crucial to the formation of the Nunavut Territory, *Footprints in New Snow* (1995) and *Footprints II* (1996), employ the image of print(s) to name written texts that lead to a new historical era.

Most importantly, Aboriginal attitudes towards books, writing, and the English language were and are shaped by the fact that they were and are used as tools of deception, destruction, and dispossession. Many authors have expressed outrage at the missionaries' use of the Bible to shatter Aboriginal world-views, and at governments' use of treaties and written laws, backed up by guns and prisons, to control and subjugate Aboriginal peoples.[19] While alphabetic script, books, and the English language remain tainted by their history, Aboriginal authors have now appropriated the power of these weapons for their own purposes.

The nineteenth century

As Aboriginal peoples have evaluated writing and books in light of their own respective cultures and histories, Europeans have assessed Aboriginal verbal artistry in terms of their own cultural paradigms. When praising Native orators for their eloquence, reasoning, dramatic flair, and prodigious memories, Europeans usually evaluated these accomplishments in terms of Classical or Renaissance European rhetorical conventions, or romantic notions of the noble savage – an ambivalent stereotype potentially both degrading and empowering to Native writers.

In their search for inspiration, authority, and financial support, most nineteenth-century Native writers had little option but to play the noble savage on occasions, and reap whatever benefits they could from Europe's fascination with "primitives" and "disappearing races." Peter Jones (Kahkewaquonaby), for example, dressed in buckskin and moccasins when he spoke to thrilled crowds during his three tours of Great Britain in the 1830s and 40s (Petrone, *Native Literature,* p. 36). Jones was among the first generation of young Ojibway men to be formally educated by the Wesleyan Methodist Missionary Society in Upper Canada in the mid-1820s. He played a central role in the first Native literary coterie, which included George Copway, George Henry, Peter Jacobs, John Sunday, Allen Salt, and Henry Steinhauer.[20] These young Ojibway men made their names through preaching, traveling nationally and internationally on public speaking tours, giving lectures to academic bodies, and performing dramatic readings and orations of their works on the stage, clad in traditional Native dress.

Peter Jones and his colleagues founded the Canadian Native literary tradition not through a decisive shift from Native orality to European literacy, but rather by moving back and forth between oral and literary institutions *within* European culture, as well as *between* European and Native cultures. Far from putting an end to talk, the writings of these young men fueled their speaking careers, which in turn boosted their popularity as writers. On his first trip to Britain in 1831–2, Jones delivered over 150 addresses and sermons, many of which were later published in pamphlets, Methodist periodicals, and local newspapers (Petrone, *Native Literature,* p. 36). He also mediated between Indigenous oral and European literate cultures, translating and transcribing messages from Native leaders and conveying them to the relevant white authorities.[21] Whether in theatrical performances, sermons, or political negotiations, oratorical skills became more, rather than less, important at the interface between Aboriginal and European cultures. In view of the power traditionally accorded to men gifted in the oral verbal arts, it is not surprising that the first generation of formally schooled Native writers adopted leadership roles as preachers, lecturers, and performers. These were (male) roles they would probably have recognized as authoritative and prestigious, not only in European terms but also in terms of traditional Native cultural criteria.

Early Métis writing was also grounded in oral cultural practices. Pierre Falcon's "La chanson de la Grenouillère," which celebrated Métis leader Cuthbert Grant's routing of Governor Semple and his men at Seven Oaks in 1816, was the first of six songs by Falcon that remain extant in written form today. Falcon's songs were not written for silent, solitary reading. They came to life in the mouths, ears, and hearts of the many Métis who sung them together, expressing their emerging sense of themselves as a distinct people with their own history and culture.[22] Métis leader Louis Riel, celebrated in Falcon's song about the Red River Rebellion, "Les tribulations d'un roi malheureux," was a prolific author of political and religious writings, diaries, speeches, and poetry.[23] With Gabriel Dumont, he is honored in Métis writing today.

Fewer Native women than men became authors and scribes during the nineteenth century. While women had their own traditional leadership roles, they did not customarily serve as spokespeople for their communities. Nor were they elevated into leadership roles through the church-based patronage systems that supported the literary activities of their menfolk. Like most of their non-Native contemporaries, Native women's literary efforts were confined to private and domestic spheres. The first Inuk autobiography, Lydia Campbell's *Sketches of Labrador Life* (1894), was an exception to the general tendency for women to write poetry rather than book-length histories, travelogues, sermons, or autobiographies. Jane Schoolcraft, for example, whose Ojibway mother and grandfather were both distinguished storytellers, published poetry under the pseudonym "Rosa." Whatever contributions she made to the books on Native culture produced by her husband, Henry Rowe Schoolcraft, he alone is named as their author. Ojibway Catherine Soneegoh Sutton (Nahnebahwequa) also wrote poetry, and petitioned Queen Victoria to regain some of her land.

By far the most famous and prolific late nineteenth-century woman writer was Emily Pauline Johnson (Tekahionwake). Her Mohawk education came from her father, and also from her grandfather, who served as Speaker in the Great Council of the Six Nations Confederacy. Her English education came mainly from her governess, and from her English mother who introduced her to Shakespearean drama and the major nineteenth-century dramatic and narrative poets (Petrone, *Native Literature*, p. 78) – that is, to the orally grounded tradition within the English literary canon. From 1892, when she recited her "Cry of an Indian Wife" and "As Red Men Die" before a gathering of Toronto literati, it was obvious that her success depended as much on her abilities as an orator as on her talents as a writer. Her poetry took the form of lyrics, narratives, and dramatic monologues, with titles such as "The Song My Paddle Sings," "Lullaby of the Iroquois," and "Cry of an Indian Wife" highlighting its oral grounding. The title of Johnson's first published poetry collection, *The White Wampum* (1895), is quietly political and ironic, given that most of the poems were written for oral recitation, and that wampum was a readable medium developed by the Iroquois peoples in pre-Columbian times. Johnson's *Legends of Vancouver* (1911) records stories told by Coast Salish Chief Capilano. Pauline Johnson's career raises complex questions about cultural transmission, identity, gender, agency, and performance. Her life and writings have come under renewed scrutiny by Native and non-Native feminist critics, including Beth Brant, Carole Gerson, Veronica Strong-Boag, and Charlotte Gray.[24]

The decades between Johnson's death and the late 1960s were a barren time for Aboriginal literature and politics. Non-Aboriginal writers published Aboriginal stories as fairytales and ethnographic data, while pseudo-Indians such as Grey Owl (Archibald Belaney) and Chief Buffalo Child Long Lance (Sylvester Clark Long) consolidated white complacency by romanticizing Native life in ways that diverted attention from the real oppression and hardship that Native peoples were suffering. While Belaney and Long were pretending to be quintessential "Indians," Tuscarora journalist and war veteran Frederick Ogilvie Loft was using the medium of print to disseminate his vision of Canada's first peoples as a single, pan-Canadian Aboriginal nation. In 1919, he sent a written circular to chiefs across Canada inviting them to join the first national Indigenous organization, the League of Indians of Canada. Having been used to divide and conquer, writing was now being used to build a national Aboriginal political constituency.

World War II veterans were also politically active. They highlighted Native and Métis contributions to the allied war effort, and noted the contradiction between Canada's abhorrence of German anti-Semitism and the grinding down of Canada's Aboriginal peoples by racially discriminatory laws and policies. In 1942, Squamish leader Andrew Paull founded the North American Brotherhood, and went on to publish two newspapers, the *Thunderbird* (1949–55) and *The Totem Speaks* (1953) (Petrone, *Native Literature*, p. 105). Aboriginal protests and the founding of many organizations, newspapers, and periodicals formed part of the political ferment that developed throughout the western world in the 1960s.

Paper against paper

Having been voted into office in 1968, under the banners of "a just society" and "participatory democracy," Prime Minister Pierre Trudeau argued that, in the name of social justice, "We must all be equal . . . We can't recognize aboriginal rights."[25] Jean Chrétien, Trudeau's Indian Affairs Minister, disregarded Native advice on how best to redress long-standing disadvantages in Native communities, and proposed in his controversial 1969 "White Paper"[26] that Indian status be abolished, Native services be mainstreamed, and Aboriginal peoples become just another element in Canada's multicultural society. The White Paper provoked a flood of anger that did not abate when Trudeau and Chrétien abandoned the White Paper's key proposals.

Dismayed at the government's lack of understanding and concern for their needs, Aboriginal leaders galvanized into a nationally organized force, and Aboriginal writing became overtly political. In *The Unjust Society* (1969) Alberta Cree writer Harold Cardinal accused the government of "extermination through assimilation," and of implying that "the only good Indian is a non-Indian."[27] A chorus of voices, including Enos T. Montour, Howard Adams, Duke Redbird, Emile Pelletier, Antoine Lussier, George Manuel, and Chief John Snow, emphasized the need for governments to recognize and redress the continuing legacies of past discrimination.[28]

Emma LaRocque suggests that from the mid-1970s strident protest literature gave way to a more "soft-sell" approach in personal narratives, autobiographies, children's stories, interviews with elders, and other non-confronting kinds of writing. Yet these types of story, as LaRocque points out, were politically effective in their own way.[29] Life narratives, for example, asserted distinct cultural identities. Inuit autobiographies such as Bernard Irqugaqtuq's "The Autobiography of a Pelly Bay Eskimo"[30] and "The Song of the Aircraft,"[31] and Peter Pitseolak's *People from Our Side* (1975) contain incidents, characters, and structural elements based on traditional Inuit legends (McGrath, "Oral Influences in Contemporary Inuit Literature," pp. 159–60). Life narratives also reveal hidden histories by documenting the lives of individuals within their communities. Although each life narrative is unique, common concerns and patterns of experience emerged. To say this is neither to essentialize Aboriginal peoples, nor to deny their historical and cultural differences, but rather to recognize that racially discriminatory laws and policies affected disparate groups of people in systematically damaging ways, so that they came to share common elements of history and identity ([Akiwenzie-] Damm, "Says Who," p. 14). Petrone's *Native Literature in Canada* describes a comprehensive range of 1970s and 80s life writings (pp. 114–20, 127–9, and 148–54). While her bibliographic work has produced a valuable resource, her aesthetic judgments regarding the tone and style of these writings subject them inappropriately to conservative European standards of literary decorum, without adequately considering how the life writings met the needs of Native and Métis communities.

As well as articulating a strong sense of personal and communal identity, many life narratives in the 1970s and 80s challenged white ignorance and apathy, revealing the hidden history of Native and Métis peoples, and developing oral modes of literary address that engaged readers on a personal level. Maria Campbell's *Halfbreed* (1973), for example, situates readers as unknowing outsiders to whom she is speaking face-to-face: "I write this for all of you, to tell you what it is like to be a Halfbreed woman in our country. I want to tell you about the joys and sorrows, the oppressing poverty, the frustrations and the dreams."³² This personal manner of address makes it difficult for readers *not* to care about the problems facing the author and other Métis women in her position. By identifying herself as "a Halfbreed woman" rather than as a unique individual, Campbell underlines the historical relevance of her story. This is important work, given the number of Aboriginal people who, as Ron Hamilton puts it, are "prisoners of [a] history . . . compiled by their enemies."³³

Numerous life narratives were produced in collaboration with non-Native interviewers, transcribers, and editors. These co-produced texts highlighted the potential risks of transforming oral discourse into printed books. Disputes and misunderstandings arose over ownership and control of these co-produced texts. Lee Maracle's *Bobbi Lee: Indian Rebel* (1975), for example, was initially published under the name of non-Native interviewer and editor Don Barnett. Non-Native editors who imagined they were merely assisting a Native authorial process often exploited the power advantage conventionally attached to the editorial role. While seeing themselves as "helpers," numerous white editors have appropriated Aboriginal oral life narratives, demoting the autobiographical subject to the subordinate role of "Native informant."

The 1970s saw the emergence of several anthologies and collections of Native poetry and stories including *Sweetgrass* (1971), *Okanagan Indian Poems and Short Stories* (1974), *Wisdom of Indian Poetry* (1976), *Native Sons* (1977), and *Many Voices: An Anthology of Contemporary Indian Poetry* (1977). Jeannette Armstrong, Ben Abele, George Clutesi, Duke Redbird, Sarain Stump, and brothers Wayne, Ronald, and Orville Keon were gaining prominence. Riding the tidal wave of anger provoked by the 1969 White Paper, much Aboriginal poetry of the 1970s addressed political issues head-on. To conservative literary critics who dismissed protest poetry as lacking in subtlety and universal relevance, the poets replied that they had to shout to be heard.³⁴ Some explored more oblique modes of political self-assertion, devising ways of rendering Native speech on the page and using elements of traditional culture to build their metaphors and structure their narratives. These kinds of strategy were refined through the 1980s and 90s, for example in Wayne Keon's poem "I'm Not in Charge of This Ritual," where elision and an absence of punctuation and capitals produce a written rendition of the voice tones of a Native man who describes his life as an endless Sun Dance in which he hangs in agony from strings pierced through the flesh of his chest.³⁵

Other poets in the 1980s viewed political issues through the lens of personal reflections and meditations on the relation between culture and power. Duke Redbird moved into a more introspective mood in *Loveshine and*

Red Wine (1981) which also included some of his earlier protest poems. Beth Cuthand's *Horse Dance to Emerald Mountain* (1987) narrated her allegorical journey towards a physical place and spiritual state, bringing into a present-day setting elements of the horse-dance ceremony that her grandfather performed. Joan Crate's sequence *Pale as Real Ladies: Poems for Pauline Johnson* (1989) joins Beth Brant's *A Gathering of Spirit* anthology (1984/1988) and Jordan Wheeler's trilogy of novellas *Brothers in Arms* (1989) to explore gender and sexuality in relation to Mohawk and Métis identities.

Daniel David Moses (Delaware) published his first collection of poetry, *Delicate Bodies,* in 1980.[36] Having spent his childhood on a farm on the Six Nations lands in southern Ontario, Moses writes out of an intimate familiarity with particular rural landscapes in all their seasonal transformations. The "Calendar" series in *Delicate Bodies* documents each month of the year, using striking images and metaphors that appeal to all of the senses. Moses' poems also dramatize relationships with family and other loved ones. His tonal palette is broad. At times his words are ironic and ambivalent, particularly in poems such as "Breakdown Moon,"[37] which have a sharp, brittly cheerful edge that simultaneously conceals and opens up deep veins of feeling.

Emotionally and politically, Moses' poems are intense yet oblique, especially those that deal with the passing of his grandparents and the world they knew. Linguistically, Moses is a Trickster, a master of subtle virtuosity. His line breaks make words mutate: objects become subjects, adjectives become nouns, new patterns of meaning and sound unfold, as in the opening of his moving poem "A Visit in Midsummer":

> You are now little
> more, Grand
> father, than the blue wool
> rumples of your blanket.[38]

Moses published nineteen poems in the *First Person Plural* anthology (1988) where he experiments with diverse poetic forms and strategies including postmodern modes of allusion to European genres and fairytale characters. Moses' second collection, *The White Line* (1990), includes self-referential poems about the phenomenon of poetry. As well as being objects, rows of marks on a page, poems are also sensual oral-aural events that happen between bodies, a mystery he explores in "The Line":

> something like a snout starts
> nudging at your ear, nibbling
> near my mouth[39]

Picturing the poem as an elusive fish the poet tries to catch, Moses also casts beautifully baited lines out to the reader, and reels us in by leaving plenty of play in the line. "The Line," however, is not just about poetry per se; the "we" does not denote people in general. Much more than a fish (or a reader) is lost if a people's lines of cultural transmission break.

Rita Joe's second poetry collection, *Song of Eskasoni* (1988), is also concerned with lines of cultural transmission. "I Lost My Talk" expresses anger that, because of her schooling, "I speak like you / I think like you / I create like you." A hand is disarmingly held out, however, to those who have themselves lost the opportunity to learn by taking her talk away: "Let me find my talk / So I can teach you about me." In "My Spirit Celebrates" Rita Joe suggests that the term "art" accommodates Native creativity not on its own terms, but rather as a misunderstood prisoner of Eurocentric cultural categories and values. Rita Joe emphasizes that, "If we consider our Native culture important, we the Native people must put it down on paper our way" (Moses and Goldie, *An Anthology of Canadian Native Literature in English*, p. 377).

The need to use writing "our own way" inspired Jeannette C. Armstrong to establish the En'owkin International School of Writing for First Nations students, which grants diplomas through the University of Victoria. Armstrong, a relation of Washington State Okanagan novelist and autobiographer Christine Quintasket (Mourning Dove),[40] is a prolific writer and editor and an innovative educator. She sees literature as a way of showing how traditional Native spiritual knowledge and cultural values can be a source of guidance in today's "snap crackle pop" world.[41] Much of Armstrong's writing has been produced for use in schools, to counter the biases of colonialist versions of history, so that people can understand clearly the political causes of present-day Aboriginal disadvantage.

Like Peter Jones and Pauline Johnson, Armstrong works at the interface between oral and literary institutions through her interviews, essays, and talks, and her children's books, poetry, and novels. Armstrong's poetry is widely anthologized, and is collected in *Breath Tracks* (1991). With Lally Grauer, she has edited *Native Poetry in Canada: A Contemporary Anthology* (2001). Her first novel, *Slash* (1985), documented the North American Indian protest movement from the 1960s to the 1980s. Armstrong's poetic second novel, *Whispering in Shadows* (2000), along with Tomson Highway's *Kiss of the Fur Queen* (1998) and Thomas King's *Green Grass, Running Water* (1993), shows the diversity of ways in which recent Native novels have moved away from the ostensibly plain-speaking realist modes of the eighties.

Armstrong was one of three Aboriginal writers to publish novels in the 1980s, along with Ruby Slipperjack (*Honour the Sun* [1987]), and Beatrice

Culleton, whose *In Search of April Raintree* (1983) was the first modern novel published by an Aboriginal writer.[42] Culleton's novel incorporates autobiographical elements to tell the story of two Métis sisters, April and Cheryl, who are taken from their parents and placed in an orphanage before being sent out to separate foster homes, April with white families who abuse her and make her ashamed of being Métis, and Cheryl in a family setting (also white) where her Métis heritage is respected and her pride in her identity nurtured. Both girls are searching for stories to live by, giving the novel a metafictional dimension, despite its apparently transparent, unselfconscious prose. April, whose skin is light in color, denies her Métis identity and tries to pass as white. She marries a rich white fairytale prince and sets up an affluent home under the poisonous gaze of her wicked, white, racist mother-in-law. Cheryl, who has darker skin, proudly identifies as Métis, involves herself in Métis community life, and yearns to find her parents. When April is brutally raped by a group of white men who mistake her for her sister, she is forced to acknowledge the rape as an act of both racial and sexual abuse. Culleton's novel, somewhat revised for school use, was republished as *April Raintree* (1984). Both versions, however, serve as a reminder that Aboriginal-white relations cannot be understood in isolation from gender and sexual politics.

The 1980s also saw the first anthologies of short fiction: *Achimoona* (1985), a product of writing workshops conducted by Maria Campbell, and *All My Relations* (1990) edited by Cherokee/ Greek writer Thomas King, who also edited a special "Native Fiction" issue of the literary journal *Canadian Fiction* (vol. 60, 1987). These anthologies included work by the distinguished Ojibway writer and educator Basil H. Johnston, who had been publishing satirical and serious stories for some years on Ojibway history, language, and culture. Another prolific, versatile, and seriously funny Ojibway writer is Drew Hayden Taylor. Trained as a radio journalist, he has published several plays, a story collection entitled *Fearless Warriors* (1998), and three collections of "errant thoughts and humorous dissertations,"[43] all subtitled *Funny, You Don't Look Like One* (1996, 1999, 2002).

Thomas King has used the short-story form to experiment with "voice pieces." While most published collections of oral narratives were edited to satisfy white literary tastes,[44] anthropologists such as Julie Cruikshank[45] and Wendy Wickwire in the 1980s and 90s devised ways of rendering the rhythms and syntax of spoken Native English on the page, complete with pauses for breath and dramatic impact, as in the following brief excerpt from Harry Robinson's "Two Men Receive Power from Two Graves":

I'll tell you this.
That's not too long ago.
They got a horses those days,
    and they got gun.
Not long ago.
Could be a hundred years ago
    or maybe not that long.[46]

Faithful transcriptions and strategic page layouts such as this made Harry Robinson's *Write It on Your Heart* (1989), and *Nature Power* (1992), compiled and edited by Wickwire, effective channels of oral cultural transmission. For authors seeking ways to render Native voices in writing, these voice-prints are a valuable resource. The turning point in Thomas King's struggle to write "voice pieces" came when Wendy Wickwire sent him some tapes and transcripts of Harry Robinson. King recalls being "blown away" by Robinson's power and skill as a storyteller, and by the potency his voice retained on the page. Robinson's influence on King can be seen in the syntax, diction, grammar, punctuation, and page layouts of the short story "One Good Story, That One":

> Alright.
> You know, I hear this story up north. Maybe Yellowknife, that one, somewhere. I hear it maybe a long time. Old story this one. One hundred years, maybe more. Maybe not so long either, this story.[47]

Exposing the exploitative politics of "collecting" (stealing) Native stories, "One Good Story, That One" is a humorous tale about an old storyteller who tricks a trio of story-hungry anthropologists out of collecting the expected kind of "traditional" Native tale. The old storyteller recycles one of their own culture's sacred stories, the biblical account of Adam and Eve, whom King renames Ah-Damn and Evening.

Tricks, transformations, and disguises are crucial both to King's handling of language and narrative, and to his mode of engaging with readers. In "One Good Story, That One," while Ah-Damn is writing down the names of the animals as they parade by, Coyote walks in circles around him, disguised as a different animal each time. From the tracks on the ground, Evening can read that Coyote has walked past Ah-Damn several times, rendering Ah-Damn's written inventory of reality unreliable. Neither words, nor the beings they refer to, are necessarily what they seem. The anthropologists, for instance, wear ingratiating grins but their bared teeth betray the predatory nature of their story-hunt. If the anthropologists stand for all who attempt to get something out of Native cultures, we are forced to see that reading itself can be an appropriative act. What the old man does to the anthropologists, King does to his non-Native readers: he protects Native cultural property by telling the collectors of otherness a story about themselves. Coyote's tracks are visible not only on the ground between the old narrator and the eager anthropologists, but also between Thomas King and his readers.

King has written essays, poems, short stories, a children's book (*A Coyote Columbus Story* [1992]), and four novels, *Medicine River* (1989), *Green Grass, Running Water* (1993) which was filmed for CBC television, *Truth and Bright Water* (1999), and (under the pen-name of Hartley GoodWeather) *DreadfulWater Shows Up* (2002). One of King's abiding themes is the re-silience of Native cultures, their ability to survive by transforming and adapting as circumstances change. In *Green Grass, Running Water*, he dramatizes the continuing importance of the Sun Dance ceremony, and uses it as a basis for the narrative and symbolic framework of the novel.[48]

King dramatizes the politics of Native acts of self-representation through Will's photography in *Medicine River*, and through his allusions to the Fort Marion Ledger Artists in *Green Grass, Running Water*. During the 1870s and 80s Plains Indians imprisoned at Fort Marion, Florida, produced autobiographic and historical drawings in ledger books, a foreign cultural medium in which they adapted their traditional practice of making pictographs on rock, buffalo-hide robes, and tipis (Goldman, "Mapping and Dreaming," p. 24). Like the ledger-book artists, King uses nontraditional media to preserve and transmit knowledge, not only in book form but also in radio and TV dramas, and film scripts.[49] Like the nineteenth-century writer-orators who toured North America and Europe, and like the ledger-book artists imprisoned at Fort Marion, King is conscious that his work will often be consumed by non-Native readers who have little understanding or respect for Native history and culture. To win contracts with major publishers, and be widely read by whites, Aboriginal people have had to write with one eye focused on the expectations of the economically and ideologically dominant white audience.

After Oka

Since 1990, questions of representation and sovereignty – governmental, legal, and cultural – have attracted much media attention. In June 1990, after the exclusion of Aboriginal representatives from the constitutional reform process, Cree-Ojibway New Democratic backbencher Elijah Harper said "No" to the Meech Lake Accord, effectively stopping a set of constitutional amendments that, while recognizing Quebec as a distinct society, offered no such recognition to Canada's Indigenous peoples. Meanwhile, in Quebec, the Mohawk community at Kanesatake had set up block-ades to prevent the town of Oka from expanding a nine-hole golf course onto Mohawk land. The Oka mayor called in heavily armed provin-cial police to enforce a court injunction to tear down the barricades. The Mohawk community at nearby Kahnawake blockaded the road run-ning through their reserve onto the Mercier Bridge, a major traffic artery for Montreal commuters. Prime Minister Brian Mulroney dismissed Mohawk sovereignty claims as "bizarre," and sent 2,500 Canadian soldiers to Kanesatake and Kahnawake. The Mohawk Warriors had little choice but to surrender.

Aboriginal writing in the 1990s registered the shock-waves of Meech Lake and Oka. These events feature prominently in Lee Maracle's novel *Sundogs* (1992), Jeannette Armstrong's poem "Indian Summer," and Beth Cuthand's dramatic monologue series "Seven Songs for Uncle Louis," where "all of us" ask Brian Mulroney

> Whose delusions brought us
> to this madness?
> Whose voice unleashed
> the rifles and the tear gas?[50]

While Cuthand is still able to use the word "us" to refer to all Canadians, Lenore Keeshig-Tobias's essay "After Oka – How Has Canada Changed?" uses the words "Indian" and "Canadian" as mutually exclusive terms, and laments the fact that nothing has fundamentally changed since colonial times.[51]

Meech Lake and Oka reignited debates about Native sovereignty, not only in relation to land and law, but also in relation to culture, language, and writing. "Oka Peace Camp – September, 1990" is the title of Lee Maracle's preface to the revised edition of her 1975 life story, *Bobbi Lee: Indian Rebel* (1990). Like the barriers erected by the Mohawk Warriors around their sovereign territories at Oka, Maracle's preface asserts her sovereignty over her story. Whether Yvonne Johnson will ever be in a position to re-claim her *Stolen Life* (1998) is another question,[52] a question that applies to numerous individuals and communities whose stories have, since colonial times, been appropriated by white authors and editors. Life narratives as di-verse as Ojibway Armand Garnet Ruffo's poetic biography *Grey Owl: The Mystery of Archie Belaney* (1997), Métis author James Tyman's prison au-tobiography *Inside Out* (1989), and Maria Campbell's and Linda Griffiths's conflict-ridden collaboration in *The Book of Jessica* (1989) all address the issue of a person's sovereign right to constitute their history and identity through stories.

Having been involved in a bitter struggle to retain some control over other people's renditions of her life story, Maria Campbell models an appropriate way to gather, translate, and transcribe oral stories into printed texts in *Stories of the Road Allowance People* (1995). One of the most powerful and brilliantly presented books published in the 1990s, *Stories of the Road Allowance People* is a collection of eight Métis narratives illustrated by Algonquin artist Sherry Farrell Racette and translated by Campbell from Mitchif (a combination of Plains Cree and French) into the Métis village oral English of her father's generation. These are "old men's stories" entrusted to Campbell by her father and other teachers, all of whom she names. The stories, which range from the humorous "Good Dog Bob" to the devastating historical tragedy "Jacob," demand to be read aloud. Carefully designed page layouts and nonstandard spellings bring the stories alive to the ear:

> "Jacob someday you'll tank the God we done dis."
> dah Prees he tell him
> an dey start loading up dah kids on dah big wagons.
> All dah kids dey was crying an screaming[53]

Plains Cree poet Louise Halfe also evokes the sounds of a voice in "My Ledders," about hypocritical white new-age healers who run Sweatlodge retreats for paying customers. Halfe's poem takes the form of a "ledder" written or spoken by a Native woman to the pope, who presided over the prohibition of "heathen rituals" such as the Sweatlodge and the Sun Dance in the time of her *nohkom* and *nimosom* (grandmother and grandfather). Ironically, Sweatlodge ceremonies survive today only because Native communities continued them in secret, yet now "some darafist . . . dell da whole world" to register for his Sweatlodge – the "fist" in "darafist" pointing to the violence implicit in the cultural theft. Halfe turns the tables on those who have turned her culture into a commodity: she asks the pope how he would like it if her people performed holy communion with no respect for or understanding of the meaning of the bread and wine. To stamp the speaker's cultural identity on her words, Halfe uses Cree words and phonetic spelling:

> i wonder if you could dell da govment
> to make dem laws dat stop dat
> whitemman from daking our *isistawina* [rituals]
> . . .
> cuz i don't have you drainin
> from doze schools.[54]

Halfe's rendition of Cree English creates puns that reinforce her political message. Instead of teaching useful knowledge and skills, "doze schools" were "drainin" Native children of their culture, and boring them off to sleep. The residential school experience has left deep scars on the thousands of families whose children were taken away, and on the thousands of children who grew up in loveless institutions where many were abused by their so-called benefactors. Alphabetic literacy came at an excessively high price. The residential school system was designed to eradicate Native cultures by separating the learning generation from the teaching generation in Native communities, a practice which the United Nations now recognizes as a form of genocide.[55] Three vivid accounts of the residential school experience are Jane Willis's *Geniesh* (1973), which documents the crushing effects of a decade spent at boarding schools, Basil H. Johnston's *Indian School Days* (1988), which recounts the story of his experiences from 1939 when, at the age of ten, he was placed in a residential school in northern Ontario, and Salish Shirley Sterling's *My Name Is Seepeetza* (1992), a novel in diary form set in the late 1950s and based on her own experiences.

During the 1990s, Aboriginal writers also challenged canonical Euro-Canadian historical visions and literary values. In "Letter to Sir John A. Macdonald," from *A Really Good Brown Girl* (1996), Marilyn Dumont, a descendant of Métis leader Gabriel Dumont, replies to Macdonald's claim that the railroad would unify Canada "from sea to shining sea." Dumont uses railway metaphors to highlight an ironic symmetry: as Macdonald's vision of unity "railroaded" Métis claims to land and political rights, Elijah Harper derailed the Meech Lake Accord. Dumont quotes F. R. Scott's poem "Laurentian Shield" (1954) to challenge his literary vision of the Canadian landscape as a empty page waiting to be written upon by the authors of a national (literary) culture. While Scott, like Macdonald, denied the Native and Métis presence, Dumont reminds her readers that "we're still here and Métis." In her powerful and moving poem "The Devil's Language," however, she dramatizes the personal cost of her people's cultural losses. She directly implicates canonical English literature and Eurocentric literary values – "the Great White way of writing English" – in the *ongoing* process of cutting Native and Métis peoples off from their mother tongues and those who speak them.

In "Circle the Wagons," Dumont satirizes superficially informed readings of Aboriginal literatures: "There it is again, the circle, that goddamned circle, as if we thought in circles, judged things on the merit of their circularity."[56] Writing out of her urban Métis experience, Dumont argues that these clichéd images are "popularly seductive but ultimately oppressive."[57] They are no less confining than the 1950s TV westerns where Indians galloped in circles around the wagon train. Dumont emphasizes how difficult it can be for people to be themselves unselfconsciously, when there is pressure to write in "the authentic voice, so you can be identified (read 'marketed') as a native Artist" (Armstrong, ed., *Looking at the Words of Our People*, p. 47). Jeannette Armstrong, Thomas King, Drew Hayden Taylor, Kateri Damm, Marie Annharte Baker, and others have also addressed the problem of stereotypes, both romantic and negative.[58]

Marie Annharte Baker approaches circles from a different direction, raising the issue of "how rigid we are becoming in drawing lines around our work and ourselves. Our circles of inclusion are exclusion for others" ("Medicine Lines," p. 115). By drawing non-Native readers imaginatively into Native and Métis life-worlds, literary texts can build bridges of understanding and empathy. Whether these bridges lead to real-world action and Native/white alliances is another question, however. As Haisla Heiltsuk author Eden Robinson implies in her story "Queen of the North," there is always a danger that white readers consume books about Native and Métis people's lives as though they were merely another material or experiential commodity to be savored intensely for a time, but soon forgotten.[59]

Baker's question about "circles of exclusion" also applies to the publishing industry. How can the need for reserved spaces (specialized publishers and journals such as *Gatherings*, dedicated anthologies, and special issues of mainstream periodicals[60]) be balanced against the need to avoid paper prisons that ghettoize Native writing, giving mainstream publishers and editors an excuse not to include Aboriginal writings in mainstream publications. Emma LaRocque fears that segregation may increase the danger that readers may overlook the universal relevance of Aboriginal writing, and may cause some Native writers to doubt that their work can compete successfully in the main arena ("Here Are Our Voices," pp. xviii–xix).

The vast majority of Aboriginal writing has been published by Native publishing houses such as Theytus Books (attached to the En'owkin Centre) in Penticton, and Pemmican in Winnipeg, or by small presses such as Polestar, Press Gang, and Talonbooks in Vancouver, Women's Press in Toronto, NeWest in Edmonton, Fifth House in Saskatoon, and Coteau Books in Regina.[61] Mainstream commercial publishers and university presses are beginning to open their doors, however. HarperCollins published Thomas King's *Green Grass, Running Water*; Knopf published Eden Robinson's *Monkey Beach* (2000) and *Traplines* (1996); Penguin Canada has recently purchased Gwich'in author Robert Arthur Alexie's *Porcupines and China Dolls* (2002) and *The Pale Indian* (forthcoming); Douglas and McIntyre published Shirley Sterling's *My Name Is Seepeetza* (1992), Richard Van Camp's *The Lesser Blessed* (1996), and anthologies that have grown out of community projects such as *Steal My Rage* (1995) and *Let the Drums Be Your Heart*

(1996). Oxford University Press published Daniel David Moses' and Terry Goldie's *An Anthology of Canadian Native Literature in English* (1992), while University of Toronto Press has recently published *E. Pauline Johnson, Tekahionwake: Collected Poems and Selected Prose* (2002).

Today, Indigenous publishing is beginning to go global, with the publication of *Skins: Contemporary Indigenous Writing* (2000), coedited by Ojibway-Pottawotami writer Kateri Akiwenzie-Damm and professional editor Josie Douglas of the Wardaman people in Australia's Northern Territory. Published jointly by Kegedonce Press on the Cape Croker Reserve in Canada and Jukurrpa Books in Alice Springs, Australia, *Skins* contains stories by First Nations, Métis and Inuit, Native American, Indigenous Australian, and Maori writers, with Canada being represented by Maria Campbell, Thomas King, Alootook Ipellie, and Richard Van Camp. *Skins* is a far-sighted venture. Despite the problems that can arise when Aboriginal texts are read through "postcolonial" lenses,[62] the advent of postcolonial studies in universities around the world means that an international audience of students and academics is now listening intently to what Native, Métis, and Inuit authors have to say.

Breaking the frame, lifting the gaze

Since Penny Petrone and Robin Gedalof [McGrath] carried out their primary research in the 1970s and 80s,[63] the turbines of academe have churned out numerous articles, chapters, theses, and books, mainly by non-Aboriginal researchers. Until recently, in special "Native Writing" issues of major literary journals, Aboriginal writers usually supplied the stories and poems, while non-Aboriginal critical essays erected the frameworks for understanding them. Recent years have seen a shift in the balance of power to confer status, meaning, and authority, as Aboriginal writers intervene increasingly in academic debates and foreground their own terms of reference in self-reflexive literature. Emma LaRocque's "Here Are Our Voices – Who Will Hear?" in *Writing the Circle* (1990), Beth Brant's *Writing as Witness* (1994), and anthologies such as *Give Back* (1992), *Looking at the Words of Our People* (1993), *(Ad)dressing Our Words: Aboriginal Perspectives on Aboriginal Literatures* (2001), and *Creating Community: A Roundtable on Canadian Aboriginal Literature* (2002) are breaking Aboriginal writings out of white-made frames. As well as speaking to Aboriginal audiences, these essays do what Kahkewaquonaby did when presenting the Ojibway petition to Queen Victoria in 1838: they mediate between Aboriginal writers and non-Aboriginal readers, guiding people such as myself who are trying to read differently, in politically accountable ways, avoiding the twin dangers of assimilating Aboriginal textual practices into western literary paradigms and of viewing Aboriginal texts as essentially pristine, change-less, and so inscrutably "other" that they have nothing to say to humanity at large.[64]

At the same time as they are breaking the frames, a number of Abo-riginal writers are lifting their gaze beyond the national arena. Armand Garnet Ruffo's powerful poetic history *At Geronimo's Grave* (2001) places Geronimo alongside French Enlightenment philosopher René Descartes and political prisoners Leonard Peltier and Nelson Mandela. Several poems in Lee Maracle's *Bent Box* (2000) have an international focus, exploring the political predicaments of oppressed groups in the Middle East, Africa, and Central and South America, from the point of view of a Native Canadian woman. In "Song to a Palestinian Child" Maracle listens to the voice of "a girl child very much like my own."[65] In "Women" she positions herself in "Can-America . . . my decadent home," where she is at once a member of an oppressed people, and an involuntary beneficiary of a US-dominated global order that oppresses others, allegedly to defend her interests. As a beneficiary of wrongs done by others in purported defense of her interests, Maracle shares the uncomfortable, politically compromised position of that minority of non-Aboriginal Canadians who, over the centuries, have know-ingly benefited from racially discriminatory political systems they sincerely abhor.

While neo-imperial economic and political realities increase inequities in Canadian society as a whole, the legacies of colonialism continue to impact on Aboriginal people's lives. Whereas the 1970s saw the building of national and continental Aboriginal constituencies, today many people see themselves also as members of an international body of Indigenous peoples, sometimes referred to as the "Fourth World," after Shuswap author George Manuel's 1974 book of the same name. The United Nations declared 1993 the Year of the World's Indigenous Peoples. Increasingly, the UN provides opportu-nities for Indigenous peoples from all parts of the globe to direct the world's gaze to injustices committed or threatened by their national governments. As Kahkewaquonaby and the Credit River Ojibway understood in 1838, writ-ing augments the voice as a means of going over the heads of colonial and national governments, to seek justice from higher powers. Today, through writing and print, the Internet, and networks developed face-to-face at in-ternational conferences and cultural events, Aboriginal writers in Canada are not only networking with Indigenous peoples outside North America, but are also speaking to readers around the world. To fight for their own rights and interests, they are using a language and writing system that were initially forced upon them, as weapons. While there is much poetic justice in this fact, as Emma LaRocque has noted,[66] the struggle for other forms of justice is far from over.

NOTES

1. I wish to thank Richard Van Camp, Helen Hoy, Thomas King, and Margery Fee for their generous assistance and invaluable advice. For reasons outlined by Lee Maracle, Jeannette C. Armstrong, Delphine Derickson, and Greg Young-Ing, eds., *We Get Our Living like Milk from the Land* (Penticton: Theytus, 1993/4) p. 78, I use the general term "Aboriginal" to refer to Native Indian, Métis, and Inuit peoples. Although naming practices vary between different contexts and speech communities, there is a general trend away from the terms "Native" and "Indian," especially as nouns, because they perpetuate colonial racial perceptions. Similarly, "Eskimo" is giving way to "Inuit," the plural of "inuk," which means "a person" or "a man" in the Inuktituk language. While many consider "First Nations" an acceptable term, Maracle et al. (p. 80) point to its adverse legal ramifications. For an explanation of the term Métis, see note 22 below. In this chapter, when identifying individual writers, I use whatever term they use to identify themselves.

2. Donald B. Smith, *Sacred Feathers: The Reverend Peter Jones (Kahkewaquonaby) and the Mississauga Indians* (Lincoln: University of Nebraska Press, 1987) p. xii.

3. Greg Young-Ing, "Aboriginal People's Estrangement: Marginalisation in the Publishing Industry," *Looking at the Words of Our People: First Nation Analysis of Literature*, ed. Jeannette Armstrong (Penticton: Theytus, 1993) p. 186.

4. Marie Annharte Baker, "Medicine Lines: The Doctoring of Story and Self," *Canadian Woman Studies / Les Cahiers de la Femme* 14.2 (Spring 1994): p. 115.

5. Olive Patricia Dickason, *Canada's First Nations* (Toronto: Oxford University Press, 1992) p. 64.

6. Penny Petrone, *Native Literature in Canada: From the Oral Tradition to the Present* (Toronto: Oxford University Press, 1990) p. 16.

7. Daniel David Moses and Terry Goldie, eds., *An Anthology of Canadian Native Literature in English* (Toronto: Oxford University Press, 1992) p. xv.

8. Tomson Highway, *Dry Lips Oughta Move to Kapuskasing* (Saskatoon: Fifth House, 1989) p. 12.

9. Hartmut Lutz, ed., *Contemporary Challenges: Conversations with Canadian Native Authors* (Saskatoon: Fifth House, 1991) p. 85.

10. Robin McGrath, "Oral Influences in Contemporary Inuit Literature," *The Native in Literature*, ed. Thomas King, Cheryl Calver, and Helen Hoy (Montreal: ECW Press, 1987) pp. 163–4.

11. Penny Petrone, *First People, First Voices* (Toronto: University of Toronto Press, 1983) p. 12.

12. Penny Petrone, "Indian Legends and Tales," *The Oxford Companion to Canadian Literature*, gen. ed. William Toye (Toronto: Oxford University Press, 1983) p. 384.

13. Richard Daly, "Writing on the Landscape," *They Write Their Dreams on the Rock Forever: Rock Writings in the Stein River Valley of British Columbia*, by Annie York, Richard Daly, and Chris Arnett (Vancouver: Talon, 1993) pp. 223–60.

14. Selwyn Dewdney, *The Sacred Scrolls of the Southern Ojibway* (Toronto: University of Toronto Press for the Glenbow-Alberta Institute, 1975) p. 20.

15. Rita Joe, "Micmac Hieroglyphics," *An Anthology of Canadian Native Literature in English*, ed. Moses and Goldie, p. 114.

16. Elizabeth Hill Boone, introduction, *Writing without Words: Alternative Literacies in Mesoamerica and the Andes*, ed. Boone and Walter D. Mignolo (Durham: Duke University Press, 1994) p. 13.

17. David L. Schmidt and Murdena Marshall, eds. and trans., *Mi'kmaq Hieroglyphic Prayers: Readings in North America's First Indigenous Script* (Halifax: Nimbus, 1995) p. 13.

18. Peter Wogan, "Perceptions of European Literacy in Early Contact Situations," *Ethnohistory* 41.3 (Summer 1994): pp. 407–29.

19. For example, Beth Brant, "From the Inside Looking at You," *Writing as Witness*, by Brant (Toronto: Women's Press, 1994) p. 50; Kateri [Akiwenzie-] Damm, "Says Who: Colonialism, Identity and Defining Indigenous Literature," *Looking at the Words of Our People*, ed. Armstrong, p. 11.

20. See Petrone, *Native Literature*, pp. 35–70 for details of the lives and writings of members of this group.

21. See, for example, Peter Jones's letter dated 14 June 1830 and petition dated 17 Feb. 1831, in Petrone, *First People, First Voices*, pp. 61–3.

22. Some of Falcon's songs survive in oral form only. See Annette Saint-Pierre, *Au pays des Bois-Brûlés* (Saint-Boniface: Collège universitaire de Saint-Boniface, 1977). Following the prevailing usage among Métis writers, and in government and legal documents, I use the term "Métis" to refer to the unique ethnic group of mixed Aboriginal French descent, who emerged in the Great Lakes and Northwest regions. Writers of mixed English Indigenous descent usually identify by their Indigenous affiliation only, or by terms such as "English-Ojibway," rather than "Metis" (without the accent). In line with their practice, I use "Métis" and have avoided the term "Metis" (without the accent), despite the fact that in English Canadian usage it is frequently employed to refer comprehensively to people of mixed Aboriginal French and/or Aboriginal English descent. Outside Canada, "métis" and "metis" (with a lower-case *m*) are sometimes used as a synonym for "hybrid" to refer to anyone of mixed Indigenous European ancestry. For further discussion of Métis writing and *métissage* in general, see Armando E. Jannetta, *Ethnopoetics of the Minority Voice: An Introduction to the Politics of Dialogism and Difference in Métis Literature* (Augsburg: Wissner, 2001).

23. See George F. Stanley, ed., *The Collected Writings of Louis Riel*, 5 vols. (Edmonton: University of Alberta Press, 1985).

24. Beth Brant, "The Good Red Road," *Writing as Witness*, by Brant, pp. 5–21; Carole Gerson and Veronica Strong-Boag, *Paddling Her Own Canoe: The Times and Texts of E. Pauline Johnson* (Toronto: University of Toronto Press, 2000); Carole Gerson and Veronica Strong-Boag, eds., *E. Pauline Johnson, Tekahionwake: Collected Poems and Selected Prose* (Toronto: University of Toronto Press, 2002); and Charlotte Gray, *Flint and Feather* (Toronto: Harper, 2002).

25. Quoted in J. R. Miller, *Skyscrapers Hide the Heavens*, rev. ed. (1989; Toronto: University of Toronto Press, 1991) p. 224.

26. Formally entitled *Statement of the Government of Canada on Indian Policy* (1969).

27. Harold Cardinal, *The Unjust Society: The Tragedy of Canada's Indians* (Edmonton: Hurtig, 1969) p. 1.

28. For more detailed information on 1960s and 70s Aboriginal writing, see Hartmut Lutz, "Canadian Native Literature and the Sixties: A Historical and Bibliographical Survey," *Canadian Literature* 152/153 (Spring/Summer 1997): pp. 167–91.

29. Emma LaRocque, "Here Are Our Voices – Who Will Hear?," preface, *Writing the Circle: Native Women of Western Canada*, comp. and ed. Jeanne Perreault and Sylvia Vance (Edmonton: NeWest, 1990) p. xvii.

30. *Eskimo* N.S. 14 (Fall/Winter 1977–8): pp. 22–5; 15 (Summer/Fall 1978): pp. 14–18; 16 (Fall/Winter 1978–9): pp. 7–10.

31. *Eskimo* N.S. 6 (Fall/Winter 1974): pp. 11–12.

32. Maria Campbell, *Halfbreed* (Toronto: McClelland, 1973) p. 8.

33. Ron Hamilton, "Our Story Not History," *BC Studies* 89 (Spring 1991): p. 87.

34. See Michael P. J. Kennedy, "The Writer as Image Maker and Breaker: An Interview with Jeannette Armstrong," *NeWest Review* 20.4 (Oct./Nov. 1994): p. 11.

35. Wayne Keon, "I'm Not in Charge of This Ritual," *Canadian Literature* 124/125 (Spring/Summer 1990): pp. 154–5.

36. Daniel David Moses, *Delicate Bodies* (Vancouver: Blewointment, 1980). *Delicate Bodies* was republished in 1992.

37. Daniel David Moses, "Breakdown Moon," *Canadian Literature* 124/125 (Spring/Summer, 1990): p. 227.

38. Moses, *Delicate Bodies*, p. 17.

39. Daniel David Moses, "The Line," *An Anthology of Canadian Native Literature in English*, ed. Moses and Goldie, p. 299.

40. Mourning Dove (c.1888–1936) authored four books: her novel *Co-Ge-We-A, the Half-Blood* (1927), *Coyote Stories* (1933), *Tales of the Okanagans* (1976), and *Mourning Dove: A Salishan Autobiography* (1990).

41. See, for example, Jeannette Armstrong, "History Lesson," *An Anthology of Canadian Native Literature in English*, ed. Moses and Goldie, p. 203.

42. Mourning Dove's *Co-Ge-We-A* (1927) is usually considered the first Canadian Native-authored novel because Mourning Dove lived in Canada for part of her life.

43. Drew Heyden Taylor, introduction, *Further Adventures of a Blue-Eyed Ojibway: Funny, You Don't Look Like One Two* (Penticton: Theytus, 1999) n. pag.

44. See Penny Petrone's listings in "Indian Legends and Tales," pp. 377–83; and her *Native Literature*, pp. 120–6 and 154–8.

45. Angela Sidney's *Tagish Tlaagu (Tagish Stories)* (1982) was recorded by Julie Cruikshank, who also authored *Life Lived like a Story* (1990) in collaboration with Angela Sidney, Kitty Smith, and Annie Ned.

46. Harry Robinson, "Two Men Receive Power from Two Graves," *Write It on Your Heart: The Epic World of an Okanagan Storyteller*, comp. and ed. Wendy Wickwire (Vancouver: Theytus/Talon, 1989) p. 224.

47. Thomas King, "One Good Story, That One," *One Good Story, That One: Stories by Thomas King* (Toronto: Harper, 1993) p. 3.

48. See Marlene Goldman, "Mapping and Dreaming: Narrative Resistance in *Green Grass, Running Water*," *Canadian Literature* 161/162 (Summer/Autumn 1999): pp. 18–41.

49. Back cover flap of King, *One Good Story, That One*.

50. Beth Cuthand, *Voices in the Waterfall* (1989; Penticton: Theytus, 1992) p. 39.

51. Lenore Keeshig-Tobias, "After Oka – How Has Canada Changed?," *An Anthology of Canadian Native Literature in English*, ed. Moses and Goldie, pp. 234–5.

52. See Susanna Egan, "Telling Trauma: Generic Dissonance in the Production of *Stolen Life*," *Canadian Literature* 167 (Winter 2000): pp. 10–39.

53. *Stories of the Road Allowance People*, trans. Maria Campbell, illus. Sherry Farrell Racette (Penticton: Theytus, 1995) pp. 97–8.

54. Louise Halfe, "My Ledders," *Bear Bones and Feathers* (Regina: Coteau, 1994) p. 103.

55. Human Rights and Equal Opportunity Commission, *Bringing Them Home: Report of the National Inquiry into the Separation of Aboriginal Children from Their Families* (Commonwealth of Australia, 1997) pp. 270–6.

56. Marilyn Dumont, "Circle the Wagons," *A Really Good Brown Girl* (London: Brick, 1996) p. 57.

57. Marilyn Dumont, "Popular Images of Nativeness," *Looking at the Words of Our People*, ed. Armstrong, p. 49.

58. Jeannette Armstrong, editor's note, *Looking at the Words of Our People*, ed. Armstrong, p. 7; Thomas King, introduction, *All My Relations: An Anthology of Contemporary Canadian Native Fiction*, ed. King (Toronto: McClelland, 1990) pp. x–xi; Drew Hayden Taylor, numerous publications including "Are You a Chip off the Old Block?," *Further Adventures of a Blue-Eyed Ojibway*, pp. 75–6; [Akiwenzie-] Damm, "Says Who," p. 14; Baker, "Medicine Lines"; Dumont, "Popular Images of Nativeness," p. 47.

59. Eden Robinson, "Queen of the North," *Traplines* (Toronto: Knopf, 1996) pp. 207–8; see also Helen Hoy, *How Should I Read These? Native Women Writers in Canada* (Toronto: University of Toronto Press, 2001).

60. Recent examples of special Native issues of literature journals include *Canadian Fiction* 60 (1987); and *Canadian Literature* 124/125 (Spring/Summer 1990), 161/162 (Summer/Autumn 1999), and 167 (Winter 2000).

61. On Native and Métis publishing, see Young-Ing, "Aboriginal People's Estrangement," pp. 177–87.

62. Thomas King, "Godzilla vs. Post-Colonial," *World Literature Written in English* 30.2 (1990): pp. 10–16.

63. Robin Gedalof [McGrath], ed., *Paper Stays Put: A Collection of Inuit Writing*, with drawings by Alootook Ipellie (Edmonton: Hurtig, 1980).

64. Helen Hoy has documented this learning process most explicitly in *How Should I Read These?*

65. *Bent Box* (Theytus: Penticton, 2000) p. 33.

66. LaRocque, "Here Are Our Voices," p. xxvi.

2

Francophone writing

E. D. BLODGETT

La Nouvelle-France (1534–1760)

One of the undeniable pleasures of reading the francophone writing of Canada as a historical project is to observe how it takes shape. Although it is produced for the most part in Quebec, in its initial phase it was published in France. A printing press was not established in Quebec until 1764 when the first periodical, *La Gazette de Québec/The Quebec Gazette*, appeared. The point of departure for subsequent writing in French is New France, which included what are now known as the regions of Acadia and Franco-Ontario. Subsequent writing from the Prairies did not appear until the nineteenth century. It also includes Aboriginal writing, which holds a distinct, if often neglected, place. Although critics of both the nineteenth and twentieth centuries consider francophone writing to be a literature of resistance, the cultures resisted are not always the same, inasmuch as French Canada would variously oppose Great Britain and France, and often the differing ideologies and regions of French Canada itself would be in opposition. Consequently, francophone writing is not so homogeneous as it is sometimes presented as being. Its heterogeneity is apparent from its variety of audiences. It is also apparent in its regional diversity. If one were, however, to speak of the francophone literatures of Canada in general, one should remark that their dominant note is their self-awareness as minority literatures. Because of that awareness, these are literatures that are always engaged in a process of identity construction as a means of social self-discovery or self-definition which it will be the task of this chapter to describe.

Of course, such a tendency is often only apparent in hindsight. The reports of Jacques Cartier's voyages to North America (1534, 1535, 1541, and 1545), which constitute the first written records of what was to be New France, are initially efforts of definition and in translation by which the unknown cultures and geography of the region were prepared for a French public. Although the first French version of the first voyage did not appear until 1598, its publication gives some indication of French interest, belated as it was, in the "new" world. Perhaps because of this delay and because Cartier abandoned his colony in 1542, Samuel de Champlain is credited as the founder of New France, following upon his *Des sauvages, ou voyage de Samuel Champlain, de Brouage* (1603), a text which forms the beginning of a number of exploratory reports on North America. It is the seminal text for the theme of the *voyageur*, a recurrent theme in francophone writing, which also prepared the way for its regional diversity. A second mode of definition was provided by the Jesuit *Relations*, letters sent by missionaries to their superiors from 1610 to 1673 which brought about, among their lasting results, the founding of such religious institutions as the *Grand Séminaire de Québec* (1663) and the Ursuline convent (1639). The letters of the Ursulines' founder in Quebec, Marie de l'Incarnation (1599–1672), to her son, along with her theological treatises and dictionaries of Algonquian and Iroquois, mark her as among the most significant writers of the seventeenth century.

Post-Conquest (1760–1839)

The Seven Years' War in Europe was concluded by the Treaty of Paris (1763) by which New France (Canada) and Île Royale (Cape Breton) were ceded to England. What had been a settler colony became, in turn, an occupied colony, and the long process of self-definition that constitutes francophone writing began. The same treaty signified the end of Acadian[1] settlement, which had already lost much of its colony following the war of the Austrian Succession when the deportation of Acadian settlers from Nova Scotia took place (1755–62). The deportation constitutes a central theme in Acadian literature and was made internationally famous in the poem by the American poet Henry Wadsworth Longfellow, "Evangeline: A Tale of Acadie" (1847), which became widely available to francophone readers in a translation (1883) by Pamphile Lemay, poet and member of the *Ecole littéraire de Montréal*. The deportation, by emphasizing the process of exile and the effort of finding a way back, may be attached, even if negatively, to the theme of the *voyageur*. The 65,000 inhabitants who remained in the colony that had become Quebec had only one choice: either become French Canadian or disappear. What "French Canadian" would mean was very much the task of French Canadian writing to declare, which is why its primary function was to assist in the task of self-definition as various labels were adopted, such as *"Canadien," "Canadien-français,"* and, since 1960, *"Québécois."*

Its initial efforts were in the genres of drama, poetry, and polemical and oratorical nonfiction. Drama, the oldest literary genre of New France, appeared as early as Marc Lescarbot's *Le théâtre de Neptune*, a *réception* (welcome) masque designed to celebrate the return of the explorer Poutrincourt to the colony at Port-Royal (1606). Because of the Church's opposition to drama, plays were not professionally staged until the first theatre building, the Théâtre Royal, was erected in 1825. Some of the plays of the French writer Joseph Quesnel (1746–1809) were produced by amateur groups, despite attacks from the Church. Quesnel also published poetry in periodicals, largely of a satirical and epigrammatic character. Significantly, the patriotic verse of the period was marked by both pride in being *canadien* and loyalty to England. The first book of French Canadian poetry, *Épîtres, satires, chansons, épigrammes et autres pièces en vers* (1830), published by Michel Bibaud (1782–1857), covers all the preferred genres, displays this literature's neoclassical style, and assumes the stance of the convinced moralist.

The most assertive mode of publication in the period was the periodical, bestowing an enormous degree of power on such editors as Etienne Parent (1802–74), who edited *Le Canadien* from 1822 to 1825, and resumed its editorship in 1831 with the motto, "Nos institutions, notre langue et nos lois." Although Parent's nationalism was more moderate than that of such *patriotes* as Louis-Joseph Papineau (1786–1871), his pragmatic and ethical influence, as witnessed in his later lectures (1846–52), may prove to have been the more profound. The earliest fiction also appeared in periodicals, usually in the form of short stories. As is characteristic of the era, the first of these to have any importance was a translation in 1827 by Bibaud of an American tale entitled "L'Iroquoise." Its debt to the exoticism and the Aboriginal themes of François René Chateaubriand and James Fenimore Cooper is evident.

The first two francophone novels both appeared as the Rebellion began (1837), and each testifies to a romantic interest in crime, violence, and fantasy. The first was *Les révélations du crime ou Cambray et ses complices* by François-Réal Angers (1812–60). It featured tales of crime and banditry, as well as the author's assertion that Canada had one of the highest crime rates in the world. The statistics alone caused a brief quarrel in the periodicals of the time. Of greater significance is *Le chercheur de trésors ou l'influence d'un livre* by Philippe Aubert de Gaspé, *fils* (1814–41). The author asserts in his preface that it is "le premier roman de mœurs canadien." Beneath the surface of realism, however, the embedded character of its narration develops levels of the fantastic and legend that endeavor to portray its characters in a supernatural light. It anticipated a tendency that was followed in such adventure novels as *Les fiancés de 1812* (1844) by Joseph Doutre (1825–86) and *Une de perdue, deux de trouvées* (1849–51 and 1864–5) by Georges Boucher de Boucherville (1814–94). Possibilities evident in Aubert de Gaspé's novel for developing the fantastic, however, were held in abeyance by more pressing concerns.

The Durham effect (1839–66)

The unrest and repression involved in the effort to democratize Lower Canada in the 1830s resulted in the Rebellion of 1837–8 – which the British army successfully quelled – and the hanging or exiling of many of the participants. On the one hand, the response confirmed the colonial status of French Canada; on the other, by creating the single Province of Canada, it made the matter of self-definition a more serious issue than it had been before. The construction of a French Canadian identity was developed against the discourse of the *Durham Report* (1839), which castigated the people of Lower Canada, without reference to Upper Canada, for their alleged lack of literature and history, making assimilation appear the only viable choice for French Canada. Among the many responses to this attitude, *L'histoire du Canada depuis sa découverte jusqu'à nos jours* by François-Xavier Garneau (1809–66), published in three volumes from 1844 to 1848 with a supplement in 1852, provided both the history and the literature. Its espousal of gallicanism, that is, a close adhesion of church and state to the detriment of the pope, prompted the Church to reshape the *Histoire's* ideology in favour of less liberal attitudes. The conflict is a grand template of an argument in francophone culture during this period, anticipating the eventual dominant position of conservative ultramontanism, which defended papal infallibility over and against gallican liberalism. Nevertheless, Garneau's *Histoire* provided a usable past for historians, novelists, poets, and playwrights.

Just as Garneau was considered the national historian, so Octave Crémazie was its poet (1827–79). Playing upon the themes of French Canada's glorious past, his poetry fitted Garneau's implied program perfectly, particularly in such poems as "Le vieux soldat" (1855) and "Le drapeau de Carillon" (1858). He was also a founder of the *Institut canadien* (1844–85), an association of liberal intellectuals and writers which was sufficiently undermined in the year Crémazie was president (1858–9) by the Bishop of Montreal, Ignace Bourget, that it barely continued to exist. Among the poets who rose to prominence during this period, such as Léon Pamphile Lemay (1837–1918), the most significant was Louis-Honoré Fréchette (1839–1908). Although international fame did not come until the 1870s, his debuts were auspicious with a collection of poetry (1863) and a very well-received comedy, *Felix Poutré* (published in 1871, first performed in 1862), that evokes the Rebellion to the advantage of the *patriotes*.

The novel took two directions in this period. The first, following Garneau, was the development of the historical novel. *Une de perdue, deux de trouvées*, a novel written in two parts between the years 1849–51 and 1864–5 by Georges Boucher de Boucherville, marks the transition from Gothic fantasy to history. An adventure novel set in Louisiana, the first part responds to an interest in the theme of the *voyageur*. The second part is a reflection on the Rebellion, particularly the misguided efforts of the *patriotes*. The second part represents a shift in attitude from liberal romanticism to the conservative attitudes that governed French Canada for the rest of the century. *Les anciens Canadiens* (1863) combines adventure, history, legend, travel, and the Conquest into a plot addressing the relations between British and French in the eighteenth century, and it is generally considered the major novel of the century, bringing almost immediate fame to its author Aubert de Gaspé, *père* (1786–1871). Part of its success lay in presenting an image of French Canada to its readers that fitted a desired self-definition of the time through its celebration of New France, but it appealed also to English readers, possibly because of its lack of overt rancor and its strong echoes of Walter Scott.

The second direction was taken by what has come to be known as the *roman du terroir*, taking its name from the fact that it privileged the *habitant* as protagonist. It shared little thematically and stylistically with either fantastic or historical novels, espousing instead a kind of utopian or socialist realism. Three novelists, Patrice Lacombe (1807–63), Pierre-Joseph-Olivier Chauveau (1820–90), and Antoine Gérin-Lajoie (1824–82), dominate its history. Ponderous as they may appear to the modern reader, their difference from novelists popular at the time, notably Walter Scott and Eugène Sue, confers upon them a certain originality. Their theme and ideology, that of a young man venturing forth to build a farm and turning his back on the liberalism of urban Canadian capitalist economy, responded well to problems in French Canada in this period. Because of their increasingly didactic character and their reliance on propaganda, leaning frequently on advice from local priests, these novels seem less like novels than agricultural tracts. It would be wrong to take Gérin-Lajoie entirely literally, however, when he remarks in the preface to *Jean Rivard* that he is not offering a novel to the public. The genre was normally understood, especially in its French context, as mere *divertissement*, and between the severity of the Church and the social positions taken by such writers as Parent, the *roman du terroir* proposed in the simplicity of its plot and the virtue of its protagonists a master discourse that continued almost unchallenged until the 1930s. The hero of Gérin Lajoie's *Jean Rivard* (1862, 1864), like his American counterpart Horatio Alger, was exemplary of how a man could rise from humble circumstances, have a town named after him, and give dissertations on success like a revered philosopher-king. Paradoxically, the ideal world proposed by these novels echoes the ideal of the *ancien régime* and, as a consequence, reflects the growing conservatism of the later nineteenth century. Not all fiction privileged the *habitant*, and writers like Joseph-Charles Taché (1820–94), as well as a number of travel-writers, satisfied an interest in the *pays d'en haut*, as well as larger regions of the continent.

The new province (1867–95)

The year that brought to a close the new constitutional arrangements that issued in the British North America Act marked the beginning of a new opportunity for French Canada to define itself. The gradual consolidation of ecclesiastical interests from the middle of the century assured that the liberal attitudes that were repressed after the Revolt rarely surfaced, and literature was largely devoted to forms of escapism, mainly manifest in adventure novels. Poets chose themes that reflected interests in religion, the nation, and nature. Although drama, which began to flourish earlier in the century, continued to develop at both the professional and amateur levels, the professional stage was dominated by touring American and French troupes, which relegated French Canadian plays to amateur circles, particularly in colleges where the surveillance of the Church was closely felt.

"O Canada" (1880) by Adolphe-Basile Routhier (1839–1920), now Canada's national anthem, inscribes both religious and patriotic themes and may be considered emblematic of the poetry of the time. It glorifies both the past and Christ in a combined utterance, and Routhier collected poems in the same vein under the title *Les échos* (1882). Fréchette also composed poems with such themes, notably "Jean-Baptiste La Salle, fondateur des écoles chrétiennes" (1889), but his true métier was the historical poem, and nothing compared with the success of his *La légende d'un peuple* (1887), often noted as an echo of Victor Hugo's *La légende des siècles*, but owing its thematic inspiration to Garneau's *Histoire*. Its three parts draw on events of the seventeenth, eighteenth, and nineteenth centuries, and despite its uneven character it remains the major poetic text of the nineteenth century. The other significant book of the period is *Les Laurentiennes* (1870) by Benjamin Sulte (1841–1923), whose interest in the particularities of country life in the new province was reflected in the poetry of Lemay that flourished in this period.

Lemay also tried his hand at the adventure novel in *Le pélerin de Sainte-Anne* (1877) and its sequel *Picounoc le maudit* (1878). Although they did not pass the moral scrutiny of their initial critics, they were often reprinted together, separately, and in abridged forms both in France and Quebec, suggesting that there was an interest in unbelievable events occurring within a cosmos where God's justice always prevails. Lemay also published a translation of William Kirby's *The Golden Dog* (1877; *Le chien d'or* 1884), but the more famous representative of the historical genre was Joseph Marmette (1844–95), whose *L'intendant Bigot* (1872), set during the period of the Conquest, testifies to Garneau's long influence in shaping a sense of the national through developing significant moments of the past. The historical novels of Laure Conan (Félicité Angers [1845–1924]) have now been overshadowed by her first novel, *Angéline de Montbrun* (1881–2), but until the latter half of the twentieth century Conan was cherished for these novels which she undertook at the suggestion of Abbé Henri-Raymond Casgrain (1831–1904), the most significant man of letters in the second half of the nineteenth century. Surpassing her predecessors, Conan added a psychological dimension to history, a talent she displayed in her first two texts. The theme of her first historical novel, *A l'œuvre et à l'épreuve* (1891), is that of self-sacrifice: the protagonist, Charles Garnier, decides against marrying Gisèle Méliande, his parents' foster-child, becomes a missionary, and dies a martyr's death among the Iroquois. It is a recurrent theme in Conan and one used to poignant effect in *Angéline de Montbrun*, which is unique both among her collected works and among nineteenth-century novels in general. First, it is written as a combination of letters and diary entries, for the most part, and, second, its protagonist is a woman. To a large degree autobiographical, it transposes a failed relationship into a novel of a woman who renounces the man who loves her after she suffers a disfiguring accident. As a consequence, she becomes a recluse and spends the rest of her life with her father in a relationship that has incestuous overtones. Another significant novel, *Pour la patrie* (1895), by the American immigrant and ultramontanist Jules-Paul Tardivel (1851–1905), has the distinction of being the first overtly separatist novel. As is typical of the dominant ideology of the period, the perspective is ultramontanist, not liberal. The plot turns on the discovery of a group of devil-worshippers and freemasons in the federal government who plan to quell the autonomy of Quebec. Although the warnings of the French Canadian MP who is the protagonist fall on deaf ears, his self-sacrifice and acceptance of God's will leads to the defeat of the federal party and eventual separation. Inasmuch as it is set in the years 1945–6, it may be considered science fiction, and it continues to be reprinted, despite its curious *fin-de-siècle* parochialism characteristic of the religious conservatism of the period.

Constructing a nation (1895–1938)

The year 1895 is pivotal in the sense that, along with seeing the appearance of *Pour la patrie*, it was also the year in which the *Ecole littéraire de Montréal* came into being. It testified to the influence of European modernity in Montreal, particularly French and Belgian Parnassian and decadent poetry. Although the movement endured for over three decades, its high moments were its first five years and the years 1907–12. As one of its founders, Jean Charbonneau (1875–1960), argued, the *Ecole* was in many ways a protest against late nineteenth-century neo-romanticism. Its most distinguished, if intermittent, member was Emile Nelligan (1879–1941), whose work shows his familiarity with the French poets Charles Baudelaire and Paul Verlaine, among others. He was particularly preoccupied with melancholic nostalgia for his childhood. His last public reading, including his "La romance du vin," took place in 1899, and later in the year he entered an asylum, never to leave. Two other prominent members of the group were Charles Gill (1871–1918) and Charles Lozeau (1878–1924). The inclusive character of the group may be seen in Gill's neo-romanticism and Lozeau's decadence with its overtones of Verlaine. Much of Lozeau's melancholy may be attributed to his spinal tuberculosis which left him paralyzed and confined to his bedroom from the age of thirteen.

The early years of the twentieth century in Canada were marked by the excitement over the Boer War and Canada's close ties with the British Empire. Its imperial character prompted in Quebec strong opposition and a rise of intense national sentiment led by Henri Bourassa (1868–1952), and part of the cultural effect of this nationalism may be seen in the poets clustered around the short-lived periodical *Le Terroir* (1909), which encouraged a more regional poetry than that of the *Ecole Littéraire*. Although most of its poets are minor, some continue to be remembered, such as Blanche Lamontagne-Beauregard (1889–1958) and Lionel Léveillé (1875–1955). The inspiration of the group was the work of Nérée Beauchemin (1850–1931); the two words of the title of his collection, *Patrie intime* (1928), evoke both aspects of what was sought by the regionalists, to which one might add the perennial theme of religion. A renewal of the spirit of the *Ecole Littéraire* is apparent in the work of René Chopin (1885–1953) and Paul Morin (1889–1963). Both supported the principles of neoclassicism as found in the Parnassians and encouraged a poetics of the exotic. The latter was a cofounder of *Le Nigog* (1918), whose influence was more lasting than that of *Le Terroir*.

Although a number of regional novels found a wide public in this period, few have found a place in the canon. An exception is the work of Adjutor Rivard (1868–1945), the titles of whose novels, *Chez nous* (1914) and *Chez nos gens* (1918), clearly express their themes. The enduring classic, however, is *Marie Chapdelaine* (1914) by the French adventurer Louis Hémon (1880–1913). It is significant both for its use of character types and for the debate it has stirred among various critics. Although a *roman du terroir*, it differs profoundly from nineteenth-century versions of the genre, inasmuch as its central character is a woman. Its action turns on whom she will accept to marry. Her choices are limited to François Paradis, a *coureur de bois*, Lorenzo Surprenant, an emigrant living in New England, and Eutrope Gagnon. Because her first choice, Paradis, dies in an accident in the forest, and because Surprenant represents the threat of godless materialism, she settles on the one who is left. Everything in the novel supports her decision, no matter how much against her will, to remain faithful to Quebec and the Church. The power of the novel derives from the deployment of the ideological positions the men represent, all of them drawn on mythic possibilities in the history of Quebec. Their names reveal them as allegories, her husband possessing the best qualities of an *habitant*: Well-Bred Earner. Marie is a victim of the same tradition that may be noted in *Angéline de Montbrun*, and self-sacrifice appears inescapable in the dominant ideology of Quebec since at least 1850. In one of the last novels in this tradition, *Menaud Maître-Draveur* (1937) by Félix-Antoine Savard (1896–1982), not only does a similar configuration of males exist around Maria, Menaud's daughter, but also Hémon's narrative is intertextually repeated in *Menaud* to emphasize the necessity of remaining faithful, especially, in this case, as one of the suitors is an agent for Anglo-American capitalist interests. One cannot fail to notice, however, that the words of Hémon's narrator are spoken by a man gone mad over the death of his son, and they form one of the many anguished cries that testify to the erosion of the way of life that these novels encourage.

The first blow had already been struck in *La Scouine* (1918), a naturalistic novel by Albert Laberge (1871–1960); however, only sixty copies of this novel were printed, and its full impact is therefore difficult to measure. The second blow was *Les demi-civilisés* (1934), an autobiographical satire by the polemical journalist Jean-Charles Harvey (1891–1967). Its intent was to expose the repressive character of the Church, capitalist interests, and the abuse of political power. It succeeded so well that it caused a scandal, as a consequence of which Harvey lost his job. He later obtained another position, but the major effect of the scandal was that he became largely an outsider until the Quiet Revolution[2] of which he was a precursor. Finally, Ringuet's (Philippe Panneton [1895–60]) *Trente arpents* (1938), linked to *La Scouine* through Claude-Henri Grignon's (1894–1976) *Un homme et son péché* (1933), dramatizes the breakdown of a patriarchal family whose ruined father is virtually exiled from Quebec by his eldest son and spends his old age as a night-watchman in the United States, unable to talk with the son who takes him in or his monolingual daughter-in-law. Inexorable in its dismissal of the father and all he represents, the novel brings the *roman du terroir* to a tragic conclusion. Its significance was immediately recognized, particularly in the number of awards it received, notably the Governor-General's Award (1940, for the English translation *Thirty Acres*), the Prix de l'Académie Française (1939), and the Prix de la Province de Québec (1940).

Just as the figure of the *habitant* was losing its signifying power in the novels written between the two world wars, so the firm attachment to the *terroir* frequently found in earlier poetry moved in new directions. The most touching of the new poets is Jean Narrache (1893–1970), who makes his poetry speak an unvarnished, spoken language sympathetic to the plights of the poor, unlike Robert Choquette (1905–91), whose *A travers les vents* (1925) initiated the effusion of the romantics while emphasizing the figure of the *coureur de bois*. Narrache stands apart in the simplicity of his diction and imagery. Nevertheless, it fell to Alfred Desrochers (1901–78) to be the central poet of the era, and his *A l'ombre d'Orford* (1929), also depicting various kinds of *coureur de bois*, celebrated a North America which, despite the title, extended its range beyond the regional.

If Desrochers shared with Narrache the merit of being the distinctive voice of the poetry of this period, a newer note was inaugurated by a number of women, notably Medjé Vézina (1896–1981), Simone Routier (1901–87), and Eva Sénécal (1905–98), whose work was characterized by a combination of a romantic attitude toward nature and levels of intimacy and longing that set them apart from the men of their generation. Although grandeur becomes human in their poetry, none of them prepares one for the achievements of Rina Lasnier and Anne Hébert in the next generation.

The century opened in theatre with a play entitled *Les boules de neige* (1903) by Louvigny de Montigny (1876–1955), a comedy of manners about gossip and the conflict of urban freedom and country conformism, but a genuinely French Canadian theatre does not appear to begin to take root until the 1930s, especially in the plays of Léopold Houlé (1883–1953) and Gustave Lamarche (1895–1987), and what the former possessed in lightness, the latter compensated with a moral vision heavily indebted to biblical and mythological themes: the most extravagant of his works was *La défaite de l'enfer* (1938), a play for chorus staged on a mountain with an audience of thousands. Both playwrights attest to the long ecclesiastical tradition in Quebec.

Longing for a larger space, however, is the dominant note in the poetry and some of the novels of Quebec in this period, and the same chord is struck in the work of the French adventure writer Maurice Constantin-Weyer

(1881–1964), who was among the first writers to draw upon the Red River Colony and the North. His recurrent theme is the plight of the Métis, and his most significant novel is the autobiographical text *Un homme se penche sur son passé* (1928), which earned him the Prix Goncourt. Its central figure is the *coureur de bois*, which interested his French audience, but also had its attractions for Quebec readers. His contemporary Georges Bugnet (1879–1981) after immigrating spent most of his life near Edmonton, Alberta, where his major fiction is set. Like Constantin-Weyer, he was also attracted to the Métis (*Nipsya* [1924]), but it is the plight of the pioneer-immigrant that is dramatized in his major novel, *La forêt* (1935), in which the protagonists are doomed for not trying to live in harmony with nature. Both novelists are significant as forming the basis of prairie francophone writing.

Quebec as self-discovery (1939–58)

It was apparent by the end of the 1930s that the old model of the *habitant* was losing significance and the early model of the *coureur du bois* was acquiring new, more psychological meanings. During the period of Maurice Duplessis's years as premier (1936–9 and 1944–59), a period known as *la grande noirceur* because of the repressive complicity between his government and the Church, it would have been difficult to foresee how the Quiet Revolution would occur. Although the Quiet Revolution is generally seen as the work of the liberal government that replaced Duplessis's Union Nationale, it was prepared for culturally by the quiet revolution that occurred in two decades of poetry and poetic thought, beginning with *Regards et jeux dans l'espace* (1937) and the published sections of the *Journal* (1954) of Hector de Saint-Denys Garneau (1912–43). Unquestionably the first significant francophone poet of the twentieth century, Garneau's exploration of the spirit suggests affinities with Nelligan, and his cultivation of interiority places him on the threshold of a period of extraordinary illumination in the writings of Alain Grandbois (1900–75), Rina Lasnier (1915–97), and Anne Hébert (1916–2000). They all shared with Garneau a profound sense of circumscription from which Grandbois escaped by becoming in his early years a world traveler, following a family tradition. Lasnier escaped through religion; Hébert, through the labyrinths of the unconscious. Each an existentialist *sui generis*, they understood life, to use the expression of Paul-Marie Lapointe (1929–), as *le réel absolu* (the real made absolute), and each poet posed mortality as the central human question articulated as an adventure of the spirit. Such an adventure need not manifest itself in recognizable religious imagery, such as that of Lasnier and Hébert, and its matrix is at least metaphysical. And in this way such texts as Lasnier's *Escales* (1950), Hébert's *Le tombeau*

des rois (1953), and Grandbois's *L'étoile pourpre* (1957) all mark a constellation around the explosion of Paul-Emile Borduas's (1905–60) equally
remarkable *Refus global* (1948), a surrealistic manifesto claiming that art
and freedom are coterminous. A clear call to revolt against the limitations
of North-American economic utilitarianism and the oppression of the spirit,
it cost Borduas his job, ironically proving his point.

The novels of the period develop similar themes, and those of Gabrielle
Roy (1909–83) reached the largest audience, possibly because of her
Manitoba childhood that allowed her to engage both of the Charter cultures of Canada. The novel that assured her lasting recognition, *Bonheur
d'occasion* (1945), is the first successful realistic narrative of a working-class
family set in Montreal in the early years of World War II. Despite the ambitious character of this novel and *Alexandre Chênevert* (1954), Roy is more at
ease in her idyllic texts set in Manitoba, such as *La petite poule d'eau* (1950)
and *La route d'Altamont* (1966). Roger Lemelin (1919–92) developed similar themes, particularly that of mother and parish priest, in a series of novels
set in working-class neighborhoods entitled *Les Plouffe* (1948), acquiring a
large audience as a subsequent television series. Finally, the last vestiges of
the *roman du terroir* appeared in the work of Germaine Guèvremont (1893–
1968), notably *Le survenant* (1945) and *Marie-Didace* (1947), and like the
novels of many of her contemporaries they trace the disintegration of the
rural family and especially the weakening of the role of the father. Like that
of Lemelin and Grignon, her work was also turned into radio and television
series.

At the same time, novels with a clearly introspective character were produced, initially by Robert Charbonneau (1911–67), which attest to a long
tradition in French, but also to the inward turn stimulated by *la grande
noirceur*. *Ils posséderont la terre* (1941) was the first volume of a trilogy
that has as its theme the unattainable ideals of adolescent friendship. *Au-
delà des visages* (1948) by André Giroux (1916–77) addresses the menace
of a godless world from a variety of psychological perspectives, and Robert
Elie (1915–73) in his *La fin des songes* (1950) pursues the problems of adolescence. The major exponents of this type of novel remain, however, André
Langevin (1927–) and Anne Hébert. The former's *Poussière sur la ville* (1953)
is set beneath a pall of asbestos dust that suggests symbolically an aspect of
la grande noirceur and traces the vain efforts of a man existentially facing his destiny. Hébert's *Les chambres de bois* (1958) poetically evokes the
child-like obsession of a girl for a man from which she is finally released.
The exception to the cultivation of interiority is Yves Thériault (1915–83).
Highly prolific, Thériault published his first novels in the 1940s, and his success was established with *Agaguk* (1958), whose sexuality has none of the

self-torture or awkwardness of many of the other novelists of the same period. But this is a central theme – the overcoming of human repression – and in this respect Thériault shares with most poets and novelists of the period an antagonism to various kinds of authority. Like them, he too searches for individual autonomy and, often, the absolute.

A rather different note was struck by drama, a genre which finally found its voice in this period and inaugurated an enduring native theatre. It did not generally seek an absolute, but it declared, nevertheless, its particular autonomy in *Tit Coq* (1948), Gratien Gélinas's (1909–99) first major play. The plot turns on the thwarted marriage of a soldier in World War II, and the success of a parish priest in preventing an adulterous affair. The play was highly successful, and its theme of an emotionally damaged orphan and a repressive Church echoes the circumscribed character of the time. Marcel Dubé (1930–) began his prolific career with *Zone* (1953) and confirmed it with *Un simple soldat* (1958). The latter's themes are similar to those of psychological novels in particular: the protagonist is an idealist who, like the central figures in *Les demi-civilisés*, exposes the hypocrisy of his milieu, a frequent preoccupation of Dubé's drama. Anne Hébert also turned her hand to playwriting, and her earliest produced play, *L'invité au process* (1952; published 1967), was aired on Radio-Canada. The guest is Satan; the trial, human sin, represented by a black flower. Because it is Hébert, the world is seen *sub specie aeternitatis*, and, as in her prose, fantasy is difficult to distinguish from the real.

Le Nouveau Québec (1959–69)

Coincident with the bicentenary of the Conquest of Quebec, Maurice Duplessis died, which opened the way for a Liberal government that in many ways brought Quebec out of its traditionalism. At the same time the Church lost much of its power and influence in the process of secularization that occurred. Although the impact of these events on literature cannot be fully measured, there is no question that the climate of reception had changed. The repression the previous generation had known was no longer perceived as effective. Much of the ground for the great flowering of writing that has occurred since the 1960s was prepared by the establishment of small, indigenous presses that emerged beside French publishers, on the one hand, and ecclesiastical publishers, on the other. Especially important among these were Erta, founded in 1949 by the poet and painter Roland Giguère (1929–), and Hexagone, founded in 1953 by Gaston Miron (1928–96) and friends. In many respects Hexagone was an era in itself, publishing *Le réel absolu: poèmes 1948–1965* (1971) by Paul-Marie Lapointe, Roland Giguère's *L'âge de la parole: poèmes inédits 1949–1960* (1965), *Poésie: poèmes 1953–1971* (1972) by Fernand Ouellette (1930–), and *Pays sans parole* (1967) by Yves Préfontaine (1937–). No survey can adequately capture the explosive significance of the work of these poets, who draw upon the techniques of surrealism to explore erotic and nationalist themes. The echo of the word *parole* in the texts of Giguère and Préfontaine indicates the heart of their intent, asserting that language makes the world and its creatures. Miron himself did not publish through his own press, and his *L'homme rapaillé* (1970), sections of which had appeared in the *independantiste* journal *Parti pris*, is a text of absolute dispossession and reinvention in which the agony of the poet is the agony of Quebec. Others who have found themselves in the same position are Préfontaine, Paul Chamberland (1939–), who chose the voice of the prophet in *Terre Québec* (1964); and Michèle Lalonde (1937–), whose *Speak White* (1974) famously attacks oppression. An equally intimate rapport between Quebec, self, and *parole* may be found, in the early work at least, of Gatien Lapointe (1931–83), especially in the suite "J'appartiens à la terre" (1963). Jacques Brault (1933–), whose early poetry in *Mémoire* (1965) meditated on the plight of Quebec, the small things of life, and the tragic loss of his brother in World War II, became more esoteric as his work developed, without entirely losing touch with the quotidian character of daily life, many of these themes recurring in *Au fond du jardin* (1996).

The dominant stance of the poets of this generation, apart from nationalist and erotic themes, is the desire, to paraphrase a line from Gatien Lapointe, to be born in a word, manifesting this poetry's profoundly romantic roots. The novel has other intentions – less overtly didactic, but equally existential. A number of significant novelists appeared in the early 1960s, and of these the most restrained and refined in her use of language was Claire Martin (Claire Montreuil [1914–]). One of her psychological novels *Doux-amer* (1960), is narrated by a man who suffers the fate of having married a woman who displays characteristics and assumes privileges normally reserved for men, such as preferring her career to her love. Yet the protagonist, Gabrielle Lubin, and, in many respects, the sardonic bookseller who narrates *Le libraire* (1960) by Gérard Bessette (1920–) are both fitting figures for the threshold of the Quiet Revolution. Ostensibly keeping a Sunday diary to kill time, the protagonist of *Le libraire* exposes starkly the extent of censorship during the Duplessis era. Although initially a playwright and founder of the Rhinoceros Party, Jacques Ferron (1921–85) is known mostly for his compassionate, if satirical, prose, the variety of whose styles is well displayed in his *Contes d'un pays incertain* (1962) in which legend, fable, and surrealist techniques are drawn upon to address the uncertain future of Quebec. A more violent attack on the repressive character of the period emerges in the work of Marie-Claire Blais

(1939–), whose *Une saison dans la vie d'Emmanuel* (1965) assured her the celebrity which she continues to enjoy. The season to which the title refers is the eternal winter in which the children protagonists suffer sexual and physical abuse sufficient to make it a season in hell. Although the sources of Blais's style may be indirectly those of naturalism, the variety of narrative strategies and nightmarish qualities mark her work as modern in a way that surpasses the realism of the novel since the end of World War II. In the same year, Hubert Aquin (1929–77), probably the most charismatic writer of his generation, published *Prochain épisode* (1965), which was an immediate critical success; it was written while the author was under psychiatric observation. The narrator of *Prochain épisode* recounts his unsuccessful attempt to assassinate H. de Heutz. At once a spy thriller and revolutionary novel, the style foreshadows Aquin's interest in metanarrative in which the play of writing makes the narrated events difficult to measure as the line between the real and the imagined is blurred. Réjean Ducharme (1941–) began his career as a playwright and novelist with *L'avalée des avalés* (1966), a novel situated on an island in the St. Lawrence where the protagonist, Bérénice, creates a closed adolescent world with its own language, characterized by the veneration of such poets as Emile Nelligan. If not as grotesque as that of Blais or as fraught with intrigue as that of Aquin, Ducharme's world is a function of the language that summons it into being.

In a lighter vein, the protagonist of *Salut Galarneau!* (1967) by filmmaker and novelist Jacques Godbout (1933–) endeavors to control the chaos of his world by walling himself in and keeping a series of notebooks that become the novel, headed by an epigraph by the surrealist André Breton. So close is the intimacy between writing and living that Galarneau invents the term *vécrire* (composed of the verbs *vivre* and *écrire*) to explain the relationship between language and the world. Making use of surrealist imagery and puns that often unravel the language of the Church, *La guerre, yes sir!* (1968) by Roch Carrier (1937–) is the first of a trilogy that exposes the grotesque aspects of village life. Although it addresses a number of significant themes – the Conscription Crisis of 1942, *les maudits Anglais* as the source of misfortune, the effects of Jansenism, the endurance of the "little guy" – the success of the novel was greater in English translation than in French. In Quebec it was perceived more as distorting caricature than fair portrayal. More ambitious is the career of Victor-Lévy Beaulieu (1945–), launched in *La race du monde* (1969), a saga of the sprawling Beauchemin family, with some echoes of the family in *Une saison dans la vie d'Emmanuel*. The narrator is a novelist who appears to revel in the misery of the world in which he finds himself – dispossessed, alienated, limited in an equivocal world – and the novelist seeks issue in a search for the absolute in subsequent novels, privileging on a metaphysical level the *voyageur* rather than the *habitant*, the centrifugal and centripetal poles of Quebec culture.

Although Ferron and Beaulieu also wrote for the theatre, the superior playwright of this period and beyond was Michel Tremblay (1942–), whose *Les belles-sœurs* (1968) turned the local (East Montreal, the use of *joual*) into a universal statement with its echoes of Greek theatre and Shakespeare. It is realism leavened by the poignancy of its themes, particularly the oppression and marginalization of women, and by its structure based on musical principles. Influenced in equal measure by popular and highbrow genres like radio serials, opera, animation, and the string quartet, Tremblay has consistently tackled controversial subjects. Working with some of the most distinguished directors of his generation, André Brassard among them, he has written plays about the subculture of Montreal's gay night-clubs (*Demain matin Montréal m'attend* [1972]; *Hosanna* [1973]), the hell of a bigoted society and its effect on personal relationships (*A toi pour toujours, Marie-Lou* [1971]), and fanatical religiosity (*Damnée Manon, sacrée Sandra* [1981]), and he has been consistently influential in anglophone Canada as well. Although he began his career as a fiction writer, it was his experience as a playwright that made his multivolume saga *Les chroniques du Plateau Mont-Royal*, especially the first volume *La grosse femme d'à côté est enceinte* (1978), an instant success. The "fat woman" in the title is Tremblay's own mother, pregnant with her son Michel, and the entire book draws on the autobiographical experience of growing up in wartime Montreal. At the same time, the narrative backtracks the lives of major characters in Tremblay's plays to their childhood, and the juxtaposition of their youthful dreams with their later disillusionment can be very painful. It is, however, also exhilarating, because Tremblay depicts childhood as a source of energy and inspiration that he urges his reader to translate into political activism. The autobiographical strain in *Les chroniques* has since come even more strongly to the fore in Tremblay's *oeuvre*, for example in *Les vues animées* (1990), *Douze coups de théâtre* (1992), and *Un ange cornu avec des ailes de toiles* (1994).

The post-national nation (1970–)

Despite the limitations of Carrier's novel, it shared with other fiction of the 1960s the sense of circumscription already mentioned. Enclosure, idealized adolescence, and a use of narrative in which the real and the fantastic are often indistinguishable are themes and strategies echoed in the poetry of the period. Violence, pain, and transgression recur to evoke what several writers refer to as a difficulty of being,[3] where "being" is not simply survival or existence, but living with full comprehension of the circumstance.

Hence, the evocation of language and narration becomes central in such a project, especially a use of language which refuses precise referentiality. Hébert's *Kamouraska* (1970) is centered exactly on the problem of being, both through its shifts of narrative perspective and through its corresponding evocation of transgression. Set in the years of the Rebellion of 1837–8 and its aftermath, it addresses the murder of the protagonist's husband by her lover. The consequences of the murder force into being a profoundly divided woman driven to relive the events by re-narrating them as she awaits the death of her second husband. Although the protagonist lives vicariously through her lover's great voyage to murder her husband, she herself is portrayed as trapped, enclosed, unable to be.

Difficulty of being marks the work of three other women, Antonine Maillet (1929–), Jovette Marchessault (1938–), and An Antane Kapesh (1926–). As an Acadian, Maillet's work is part of a vast enterprise of self-recovery that began with the gradual return of the Acadians after the *grand dérangement* or deportation of 1755. After Maillet's success with the dramatic monologues of *La Sagouine* (1971), she continued to develop her interest in the Acadian past, especially in the achievement of *Pélagie-la-Charette* (1979). Pélagie's nickname derives from her becoming symbolically the great cart that brings the scattered Acadians home. Part of the success of this novel and other texts is the use of sixteenth-century French, which remains part of the Acadian heritage and the celebration of the past as a living present, and in this instance coincides with the theme of the *voyageur*. An Antane Kapesh's *Qu'as-tu fait de mon pays?* (1979) is one of the many First Nations texts that followed the negative reaction to *The Statement of the Government of Canada on Indian Policy* (1969), the so-called "White Paper," marking the serious transition from oral to written literature. Although a translation from Montagnais (Innu), it is a significant aspect of the francophone literary system. It is also a collective autobiographical novel, a widely used Aboriginal genre, which dramatizes the dispossession of First Nations perceived from a child's point of view. Marchessault, who is Métis, draws upon her Aboriginal heritage in *Comme une enfant de la terre/1. Le crachat solaire* (1975), the first of a trilogy of a collective autobiography situated in the world of spiritual quests by a narrator born of "solar spittle." Subsequent novels and plays by the same author both celebrate French Canadian novelists (for example, Roy and Hébert) and denounce male domination from a lesbian perspective.

In many respects, the writing of the last decades of the twentieth century eclipses the nationalist themes so prevalent in the 1960s and early 1970s. Part of this development is due to the increasing prominence of immigrant writers, to publications by gay and lesbian authors, and to the work of multi-talents like Robert Lepage. Among the former, Régine Robin (1939–), born of Polish Jewish parents in Paris, uses her prose to explore herself in a social context. Her *La Québécoite* (1983) is a novel yet to be written, which turns on the problem of the immigrant as silenced (*coi*: silent, speechless) and consists of the narrator's notes reflecting her efforts to acquire a voice. As the author notes in her later appended postface (1993), it constructs a Borgesian, postmodern Quebec of continually interrelated borders. Writing *hors Québec* is notable in the fiction of Marguerite-A. Primeau (1914–), whose *Sauvage Sauvageon* (1984), an autobiographical novel with echoes of *Kamouraska*, dramatizes what appear to be the final reflections of a 38-year-old woman on the verge of suicide. Traumatized by the early gift and loss of a magical childhood in Alberta, her life consists of self-punishment for the damage she feels she has inflicted on those with whom she is intimate. Set in Alberta, France, and British Columbia, it is at once a physical and psychological journey towards self-understanding that evokes a *voyageur* past.

The best parodies are implicit acts of celebration, and Jacques Poulin (1937–) in his *Volkswagen Blues* (1984), by having his narrator Jack Waterman (whose first name echoes the author's and Jack Kerouac's) set off across the American continent in the company of a young Métis woman in search of his brother, at once honors and deconstructs the long memory of French exploration of the continent. Making use of a number of post-modern touches – gender role reversal, blurring geographical and temporal borders, interweaving cinematic and historical heroes – the novel guarantees the continuing shade that Garneau's *Histoire* casts over francophone writing, notably in the validation of the theme of the *voyageur*, especially in respect of plot and content. Like the narrator of *Volkswagen Blues*, the narrator of Dany Laferrière's (1953–) *Comment faire l'amour avec un nègre sans se fatiguer* (1985) is a writer seeking a kind of identity in a minority culture, but Laferrière's widely read narrator is writing less to find francophone culture in North America than to affirm a black, immigrant presence in a white, imperialist world in which all racial stereotypes are taken apart. Two other writers who have also refashioned the theme of the *voyageur* are Nicole Brossard (1943–) and Ronald Lavallée (1954–). The former, a major feminist poet and essayist, displays it particularly in the polysemous use of language in *Le désert mauve* (1987), a novel inset with the narrator's story followed by a translation (into French) with translator's notes. So fine is the line between the real and the fictional that in the end the translator slips anonymously into her text. Hardly postmodern, Lavallée's epic novel *Tchipayuk ou le chemin du loup* (1987) firmly and grandly dramatizes the life and plight of the Métis in the West during the period of the Riel Rebellions (1869–85). It ranges in scope from the protagonist's childhood among the

Manitoba Ojibway and his education in Montreal to his later return to the West, not only celebrating the *coureur de bois* but also suggesting the difficulty of being Métis in a world dominated by people of French and English origin.

The Franco-Ontarian novelist and translator Daniel Poliquin (1953–) comes perhaps as near as one can to producing a pan-Canadian francophone novel in his *Visions de Jude* (1990). Set in Ottawa, it is told by four women known to each other – a young widow, her daughter, her daughter's music teacher, and the hero's landlady – and all at one time or another the hero's lover. Jude is described as a sailor, geographer, writer, founder of an Arctic institute, adventurer, discoverer, and a courageous, erudite Don Juan. Asked if he thinks of himself as a *coureur de bois* or something closer to an *habitant*, he claims to be both, thus assuming for himself the two central roles in francophone culture. In action, however, he is closer to the former, and one who is always departing from the lives of those who love him. As told by the women whose lives he damages, the myth of the adventurer is developed with ironic sympathy.

Significantly, one of the major plays of the period, Denise Boucher's (1935–) *Les fées ont soif* (1978), examines another powerful theme in francophone culture, that is, that of the Virgin Mary, whose presence in French Canadian culture is as old as New France. Woman as virgin, mother, and prostitute are all roles that are carefully deconstructed. The play was for a few years on the verge of attracting the Church's censor because of its perceived scandalous character. After so many generations of proposing modes of self-definition, it has become generally agreed in French Canada that all of them are flawed. Contemporary theatre reaches its apogee in the work of Robert Lepage (1957–), whose career has risen steadily since his highly experimental *Circulation* was produced (1984). *Les sept branches de la rivière Ota* (1994), a play that takes seven hours to produce, is arguably among the most ambitious theatrical stage plays ever mounted in Canada. Highly varied, his theatre is at once confessional and universal, and he does not hesitate, for example, to represent the French surrealist Jean Cocteau and jazz musician Miles Davies in an intensely personal play about a failed love affair (*Les aiguilles et l'opium* [1991]). Not entirely at home in Quebec, Lepage frequently directs work in Europe and Japan, testifying to the growing international importance of Quebec theatre. Also widely translated is the work of Michel Marc Bouchard (1958–), who made his breakthrough with *Les feluettes ou la répétition d'un drame romantique* (1987), a play about a Roman Catholic bishop who, forced at knifepoint to watch a prison amateur production about gay love, must confront his own past.

To appear flawed, however, is merely to be subject to time. Myths that have grown and been modified since the early visits of Cartier and subsequent European adventurers and missionaries have endured with great tenacity. The sense of mission continues to prevail in Quebec if only in a secularized form, and the narrative of venturing into unknown spaces has moved from geography into metaphysics. If not the sustaining myth of Quebec, it has, at least, a lasting resilience, and it is well represented in other forms elsewhere in francophone Canada. Inasmuch as francophone Canada is not entirely the culture of Quebec or of a people primarily of French descent, it is a myth used to assert several identities for a number of constituencies endeavoring to preserve their *patries intimes*. The myth of the *voyageur*, however, remains volatile because it always implies a movement away from an imagined center and yet one that holds the moving outer edge to the center by means of the space between. The dangers incurred by historical adventurers are lived in another, but corresponding, way by writers always aware that such ventures are risks of being. This is particularly true for those literatures, like that of Quebec, which feel themselves overshadowed by larger, more internationally powerful cultures. It is therefore a condition of their *habitus* as a culture that they must continually assert a kind of identity. In the instance of the francophone writing of Canada, such an assertion is complicated by the fact that it is not a unified culture, particularly now, but rather one that is composed of layers of strength, all in some way in transition, while some layers are more firmly anchored than others.

NOTES

1. The geographical region of Acadia extends to various parts of the Maritime Provinces, not including Newfoundland. Its name may be derived from two possible sources. It is either a corruption of "Archadia," the name proposed by the explorer Giovanni da Verrazano (1524), or derived from an Algonquian root. It was settled by French immigrants who were later for the most part deported (*le grand dérangement*) by the British during the years 1755–62 for their failure to swear allegiance to the British Crown and, it should be added, to the French Crown. Although many settled in Louisiana, a great number also returned (see Craig Brown, ed., *The Illustrated History of Canada* [Toronto: Lester, 1987] pp. 124, 181–2).

2. A term invented by a journalist for the *Globe and Mail*, the "Quiet Revolution" designated the modernization of Quebec that began to take place between the years 1960 and 1966. Its roots extend into the period when the province was governed by Maurice Duplessis, a period known as *la grande noirceur* and characterized by his close association with the Roman Catholic Church. The revolution, whose impact is still the object of analysis, amounted, on the one hand, to a thorough secularization of the state apparatus and, on the other hand, to a reconsideration of French Canada's sense of mission in North America, resulting in an intensification

of national and autonomous aspirations. Its effect on cultural renewal has been incalculable.

3. This phrase, uttered by the seventeenth-century philosopher Fontenelle on his death-bed, has been significantly echoed by several francophone writers, and notably by Hubert Aquin and Anne Hébert, as a means of expressing Quebec's ontologically precarious position in North America (see Anthony Purdy, *A Certain Difficulty of Being: Essays on the Quebec Novel* [Montreal: McGill-Queen's University Press, 1990] p. 9 *et passim*).

3

Exploration and travel

EVA-MARIE KRÖLLER

"Discovery" and ideology

In their introduction to Walter Cheadle's *Journal of Trip across Canada, 1862–1863* (1931), editors A. G. Doughty and Gustave Lanctot boldly declare that "[t]his is the journal of the first transcanadian tourist."[1] The editors are equally categorical about *The North-West Passage by Land. Being the Narrative of an Expedition from the Atlantic to the Pacific, Undertaken with the View of Exploring a Route across the Continent to British Columbia through British Territory, by One of the Northern Passes of the Rocky Mountains*, an earlier publication based on the trip and co-authored by Cheadle and his fellow traveler Viscount Milton. Doughty and Lanctot write that "in the title of the book, the tourist trip of the authors is raised to the dignity of an exploration. To it is ascribed a purpose of greater importance, probably as bearing a larger public appeal" (pp. 9–10). The implication is that exploration and tourism are two different things, and that one is significant and the other trivial. However, for a reader confronted with the rich and varied history of Canadian travel-writing, which includes seventy-odd years of which Doughty and Lanctot were not yet aware, it can be quite difficult to make such distinctions. Exploration and tourism, and the writing resulting from them, often overlap in a country where travelers are called upon to match the pragmatic and aesthetic principles to which they have become accustomed (and which they are determined to pursue) against extraordinary geographical, climatic, and cultural challenges. The literature of exploration and travel cuts a broad swath through histories, genres, disciplines, and readerships, and it has frequently been a place where evolving ideas about Canadian and North American identity are being played out. The study of this writing and the mapmaking associated with it instantly and dramatically modifies the notion that Canada, despite its enormous size, is essentially a narrow band of settlements strung along the forty-ninth parallel. Tracing the trade routes through the intricate river and lake systems that thread their way throughout the northern part of the continent provides an understanding of complex historical communication networks that are not dependent on roads or railways. Many of these networks pre-date European contact, but they also illustrate how western commercial interests, appropriating Indigenous skills, established themselves along these routes and made them part of an ever-expanding mercantile network of their own. Canadian literature and culture continues to draw inspiration from the journals, letters, and reports that record these travels, among them Rudy Wiebe, *A Discovery of Strangers* (1994), Fred Stenson, *The Trade* (2000), and Wayne Johnston, *The Navigator of New York* (2002) to mention only a few.

Because exploration- and travel-writing is one of the mainstays of popular culture, typically combining large helpings of instruction and entertainment, it can easily be used for imperial, national, and other propaganda. In juvenile literature, such intentions can be especially obvious. Everett McNeil's *For the Glory of France* (1927), for example, tells the story of Samuel de Champlain through the eyes of fictitious stowaways, "Noel Bidoux...and Robert de Boville, two French boys," but in the wake of the tensions between English and French Canadians during World War I, the book makes sure that the English are in the picture by telling the story "as set down in English by Everett McNeil."[2] Earlier in the century, the disagreements that erupted over the Boer War required similar educational action, with books like *Heralds of Empire; Being the Story of one Ramsay Stanhope, Lieutenant to Pierre Radisson in the Northern Fur Trade* (1902) including both English and French names in the title to suggest that, despite appearances, there was an *entente* of long standing that was worth preserving. On the other hand, the prolific writer Agnes Laut, who moved to the United States in search of a wider audience, included two famous American explorers in her book *Pathfinders of the West; Being the Thrilling Story of the Adventures of the Men Who Discovered the Great Northwest, Radisson, La Verendrye, Lewis, and Clark* (1904) to suit her own market. Nor were writers in the early part of the twentieth century the only ones to make such uses of the genre. As will be discussed later on, World War II, the Centennial celebrations, and the attack on the World Trade Center in New York all brought travel and travel-writing to the fore, with the specific purpose of sorting out broad questions of alliance, political and otherwise.

One of the most problematic ideological uses of exploration literature is found in the ways in which such writing asserts the invader's claim to ownership, by stipulating that he and the metropolitan power he represents are the first to survey and therefore claim the place, thus becoming "Cartier, finder of the St. Lawrence" and "Samuel de Champlain, Father of New France" or, indeed, a "Caesar of the Wilderness" (after Radisson's "We were

Cesars, being no body to contradict us"), a "Little Emperor" (to denote the Napoleonic demeanor of Hudson's Bay Company Governor George Simpson), and "King of the Fur Traders."[3] A book tracing the origin of the place-names in the Pacific Northwest, Edmund S. Meany's *Vancouver's Discovery of Puget Sound: Portraits and Biographies of the Men Honored in the Naming of Geographic Features of the North-Western America* (1907) assumes the explorer's right to appropriate a territory by giving it a name or to take quasi-sexual possession of it, as appears to be suggested in titles such as *First Crossing: Alexander Mackenzie, His Expedition across North America, and the Opening of the Continent*. Given the difficult legacy of "discovery," strenuously disputed during the bicentenary of Vancouver's arrival in America (which coincided with the 500th anniversary of that of Columbus), it is logical that the literature of exploration has also been a site where to begin the necessary revisions. Some of these are apparent in books describing the role of Aboriginal people in mapping the continent, such as *The Helping Hand: How Indian Canadians Helped Alexander Mackenzie Reach the Pacific Ocean* (1972) or, more sharply formulated, *The Helping Hand: The Debt of Alexander Mackenzie and Simon Fraser to Indian Canadians* (1973), both educational guides for use in high schools published with the collaboration of the Indian Education Resources Centre at the University of British Columbia. Other attempts at correcting the imperialist "thrust" of exploration have been to turn the itinerary into a naturalist and all too often elegiac enterprise, as in John Woodworth's *In the Steps of Alexander Mackenzie: Trail Guide* (1981), sponsored by the Nature Conservancy of Canada, or Jack Nisbet's *Sources of the River: Tracking David Thompson across Western North America* (1994).

Viscount Milton and Walter Cheadle

For a number of reasons, Cheadle's diary is an interesting book with which to begin this discussion. It records the trip undertaken in 1861–2 by Walter Cheadle, a physician, and William Fitzwilliam Viscount Milton from Eastern Canada to the Pacific when both men were in their early twenties, but the book appeared more than sixty years after the journey. The first publication resulting from the expedition was a work co-authored by Milton and Cheadle, *The North-West Passage by Land*. Including practical information on natural resources and agricultural potential and drawing on the recommendations of the Palliser-Hind expeditions, the book was instrumental in making a case for the settlement of the prairies and of British Columbia and for bringing the West into Confederation. Its description of the rugged land and the hardship endured in traversing it were thrilling enough to make

The North-West Passage by Land a very successful publication, with ten editions published by 1901 and a French translation issued as early as 1866. The book continues to have its enthusiasts: Christie Harris's *West with the White Chiefs*, a children's adaptation, appeared in 1965; Milton's great-great-grandson Michael Shaw Bond followed in his ancestor's footsteps, in an expedition described in *Way Out West: On the Trail of an Errant Ancestor* (2001), and in 2001 reporter John Stackhouse cited Milton and Cheadle as he crossed Tête Jaune Pass, where the pair had competed in naming mountains after each other. (Stackhouse was on assignment from the *Globe and Mail* which had sent him on a hitch-hiking trip across the country to find out what ordinary Canadians were thinking about the future of their country. *The North-West Passage by Land* appears to have been something of a blueprint by which to measure the answers.)

Alluding to two key terms in the title of *The North-West Passage by Land*, the editors of Cheadle's *Journal* sniff in their introduction that neither expedition nor exploration was involved as the route was well established by travelers "on business, exploration or duty" (p. 7), and in their biographical notes they do their best to depict Cheadle, the more robust of the pair, as a vacationing Cambridge man who, "selected to row in the University eight against Oxford," had been "prevented by a family bereavement from taking part in the great race and securing his full blue" (p. 12). Unlike *The North-West Passage by Land*, the *Journal* not only contains very detailed notes about social life on board the *Anglo-Saxon* from Britain to Canada ("Breakfast 8.30, Luncheon 12, Dinner 4, Tea 7, *Supper only to order*") but also a leisurely description of their return journey via the United States, during which Cheadle, after two years of deprivation, engages in much enthusiastic leering at the ladies. However, despite their reservations Doughty and Lanctot are equally clear about the all-important role Cheadle played in the undertaking, which ranged from all practical aspects of the team's daily progress to keeping the extensive notes on which the book is based (Milton was also supposed to keep a diary but did so infrequently). Indeed, it is unlikely that the trip could have been made at all without his constant medical attention. Milton suffered from epilepsy and the *Journal* frequently refers to his "symptoms" or "a turn" brought on by their exertions. Cheadle often notes that they make a late start because Milton has slept in, and it is likely that his languor has a great deal to do with his illness. At the same time, Cheadle is exasperated with "Lord M."'s moodiness and "his complaints & curses that he had ever come & wanting to stop and make a fire with every rotten stick he saw" (p. 100), not to mention the effect on their Native guides whose impatience with Milton's capriciousness sometimes knows no bounds and requires Cheadle's energetic mediation. *The North-West*

Passage by Land, by contrast, depicts Milton as never anything but mature and capable, and the relationship between the travellers as never less than collegial.

These differences become apparent elsewhere in these books as well. Along with the unusual, in the expectation of which the journey has been undertaken, the log records the daily routine which can become so numbing that days disappear without trace. Toward the end of August 1862 Cheadle writes: "Write up log. A long discussion whether it is Saturday or Sunday, decided by La Ronde in favour of former. Cook ham for Sunday dinner" (p. 50). On occasion, the diary records the tedious ("On-on-on-paddle-paddle-paddle-nothing to be seen until noon" [p. 42]) along with the wildly adventurous in ways that confusingly mix recorded speech and first-person narrative. On Friday 8 August, for example, at the beginning of their journey in the Red River country, Cheadle lists "Breakfast in La Ronde's House," followed by attending to Milton's numerous ailments and to other patients ("Son got abscess in kidney. Old boy very hospitable; cold roast beef; delicious, left England at 13"), making an unsuccessful trip to the Post Office, and listening to a story about six grizzly bears which, without apparent transition, becomes a sighting of buffaloes: "Go up to them very quick, raised tail, &c., &c." The day concludes with "Port wine & pipe with Dr. Bird" and the observation that "Things at Fort stores dear & Messiter frantic with many preparations & packings. Half breeds & drunken Indians. Tom-tom going all night" (p. 44). In *The North-West Passage by Land*, by comparison, the monotony is tamed by complex vocabulary and syntax suggesting that the writer remained in charge of his tasks, no matter how tedious, and that the fatigue was an insignificant aspect of an important undertaking: "The unvarying sameness of the river, and the limited prospect shut in by rising banks on either side, gave a monotony to our daily journey; and the routine of cooking, chopping, loading and unloading canoes, paddling, and shooting, amusing enough at first, began to grow rather tiresome" (p. 24). The book also "tidies up" the hierarchies, often blurred in the *Journal*, between the men, their guides, and the numerous Aboriginal people they meet en route, by drawing on narrative modes apparently borrowed from James Fenimore Cooper's *Leatherstocking* saga. The attire of a chief is given with ethnographic precision and his "oration" – "delivered . . . with much dignity" (p. 66) – rendered in direct speech, featuring the stilted prose European readers had been taught to associate with North American Indians. The book is careful to enhance the link to an adventure story by creating an ambiance of stealth, complete with ominous foreshadowings and the sighting of a headless dead Indian ("full of chrysales of maggots" in the *Journal* [p. 202], but "filled with the exuviae of chrysales" [p. 296] in *The North-West Passage*), and it provides sentimental counterpoints to all the vigorous exertions by telling the touching story of Rover the dog or lovingly describing "the footprints of the cross or silver fox, delicately impressed in the snow" (p. 117). A bothersome Irishman who attaches himself to the gullible young men and, in Cheadle's version, frequently drives them to distraction, is efficiently transformed into the "Paddy" of English stage fame, and his presence provides the comic relief to a drama that threatens to turn into tragedy as the travelers, near starvation, stumble about in the forests of British Columbia.

"Incremental" narratives

The relationship of *The North-West Passage by Land* and Cheadle's *Journal* may be unusual in its details, but it still highlights the typical textual situation of most travel-writing. Germaine Warkentin has referred to the sometimes complicated textual history involved in travel-writing as "incremental,"[4] with several authors, different readerships and different ideological purposes to be accommodated over different periods of time. Some travelogues were published almost immediately after completion of the journey, such as George Vancouver's *A Voyage of Discovery to the North Pacific Ocean, and round the World: in Which the Coast of North-West America Has Been Carefully Examined and Accurately Surveyed: Undertaken by His Majesty's Command, Principally with a View to Ascertain the Existence of Any Navigable Communication between the North Pacific and North Atlantic Oceans; and Performed in the Years 1790, 1791, 1792, 1793, 1794, and 1795, in the Discovery Sloop of War, and Armed Tender Chatham, under the Command of Captain George Vancouver.* The book appeared in 1798, a swift three years after his return, but there are more than 200 years between Radisson's travels in 1660 and the time they were published in 1885. In this case, the situation is complicated by the fact that Radisson, a Provençal whose allegiance to the French king was somewhat casual, also worked for the Stuarts and had learned some English. Victor Hopwood points out that the available English manuscript is distinguished by its "almost dazzling illiteracy,"[5] the result, so he and others concluded, either of Radisson's own imperfect grasp of grammar or the incompetence of a translator hired by the Hudson's Bay Company, but the textual status of these documents remains the subject of scholarly debate and detective work.[6] Readers familiar with the tortured textual history that arises out of the corporate authorship involved in producing Captain James Cook's travels[7] will find similar complications in the narratives of the Franklin expeditions and in Samuel de Champlain's travelogues. Alexander Mackenzie's journals differ greatly from the version prepared by his editor William Combe who embellished the original with the lofty tone that was his trademark. David Thompson, a brilliant mapmaker and humble observer, is a favorite with critics of Canadian exploration literature who praise him for his "breadth of vision and sense of wonder [that] are unique among his peers"[8] but, her admiration for the author notwithstanding, Germaine Warkentin's notes often read like those supplied by Barney's son to complement "Barney's Version" in Mordecai Richler's eponymous novel (1997); time and again, the annotations point out how the narrator's memory is slipping. Settled into retirement when he began writing and with his eyesight failing, Thompson muddles dates and places, confuses people with similar names, and has difficulty keeping the time in which he is writing separate from the one he is writing about.[9]

While these kinds of discrepancies are mostly involuntary, other inconsistencies in travel-writing are clearly intended. Because its proximity to sensationalism makes it popular, revision for profit, performed by an editor or the author himself, can be extensive, and the borderline between truth and fiction becomes blurred. Thus, Samuel Hearne's account of the so-called "Coppermine Massacre" (1771) of a group of Copper Inuit by Chipewyan and Copper Indians features a memorable scene in which "a young girl" is killed so close to the narrator that she "twist[s] round [his] legs."[10] Close study of the various textual stages involved in producing this episode has made it likely, however, that its poignancy has more to do with the literary vogue of the Gothic than with historical accuracy and that the whole scene may not have taken place in this way at all.[11] If it is difficult to follow the transitions between recorded and direct speech in unpolished journals like Cheadle's, the task can be even more complicated when the rendition of speech becomes subject to the same kind of considerations that make it important to reassert the hierarchies between traveler and guide. Travelogues are valuable historical sources for Indigenous people's customs and speech, including the Piegan chief Saukamapee's narration recorded in David Thompson's *Narrative*. The book confirms that "the speeches of the Indians on both sides of the Mountains are in plain language, sensible and to the purpose [and] I never heard a speech in the florid, bombastic style, I have often seen published as spoken to white men,"[12] but phonetic transcriptions or inventive translations of oral culture can create serious misinterpretation.

Nor is language the only form of representation to consider. Travel-writing characteristically features maps, and the history of exploration hinges on the availability of reliable surveys and charts. On his way to the Arctic Ocean and the Pacific, Alexander Mackenzie frequently consulted with Native people who advised him on the location of rivers, trails, and natural obstacles and provided him with maps drawn "upon a large piece of bark,"[13] while Simon Fraser, together with a chart of the river that now bears his name, received a severe scolding "for venturing so far with our canoes, & for not going by land as advised by the Old Chief on a former occasion" and for generally taking on a route to "be found impracticable to strangers, as we shall have to ascend and descend mountains and precipices by means of rope ladders &c."[14] Fraser's rendition of this dressing-down in indirect speech may be intended to convey his own exasperated amusement at being lectured, but the information undoubtedly made its way into his own evaluation of the itinerary, and maps are frequently drawn at his request. Charting became closely associated, even equated, with imperial enterprise, and because of the immensity of the assumptions, the failures were sometimes equally spectacular. Thus, Captain George Vancouver includes nautical astronomy among the developments that make the unstoppable expansion of the British Empire possible, but his own assiduous activities on the Pacific West Coast were brought up short by the unexpected appearance of the Spanish fleet, clearly engaged in a similar pursuit. As proof of their prior claim to the area, "Sen' Galiano, who spoke a little English"[15] produces a chart documenting their surveying activities the previous year, generously providing the greatly annoyed Vancouver with a copy. Vancouver's chance encounter with the Spanish fleet is only one instance where explorers seem to be following hard on each other's heels. Arriving at Dean Channel, for example, Mackenzie is confronted with news of the recent arrival of people in "a large canoe," including a certain "Macubah" (Vancouver) and "Bensins" (botanist Archibald Menzies).[16] Travelogues are full of cross-references to other explorers' observations, ranging from the medical recommendations to be derived from Samuel Hearne's digestive problems after breakfasting on *tripe de roche* to evaluations of Sir John Franklin's paleontological theories, and one often has the impression of mental maps being passed on from one to the other through the hands of numerous intermediaries. Their exploits may traditionally have been depicted as those of solitary men leading the forward march of western civilization, but explorers' narratives are crowded with voices both competitive and companionable.

Shadow-texts

The Milton-Cheadle narrative moreover falls into the special category of a "shadow-text,"[17] in which one version exists in contrapuntal relationship to another, adopting a textual mode and revealing aspects of the journey and its participants that were probably not meant for publication to begin with. The classic "shadow-text" is Bronislaw Malinowski's self-obsessed *A Diary in the Strict Sense of the Term* (1967), published twenty-five years after his death, which revealed the famous anthropologist of *Argonauts of the*

Western Pacific (1922) as a lecherous hypochondriac who loathed the subjects of his study. Although the *Diary* may be an extreme case, travel-writing
features many such companion texts and Canadian literature is no exception.
Because a shadow-text may reveal unflattering or even scandalous aspects
of a public person that the official record is eager to suppress (and Milton's
petulance but also his illness would have fallen into that category at the time
The North-West Passage by Land was published), considerable sleuthing may
be required to ferret the missing information out. One particularly complex
case is that of George Simpson, Governor of the Hudson's Bay Company,
his wife Frances, and his country-wife Margaret Taylor. Simpson's reports
of his numerous travels, conducted at frenzied pace the length and breadth
of HBC trade routes, including *Peace River: A Canoe Voyage from Hudson's Bay to Pacific...in 1828* (1872) and *Fur Trade and Empire: George
Simpson's Journal. Remarks Connected with the Fur Trade in the Course
of a Voyage from York Factory to Fort George and back to York Factory
1824–1825* (1931), belong to the classics of Canadian exploration and travel
literature, as does his *Narrative of a Journey round the World, during the
Years 1841 and 1842* (1847) in pursuit of expanding HBC interests in the
Sandwich Islands and Russia. His "Character Book," with sharply observed
sketches of the factors, traders, and clerks at York Factory and not intended
for publication, did reveal an unofficial side of a closely guarded official
when it appeared many years after his death, but it is his relationships with
women that have been the darkest "shadows" in his texts.

The "Journal of a Voyage from Montreal, thro' the Interior of Canada,
to York Factory on the Shores of Hudson's Bay," serialized in 1954 in the
Beaver (a history magazine founded by the HBC in 1920), describes the
journey to her new home of the eighteen-year-old Frances, the cousin whom
Simpson married in 1830 while on a two-year leave in Britain. However,
there is no written record by Margaret Taylor, a Métis who had borne
Simpson two sons and whom he had left in the care of senior HBC em-
ployees while he was away with the understanding that their relationship
would be resumed when he returned. But with Frances installed in the
Governor's mansion, Taylor was married off to *voyageur* Amable Hogue
and tongues wagged: "The Govrs little tit bit Peggy Taylor is . . . Married
to Amable Hogue . . . what a downfall is here . . . from a Governess to
Sow."[18] Taylor's missing voice has since been supplied by her descendant,
filmmaker Christine Welsh, whose documentary *Women in the Shadows*
(1991) and memoir "Voices of the Grandmothers" (1991) are both subtitled "Reclaiming a Métis Heritage."[19] Some of the most stirring footage in
Welsh's film occurs when she is shown around the Governor's house, taken
to the flat rocks near York Factory where some of the HBC men, including

George Simpson, carved their names, and when she looks around the overgrown cemetery heaved up by the permafrost, with elaborate tombstones marking the "important" graves.

Welsh's travels in search of her ancestor and her conversations with family members who do their best to explain their silences (or, in the case of one feisty aunt, insist on their right to refuse information), are an undertaking in "relational biography."[20] More specifically, they are part of an emerging genre of collective memoirs in which young authors and filmmakers research the story of their ethnic backgrounds by seeking out the "ghosts" that populate their families' histories. The Chinese cooks and workmen that Cheadle and Milton saw in the interior of British Columbia and on the coast were often widely connected with other Chinese immigrants in North America and maintained strong relationships with their families in China. In Denise Chong's *The Concubine's Children* (1994) and filmmaker Colleen Leung's *Letters from Home* (2001), researchers retrace the networks that their families maintained over two continents, the journeys that had to be undertaken, sometimes with decades in between, to fulfill obligations on both sides of the Pacific, and the difficulties that resulted from racist legislation like the Headtax and the Chinese Exclusion Act. The search may be complicated by the descendant's lack of proficiency in the language but, as in Christine Welsh's case, faces can be powerfully effective family "archives" over several generations.[21] The irrefutable visual evidence that family resemblance provides is surely one reason why this type of family memoir and the often extensive travel associated with it have been a favorite with filmmakers.

Mails, railways, and canoes

As the title of Colleen Leung's film indicates, letters were an important means of maintaining family connections and numerous published travel reports have their origin in letters home. Given the vast distances between country of origin and Canada, not to mention those within Canada itself, letters and the speed with which they were delivered reflect on the state of the available communication network at any given time and on the numerous ways in which it could be interrupted. Marie de l'Incarnation (1599–1672), founder of the first Ursuline order in North America, wrote some 13,000 letters in the thirty-odd years she lived in New France. Many of these were official letters, commenting on her order's missionary and educational work and soliciting support from the appropriate authorities, but she also maintained an extensive correspondence with members of her family in France, especially her son Claude, whom she had left behind in France at the age of eleven. The rhythms in her writing and receiving of letters were determined by the months when the St. Lawrence was open to receive ships, by the length of time vessels were able to spend in port, and by the time her onerous duties allowed her to lavish on her private correspondence. Letters requiring a quick turnaround because a vessel had arrived late in the season, obliging it to depart in some haste to avoid the freeze-up of the river, usually meant that a question requiring a thoughtful response had to wait till the following year. The vicissitudes of transport also affected the way correspondents composed their letters. For particularly important correspondence, letter-writers sent several copies with different vessels, and the constant possibility that letters would go missing necessitated, at the beginning of each new letter, a provisional summary of previous exchanges in order to ensure that the chain of communication – often maintained with long gaps in between – was not broken.[22] Two hundred years after Marie de l'Incarnation, letters from home remained a keen concern with Milton and Cheadle as well, especially as services were disrupted by political events. Thus, they are greatly disappointed when "the packet from Red River via Norway House & La Corne" arrives and "the letter boxes [contained] none for Milton or myself! The rascally Sioux the cause, I presume, for only 2 or 3 letters have reached here from Red River" (Cheadle, *Journal*, p. 107). A reminder of the extensive difficulties that attended the punctual delivery of letters to ships and remote outposts or to men working as *voyageurs*, an annotated edition of *Undelivered Letters to Hudson's Bay Company Men on the Northwest Coast of America, 1830–57* (2003)[23] also provides a richly varied chorus of voices from the people who are often absent from the official accounts, in particular members of the working class and lower-middle class. These letters (if successfully delivered) furthermore circulated valuable information that would have assisted people from these backgrounds in making up their minds about whether or not to contemplate emigration.

Lady Dufferin was more fortunate than Cheadle and Milton or any of the unfortunate correspondents in *Undelivered Letters*. On her arrival in Vancouver after traveling across the continent and along the Pacific coast, the perusal of forty letters, "so many from the children," gave her "quite a headache,"[24] although there are also occasions during the Dufferins' tours when the Governor-General and his aides have to engage in frantic letter-writing to catch a departing ship. If *The North-West Passage by Land* helped promote the settlement of the West, the Dufferins' tour of British Columbia in 1876 furthered the cause of those who wanted British Columbia to join the Confederation and to promote the building of a transnational railway to provide the necessary linkage. "At present the feeling here is British, but anti-Canadian, on account of the railroad, which can't be made yet," Lady Dufferin writes about their arrival in Victoria where the Governor-General "was obliged to refuse to go under [an arch]" with "Our Railroad or Separation" written on it, although he recommended that turning the "S" into an "R" would solve an impasse in the protocol (*My Canadian Journal*, p. 200). A few years earlier, George Munro Grant, who served as secretary to Sir Sandford Fleming, engineer-in-chief of the Canadian Pacific Railway, produced *Ocean to Ocean: Sandford Fleming's Expedition through Canada in 1872* (1873), reporting on Fleming's travels west, by canoe, stage-coach, train, and every other conceivable means of transportation, to study a likely route for the transcontinental railroad. Fleming followed up with *England and Canada: A Summer Tour between Old and New Westminster* (1884), an assured and elegant narrative written in the knowledge that the plans sketched out in *Ocean to Ocean* had now come to fruition. This is not to say that train travel has always served the cause of Canadian unity. In his memoir *Baltimore's Mansion* (2000), Wayne Johnston describes a train journey through Newfoundland with his passionately anti-Confederation father. The trip becomes a manic celebration of independence, doomed like the train itself which is about to yield to the more economical service by bus.

On their arrival in Canada, the Dufferins had set a maid to work fabricating a Canadian flag ("all suppose there must be a beaver and a maple-leaf in it" [*My Canadian Journal*, p. 2]), but there was no tentativeness in Lady Dufferin's much-quoted description of fall in Tadoussac:

> The hills all round...are of the most lovely autumn colours, and, covered as they are with red and orange trees, they really look like flames in the distance, or like gigantic flower-gardens; for our *trees* are quite as brilliant as your best *flowers*, and if you can imagine your conservatory magnified a million times and spread over miles and miles of hill and dale, you will begin to understand how we do things in this Canada of ours. (pp. 25–6)

The description exudes the kind of panoramic grandeur that associates landscape with nationalism and was vigorously promoted by the Canadian Pacific Railway as the railroad neared completion. The CPR, especially Sir William van Horne, president (1888–99) and chairman of the Board (1899–1915), gave away free passes and commissions to artists. Painters like Lucius O'Brien and Frederic Marlett Bell-Smith took to the trains in the pursuit of majestic scenery, and some of the artists provided leading magazines like the *Week* with a running commentary on their impressions. Influenced by the American Hudson River School, these painters developed a grandiose aesthetic to go with the size of the country. These expeditions also provided an opportunity to use the camera, as an *aide-mémoire* to painters or as a handy substitute, resulting in such travel narratives as Lady Aberdeen's *Through*

Canada with a Kodak (1893), which combined travel impressions with photographic snapshots.

The promotional activity of the CPR painters and the building of CPR hotels in the style of French *châteaux* in major scenic locations along the route of the railroad are closely connected to the advent of organized tourism that made it possible for travelers of a less adventurous inclination than Milton and Cheadle to see the country. The completion of Château Frontenac in Quebec was linked to the 1893 Columbian Fair in Chicago, and Quebec City was increasingly marketed as a substitute Europe and honeymoon destination for American couples. Here too, Lord Dufferin played a significant role. Appalled at the dilapidated state of the walls and gates of the old town, he had instigated their repair, but they had also been "improved" so as not to interfere with the traffic flow generated in part because the restoration was expected to enhance the city's attractiveness to tourists. Subsequent Governors-General enthusiastically furthered the cause, so that at the time of the 1908 tercentenary of Champlain's founding of Quebec, the Château Frontenac, the Dufferin Terrace in front of it, and the picturesque city surrounding them had become a flawless theatrical backdrop for the pageantry.[25] Scenic spots like Niagara Falls were formalized as tourist attractions, a process facilitated by the descriptions that every visitor – from Father Louis Hennepin in the late seventeenth century to Anna Jameson on an 1830s visit to her estranged husband, attorney-general of Upper Canada – had provided of them, not to mention a "fungus" of tourist facilities ("Chinese pagoda, menagerie, camera obscura, museum, watch-tower, wooden monument, sea gardens, and 'old curiosity shops'").[26] Like the carefully staged scenery of Quebec, Niagara Falls was also marketed as a site of Canadian and American confrontation because of its fortuitous proximity to Queenston Heights which allowed battlefield tourists "to hear the sound of guns mingling with the roar of the cataract at Lundy's Lane" (Jasen, *Wild Things*, p. 38).

Inevitably, commodification of these places required the discovery of "untouched" wildernesses, such as the Muskoka region north of Toronto which rapidly became a highly developed place where urban dwellers could recuperate from their business in the city and employ Native guides to take them duck-shooting. As is typical for travel-writing with the advent of nineteenth-century organized tourism, narratives describing the sights appear side by side with others lamenting the environmental destruction necessary to make these sights accessible. With the wisdom of hindsight, scientific reports like Henry Youle Hind's *Narrative of the Canadian Red River Exploring Expedition of 1857 and of the Assiniboine and Saskatchewan Exploring Expedition of 1858* (1860) and *The Papers of the Palliser Expedition* (1857; publ. 1968) may also be read as elegies for a vanishing world. Norman Henderson's memoir *Rediscovering the Great Plains: Journeys by Dog, Canoe, and Horse* (2001) is infused with a good dose of nostalgia, but it also comes with some belligerently practical observations. The author is a senior policy advisor on resource and environmental management issues to the government of Saskatchewan, who has studied grasslands worldwide. As an experiment to research the conditions of historical travel through the prairies, Henderson makes three trips through the Qu'Appelle Valley by dog-and-*travois*, canoe, and horse-and-*travois*. Although the journey has its adventures and tense moments, its purpose is not extreme sports. The narrative takes the time "to travel through [the landscape] slowly, and as exposed to the elements as reasonably possible."[27] It cites the observations of HBC men and other travelers through the prairies, looks at the impact of agriculture and the constitution of the grassland, studies animals and their habitats, and formulates some practical recommendations. The book comes with a scholarly apparatus, but it is also a spiritual autobiography leavened by self-irony.

Henderson warily reviews the "nation-building agenda that underlies the promotion of a canoe ideology" (*Rediscovering the Great Plains*, p. 67). He cites Prime Minister Trudeau's essay "Exhaustion and Fulfillment: The Ascetic in a Canoe" (1944), and one might add Governor-General Adrienne Clarkson's "mystical love of the land" which impelled her to ask in her inaugural speech, "what were Cavalier de la Salle, La Verendrye, Hearne and Mackenzie doing if not imagining this astonishing space?" and which made her promise "to travel this whole country by plane, train, car, canoe and kayak."[28] But there is an undercurrent of patriotism in *Rediscovering the Great Plains* as well, updated as global responsibility. Nation-building was certainly part of the agenda when a crew traveled the historical 3,283-mile *voyageur* route from North Saskatchewan to Montreal during the Centennial year. A similar feat was performed in 2002 when History Television – inspired by the success of the CBC's *Canada: A People's History* and *Pioneer Quest*, a reality television show simulating life among the pioneers – produced "Quest for the Bay," a York boat trip from Lake Winnipeg to York Factory under nineteenth-century conditions.

Travel to Europe

When historian François-Xavier Garneau traveled to Europe in 1831, he spent twenty-one days on board the *Strathisla* in a crossing still to be considered brisk compared to Susanna Moodie's nine-week crossing in the other direction the year after. On their journey to attend Queen Victoria's coronation in 1838, however, Joseph Howe and Thomas Chandler Haliburton were thrilled with a sighting of the *Sirius*, an English steamer moving along "in gallant style with the speed of a hunter,"[29] which was expected to complete the crossing in twelve to fifteen days. A year later, Samuel Cunard of Halifax founded the British and North American Royal Mail Steam Packet Company, and in 1840 the first Cunard liner, the *Britannia*, made its way across the Atlantic. After 1850, excavations in the St. Lawrence and an extensive improvement of pilotage service and sounding systems eased the way for oceangoing vessels to Quebec and Montreal, both of which quickly overtook Halifax in their importance as ports. Hugh Allan of Montreal became one of the most prominent shipping magnates of the Empire and, like Cunard, he was knighted for his endeavors. By 1891, the fastest crossing was clocked at five days, sixteen hours, and thirty-one minutes. Although travel remained a privilege of the well-to-do for some time to come, the journey to Canada was no longer the inexorable one-way trip that it had been for many emigrants at the time of Marie de l'Incarnation and for many years after. Journeys to Europe were now undertaken to visit family, to conduct a pilgrimage associated with one's cultural origins, and to ensure that the younger generation was exposed to the traditions that their elders held high.

Thomas Stinson Jarvis, offspring of a prominent Loyalist family and later a well-known lawyer, produced a series of lively and precocious sketches describing his grand tour. His *Letters from East Longitudes: Sketches of Travel in Egypt, the Holy Land, Greece, and Cities of the Levant* (1875) give evidence of the classical and contemporary reading he had done as a graduate of Upper Canada College, of the prejudices of his class, and of his adolescent preoccupations with "half-clad women."[30] Jarvis traveled alone, as did William Henry Parker who in 1855 enjoyed upsetting his family back in Canada with reports of "bandits" in Italy whom he intended to fight with "colts [and] revolvers" should they become "bould" [sic],[31] but other parents wisely kept an eye on their children's progress at all times. Egerton Ryerson, chief superintendent for education, Canada West, supervised his son's progress personally, requiring him to pursue a formidable program of language lessons, opera, and art appreciation. Ryerson himself intently studied the educational systems of France and Germany, and brought home stacks of paintings and plaster casts for use as educational material.

Margaret Addison's *Diary of a European Tour 1900* (1999) provides a rare feminine complement to Ryerson's preoccupations. Addison, the first dean of Annesley Hall at Toronto's Victoria College, studied women's education in Switzerland and Great Britain, writing enthusiastically about Newnham and Girton Colleges and using the opportunity to form friendships that were to prove helpful in her profession. In addition to acquiring information and building a network, Addison was also traveling to improve her health and recover from a nervous disposition. In 1891, Sandford Fleming's daughter-in-law Gertrude was overcome by neurasthenia while traveling through Europe on her honeymoon and consulted an avuncular Walter Cheadle (by then an advocate of women's right to practice medicine) in London who prescribed burgundy and rest and took his patient for a drive.[32] Canadians who could afford it consulted with European doctors and removed themselves to the hot climates of France, Italy, and North Africa in the hope of curing their tuberculosis when the salubrious environment of the Muskoka Lakes or the sanatoriums in the St. Lawrence Valley failed them.

Although Ryerson made some very unorthodox friendships during his travels, including one with an eccentric Librarian to the Pope, and was well known for his occasional extravagant spending on vintage wines and other luxuries, he was guided by his Methodism to account for his time and actions, as was Addison who throughout her life was given to keeping meticulous lists of her activities. She traveled to Europe on a tour led by William Withrow, a Methodist minister believed to have completed much of his copious reading while on horseback as a circuit rider, and a recipient of many of the Dominion's highest honors for his contributions to education, publishing, and the arts, including his work with William Hay, a disciple of Augustus Welby Pugin. His letters to the *Canadian Methodist Magazine* were later gathered in *A Canadian in Europe: Being Sketches of Travel in France, Italy, Switzerland, Germany, Holland and Belgium, Great Britain and Ireland* (1881), and he also wrote about early Christianity and the catacombs in his novel *Valeria: The Martyr of the Catacombs; a Tale of Early Christian Life in Rome* (1882), which fictionalized material from his travel sketches. Pedestrian as some of these writings may be, they are an important source of influential views on art in nineteenth-century Canada, especially if compared with similarly conservative views forwarded by French Canadian travelers, many of them priests, in the same time period. However, while some of the artists who traveled to Europe to work in its studios had imbibed the lessons of the likes of Withrow and his counterparts among French Canadian arbiters, others certainly did not. Sara Jeannette Duncan and Alice Jones both wrote slightly risqué novels about the artists' milieu in Paris, and Jones, daughter of Lieutenant-Governor Alfred Gilpin Jones of Nova Scotia and sister of the painter Frances Bannerman, published some exceptionally elegant and nuanced sketches in the *Week* based on her extensive travels in France and Italy in the 1880s and 90s.

A welcome opportunity to compare Canada's accomplishments with those of Europe and with those of the other members of the British Empire was provided by the international exhibitions that, from the Great Exhibition in 1851 onwards, served as powerful tourist attractions. In 1900 Addison dutifully visited as many pavilions as she could, but she was disappointed by the disorganized Canadian display, consisting of "gold, minerals, fruits, cold storage, furs, birds and animals peculiar to the country, graniteware, stoves, agricultural implements, pianos, bicycles, leather, paper, pictures of the mountains, exhibits of the C.P.R. even to a sleeping car made up."[33] She did not go so far as the lawyer Thomas Langton who began to think of his country as a "hobbledehoy-nation" when he had been mistaken once too often as American or British,[34] or the schoolteacher Andrew Spedon whose description of Canada's display at the 1867 Paris exhibition turns into full-blown satire. Spedon tells of his painful search for the display and for his failure to locate anyone to give him directions, until by sheer accident he comes upon an "alcove" headed by the word "CANADA in insignificant letters, surrounded by maple-leaves, and surmounted by the figure of a '*Beaver*' chewing at a *maple-branch*."[35] While it found itself in close proximity to more glamorous members of the Empire, especially India, Canada was a regular disappointment to visitors from home, but there was rich compensation when Expo '67 in Montreal proved a spectacular success, showing off the country's accomplishments on its own home ground.[36] Other welcome opportunities to compare Canada's public image to that of other nations were Queen Victoria's Jubilees. Writing in *To London for the Jubilee* (1897), Kathleen ("Kit") Coleman, acerbic journalist of the *Globe* (later *Globe and Empire*), reported on the pageantry of the Diamond Jubilee in London, dutifully including the fashion notes that were expected of her although she was herself notorious for her unkempt appearance.

Travel and war

The time when tourists began to haunt Queenston Heights, digging "up the bones of the dead" to take away as relics (Jasen, *Wild Things*, p. 40) coincided roughly with the time when the Battle of Waterloo generated an entire battlefield industry. Throughout the nineteenth century, travelers on their way to the Holy Land detoured to the sights of the Crimean War, and others were barely dissuaded from pocketing unexploded shells from the ruins of Paris after the Franco-Prussian War. For Canadians, World War I was a nation-defining event in numerous ways, and battles like Vimy Ridge generated entire iconographies to go with them. A Michelin guide to the Front was available as early as 1919, and travel agencies specialized in affordable tours. For the unveiling of the Walter Allward memorial (which has since become the subject of Jane Urquhart's novel *The Stone Carvers* [2001]) at Vimy Ridge 6,000 Canadians made the pilgrimage, and many brought back "[b]its of rubble, shards of glass, and bags of dirt"[37] as souvenirs.

While some of these activities developed with hostile action scarcely over, some tourists found their movements suddenly and alarmingly curtailed when war broke out while they were on their travels. Passenger ships were immediately requisitioned for the troops, and Hugh Allan's shipping company gained praise for the commendable speed with which he made his fleet available during the Crimean and Boer Wars. In 1914 Joseph Whitman Bailey, a lawyer from New Brunswick, spent a tense week or so on board a ship painted "the steel gray coloring of a ship of war"[38] with all the lights dimmed. He was fortunate to have obtained passage at all. In order to replace the travel-writing that had become a staple of weekly leisure reading and in order to educate Canadians in their patriotic duty, the *Canadian Magazine* and *Maclean's* turned to local tourism, alerting readers to the beauties of the West Coast and the prairies, and substituting some of its more "exotic" immigrants for the ones who could not be visited in their own countries. However, travel books are also major sources for the ethnic phobias that erupt during times of war. Two such works are Bruce Hutchison's *The Unknown Country: Canada and Her People* (1942), winner of a Governor-General's Award, and Dorothy Duncan's *Here's to Canada!* (1941), both cross-country journeys. A highly respected journalist, Hutchison produced an idiosyncratic narrative, alternating regionalist sketches with political journalism and high-toned lyrical reflections. His description of Vancouver at night, for instance, resembles Earle Birney's poem "Vancouver Lights" (1941) in its pathos, and both Hutchison and Birney won Governor-General's Awards in 1942 for work that evoked the effects of war on Canada. Hutchison's book was very popular, going through thirteen printings between 1942 and 1965, with excerpts included in such patriotic anthologies as John D. Robins's *A Pocketful of Canada* (1946) and McClelland and Stewart featuring the first paperback version in its "Canadian Best-Seller Library" in 1965. It is when he talks about the "Orientals" on the West Coast that the wartime propaganda that runs through the narrative as a not-so-subtle undercurrent is openly revealed. Expressing alarm at their "control" of gardening, fishing, and other businesses, Hutchison is convinced that "[t]here is no hope either of their absorption or their decline."[39] The book was revised in 1948 and some of the comments on the Chinese and Japanese have been muted, but what remains in the 1965 edition is still highly prejudiced. Duncan, American-born wife of the novelist Hugh MacLennan, also mixes genres in her book which presents Canada as an emergency tourist land for wartime Americans, combining regional sketches with information on how to get to places and what sorts of souvenir to buy. Writing about Halifax, she does offer interesting information on life in a wartime port, but when her itinerary reaches British Columbia, the guidebook disguise of the book is suddenly swept aside in favor of unalloyed prejudice against the Japanese in particular who, although "these hard-working little men were needed as cheap labour in the building of the railroads," are now a menace because "there are urgent war activities going on which cannot run the risk of being sabotaged or spied upon."[40]

The connection between war and travel was brought home powerfully during the attack on the World Trade Center in New York. Thousands of passengers stranded in Canada and their encounters with the locals in Gander, Newfoundland, and elsewhere were celebrated in newspaper articles by the likes of Stephen Jay Gould, in television specials, and in a number of commemorative books, including *The Day the World Came to Town: 9/11 in Gander, Newfoundland* and *A Diary between Friends*, both published in 2002. The travel section of the *Sunday New York Times*, generally the bulk of a doorstop, shriveled to minimal size for several weeks because the logistics of travel suddenly seemed insurmountable. One of the few travel essays that made it into publication on 22 September offered a railway journey through Canada as a safe and comforting alternative while 7 October brought a special on "America, Grandly Familiar."[41] The 2003 war in Iraq provoked similar publications in Canada and the United States.

Literary travel

Many Canadian writers have published books about their travels around the world. The inward-gazing scholarship of the 1960s and 70s paid little attention to these narratives, but recent research has taken another look at Margaret Laurence's writing about Ghana and Somalia, especially *The Prophet's Camel Bell* (1963), at Daryl Hine's charming if superficial notes on Cold-War Poland in *Polish Subtitles: Impressions from a Journey* (1962), and at P. K. Page's reflections about her time as an ambassador's wife in Rio de Janeiro in *Brazilian Journal* (1987).[42] Diplomat Charles Ritchie, in *The Siren Years* (1974), writes of wartime duty in London's Canada House, telling of assignations with a ballerina and lunches with "Sachie" Sitwell, Margot Asquith, and the Princess Callimachi. All of this still left enough leisure to admire "the white lilacs leaning over the garden wall at Apsley House."[43] Pierre Elliott Trudeau and Jacques Hébert's *Deux innocents en Chine Rouge* (1961; translated as *Two Innocents in Red China*) has been mined for its biographical and political information, but deserves analysis as a piece of travel-writing. In her Governor-General's Award-winning *Touch the Dragon: A Thai Journal* (1992), Karen Connelly writes about a year teaching English in Thailand, and language teaching is also one of the subjects in Gabrielle Bauer's *Tokyo, My Everest: A Canadian Woman in Tokyo*

(1995). The travel books of George Woodcock are legion, including *To the City of the Dead: An Account of Travels in Mexico* (1957) and *Faces of India: A Travel Narrative* (1964). Ronald Wright has also been prolific, with *Cut Stones and Crossroads: A Journey in the Two Worlds of Peru* (1984) and *Time among the Maya: Travels in Belize, Guatemala and Mexico* (1989) among his publications. Of particular note are the travel sketches in *Writing Away: The PEN Canada Travel Anthology* (1994), edited by Constance Rooke, with contributions by Daniel David Moses, Thomas King, George Elliott Clarke, and Rohinton Mistry which steadfastly return the gaze that tourists have directed at their forebears.

A complex and growing subcategory is the literature of travel by Canadian writers to their families' homeland. Journalist Jan Wong's bestselling *Red-China Blues* (1996) offers a *bildungsroman* of the author's disillusionment with Maoism, while filmmaker Yi Sun-Kyung's *Inside the Hermit Kingdom: A Memoir* (1997) is a bitter account of the author's exposure to the regime of North Korea. A particularly accomplished work, Dionne Brand's *A Map to the Door of No Return: Notes to Belonging* (2001), moves between Canada, Trinidad, Europe, and Africa, combining travel-writing with memoir, history, linguistic study, and a dozen other genres. Drawing on her background in philosophy, history, education, and English, Brand provides brief essays in which she interrogates and thus revives terms like "migration" and "diaspora" that have become something of a cliché in postcolonial studies, losing much of their experiential poignancy in the process. Her approach is one of question and answer, with repeated runs at a topic or formulation and with provisional conclusions. Clarke Blaise and Bharati Mukherjee's *Days and Nights in Calcutta* (1977), a relatively early example of such return journeys, describes the complications of cross-cultural marriage. The book has reappeared, with updated introductory comments by both authors, in the wake of the current interest in collaborative and ethnic autobiographical writing. Michael Ondaatje's *Running in the Family* (1982) also belongs to this genre, although its inventiveness and crossovers into fiction put it in a category of its own.

Because their authors come from privileged backgrounds, however, neither Blaise/Mukherjee nor Ondaatje conveys the sense of exile that complicates the travels in the flood of recent books written by immigrants from Eastern European countries or by their descendants, such as Myrna Kostash's *Bloodlines: A Journey into Europe* (1993), Eva Hoffman's *Exit into History: A Journey through the New Eastern Europe* (1993),[44] Irena Karafilly's *Ashes and Miracles: A Polish Journey* (1998), Janice Kulyk Keefer's *Honey and Ashes: A Story of Family* (1998), and Lisa Appignanesi's *Losing the Dead* (1999). With the exception of Kostash who completed her travels before the fall of the Wall, these books recount journeys long delayed by restrictions imposed by Eastern European communist regimes. Their purpose is wide-ranging: to be reunited with family the narrator barely knows, to visit a village or city conjured up in stories and photographs, and to deal with the traumas – often the Holocaust – that have forced their families to emigrate and that, as Karafilly poignantly relates in *The Stranger in the Plumed Hat: A Memoir* (2000), have been repressed until the onset of a personal crisis, such as Alzheimer's, releases them. Historian Modris Eksteins's *Walking since Daybreak: A Story of Eastern Europe, World War II, and the Heart of Our Century* (1999) has attracted attention for its experimental narrative which juxtaposes his prodigiously successful contemporary self (Upper Canada College student, Rhodes scholar, university professor) with the humiliations his family endured in fleeing from Latvia and settling in Canada. Bristling with scholarly footnotes that document in painful detail how impromptu changes in political expediency determined the lives of thousands, including that of his family, Eksteins's book dwells with bitterness on terms like "Displaced Persons" that convey their full impact only to those who have lived through the experience.

These visits are hazardous because they can expose collusion and guilt that the traveler is not prepared for, and they open difficult questions about ethnicity in Canada. Janice Kulyk Keefer's response, in "'The Sacredness of Bridges': Writing Immigrant Experience," to Himani Bannerji's blanket criticism of East Europeans illustrates the resulting conflicts particularly well.[45] For her part, Myrna Kostash is a traveler who resolutely confronts the difficult personal consequences when ethnic identities shift between those of victim and victor. She is equally resolute about de-romanticizing globalism. Instead, she calls "for a rearticulated idea of the common cause" which is all the more necessary because "the new capitalism [is] the one 'meta-narrative' that has not been deconstructed."[46] From its beginnings, Canadian travelwriting has provided ways of drafting and continually revising the meaning of Canada, and the recent wealth of publications and the discussions about them indicate that the process is far from completed.

NOTES

1. A. G. Doughty and Gustave Lanctot, introduction, *Cheadle's Journal of Trip across Canada 1862–1863*, by Walter B. Cheadle (1931; Edmonton: Hurtig, 1971) p. 7.
2. Everett McNeil, *For the Glory of France; Being the Tale Told by Noel Bidoux of How He and Robert de Boville, Two French Boys . . . Hid Themselves in the Hold of the Ship of Samuel de Champlain Just before He Sailed for the New World . . . / as Set down in English by Everett McNeil* (New York: Dutton, 1927).

3. See Ronald Syme, *Cartier, Finder of the St. Lawrence* (New York: Morrow, 1958), Samuel Eliot Morison, *Samuel de Champlain, Father of New France* (Boston: Little, 1972), Grace Lee Nute, *Caesars of the Wilderness: Medard Chouart, Sieur des Groseilliers, and Pierre Esprit Radisson, 1618–1710* (1943; New York: Arno, 1977), Stanley Vestal, *King of the Fur Traders; The Deeds and Deviltry of Pierre Esprit Radisson* (Boston: Houghton, 1940).

4. Germaine Warkentin, introduction, *Canadian Exploration Literature*, ed. Warkentin (Toronto: Oxford University Press, 1993) p. x.

5. Victor Hopwood, "Explorers by Land (to 1867)," *Literary History of Canada*, ed. Carl F. Klinck, vol. I (1965; Toronto: University of Toronto Press, 1976) p. 23.

6. See Germaine Warkentin, "Who Was the Scribe of the Radisson Manuscript?," *Archivaria* 53 (Spring 2002): pp. 46–63.

7. See Neil Rennie, *Far-Fetched Facts: The Literature of Travel and the Idea of the South Seas* (Oxford: Clarendon, 1995).

8. Bill Moreau, "Exploration Literature," W. H. New, ed., *Encyclopedia of Literature in Canada* (Toronto: University of Toronto Press, 2002) p. 348.

9. See Warkentin, *Canadian Exploration Literature*, pp. 230–3.

10. Samuel Hearne, *Journey from Prince of Wales's Fort in Hudson's Bay to the Northern Ocean in the Years 1769, 1770, 1771, and 1772* (Toronto: Champlain Society, 1911) p. 179.

11. See Ian MacLaren, "Samuel Hearne's Accounts of the Massacre at Bloody Fall, 17 July 1771," *Ariel* 22.1 (Jan. 1991): pp. 25–51.

12. David Thompson, *David Thompson's Narrative 1784–1812*, ed. Richard Glover (Toronto: Champlain Society, 1962) p. 279.

13. Sir Alexander Mackenzie, *The Journals and Letters of Sir Alexander Mackenzie*, ed. W. Kaye Lamb (Cambridge: for the Hakluyt Society at the University Press, 1970) p. 319.

14. Simon Fraser, *The Letters and Journals of Simon Fraser, 1806–1808*, ed. W. Kaye Lamb (Toronto: Macmillan, 1960) p. 76.

15. George Vancouver, *A Voyage of Discovery to the North Pacific Ocean and round the World, 1791–1795*, ed. W. Kaye Lamb, vol. II (London: Hakluyt Society, 1984) p. 591.

16. Mackenzie, *Journals and Letters*, p. 375.

17. See Dennis Porter, *Haunted Journeys: Desire and Transgression in European Travel Writing* (Princeton: Princeton University Press, 1991).

18. W. Sinclair, letter to Edward Ermatinger, 15 Aug. 1831, Ermatinger Papers, Provincial Archives of British Columbia (AB 40 Er 62.3), quoted. in John S. Galbraith, *The Little Emperor: Governor Simpson of the Hudson's Bay Company* (Toronto: Macmillan, 1976) p. 109.

19. See also Christine Welsh, "*Women in the Shadows*: Reclaiming a Métis Heritage," *Descant* 24.3 (1993): pp. 89–104; Christine Welsh, "Voices of the Grandmothers: Reclaiming a Métis Heritage," *Canadian Literature* 131 (Winter 1991): pp. 15–24.

20. See Paul John Eakin, "Relational Selves, Relational Lives: Autobiography and the Myth of Autonomy," *How Our Lives Become Stories: Making Selves*, by Eakin (Ithaca: Cornell University Press, 1999) pp. 43–98.

21. See the memoirs in Josephine Khu, ed., *Cultural Curiosity: Thirteen Stories about the Search for Chinese Roots* (Berkeley: University of California Press, 2001).

22. See Jane E. Harrison, *Until Next Year: Letter Writing and the Mails in the Canadas, 1640–1830* (Ottawa: Wilfrid Laurier University Press, 1997).

23. See Judith Hudson Beattie and Helen M. Buss, eds., *Undelivered Letters to Hudson's Bay Company Men on the Northwest Coast of America, 1830–57* (Vancouver: University of British Columbia Press, 2003).

24. Marchioness of Dufferin and Ava, Hariot Georgina Blackwood, *My Canadian Journal 1872–1878* (Toronto: Longmans, 1969) p. 210.

25. See H. V. Nelles, *The Art of Nation-Building: Pageantry and Spectacle at Quebec's Tercentenary* (Toronto: University of Toronto Press, 1999).

26. Patricia Jasen, *Wild Things: Nature, Culture, and Tourism in Ontario 1790–1914* (Toronto: University of Toronto Press, 1995) p. 43.

27. Norman Henderson, *Rediscovering the Great Plains: Journeys by Dog, Canoe, and Horse* (Baltimore: Johns Hopkins University Press, 2001) p. XIII.

28. John Fraser, "Excellency," *National Post* 1 Feb. 2003: p. B6; "Adrienne Clarkson: 'To Be Complex Does Not Mean to Be Fragmented'," *Globe and Mail* 8 Oct. 1999: p. A11.

29. Joseph Howe, "The Novascotian Afloat," *Novascotian* 12 July 1838: p. 1. For nineteenth-century Canadian travel, see Eva-Marie Kröller, *Canadian Travellers in Europe: 1851–1900* (Vancouver: University of British Columbia Press, 1987).

30. Thomas Stinson Jarvis, *Letters from East Longitudes: Sketches of Travel in Egypt, the Holy Land, Greece, and Cities of the Levant* (Toronto: Campbell, 1875) p. 46.

31. See William Henry Parker Papers, National Archives of Canada.

32. Gertrude Fleming Papers, National Archives of Canada.

33. Margaret Addison, *Diary of a European Tour 1900*, ed. Jean O'Grady (Montreal: McGill-Queen's University Press, 1999) p. 30.

34. Thomas Langton Papers, National Archives of Canada.

35. Andrew Spedon, *Sketches of a Tour from Canada to Paris, by Way of the British Isles, during the Summer of 1867* (Montreal: Lovell, 1868) p. 199.

36. See Eva-Marie Kröller, "Expo 67: Canada's Camelot?," "Remembering the Sixties," special issue of *Canadian Literature* 152/153 (Spring/Summer 1997): pp. 36–51.

37. Jonathan Vance, *Death So Noble: Memory, Meaning, and the First World War* (1997; Vancouver: University of British Columbia Press, 2000) p. 70.

38. J. W. Bailey Papers, Harriet Irving Library, University of New Brunswick.

39. Bruce Hutchison, *The Unknown Country: Canada and Her People* (Toronto: Longmans, 1942) p. 287.

40. Dorothy Duncan, *Here's to Canada!* (New York: Harper's, 1941) p. 275.

41. See Adam Clymer, "Upstairs, Downstairs on Rails," *New York Times* 23 Sept. 2001: pp. 9–10.

42. See *Canadian Literature* 174 (Autumn 2002), a special issue on travel, for recent scholarship.

43. Charles Ritchie, *The Siren Years: A Canadian Diplomat Abroad, 1937–1945* (1974; Toronto: Macmillan, 1984) p. 106

44. Hoffman spent several years in Vancouver after emigrating to North America. She recounts her experience in *Lost in Translation: A Life in a New Language* (New York: Dutton, 1989).

45. Janice Kulyk Keefer, "'The Sacredness of Bridges': Writing Immigrant Experience," *Literary Pluralities*, ed. Christl Verduyn (Peterborough: Broadview, 1998) pp. 97–110.

46. Myrna Kostash, "Immigration, Representation, and Culture," *Literary Pluralities*, ed. Verduyn, p. 94.

4

Nature-writing

CHRISTOPH IRMSCHER

A challenge to representation

In 1801, the fur trader Alexander Mackenzie (1764?–1820), the first European to see the mighty river that would be named after him and the first to cross the North American continent, published a book about his travel experiences. Surprisingly, his account begins on a rather apologetic note. Do not expect any "variety" from my narrative, he told his readers, ticking off the challenges he had encountered along the way: "Mountains and valleys, the dreary wastes, and the wide-spreading forests, the lakes and rivers succeed each other in general description."[1] Even a trained naturalist would have found little to write about in this inhospitable terrain, which he and his men, raw-mannered *coureurs de bois*, had been forced to traverse with "rapid steps," constantly afraid of "savages" lurking in dark corners.

In October 1792, Mackenzie's party had set out from Ford Chipewyan on Lake Athapasca to try again to find a route to the Pacific. As they were traveling up the Peace River, the frost became so severe that their axes seemed "as brittle as glass" (vol. I, p. 352). On 2 December, Mackenzie's thermometer broke. As he was walking in the woods, however, he heard, to his utter surprise, birds singing in the trees (vol. I, p. 355). On 29 December, the sky suddenly cleared and the weather became so warm "that it dissolved all the snow on the ground." Puddles of water gathered on the ice, as if it were about to break up. But then a northeasterly wind arose, and with it came rain and hail. In two days, the snow was back. On 5 January 1793, another warm wind brought thaw conditions again, a soft greeting, Mackenzie felt, from the place he longed to reach, the Pacific Ocean (vol. II, pp. 10, 13). The only thing that seemed predictable about this land was its unpredictability.

No wonder that Mackenzie, by his own account "a man...not disposed to think too highly of himself" (vol. I, p. xiii), saw his narrative determined not by writerly concerns but by external factors, the dull exigencies and hardships of travel. And yet there is also his description of the birds singing in the snow, rendered in such loving detail that the hired hack who helped him write the book could not have invented it. The body of the male bird Mackenzie found to be a delicate "fawn color"; its neck, breast, and belly were colored "a deep scarlet," the wings were black and had two white bands running across them, and the head was crowned with a "tuft." The female was fawn-colored throughout, though her neck was "enlivened by an hue of glossy yellow." These strange birds (most likely pine grosbeaks) were "constant inhabitants of this climate," perfectly at ease in a world in which Mackenzie and his men were struggling to survive (vol. I, p. 355).

Mackenzie's narrative raises a number of interesting points about the body of texts, ranging from travelogue to gardening handbook, which will be discussed in this chapter. Canadian nature is, first and foremost, a physical challenge. But it is also, because it follows none of the established rules, a challenge to the powers of the writer. Like Mackenzie, other writers on Canadian nature have felt uncertain about their presence in an environment that so often confuses the human observer, reducing him or her, as the naturalist John Keast Lord felt in 1866, to the size of a diatom.[2] And, like him, some of these writers have gone on to question, more specifically, the adequacy of the human point of view as a "central focalizing device" in representations of nature, doubting that humans should consider themselves exempt from, or superior to, the "rhythms" of nature.[3] In spite of their differences, critical models of Canadian identity – from Northrop Frye's "garrison mentality" to Margaret Atwood's "survival" to Robert Kroetsch's "disunity as unity" to Frank Davey's definition of Canada as a "site of social contestation" – have remained stubbornly anthropocentric rather than ecocentric, focused not on the environment, that is, but on its human inhabitants.[4] This is a striking limitation, given the rather marginal presence of humans in a territory that includes such vastly different landscapes as Mackenzie encountered on his journey (mountains, lakes, grasslands, forests, and seashores). While the majority of recent "ecocritical" studies published in the United States have bypassed works written north of the border, the few existing treatments of Canadian nature-writing have tended to emphasize works traditionally regarded as "literary."[5] In his introduction to *This Incomperable Lande: A Book of American Nature Writing*, Thomas J. Lyon proudly describes nature-writing as a specifically US preoccupation, offering as it does a "lifting and a clarifying of perception" that is "very much in the American grain."[6]

This chapter counters such exceptionalist readings of the genre, vigorously criticized by Lawrence Buell,[7] as well as narrowly literary definitions of nature-writing by reviewing the contributions of Canadians who have frequently been more radical than their US peers in noting that there are concerns more important than the self or human society. Only 10 percent of the present Canadian territory is permanently settled, yet if we turn to the works discussed here we find little evidence that, as Northrop Frye claimed, humans have felt "silently swallowed by an alien continent" (conclusion, *Literary History of Canada*, p. 824). In fact, the question inherent in the answers given by Canadian nature-writers from Alexander Mackenzie to Mark Hume is less Frye's puzzled "Where is here?" (p. 826) than, more typically, a patiently repeated, genuinely amazed "*What* is here?"

Man sliding

Samuel Hearne's *Journey from Prince of Wales's Fort in Hudson's Bay*, published posthumously in 1795, paved the way for the success of Mackenzie's book. On the surface, Hearne (1745–92) had been singularly unsuccessful as an explorer. Ordered by the governor of the Hudson's Bay Company to find a legendary copper mine to the northwest, he attempted three times to reach what he finally discovered was only a heap of scattered rocks. In the winter of 1772, Hearne's party, on their way back from the mouth of the Coppermine River, arrived at Lake Athapasca. The southern side of the lake was a surreal sight, dotted with small, flat, wooded islands that, to the men's delight, were full of deer. One of Hearne's engravings, called *A Winter View in the Athapuscow Lake*, evokes a landscape where nothing speaks of the presence of humans, whose ordinary sense of proportion simply doesn't apply here (plate 1). The image has been criticized as "far too symmetrical and disproportionate" to count as a faithful representation of reality.[8] But by emphasizing, through stylization, the starkness of a terrain that to him was a source of continuing amazement, Hearne in fact testifies to his unique experience.

If the land was strange, some of the animals Hearne encountered were even stranger. Either they didn't care about the human intruders or they took shameless advantage of their unbidden presence: the arctic foxes, turning white like ash in the winter when they clustered around the forts in disconcerting numbers; the brown bears, whose warm breath Hearne saw rising from their dens on brittle winter nights; the ermines, given to raiding the Hudson's Bay Company's provision-sheds but unwilling to let themselves be domesticated (the longer he kept such an animal, Hearne said, the more "impatient and restless it became"). What impressed him the most was the beavers. As the workmanship of their dams showed, they had such a degree of "sagacity and foresight ... of approaching evils, as is little inferior to that of the human species, and is certainly peculiar to these animals."[9]

The pragmatic Welsh-born trader David Thompson (1770–1857), who found the trade route across the Rockies that Mackenzie had missed, was

Plate 1: Samuel Hearne, "A Winter View in the Athapuscow Lake," from Hearne, *Journey from Prince of Wales's Fort* (1795). Courtesy of Houghton Library, Harvard University.

interested in beavers mostly as a commodity, though even he couldn't help admiring their "fine houses." The journals Thompson kept from 1800 to 1811 are a messy jumble of notes, but they fit perfectly a landscape not intended for the limited perspective of the human observer: "the Eye had not Strength to discriminate its Termination," Thompson wrote, looking eastward from Loder Peak, his vantage point in the Rockies.[10] To the west he saw snow-capped mountains, rising and subsiding like "the Waves of the Ocean in the wintry Storm." He wanted to believe that "these stupendous heights" had actually been created for the "convenience and comfort of mankind," since in the spring the thawing snow and ice would fill the rivers and irrigate the earth (*Columbia Journals*, p. 201). But he also had to admit that he and his men were simply not adapted to a terrain in which other creatures moved so nimbly, like the mountain goats scurrying up the steep banks of the Bow River. The bucks especially, with their large, weighty horns, had "an Air [of] daring with a Dash of the Formidable" (p. 18). Seven years later, while following the Howse Pass, Thompson pursued some of these animals, only to find himself clinging to the side of the mountain with his "Nails & feet to prevent myself sliding down" (p. 46), a memorable and comical image of human ineffectiveness and nature's indifference to those not fit to meet its demands.

Thompson's hand-drawn maps laid the groundwork for further western exploratory efforts in the nineteenth century. But by 1858, when John Keast Lord (1818–72) was named to serve as naturalist on the English Boundary Commission, charged with establishing the border along the 49th parallel between British Columbia and the United States, discovery had already given way to property distribution. In *The Naturalist in Vancouver Island and British Columbia* (1866), Lord's breezy style for the most part eschews technical terminology, except in his taxonomic appendix, and he refers to the "scientific world" as if he himself weren't part of it (vol. II, p. 46). In the fantastically exotic landscapes inhabited by his animals, the skunk cabbage grows in "rank luxuriance" and "flabby fungoid growths spring like huge ears from moist-decaying wood" (vol. II, p. 39).

But Lord's book has a serious agenda. To mark the boundary line, his men had to cut through mountain ranges, rocky ravines, and impenetrable forests. How, asks Lord, aware of the absurdity of their task, were they to make good political sense of this "chaos of rocks and trees" (vol. II, p. 75)? The frontispiece to the second volume of his book (plate 2) shows, in stark contrast with Hearne's vision of a pristine Lake Athapasca, a scene of nightmarish destruction, a bleak landscape filled with the severed, tangled trunks of trees. A melancholy human observer – the agent of all that devastation? – sits exhausted, his back turned to us, next to the hollowed-out ruin of a once enormous tree. The stumps in the foreground look like decaying teeth in a giant's mouth.

In *The Naturalist in Vancouver Island*, Lord's professional rage for order runs afoul of the actual diversity of the natural world he encounters. The most memorable of his animals are the ones that don't fit the categories of the naturalist – the viviparous fish, for example, in whose placental sacs the offspring are arranged like the wedge-shaped pieces of an orange; the urotrichus, a blind, pig-snouted, subterranean furry animal with forefeet like garden trowels; the muskrat-like sewellel, with teeth as sharp as a carpenter's chisels and rounded ears that seem almost human. Especially in the case of the last creature, which passes its life in dark burrows and eats vegetable matter only, he finds it hard to decide "what purpose it serves in the great chain of Nature" (vol. I, p. 357). But despite Lord's unabashed colonialist agenda (he waxes rhapsodic about the possibilities for industrial salmon-harvesting in British Columbia) he readily acknowledges the presence of a world that exists apart from all our attempts to understand and commodify it: "Why did He, who made the world, the sun, and the stars, deck the butterfly's wing with tiny scales, that by a simple change in arrangement produce patterns beside which the most finished painting is a bungling daub?" (vol. I, p. 358).

Plate 2: "A Camp on the Boundary Line," frontispiece to vol. II of John Keast Lord, *The Naturalist in Vancouver Island and British Columbia* (1866). Author's collection. Photograph: Tim Ford.

Not coincidentally, Lord, who spends his time along the future Canadian border living in mosquito-infested canvas tents, feels magnetically drawn to the habitations of animals who have a clearer sense of belonging than he does. Ospreys, he notes, use the same nest year after year; crows are so attached to their nest that they hover around it even after a falling tree has smashed it to pieces; and under the muskrat's cleverly domed roof of bulrushes he uncovers a cozy suite of apartments (vol. II, pp. 161, 128, 78).

Local knowledge

In the course of the nineteenth century, a strand of nature-writing ostensibly different from the exploration narratives with their emphasis on vast spaces and personal daring began to develop as authors turned to more circumscribed locations. But the main intellectual concerns, even if shrunk to the size of a writer's own garden, remained similar. A landmark book was Philip Henry Gosse's *The Canadian Naturalist* (1840), a reflection of the author's own experiences in Compton, Lower Canada, where, on harsh ground, he tried to eke out a living as a farmer from 1835 to 1838. Throughout the book, written in a series of dialogues between a Canadian father and his son (the latter having recently arrived from England), Gosse (1810–88) mocks the inappropriateness of human concepts and terms in descriptions of nonhuman nature. For Gosse, Canadian nature is marked by its capacity to surprise and confound the human observer, a tendency particularly evident in the metamorphosis of insects.[11] A "large and handsome" caterpillar found today will transform itself tomorrow into a pupa "with a remarkable prominence on the back," out of which, a fortnight later, will arise the Banded Purple Butterfly. Nature pokes fun at the naturalist's attempts to grasp and label it. Thus the father warns his son – who is depressed by the landscapes of Quebec, with their unbroken fields of snow and impenetrable woods full of "logs, roots and fallen trees" – to stay clear of all unwarranted generalizations.[12]

Gosse's farming experiment failed miserably. And while he eventually returned to England, where he became one of the Victorian period's most distinguished experts on marine organisms, Catharine Parr Traill (1802–99) had come to stay. Born into a Suffolk family that would include several accomplished writers, among them her sister and fellow emigrant, Susanna Moodie (1803–85), she followed her husband, a half-pay officer in the British army, to Upper Canada. Determined, as she later put it, "to claim all the loveliness for Canada,"[13] Traill weathered a series of personal and economic disasters, including the loss of her farm by fire and the death of her chronically depressed husband in 1859. Her first Canadian books, *The Backwoods of Canada* and *The Canadian Settler's Guide*, earned her a reputation as a "practical coper."[14] But her success was not limited to stamina and good domestic skills. In 1868, one year after the formation of the Canadian Dominion, Traill's *Canadian Wild Flowers* appeared, with color plates hand-produced by her artist niece Agnes Moodie Fitzgibbon (1833–1913). A sequel, *Studies of Plant Life in Canada*, came out nearly twenty years later, in 1885. In her preface to *Wild Flowers*, Traill expressed the hope that the book, written and illustrated by two Canadians and issued by a Canadian publisher, would teach the newly united Canadians to recognize and love their native plants.[15]

Traill's text and Fitzgibbon's lithographs beautifully complement each other. Traill delights in her knowledge of botanical language but, in prose laced with quotations from her favorite poets, she also engages freely in poetic conceits, comparing, for example, the buds of the showy lady's slipper to "the appearance of slightly flattened globes of delicately-tinted primrose coloured rice-paper" (*Wild Flowers*, p. 60). In similar fashion, Fitzgibbon's illustrations seem to have been made with both a scientific and a literary audience in mind. Consider plate 3, where Traill's favorite lady's slipper is paired with a "Wild Orange Lily" (now known as the red lily or Philadelphia lily), whose rich orange, scarlet, and yellow colors offer an effective contrast to the more subdued, if equally spectacular, hues of the lady's slipper. The smaller pale-blue flowers of the harebell provide an ornamental frame for the composition as a whole, an effect enhanced by the parallel the artist has established, at the top of her picture, between the open blossom of the harebell and the closed bud of the red lily. But Fitzgibbon is also mindful of the more concrete demands of taxonomy, and she bends and turns her specimens in such a way that the viewer can see both sides of the leaf and look right into the flower, even to the point of being able to count its stamens.

Fitzgibbon's compositional tricks, like Traill's taxonomic exercises and poetic personifications, serve to civilize the wildflowers, bending them into frames and patterns that are no longer those of nature herself. Traill is aware of this distortion. All wildflowers, she admits in her preface, are "destined sooner or later to be swept away, as the onward march of civilization clears away the primeval forest" (p. 8). On the cusp of extinction, however, Traill's beautiful plants acquire provocative political significance. "Types are they," writes Traill, "of the native race, the Indian children of the land, fast passing away" (*Pearls*, p. 69). She views with regret the disappearance of a whole way of life. Proud of her own Ojibway name, *Peta-wan-noo-ka*, "red cloud of dawn," given to her on account of her "rosy English complexion," she also prefers the Native names for plants to those given them by zealous naturalists: "How much prettier is the Indian name for Spring Beauty, 'Misko-deed,' than the unmeaning botanical one of *Claytonia Virginica*. In the

Plate 3: Agnes Fitzgibbon, Plate VI, facing p. 48, in Catharine Parr Traill, *Canadian Wild Flowers* (1868). Courtesy of the Canadian Museum of Nature. Photograph: Anne Botman.

latter some botanist has perpetuated his own insignificant name of Clayton" (*Pearls*, p. 104). The author of *Wild Flowers* has special affection for the "herb-seeking medicine men of the native tribes," frequently interrupting her descriptions to dispense the kind of advice that would have been given by them. The large leaves of the water lily are "good dressing for blisters" (*Wild Flowers*, p. 69), wintergreen alleviates rheumatism, and the juices of the Indian turnip, though poisonous when uncooked, help end violent colics and even cure consumption.

Like her Native herbalists, Traill the naturalist has smelled, touched, and tasted the plants she writes about. She has felt their leaves, has rolled them in her palms, has run her fingers along their hairy stalks, and eaten their roots. She doesn't doubt that nature has been created, first of all, for human contemplation and consumption, and her text is littered with encouragements to transfer wildflowers into the more ordered environment of the garden or the greenhouse. But in passages like the one about the water lily we also begin to see a contrary notion at work, the realization that the wilderness, threatened as it is, might be the only place left where such flowers can be enjoyed in their full beauty. In spite of the writer's temptation to personify them, Canadian wildflowers are so attractive precisely because they are *not* human. Nature in these texts is not the world of Adam separated from his Creator, "cast out of Eden to wander in the wilderness."[16] Rather, it is a world in which Adam's (or, for that matter, Eve's) presence is an almost incidental fact. Flowers like the water lily are, Traill realizes, more native in Canada than she, the immigrant from England, will ever be, and their mysterious watery habitats make them well-nigh inaccessible to the grabby hands of humans. Note how Traill's syntax here imitates the undulating motions of the water on which her lilies gracefully float. The human subject is represented only by her outstretched hand and desiring eyes:

> Who that has ever floated upon one of our calm inland lakes, on a warm July or August day, but has been tempted, at the risk of upsetting the frail birch-bark canoe or shallow skiff, to put forth a hand to snatch one of those matchless ivory cups that rest in spotless purity upon the tranquil water, just rising and falling with the movement of the stream; or have [sic] gazed with wishful and admiring eyes into the still clear water, at the exquisite buds and half unfolded blossoms that are springing upwards to the air and sun-light. (p. 68)

Taking stock

Traill's love of native Canadian flowers seems even more amazing when we bear in mind the gardening interests of her contemporaries, who deplored the length of the Canadian winters and longed for the bulbs of hyacinths, narcissi, and tulips they were ordering from home, in hopes of re-creating their own little piece of England in the midst of the Canadian wasteland.[17] The first genuinely Canadian gardening handbook, written by a Canadian and offered to "all who love good fruit, pretty flowers, and choice vegetables," was not published until 1872. The author, Delos White Beadle (1823– 1905), editor of *The Canadian Horticulturist*, saw himself as a pioneer, but not only in a literary sense. Ontario is populated with farmers who do not eat well, he complained, because they don't know how to cultivate their own kitchen gardens: "The consumption of the coarsest products only, will tend to make coarse men."[18] Hence his *Canadian Fruit, Flower, and Kitchen Gardener*, chock-full of good gardening and grafting advice and ranging over an impressive terrain (including Ontario, Quebec, Nova Scotia, and New Brunswick). The author's vision is to see all of Canada transformed into a flourishing garden, in which everything is both practical and aesthetically pleasing, a notion that is evident in one of the lithographs accompanying his book, a still life featuring an unusual ensemble of fruits and vegetables, bursting with juice (plate 4). These well-ripened, ruddy tomatoes, carrots, strawberries, and raspberries, the beet, squash, and asparagus (note also the light compositional touch of the two radishes placed in the foreground!) are obviously intended to dispel the notion that the useful cannot also be beautiful.

Plate 4: From Delos White Beadle, *Canadian Fruit, Flower, and Kitchen Gardener* (1872). Author's collection. Photograph: Tim Ford.

Living in Canada is hard work, and flowers, like new immigrants, won't last long if they are not sturdy enough. But a little "thought and care" bestowed upon desirable plants and trees will go a long way. Take courage, then, recommends Beadle, and remember the Canadian's motto, which is "to make a path where he cannot find one" (p. 270). Interestingly enough, his anthropocentric concerns also led the author to lash out against the indiscriminate logging practiced by his fellow citizens, who do not "understand the influence of frequent belts of timber...upon the life and health of ourselves" (p. 94). But Beadle knows that in an "age of haste," any "enlarged and enlightened policy" which considers long-term prospects will inevitably yield to the usual "thoughts of immediate advantage" (p. 33).

Such fears were shared by the Scottish-born naturalist Thomas McIlwraith (1824–1903). A coal merchant in Hamilton, Ontario, McIlwraith was also a founding member of the American Ornithological Union. In 1886, he published *The Birds of Ontario*, perhaps the most remarkable achievement in nineteenth-century Canadian nature-writing (a second, illustrated edition appeared in 1894).[19] Local in emphasis (McIlwraith repeatedly reminds the reader that he is "writing from Hamilton"), the book was practical in intent. His audience were not gun-toting hunters but aspiring field ornithologists and bird collectors, enamored of their "feathered friends."[20] The proudly regional perspective of *Birds of Ontario* sets it apart from previous approaches, notably Audubon's grandly conceived *Birds of America*. McIlwraith jots down his observations as if he were participating in a conversation among friends, and his chatty comments on the birds that he has gathered in and around Hamilton almost make the reader forget that killings have preceded the act of writing. References to Mr. John Bates "whose farm is on the shore of Hamilton Bay, near the waterworks" (p. 68), "young Mr. Reid, gardener, York Street, Hamilton" (p. 223), and Mr. Dickson "who is station-master on the G.T.R. [Grand Trunk Railway] at Waterdown" (p. 380) lend an aura of masculine intimacy to the book. But they also create an effective contrast between the people, who are individualized, and the real protagonists of the books – the birds, which refuse to be recognized as individuals until they are safely dead. Their comings and goings structure the year for humans. But, incorrigible migrants that they are, most birds, unlike the humans who watch them, do not become permanent residents here.

In a sense, then, the title of McIlwraith's book is a deception, a convenient lie. Few of the birds represented here are *of* Ontario: owned by no one and unconstrained by arbitrary human boundaries, they alight where they please. For some birds, southern Ontario is the north; for others, it is a stopping-point on their way south. Some, like the sora, arrive as summer residents; others, such as the snowy heron or the whistling swan, are in Ontario only because they got lost. Birds are picky and unpredictable, and often it seems as if they were mocking the eager ornithologist, who must trudge a long way to get a glimpse of them: "All the nests I have seen have been so placed that they could only be reached by wading or in a boat," writes a miffed McIlwraith about the long-billed marsh wren, "and sometimes they were among the reeds on a quaking bog where approach was impossible" (p. 397).

On occasion, a sense of personal deprivation creeps into McIlwraith's prose. In truth, he cannot understand why birds even *have* to migrate, leaving behind the land that he, the Scottish immigrant, has embraced as his home. Imperceptibly the reader ends up in McIlwraith's home, where sleep won't come easily to the author at night as he is listening to sounds of his faithless birds taking wing: "In the latter part of August, while lying awake with the windows open during the warm summer night, we can hear the skirling of the Sandpipers as they pass overhead on their way southward, leaving a land of plenty behind them" (pp. 13–14). A few birds, of course, stay for the year, like the white-breasted nuthatch, whose "*quank, quank*" is often the only sign of animal life in winter, cheering up the country lads as they are chopping wood (p. 399). However, inevitably, "as the country becomes more thickly settled, the birds seek for greater retirement elsewhere" (p. 210). A case in point are the wood ducks, featured in the second edition of McIlwraith's book in a beautiful line drawing provided by Ernest E. Thompson ("E. E. T."), soon better known as Ernest Thompson Seton (plate 5).[21] Twenty-five years earlier, McIlwraith had still seen them frequently, "leading out their young from one of the inlets of the Dundas marsh." Their extraordinary beauty, however, had attracted "all classes of sportsmen," and now they were just "passing migrants" (pp. 76–7).

A few species, it is true, have learned to coexist with the wasteful humans. The American herring gulls, for example, feeding on the morsels they glean from the city sewers that empty into the bay, which are now "regarded by the 'boys' as belonging to the place, are not much disturbed" (p. 47). But what nourishes the gulls may kill other birds. White-winged scoters, which show up towards the end of April, soon afterwards wash up dead on the beach – poisoned by the polluted water.

"When will some divinely gifted Canadian appear," sighs McIlwraith, "to sing the praises of our native birds, as men of other lands have done for theirs?" (p. 406). But *Birds of Ontario* is as beautiful and eloquent an evocation of Canadian birds as any. Aesthetic judgments pervade McIlwraith's ornithological observations, and even the taxonomic descriptions – the fine print of the birder's handbook, intended to be serviceable rather than imaginative – are often richly poetic. The head and neck of the bronzed grackle, for example, are "silky steel-blue," "varying in shade from an intense Prussian

Plate 5: "E. E. T." (Ernest E. Thompson [Seton]), Wood Ducks, from Thomas McIlwraith, *Birds of Ontario*, 2nd edn. (1894). Author's collection. Photograph: Tim Ford.

blue to brassy-greenish," while the body is of a "metallic brassy-olive" color (p. 289). And the rusty blackbird is "lustrous black," its feathers "skirted with warm brown above and brownish-yellow below" (p. 287). It seems that for Thomas McIlwraith there is never a mere black, never an ordinary blue. In *Birds of Ontario*, writing becomes an act of mourning for the lost connection between humans and birds, all the more poignant because the author's rifle, a rough collector's tool, also participates in the violence that has rent them apart.

Telling stories

The most unabashedly anthropocentric examples of Canadian nature-writing in the late nineteenth century are perhaps the animal stories by McIlwraith's disciple, Ernest Thompson Seton (1860–1946). Born in South Shields, England, Seton came to Ontario with his family in 1866, where he embarked on a dual career as a painter of animal scenes and a naturalist. But Seton's enduring fame rests on his numerous animal stories. Here, the narrator's central perspective typically dominates the representations of the natural environment, although the role of humans in the network of natural relationships is far from unambiguous.

Most of Seton's animals are humanized, sometimes insistently so. The vixen in "The Springfield Fox" is, in her own way, quite the scientist: "old Vixen was up in natural history – she knew squirrel nature and took the case in hand when the proper time came." But she actually uses her knowledge to keep the humans, as the only predators that she and her family must fear, at bay. One night, she takes her little ones to a field "where was a strange black flat thing" (a man's jacket) on the ground. At the first whiff, the young foxes' "every hair stood on end . . . And when she saw its full effect she told them – 'That is man-scent.'"[22] Of course, the vixen's raids on the henhouses must be stopped, but the humans who invade her den and then take her last surviving cub away are far from irreproachable either. When the old fox returns every night to work on freeing her child, the sturdy chain she gnaws on seems like a perverted, man-made umbilical cord. While the most "humane" behavior in Seton's stories frequently appears to be that of the animals, the practical differences between their world and the (much easier) world of humans are never in doubt either: "There are no hospitals for sick crows," explains the narrator at the end of "Silverspot: The Story of a Crow" (*Wild Animals I Have Known*, p. 83).

Inspired by Seton's success, Charles G. D. Roberts from New Brunswick (1860–1943) published, over the course of his long career, more than a dozen books of animal stories. Like Seton, Roberts insists on the "scrupulous" scientific accuracy of his work,[23] but in the Darwinian universe of his stories humans are active participants. The gulf separating "the lowest of the human species from the highest of the animals" (*Kindred of the Wild*, p. 23) has become a narrow fissure: in the wilderness, animals assume humanlike characteristics, while humans discover the extent to which they, too, can become like animals. The logger in "The Watchers of the Campfire" from *Kindred of the Wild* (1902) doesn't know that he is being watched by a panther but nevertheless feels it, in the form of "a creeping sensation along his backbone and in the roots of the hair on his neck" (p. 265). And the boy trapping rabbits in "The Moonlight Trails" suddenly senses rising in him instinctive impulses "handed down to him from his primeval ancestors," completely obliterating the acquired markers of civilization, such as "tenderness of heart" and "sympathy with the four-footed kindred" (p. 46). At the sight of the first trapped rabbit, the boy springs "forward, with a little cry, as a young beast might in sighting its first quarry" (p. 51). Roberts's stories, in which hunters' eyes peer "through the leafage with the keen glitter of those of a beast of prey in ambush" (p. 190), are filled with such transformative experiences. Civilization has become an afterthought, the comfortable place where one hides from nature's ultimate reality, death, as the end of "The Moonlight Trails" shows. "We won't snare any more rabbits, Andy," the boy cries, averting his face from the trapped animal's "half-open mouth, the small, jutting tongue, the expression of the dead eyes" (pp. 51–2).

One of Seton's most ardent admirers was Archibald Stansfeld Belaney (1888–1938) from Hastings, Sussex, who emigrated to Toronto in 1906 and soon after fled to the wilderness of Lake Temagami, Ontario, where he worked as a trapper and nature guide. In 1931, Belaney, who had been bragging about his Apache ancestry, formally announced that he was "Grey Owl" or, in (faulty) Ojibway, *Wa-sha-quon-asin*.[24] In his "Beaver Lodge" on Lake Ajawaan, Saskatchewan, tucked away deep in a spruce, pine, and aspen forest, Grey Owl shared his life with a moose and his "beaver people," casting himself in the role of a modern Hiawatha, a selfless "Messiah of the Wilderness" and prophet of nature conservation.[25] In his books, written with his "boots on" (*Tales of an Empty Cabin*, p. ix), he lamented the loss of a past in concert with uncontaminated nature and extolled the gentleness of his humanlike companions. "The inflections of a beaver's voice," wrote Grey Owl in *Tales of an Empty Cabin* (1936), "resemble greatly those of a human being; they have a wide range of sounds and can convey most of their emotions...in a manner that is remarkably intelligible" (p. 88). Given the author's rootlessness and compulsive role-playing, the passages in which he admires the "unconquerable poise" of his beavers and the seriousness with which they tackle the task of raising a family seem especially poignant. Paradoxically, the more urgently Seton, Roberts, and Grey Owl represent nature as the site of authenticity, as the point where outward appearance and inner truth coincide, the more clearly they identify it also as a human construction, the product of the writer's lively imagination. *Tales of an Empty Cabin* ends movingly with the author's plea to the reader to fill the void with "kindly understanding" (p. 335), the pathetic hope that even isolated acts of kindness could halt, or compensate for, the inevitable loss of those ancient forests in which still stands the storyteller's moldering cabin.

Losses and gains

Grey Owl, who faked his own life, ironically helped make respectable a mode of writing in popular Canadian natural history that became a winning combination – the elegiac lament for lost harmony cast in the form of an autobiographical tale of self-discovery. Farley Mowat's *Never Cry Wolf* (1963) is perhaps the best-known modern version of this genre, a serious parable about the human desire to identify with, and yet separate oneself from, the animals. Sent by a kafkaesque bureaucracy to confirm government plans to reduce the number of wolves in the Arctic, Mowat (1921–) had himself dropped off at a remote location 300 miles northwest of Churchill. Here, having sporadic contact only with Mike, a trapper of mixed white and Inuit parentage, and with an Inuit named Ootek, he watches, with increasing personal involvement, a family of wolves raising a litter of cubs. He renders these animals in overtly anthropomorphic terms, bestowing names upon them and discovering in them the paragons of a family life he never had. As he humanizes the wolves, Mowat de-humanizes himself, living the life of a "pseudo-wolf."[26] Searching for "the lost world which once was ours before we chose the *alien* role," he compiles data to sway his unsympathetic audience in Ottawa, who are interested only in statistics and wolf poop. A wolf, he argues, "never kills for fun, which is probably one of the main differences distinguishing him from man" (p. 136). But the ending of *Never Cry Wolf* leaves little hope for either the wolves or the narrator. When, shortly before his departure, Mowat finally enters the den of "George" and "Angeline," he discovers that, contrary to his expectations, two members of the family are still there, cowering in the dark. Immediately Mowat, longing for his rifle, is seized by the same old irrational anti-wolf prejudices he had set out to rectify. His narrative ends not with a bang but with a whimper, with the naturalist's appalled recognition of how easily he had forgotten "all that the summer sojourn with the wolves had taught me about them...and about myself" (p. 163). Thus, Mowat's encounter with the wolves is a story of lost opportunity, destined to fade into the mere memory of a "world which I had glimpsed and almost entered...only to be excluded, at the end, by my own self" (p. 163).

Self-awareness is not an obstacle but an opportunity in *The Perfection of the Morning* (1994), Sharon Butala's account of her removal to the prairies of southwest Saskatchewan. In luminous detail, Butala (1940–) records her own spiritual awakening in the unfamiliar environment of her new husband's cattle farm, in "the close presence of the grass and the sky."[27] Freed to the elements, Butala is at first disconcerted but then also exhilarated by the "magnificent spread of pure light across the grassy miles," her discovery of a "star-ridden, green and scented universe" (*The Perfection of the Morning*, pp. 11, 20). Soon the landscape begins to speak to her, through the animals that follow her and the remnants of Native ritual she discovers. At night she continues her "psychic journey" in intense dreams. The changing seasons help Butala become aware of the "rhythms of the feminine" in herself, as she is approaching "a level of understanding about the nature of existence that I can't imagine coming...in any other place" (pp. 160, 146). Butala compares herself to Columbus, sharing the "tremendous excitement, joy and relief" that the explorer experienced "when he first saw the shores of the New World." What a pity that her continent, too, is already "populated by people who took for granted and understood what for us was a world of immeasurable treasure and wonder" (p. 131). The author's idiosyncratic use of the Columbus image identifies her as a feminist disciple of H. D. Thoreau, who had encouraged his readers to discover a whole new universe within themselves. But Butala's self-centeredness, unrelieved by Thoreau's self-irony, ultimately throws doubt on the book's modest subtitle, "An Apprenticeship in Nature." And though she once claims that the Saskatchewan prairies are so huge that our imagination cannot grasp them, she reveals on the same page: "what nature leaves bare the human psyche fills" (p. 88).

This is a premise not shared by Mark Hume (1950–), whose tribute to the Bella Coola River, *River of the Angry Moon* (1998), is a stirring critique of human hubris and the damage humans do to ancient ecosystems. Dedicated to the "unknowable mystery of the river" (p. 142), Hume's book is part elegy, part fieldwork (the latter done in close collaboration with fellow angler Harvey Thommasen). A self-professed "salmo-centrist," Hume painstakingly records a year in the life of the Bella Coola and its fish, choosing the Nuxalk name for each month. Powerfully evoking the intricate web of ecological relationships in the temperate rainforests of British Columbia, Hume also points out how no-holds-barred logging has almost depleted the river's protective cover, while mindless "rituals of waste" practiced by commercial fishermen and catch-and-kill anglers have wreaked havoc among the salmon species returning to the Bella Coola to spawn.

Nature, warns Hume, is not a "dry goods store" (p. 27). Fly-fishing emerges as a responsible way of engaging with the vanishing steelheads, cutthroats, bull trout, and coho salmon of the Bella Coola on their own terms. The element of human deception inherent in it is more than offset by the capacity of the fish to turn their brief encounter with humans into a game in which they, in fact, have the evolutionary advantage: "The human body," writes Hume, "is blocky and cumbersome and weak. The fish, by contrast, hang effortlessly in the current, as the water sluices around their smooth bodies" (p. 99). A drawing included in the book (plate 6), which compares the ocean and the river phases of the males of different species, conveys the author's admiration for the gleaming bodies of his fish.

Fly-fishers follow their instincts, just as the salmon follow theirs (p. 114). With their rods and lines as thin "as a strand of cedar bark," they listen to the "pulse of the river" (p. 166). Hume draws the reader into a landscape still alive with sights, sounds, and scents that would have seemed familiar to the likes of Mackenzie and Lord: the mud-stained faces of bears, the buzz of pollinating insects, the snapping of lupine pods in the summer sun, the

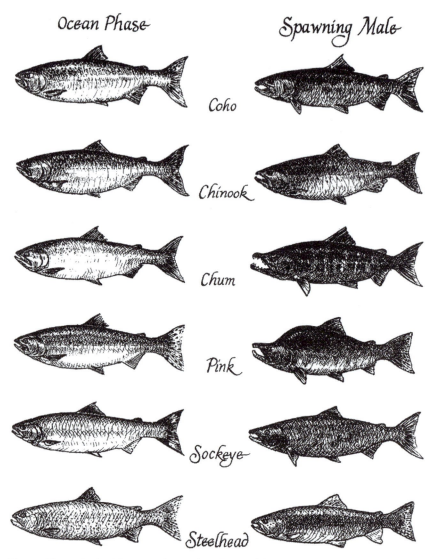

Plate 6: Illustration by Alistair Anderson, from *River of the Angry Moon* by Mark Hume with Harvey Thommasen. Copyright © 1998 by Mark Hume. Published in Canada by Greystone Books, a division of Douglas and McIntyre. Reprinted by permission of the publisher.

acrid fragrance of the skunk cabbage, the orchid's perfume, a wisp of warm breath arising from a beaver's lodge on a cold December morning. Hume's book ends with a richly symbolic scene: as he catches a coveted steelhead, his fly accidentally gores the fish, whose sharp teeth in turn scratch him. Blood flows, erasing, for a short moment, the boundaries between the angler and his victim. The steelhead, once it has been returned to the river, will die, while its captor, unwilling accomplice to the depredations wreaked on the fish of the Bella Coola, will survive to commemorate their painful encounter, writing about the ties that bind the human to the fish and the fish to the human.

NOTES

1. See Alexander Mackenzie, *Voyages from Montreal, on the River St. Lawrence, through the Continent of North America, to the Frozen and Pacific Oceans; in the Years 1789 and 1792, with an Account of the Rise and State of the Fur Trade,* vol. I (1801; New York: Allerton, 1922, 2 vols.) pp. x–xi.

2. John Keast Lord, *The Naturalist in Vancouver Island and British Columbia,* vol. II (London: Bentley, 1866, 2 vols.) p. 108.

3. Lawrence Buell, *The Environmental Imagination: Thoreau, Nature Writing, and the Formation of American Culture* (Cambridge: Belknap, 1995) p. 179; Mark Hume, with Harvey Thommasen, *River of the Angry Moon: Seasons on the Bella Coola* (Vancouver: Greystone, 1998) p. 171.

4. Northrop Frye, conclusion, *Literary History of Canada: Canadian Literature in English,* ed. Carl F. Klinck (Toronto: University of Toronto Press, 1965) pp. 821–49; Margaret Atwood, *Survival: A Thematic Guide to Canadian Literature* (Toronto: Anansi, 1972); Robert Kroetsch, "Disunity as Unity: A Canadian Strategy," *The Lovely Treachery of Words: Essays Selected and New,* by Kroetsch (Oxford: Oxford University Press, 1989) pp. 21–33; Frank Davey, "Contesting 'Post(-)Modernism,'" *Canadian Literary Power,* by Davey (Edmonton: NeWest, 1994) pp. 245–93.

5. For the most recent example, see Rebecca Raglon and Marian Scholtmeijer, "Canadian Environmental Writing," *The Literature of Nature: An International Sourcebook,* ed. Patrick D. Murphy (Chicago: Fitzroy Dearborn, 1998) pp. 130–9.

6. Thomas J. Lyon, "A Taxonomy of Nature Writing," *This Incomperable Lande: A Book of American Nature Writing,* ed. Lyon (1989; London: Penguin, 1991) pp. 3–91; p. 7.

7. Buell, *The Environmental Imagination,* p. 61.

8. Victoria Dickenson, *Drawn from Life: Science and Art in the Portrayal of the New World* (Toronto: University of Toronto Press, 1988) p. 212.

9. Samuel Hearne, *A Journey from Prince of Wales's Fort in Hudson's Bay to the Northern Ocean, 1769, 1770, 1771, 1772,* ed. Richard Glover (1795; Toronto: Macmillan, 1958) pp. 146–7.

10. David Thompson, *Columbia Journals,* ed. Barbara Belyea (Seattle: University of Washington Press, 1994) p. 19.

11. Christoph Irmscher, "Nature Laughs at Our Systems: Philip Henry Gosse's *The Canadian Naturalist,*" *Canadian Literature* 170/171 (Autumn/Winter 2001): pp. 58–86.

12. Philip Henry Gosse, *The Canadian Naturalist: A Series of Conversations on the Natural History of Lower Canada* (London: Van Voorst, 1840) pp. 194, 17, 65.

13. Catharine Parr Traill, *Pearls and Pebbles,* ed. Elizabeth Thompson (1894; Toronto: Natural Heritage, 1999) p. 11.

14. Margaret Atwood, *Strange Things: The Malevolent North in Canadian Literature* (Oxford: Clarendon, 1995) p. 99.

15. Catharine Parr Traill, *Canadian Wild Flowers. Painted and Lithographed by Agnes Fitzgibbon, with Botanical Descriptions by C. P. Traill* (Montreal: John Lovell, 1868) p. 8.

16. D. G. Jones, *Butterfly on Rock: A Study of Themes and Images in Canadian Literature* (Toronto: University of Toronto Press, 1970) p. 15.

17. See Juliana Horatia Ewing, letter to Miss Thompson, 23 February 1869, Fredericton, New Brunswick, *Garden Voices: Two Centuries of Canadian Nature Writing*, ed. Edwinna von Baeyer and Pleasance Crawford (Toronto: Random House, 1995) pp. 224–8.

18. Delos White Beadle, *Canadian Fruit, Flower, and Kitchen Gardener: A Guide in All Matters Relating to the Cultivation of Fruits, Flowers and Vegetables, and Their Value for Cultivation in This Climate* (Toronto: Campbell, 1872) p. 190.

19. See the entry on McIlwraith written by his grandson, Thomas F. McIlwraith, in *Dictionary of Canadian Biography, 1901–1910*, gen. ed. Ramsay Cook, vol. XIII (Toronto: University of Toronto Press, 1994) pp. 646–7.

20. Thomas McIlwraith, *The Birds of Ontario, Being a Concise Account of Every Species of Bird Known to Have Been Found in Ontario, with a Description of Their Nests and Eggs and Instructions for Collecting Birds and Preparing and Preserving Skins, Also Directions on How to Form a Collection of Eggs*, 2nd edn. (1886; Toronto: Briggs, 1894) p. 354.

21. McIlwraith taught Seton taxidermy and lent him stuffed birds as models.

22. Ernest Thompson Seton, "The Springfield Fox," *Wild Animals I Have Known and 200 Drawings* (1898; New York: Penguin, 1987) pp. 204, 207–8.

23. Charles G. D. Roberts, *The Kindred of the Wild: A Book of Animal Life* (New York: Blue Ribbon, 1902) p. 24.

24. See Donald B. Smith, *From the Land of Shadows: The Making of Grey Owl* (Vancouver: Greystone, 1998) pp. 91–2.

25. Grey Owl, *Tales of an Empty Cabin* (1936; Toronto: Macmillan, 1972) p. 89.

26. Farley Mowat, *Never Cry Wolf* (1963; New York: Bantam, 1984) p. 146.

27. Sharon Butala, *The Perfection of the Morning: An Apprenticeship in Nature* (Toronto: Harper, 1994) p. 183.

5

Drama

RIC KNOWLES

Canadian drama in English has always mixed forms. From the late sixteenth to the mid twentieth century this hybridity has most often involved the use of European dramaturgical structures to appropriate and contain Canadian – what was then thought of as "native" – content. More recently, previously marginalized groups have reappropriated the dramaturgical tools of the master to dismantle, or at least effect major renovations on, the master's theatrical house.

Post-contact performances

The earliest English-language theatre in what is now Canada consisted of an intermixture of neoclassical forms with neo-romantic content, professional with amateur practitioners, and English with French languages (together with occasional pidgin representations of Irish, First Nations, regional, or working-class dialects). The earliest post-contact performances took place in the sixteenth and seventeenth centuries, on occasions such as the variety show of music, Morris dancing, and Maygames ("to delight the Savage people"[1]) performed in 1583 by the crew of Sir Henry Gilbert's ship in St. John's harbor. However English in content, these performances were dramaturgical remixes, shaped by what were understood to be the tastes of First Nations audiences "whom we intended to winne by all faire means possible" (Haies in Plant, "Drama in English," p. 148). The combination of colonizing intent with hybridity of form is legible throughout the history of English Canadian drama, as European forms were revitalized by what were considered to be exotic New World settings and performative rituals, even as those forms served to domesticate the threats posed by the allegedly uncivilized other.

By the eighteenth century, performances at military garrisons mixed military personnel with the local bourgeoisie to stage adaptations of European pastoral dramas or neoclassical tragedies, exercises that exerted control through assimilation, demonstrated positions of power, and assumed the right to define colonial space that, because they failed or refused to understand its configuration and use by First Nations peoples, they represented as being empty. There were also closet dramas (plays written to be read, rather than performed) on First Nations subjects based on European models and authored by military personnel such as Massachusetts-born British army officer Robert Rogers, whose pre-Romantic *Ponteach; or, The Savages of America* in 1776 lamented the European destruction of what he called "Indian" life.[2] Outside of the garrison, meanwhile, touring productions brought so-called civilized culture to Indigenous peoples while implicitly justifying colonization and economic exploitation. Most of these productions configured local content (understood to be wild) as fodder for European forms (assumed to be civilizing), constructing the New World as raw material for European cultural and economic production.

Beginnings of post-colonial resistance

By the turn of the nineteenth century a considerable closet dramaturgy had emerged, inherently mixed in genre and depending for its impact on intertextual recognition of its European, often classical, models, in which paratheatrical satires employed familiar plots to skewer local political figures. This tradition continued well into the century and included such work as the anonymous *Measure by Measure*, a Shakespearean parody published in New Brunswick in 1871. The closet tradition merged with a satiric vein of performed drama that produced such work as Thomas Hill's lost play *The Provincial Association*, which was so inflammatory that it caused riots in Saint John in 1845, and *Dolorsolatio*, by "Sam Scribble" (1865), a good-natured "local political burlesque"[3] about that time-honored subject, the Canadian constitution, in which the characters are cities and regions of Canada, plus "two noisy neighbours" ("Mr Abe North" and "Mr Jefferson South)" and "Santa Claus," but in which there are no Indigenous peoples represented (*Dolorsolatio*, p. 56). The tradition culminated in such work as Henry Fuller's Gilbert-and-Sullivan take-off *H.M.S. Parliament* (1880), John E. P. Aldous and Jean McIlwraith's *Ptarmigan* (1895), an operetta about another time-honored topic, Canadian identity, and Johnny Burke's *The Topsail Geisha*, a 1901 Newfoundland adaptation of the British operetta *The Geisha*, in which the original "Japanese" chorus become local fishermen fanning themselves with salt cod. Although firmly linked to metropolitan tradition, many of these satiric plays acknowledge their own marginalization in ways which can be read as the beginnings of postcolonial resistance.

By the mid nineteenth century a different closet-drama tradition had evolved, with aspirations to literary merit. Writers such as Charles Mair, William Wilfred Campbell, and Charles Heavysege wrote neo-Shakespearean or neo-Romantic verse dramas with exotic settings ranging from mythical Britain or the biblical Middle East (Campbell's *Mordred* [1895] and Heavysege's *Saul* [1857]) to the New World itself and its inhabitants (Mair's *Tecumseh* [1866]). Few of these were anything but colonialist. Indeed, Mair's *Tecumseh* is paradigmatic in its construction of the land as vast, the wilderness as romantically vanishing, and the landscape, in spite of his subject, as uninhabited. Not surprisingly, the only well-developed characterization is that of the white male poet in love with an exoticized embodiment of Nature, the archetypal Indian Maiden. It is only more than a century later that Kuna-Rappahannock playwright Monique Mojica's deconstructs the subject in *Princess Pocahontas and the Blue Spots*.

More resistant in its representations of women to dominant constructions of gender in the nineteenth century, and more theatrical, are the plays of Sarah Anne Curzon (*The Sweet Girl Graduate* [1882], *Laura Secord, the Heroine of 1812* [1887]) and Eliza Lanesford Cushing (*Esther* [1838], *The Fatal Ring* [1840]). Both writers, in very different ways, present independent women and their roles in society. They range from protofeminist social critique in *The Sweet Girl Graduate*, which probes contemporary debates about the admission of women to Canadian universities, to the moralistic representation of heroic intervention in *Esther*, in which "a humble Jewish maiden becomes queen of Persia as God's instrument for saving His people from destruction."[4] Curzon's *Laura Secord* locates a more political and secular model of female heroism within nationalist and imperialist debate, aligning Canadian "patriotism" with anti-American (and anti-republican) loyalty to Great Britain.

Theatre after World War I: Nationalism and naturalism

The twentieth century arrived in Canada theatrically with the "Great War," and an amateur, European-style "Little Theatre" movement that was both nationalist and naturalistic (modeled after Dublin's Abbey Theatre), and proto-modernist (following the European avant-garde). Large professional venues featuring touring productions from the United States and Britain were eschewed by followers of small theatres featuring local arts groups where new, occasionally Canadian work was performed in styles ranging from the light rural comedy of Merrill Denison's *Brothers in Arms* (1921), through the same author's deterministically naturalistic *Marsh Hay* (1923), to Lois Reynolds Kerr's social satires *Among Those Present* (1933) and

Nellie McNabb (1934). The paradigmatic Little Theatre was Toronto's Hart House, under Roy Mitchell, out of which Vincent Massey published *Canadian Plays from Hart House Theatre* in 1926–7, and Merrill Denison his own de-romanticizing collection, *The Unheroic North*, in 1923.

One of the most significant plays, which transferred to Hart House from Montreal, was Marjorie Pickthall's *The Woodcarver's Wife* (1920), a romantic melodrama with modernist and protofeminist overtones, in which the wife and model of a woodcarver discovers the deep-seated sorrow of her role as mixed-race Pietà in her husband's work through a sexual relationship with an "Indian lover." The play functions at a crossroads between romanticist orientalism and modernist formalism, but resists easy categorization because it foregrounds its own tensions and discomforts about the role of women and Native peoples within an imperialist project. Their ambiguous role within the play's formal and moral patterns throws common-sense gendered and raced assumptions of the period productively into question. In this play, "Native" content is not convincingly or completely contained by European form, and the dismantling agent seems, here, to be gender.

More self-consciously avant-garde than Denison or Pickthall, and working under the influence of Edward Gordon Craig, Adolphe Appia, and the German expressionists, was Herman Voaden, whose "symphonic expressionism" attempted to do for drama in the 1930s what the Group of Seven did in painting. Hybrid primarily in their formalist interdisciplinarity, Voaden's plays were steeped in abstract theatricality, choreographed movement, music, and the interplay of light and shadow. They were also rooted in metaphysical theosophy and nationalist mysticism based on what Voaden and others saw as the harsh beauty of the northern landscape. Like that of his contemporary, painter Lawren Harris, Voaden's North, as empty canvas, had no room for the material realities of Native life. Voaden's most characteristic contribution to Canadian dramaturgy may be *Symphony*, "A Drama of Motion and Light for a New Theatre,"[5] consisting of five "movements" outlined entirely in stage directions evoking moods, music, light, colors, and movement, and moving from a harsh urban landscape towards a final, transcendent mysticism in a mountain setting; it is entirely without dialogue, and remains unproduced. Voaden's work represents the totalizing formalist containment of disciplinary difference within an overriding master vision rather than any more open or inter-discursive hybridity.

The bourgeois amateur theatre represented by the Dominion Drama Festival (DDF) annually brought adjudicators from abroad to judge the thespian aspirations of community practitioners, but at the opposite end of the spectrum was the left-wing Workers' Theatre, the hybridity of which was politically strategic, its internationalism that of the workers' movement, and its

modernism documentary rather than expressionist. Its best-known play was
Eight Men Speak, by Oscar Ryan, E. Cecil Smith, Frank Love, and Mildred
Goldberg. Performed for one night only on 4 December 1933 before being
shut down by the "Red Squad" of the Toronto police, this classic agit-prop
piece was inspired by the attempted assassination of Tim Buck, leader of the
outlawed Communist Party of Canada. The Workers' Theatre was arguably
the most innovative of the period, introducing the techniques of Bertolt
Brecht, Erwin Piscator, and American documentary drama to a Canadian
tradition that would later boast the documentaries of Toronto Workshop
Productions, Théâtre Passe Muraille, and The Mummers Troupe. It is also
the background against which the political plays of the 1970s, 80s, and 90s
are best read, including work emerging out of the Canadian Popular Theatre Alliance and the work of such playwrights as Arthur Milner (*Zero Hour*
[1986], *Masada* [1989]) and David Fennario (*On the Job* [1975], *Balconville*
[1979], *Joe Beef* [1991], *Banana Boots* [1994]). But like other contemporary
theatrical movements, the Workers' Theatre also ignored the presence or significance of First Nations peoples.

Even those playwrights traditionally regarded as naturalists broke with
that tradition in interestingly hybrid ways. Gwen Pharis Ringwood's *Still
Stands the House* (1939) has been considered *the* archetypal prairie realist
play, but in her later "Indian trilogy" (1959–80) she produced a complex
drama that combined Native forms and subjects with Greek tragic structures, including, in *The Stranger*, a revisioning of *Medea* complete with an
"Indian" chorus. Although Ringwood's method may be suspected of pater-
nalism, her work anticipates the postcolonial hybridities of 1980s and 90s
Native playwrights such as Tomson Highway.

After the Massey Commission: Center to periphery

The emergence of a professional theatre in Canada after World War II
in the wake of the Massey Commission (1951) and the founding of the
Canada Council (1957) was not immediately beneficial to the production of
Canadian plays, and the hybridities it produced most often had to do with
real or professed attempts to find Canadian ways of performing classical theatre. Thus Tyrone Guthrie, the British founding artistic director of
Ontario's Stratford Festival, made the case in 1953 for the establishment of
"a distinctive style of Canadian theatre" founded on Shakespeare,[6] though
his successor, Michael Langham, admitted in 1982 that "there was never
anything Canadian about Stratford... That was a diplomatic thing Guthrie
cooked up."[7] The Manitoba Theatre Centre, founded in 1958, was the proto-
type for a series of "branch-plant" regional theatres that became the visible

manifestation of the Massey Commission's center-to-periphery philosophy, based on the British model of disseminating cosmopolitan high culture to the culturally impoverished provinces. Stratford, the Regionals, and smaller companies founded in the period largely neglected Canadian work, though Sydney Risk's Everyman Theatre in Vancouver and Dora Mavor Moore's New Play Society in Toronto were exceptions, producing such work as Elsie Park Gowan's *The Last Caveman* in 1938, and the plays of Morley Callaghan, Mazo de la Roche, Lister Sinclair, and John Coulter throughout the 1940s and 50s. The Irish Canadian Coulter's best-known work, *Riel* (1950), blends Irish nationalist myth-making with Elizabethan-style staging and Canadian historical content, including Métis and Cree, in an attempt to invent a national mythology – a totalizing imagined community constructed from a curious *métissage* in which Indigenous traditions and relationships with the land played the same sentimental authenticating role as Celtic mythology had played in Ireland.

Perhaps the most significant development in the 1950s was the founding of Toronto Workshop Productions in 1959 by George Luscombe, who reintroduced to Canada, by way of his experience at Joan Littlewood's Theatre Workshop in Stratford East, London, a politically engaged dramaturgy with direct debts to Piscator and Brecht. In collaborations such as *Hey Rube!* (1961), *Mr. Bones* (1969), *Chicago '70* (1970), *Ten Lost Years* (1974), and *Ain't Lookin'* (1980), Luscombe created a hybrid documentary form that blended elements from circus and minstrelsy with mime, music, and team sports to address issues of class, revolutionary politics, and race. This mélange would continue to resonate in the work of First Nations playwrights decades later, most notably Tomson Highway, Daniel David Moses, and Monique Mojica.

Luscombe's work proved prescient, as many dominant strands of the alternative theatre movement in the late 1960s and 70s employed collective techniques in localist and/or politicized documentary dramas. This included the collaborative poetic plays of James Reaney with his director, Keith Turnbull, which documented place and history in Southwestern Ontario, and culminated in his epic trilogy *The Donnellys* (1974–7), a monumental achievement that mixed documentary with myth, classical archetypes with local history. Reaney's 1977 adaptation of John Richardson's *Wacousta* was developed through a series of workshops that included the then-unknown Tomson Highway as a Cree language coach, together with the now well-known First Nations actors Gary Farmer and Graham Green. The production modeled a blend of western and Indigenous practices and performative traditions that continue to resonate, particularly in the work of Highway himself.

Still more directly in the Luscombe tradition were collective documentary theatre by Newfoundland's Mummers Troupe, Nova Scotia's Mulgrave Road Co-op, Saskatoon's 25th Street Theatre, Edmonton's Theatre Network, and Vancouver's Tamanhous Theatre. But the preeminent exemplar of collective documentary dramaturgy was Toronto's Théâtre Passe Muraille under Paul Thompson, whose signature piece, *The Farm Show*, virtually defined the episodic form: as Thompson himself describes it somewhat disingenuously, "The show kind of bounces along one way or another and then it *stops*."[8] The real impulse behind this and much of Passe Muraille's work in the period – including landmark productions such as *1837: The Farmer's Revolt* (created with Rick Salutin), and the notorious *I Love You, Baby Blue*, documenting the Toronto sex scene – was localist. Through the documentation of local place and history, Passe Muraille participated in what was thought to be the forging of indigenous theatrical forms out of local landscapes and cultures, although the country's Indigenous peoples were largely neglected. In addition to its impact on companies across the country, Thompson's era of Passe Muraille directly influenced the work of a wide range of playwrights, most prominently John Gray (*18 Wheels* [1977], *Billy Bishop Goes to War* [1978], and *Rock and Roll* [1982]) and Linda Griffiths (*Maggie and Pierre* [1980], *OD on Paradise* [1982] with Patrick Brymer, *Jessica* [1986; published 1989] with Maria Campbell, *The Darling Family* [1991], *The Duchess, a.k.a. Wallis Simpson* [1998], and *Alien Creature* [2001]).

The tradition of collective documentary and the search for hybrid Canadian dramaturgies continued into the 1980s and 90s in productions such as *This Is for You, Anna* (1985), a mixture of documentary, fairytale, and personal narrative that emerged out of Toronto's Nightwood Theatre in 1982 to take its foundational place in Canadian feminist theatre, and in the work of Toronto's Videocabaret International, best known for Michael Hollingsworth's eight-play series *The History of the Village of the Small Huts* (1985–94). Hollingsworth employed a mélange of filmic visual styles to tell the multiple histories of the peoples of Canada in ways that deconstruct the country's founding myths. If the Native characters are knaves, rogues, and fools, it is a distinction they share with the English and French, though, more disturbingly, they disappear from the drama after 1867.

What collective creation effected as a democratization of process, a series of environmental theatre productions since the 1980s have often done for space, multiplying perspectives and introducing formal elements from the visual arts. ("Environmental theatre" refers to productions that make use of rather than efface their production environments, often breaking down the traditional naturalist "fourth wall" between the stage and the audience.)

The best known of these is John Krizanc's *Tamara*, first produced in 1981 by Necessary Angel Theatre under Richard Rose, in which audience members follow characters of their choice to encounter different, concurrent scenes occurring throughout a mansion representing the home of the nationalist poet Gabriele d'Annunzio in the fascist Italy of the 1930s. By self-consciously giving choices to the audience, Krizanc and Rose attempt to undermine what Krizanc sees as the "fascism" of traditional theatre, with its rigorous control of the audience's gaze. But environmental plays also include the not notably democratic operatic extravaganzas of R. Murray Schafer's *Patria* cycle, staged anywhere from a West-Coast beach to a Peterborough fairground, Toronto's Union Station, or the Ontario Science Centre; and the complex interactive orchestrations by Hillar Liitoja and Toronto's DNA Theatre of actions, rituals, and repetitions deriving from Ezra Pound, Shakespeare, Artaud, and – in *The Panel* and *Sick*, staged as public debates – the culture of AIDS.

But not all of the theatre considered to be alternative that has been produced since the late 1960s has been collective in process, documentary in form, or experimental in presentation. Much of that work was alternative only by virtue of a focus on social issues and a counterhegemonic nationalism or regionalism – a construction of "alternative" Canadian or regionalist hegemonies in the face of those of the colonial center, which nevertheless produced their own exclusions. Foundational plays such as George Ryga's *The Ecstasy of Rita Joe* (1967), David French's *Leaving Home* (1972), David Freeman's *Creeps* (1971), Michael Cook's *Head, Guts, and Soundbone Dance* (1973), and the early work of Sharon Pollock (*Walsh* [1973], *The Komagata Maru Incident* [1978], and *Blood Relations* [1981]) defined a dominant *literary* tradition, rooted in naturalism, that continues into the present in the plays of John Murrell (*Memoir* [1977], *Waiting for the Parade* [1980], *Farther West* [1986], *The Faraway Nearby* [1996]), Joan MacLeod (*Jewel* [1985], *Toronto, Mississippi* [1987], *2000* [1996]), and Wendy Lill *(The Occupation of Heather Rose* [1986], *Memories of You* [1988], *The Glace Bay Miner's Museum* [1995], *Corker* [1998]). Even at Toronto's Tarragon Theatre, with which the tradition is most closely identified, such work has blended stylized formal influences with naturalistic dialogue and characterization to incorporate, as had Ryga, First Nations, Ukrainian, and other marginalized traditions within the so-called Canadian mosaic. MacLeod's *Amigo's Blue Guitar* (1990) confronts a British Columbian family founded by a US draft resister with the contemporary realities of hosting a Salvadoran political refugee. Her structurally complex, metatheatrical one-woman play *The Hope Slide* (1992) links the stories of Canadian Doukhobors with the Hope, BC, landslide in 1965 and the death of a childhood friend from AIDS, all filtered through the coming-to-political-awareness of a young girl who grows up to be an actor.

But the most celebrated playwrights to emerge from the Tarragon tradition of poetic naturalism nurtured under artistic directors Bill Glassco (1971–82) and the late Urjo Kareda (1982–2002) are Judith Thompson and Jason Sherman. Since her first play, the bleakly naturalistic *The Crackwalker*, was produced at Passe Muraille in 1980, Thompson has pushed the limits of naturalism in darkly disturbing ways. *White Biting Dog* (1984), *I Am Yours* (1987), and *Lion in the Streets* (1990) blend naturalistic conceptions of character with extreme, often contradictory action and situation to push audiences to "the other side of the dark."9 In 1997 she attempted in *Sled* to capture, within one of her most brutal plots, both the rich multi-ethnic history and contemporary constitution of Toronto, as well as a northern, nationalist transcendence with roots in both First Nations mythology and the metaphysical theosophy of Voaden and his contemporaries. Since then Thompson has consolidated a less disruptive naturalistic style in *Perfect Pie* (2000) and *Habitat*, which premiered at Canadian Stage in 2001.

Sherman's work, like Thompson's, is deeply ethical. It is also rooted in naturalism, and like Thompson's exhibits a flawless ear for dialogue and the poetic rhythms of quotidian speech. Sherman's work, however, is more overtly political than Thompson's, and his hybridities are less emotionally raw, mediated as they are by his wit and intellect. Sherman is also the only major Canadian playwright who deals, in plays such as *The League of Nathans* (1992), *Reading Hebron* (1996), and *Patience* (1998), with what it means to be Jewish in the contemporary western world. The hybridities of Jewish identities in Canada also inform his struggles with what it means, in personal, political, and historical terms, to be Canadian (*Three in the Back, Two in the Head* [1994], *An Acre of Time* [1999]) and to be a writer (*The Retreat* [1996], *It's All True* [1999]).

Existing against these language- and character-based dramaturgies since the late 1960s has been the more self-consciously avant-garde work of playwrights such as Beverly Simons (*Crabdance* [1969]), Wilfred Watson (*Gramsci X 3* [1983]), Lawrence Russell (*Clay* [1982], *Tower* [1983]), Hrant Alianak (*The Blues* [1976], *Lucky Strike* [1978]), Tom Cone (*Cubistique* [1974], *Beautiful Tigers* [1976]), Don Druick (*Where Is Kabuki?* [1990]), Michael Springate (*Dog and Crow* [1990]), Margaret Hollingsworth (*Apple in the Eye* [1983], *War Babies* [1984], *Poppycock* [1987]), Lawrence Jeffrey (*Who Look in Stove* [1994]), and the prolific Morris Panych (*7 Stories* [1989], *Vigil* [1996], *Lawrence & Holloman* [1998]), together with companies such as Savage God in Vancouver, the early Factory Theatre Lab and Toronto Free Theatre in Toronto, PRIMUS Theatre in Winnipeg, and One

Yellow Rabbit in Calgary. With the exception of the work of Hollingsworth, which interrogates the modernist aesthetic from a feminist perspective, most of these plays share the tendencies of high-modernist formalism to contain anxieties and assimilate threatening otherness based on gender, culture, or social situation within tightly controlled and self-contained dramaturgical enclosures.

Perhaps the best of the Canadian neo-modernist plays have been by David Young and John Mighton. Young's *Glenn* (1992), based on the life of pianist Glenn Gould, deals with the psychologies of the modernist aesthetic and its construction of divided and alienated human subjectivity; his *Inexpressible Island* (1997), based on the survivors of the Scott expedition to the Antarctic, deals with the historical and intellectual beginnings of the modern era. Both plays have all-male casts. Mighton is a philosopher and mathematician, and his *oeuvre* deals almost exclusively with the space-time continuum, a problematic that plays itself out in both the content and structure of his plays. In *Scientific Americans* (1988), *Possible Worlds* (1990), *Body and Soul* (1994), and *The Little Years* (1995), Mighton has produced formally innovative plays about, respectively, the politics of science, parallel universes, necrophilia and "teledildonics,"[10] and the theory that "what happens [to an individual] can include much that does not take place within the boundaries of his [sic] life."[11]

The *oeuvre* of George F. Walker, Canada's most prolific playwright and the one who is most produced in Canada and abroad, is difficult to characterize, though his history of generic revisioning is clearly one of dramaturgical *métissage*. He first emerged as a modernist, writing homages to Beckett and the Theatre of the Absurd in his earliest work (*Prince of Naples* and *Ambush at Tethers End* [1971]), but he soon modulated into what Chris Johnson has called "B-Movies beyond the Absurd"[12] – dramatic revisionings in exotic settings rooted in B-movie and *film noir* conventions (*Bagdad Saloon* [1973], *Beyond Mozambique* [1974], *Ramona and the White Slaves* [1976]). This period in Walker's work culminated in his first major success, *Zastrozzi* (1977), a darkly ironic play about a master criminal who sets out to rid the world of sloppy thinking, after which he embarked on a detective trilogy, *The Power Plays* (*Gossip* [1977], *Filthy Rich* [1979], *The Art of War* [1983]), on similar themes. These plays were interspersed with the punk-rock musical *Rumours of Our Death* (1980), the darkly comic *Theatre of the Film Noir* (1981), and *Science and Madness* (1982), a throwback to the characters and archetypes of *Beyond Mozambique*.

In 1983 Walker turned for the first time (with the exception of the anomalous *Sacktown Rag* [1972]), to his own backyard, embarking, with *Criminals in Love*, on what proved to be a double trilogy of *East End Plays*

(*Criminals in Love* [1983], *Better Living* [1986], *Escape from Happiness* [1991]; and *Beautiful City* [1987], *Love and Anger* [1989], and *Tough* [1993]), set in "the working class east end of a big city" ("probably Canadian, most likely Toronto").[13] These plays betray an increasing naturalism, an increasing interest in societally marginalized characters, and an increasingly direct concern with social issues. But Walker's most widely produced incursion into large theatres across the continent and beyond, also written during this period, was his only adaptation of a classic. *Nothing Sacred* (1988), based on Ivan Turgenev's *Fathers and Sons*, is an anti-Oedipal play structured around rebellions against the Law of the Father and linking questions of biological reproduction (fathering) with critiques of capitalist reproduction (surplus value), and the reproduction of the patriarchal order.

Walker disappeared from the theatre briefly during the mid-1990s, moving from Toronto to Vancouver and writing for television. When he returned to Toronto and to the stage it was with a considerable splash, as Factory Theatre launched no less than six new plays, running in repertoire as its entire 1997–8 season.[14] Individually, several of the plays – *Problem Child*, *Adult Entertainment*, and *The End of Civilization* – are brilliant confrontations with the brutalities of late capitalism. Taken together, the interlinked plays that constitute the *Suburban Motel* series are epic in their scope, in spite of the facts that all are set in the same seedy motel room and each is restricted to four or five characters. Walker's most recent play, *Heaven*, mounted at Canadian Stage in Toronto in 2000 and set, for the first time, in the inner city, pushes his earlier work's critique of a brutal social system to expressionist extremes, including farcical scenes in a fanciful 1940s heaven. But in the end, like most of Walker's work, "it's all about pain"[15] and "shared anxiety."[16]

Clowning, mime, and movement-based theatre

In the last years of the twentieth century Canada also saw the powerful influence of European clowning, mime, and movement-based theatre on companies such as Theatre Smith Gilmour and Theatre Columbus in Toronto, Jest in Time in Halifax, and Vancouver Moving Theatre in British Columbia, through the influence of *L'Ecole Jacques LeCoq* in Paris and Toronto's Theatre Resource Centre. Many of these companies have produced plays in mixed genres, including work such as Leah Cherniak, Robert Morgan, and Martha Ross's *The Anger in Ernest and Ernestine* (1989), Karen Hines's *Pochsy's Lips* (1992), and Jennifer Brewin, Leah Cherniak, Ann-Marie MacDonald, Alisa Palmer, and Martha Ross's *The Attic, the Pearls, & Three Fine Girls* (1999). At its best this work crosses performative boundaries and results in shows that are highly theatrical, wildly funny, and productively unsettling of societal assumptions about what is "normal." The influence of mixed-genre performance pieces, often for solo actor, has also resulted in hybrid, interdisciplinary work such as the "dub theatre" of ahdri zhina mandiela (*dark diaspora...in dub* [1991]); the lesbian feminist costume-based work of Lorri Millan and Shawna Dempsey (*Mary Medusa* [1993]); the explosion of gay dramaturgies in the work of Bryden MacDonald (*Whale Riding Weather* [1992], *The Weekend Healer* [1994]), Timothy Findley (*The Stillborn Lover* [1993], *Elizabeth Rex* [2000]), Raymond Storey (*The Saints and the Apostles* [1993]), Hillar Liitoja (*The Last Supper* [1995]), and Gordon Armstrong (*Blue Dragons* [1993], *Scary Stories* [1996]), often rooted in other high and popular art forms; the lecture plays, such as Daniel Brooks and Guillermo Verdecchia's *The Noam Chomsky Lectures* (1991); and the monodrama of playwright/designer and visual artist Ken Garnhum (*Surrounded by Water* [1991], *Beuys, Buoys, Boys* [1992]).

Gay theatre

Most prominent among the gay playwrights are Brad Fraser, Sky Gilbert, and Daniel MacIvor. Fraser came to prominence in 1990 with his grotesquerie of sex and violence, *Unidentified Human Remains and the True Nature of Love*, and his reputation for sensationalist contemporary melodrama has been sustained since in productions of *Poor Superman* (1994) and *Martin Yesterday* (1997) together with publications of *The Wolf Plays* (1993) and the release of *Unidentified Human Remains* as a film by Denys Arcand (*Amour et restes humains* [1993]). Fraser's is a mannerist sensibility, and his work plays on the pop-sophisticated media knowingness of a post-*Rocky Horror Picture Show* audience. The plays revel in clever lines, shallow characterization, sex, violence, comic-book captions, and the production of Beaumont-and-Fletcheresque *frisson*. And like Beaumont and Fletcher's plays they achieve meaning less by exploring the issues of power and abuse that circulate in their represented worlds than by playing out patterns of response in audiences capable of appreciating their manipulation of style and genre expectations.

Gilbert, prominent as the founding artistic director of the largest gay and lesbian theatre in North America, Toronto's Buddies in Bad Times, remained virtually unpublished as a playwright, apart from the early *The Dressing Gown* (1984) and *Lola Starr Builds Her Dream Home* (1989), until Robert Wallace included his *Capote at Yaddo* in *Making, Out: Plays by Gay Men* in 1992. In 1995 Wallace followed with a six-play collection of Gilbert's best work, *The Unknown Flesh*, and in the same year Playwrights Canada issued *Play Murder*, Gilbert's metatheatrical historiographic exploration of "the difference between an investigation and a play."[17] In 1996

Playwrights Canada released another collection, *Painted, Sainted, Tainted*, this time bringing together Gilbert's high-camp Drag Queen plays, consolidating a canon that has continued to expand, most recently including *The Emotionalists* (2000), based on the life and opinions of Ayn Rand. Gilbert is a clever and provocative, if not always careful, playwright, dealing more in the audacious gesture than in the nuanced construction of action, language, or characterization. But at its transgressive best his dramaturgy functions effectively to implicate audiences in oppositional art, and to confront them with transgressive sexuality in a homophobic culture.

Daniel MacIvor, also included in *Making, Out*, is preeminent among the new generation of solo playwrights/performers. He first achieved prominence in 1990 with two one-person shows, *See Bob Run* and *Wild Abandon*, and has since expanded his repertoire exponentially. His is a quirky, poetic, and resonant voice that he uses to explore the minds and emotions of characters who are "fucked up": Bob, in *See Bob Run*, fleeing a lover she has murdered, trying to return to the sea and to the arms of her abusive father; Steve, in *Wild Abandon*, with his birdcage and his egg, funny and suicidal; the ironically named Victor in *House* (1992), attending "group" (therapy) and living with a dominatrix; Henry, in *Here Lies Henry* (1997), a pathological liar who returns after death to tell us something we don't already know; and a series of characters in *Monster* (1999, with Daniel Brooks) who recount, in various interconnected filmic, dramatic, and narrative forms, the movie/story/dream of a boy who hacked up his father in the basement. These characters and the plays they inhabit are sad, wildly funny, infectiously angry, and beautifully written. MacIvor's most recent addition to the fictionally autobiographical/confessional solo show is *You Are Here* (2001), which retrospectively dramatizes with a full cast the life of a woman who loses her way. MacIvor has also virtually invented the form of the poetic three-person dance play. *Two Two Tango: A Two-Man-One-Man Show* (1992) involves not only the two men of the subtitle, but also a boy with a watermelon. A gay comedy of manners for the 1990s, it acts out the rhythms, gives, and takes of gay "relationshipping" without resorting to either reductive allegory or angst-ridden realism. *Never Swim Alone* (1993), using a similar blend of coordinated speech and movement, orchestrates a story of male competition between boys at beach/men in business, played out before a woman-as-judge, in a scathingly funny representation of the gendering and engendering of conflict.

Some gay playwrights writing in French, in particular Michel Tremblay and Michel Marc Bouchard, are equally well known in anglophone Canada. Both authors are discussed in the chapter on francophone writing, as is the internationally acclaimed multimedia theatre of Robert Lepage.

Reappropriative dramaturgy

Perhaps the most significant shift to have occurred since the 1980s has been towards a fundamentally reappropriative dramaturgy that is emerging from a range of marginalized communities talking powerfully back to the center in a healthy and hybrid cacophony of voices. Sky Gilbert reclaims the lives of prominent gay artists (*Pasolini/Pelosi* [1983], *Capote at Yaddo* [1992], *My Night with Tennessee* [1992], *More Divine: A Performance for Roland Barthes* [1994]); and playwrights such as Uma Parameswaran (*Rootless but Green Are the Boulevard Trees* [1987]), Rick Shiomi (*Yellow Fever* [1982]), Marty Chan (*Mom, Dad, I'm Living with a White Girl* [1995], *The Meeting* [2002]), Rahul Varma (*Counter Offence* [1996]), Betty Quan (*Mother Tongue* [1996]), and Vittorio Rossi (*The Chain* [1988], *Scarpone* [1990], *The Last Adam* [1995], *Paradise by the River* [1998]) interject othered, ethnic, or immigrant community histories into Canadian drama. Much of this activity has consisted of a hybridization-from-the-margins of mainstream western dramaturgical forms and authorized canonical works. Thus Ann-Marie MacDonald in *Goodnight Desdemona (Good Morning, Juliet)* (1989) rewrites and claims lesbian female authorship for *Romeo and Juliet* and *Othello*; Jackie Crossland (*Collateral Damage* [1992]) and Deborah Porter (*No More Medea* [1994]) rewrite from feminist perspectives the story of Medea; Beth Herst (*A Woman's Comedy* [1990]) and Maenad Theatre (*Aphra* [1991]) reclaim for women the life of seventeenth-century playwright Aphra Behn; Tomson Highway, in *Aria* (1987), *The Rez Sisters* (1988), and *Dry Lips Oughta Move to Kapuskasing* (1989), appropriates for Native experience such western structural elements as the operatic aria, sonata form, and the Greek chorus; Marie Clements produces sophisticated multimedia *mélanges* to explore the lives and deaths of mixed-race and First Nations women in British Columbia (*The Unnatural and Accidental Women* [2000]); and Drew Hayden Taylor enters the mix with a series of sitcom revisionings with an Ojibway twist (*The Bootlegger Blues* [1991], *Someday* [1993], *alterNatives* [1998], *Only Drunks and Children Tell the Truth* [1998], *The Baby Blues* [1999]).

Almost all of Sally Clark's best work takes the form of revisionist history. Although she has produced and published other strong plays – *Moo* (1984), *Ten Ways to Abuse an Old Woman* (1990), *The Trial of Judith K* (1991), and *Wasps* (1997) – her most provocative work has rewritten the stories of historical women. *Jehane of the Witches* (1990) concerns itself with Joan of Arc, the social construction of gender, the suppression of women's mythology as witchcraft, and the retrenchment of patriarchy in the fifteenth century. It is a complex metatheatrical exercise that sets the truth claims of the old, matriarchal religions against those of Christianity. *Life without Instruction* (1994), loosely based on the life of Italian Renaissance painter Artemisia Gentileschi, is a revenge play about respect, responsibility, and the role of the artist, in which emblematic painterly tableaux play the role that metadrama did in *Jehane*. Like the earlier play, it asserts the constructed, ideological nature of character, identity, gender, and role. Finally, *Saint Frances of Hollywood* (1996) moves into the more recent history of film actress Frances Farmer. *Saint Frances* is the closest Canadian theatre has come to contemporary tragedy: in this play, consumer capitalism takes over from fate in a universe that makes the commodification and exploitation of women the equivalent of tragic inevitability, and resistance is configured as madness.

Hyphenated communities

Among the most challenging and politically committed playwrights to emerge from Canada's "hyphenated" (multi-ethnic) communities is Guillermo Verdecchia, whose *Noam Chomsky Lectures* (with Daniel Brooks) took on, in a lecture/play format, the issue of Canadian collaboration in the Chomskian "manufacture of consent" surrounding economic and military oppression in the Americas and their misrepresentation in the media. Verdecchia has also co-authored with Marcus Youssef a scathing dramatic analysis of Canadian peacekeeping atrocities (*A Line in the Sand* [1995]). But he is best known for his tri-lingual solo show *Fronteras Americanas (American Borders)* (1993), in which, from a personal/autobiographical and social/political perspective, he confronts the audience with their complicity in the production of difference and the demonization of the "other." Using an almost schizophrenic form alternating between an autobiographical subject and a wildly satiric caricature of the Latino, Verdecchia explores his own identity as neither Canadian nor Argentinian. The play finally asks that we "call off the border patrol," for "[t]he border is your home."[18]

Djanet Sears has become the leading playwright, director, and spokesperson for the African Canadian theatrical community. Her first, one-woman play, *Afrika Solo*, was in 1990 the first play published in Canada by a person of African descent; her second, *Harlem Duet* (1997), a prequel to Shakespeare's *Othello* set in contemporary Harlem and focusing on the story of Othello's first wife, Billie, won a Governor-General's Award for Drama; and her third, *Adventures of a Black Girl in Search of God*, a large-cast multicultural extravaganza, launched Toronto's Obsidian Theatre in 2002, which is devoted to the work of African Canadian playwrights. While *Afrika Solo*, like *Fronteras Americanas*, probes the situation of a divided, hybrid self (not African, perhaps Canadian, but always other), *Harlem Duet* pushes the question of Black cultural identity in North America, particularly for women, further still. The play is deeply steeped in African American history and political debate – it takes place literally and figuratively at the inter-section of Malcolm X and Martin Luther King Boulevards – but it never forgets that Black Canada is also different. It is perhaps most notable, how-ever, for taking on Shakespeare, *the* iconic figure in European high culture, within an invented, mixed genre that the playwright calls "rhapsodic blues tragedy."[19] Within a context that acknowledges, but rejects, her Othello's argument that "my culture is Wordsworth, Shaw, *Leave it to Beaver*, *Dirty Harry*, what does Africa have to do with me?,"[20] the play's postcolonial hybridities are best captured by Billie as she and Othello divide their books: "the Shakespeare's mine, but you can have it" (*Harlem Duet*, p. 52).

Sears's contribution, however, is not limited to her own work. In 2000, Playwrights Canada Press changed the face of Canadian drama by publishing *Testifyin'*, the substantial first volume of her anthology of African Canadian drama, including a wide range of work by Black playwrights from various re-gions and cultures within Canada, including Andrew Moodie (*Riot* [1995]), M. Nourbese Philip (*Coups and Calypsos* [1996]), h. jay bunyan (*Prodigals in a Promised Land* [1981]), George Elliott Clarke (*Whylah Falls* [1997]), maxine bailey and sharon m. lewis (*sistahs* [1994]), George Seremba (*Come Good Rain* [1992]), Austin Clarke (*When He Was Free and Young and He Used to Wear Silks*, unproduced), ahdri zhina mandiela (*dark diaspora...in dub* [1991]), and Walter Borden (*Tightrope Time* [1986]).

First Nations drama

But perhaps the most striking examples of postcolonial drama newly talking back to the imperial center have emerged since the 1980s among First Na-tions communities. In 1989 Cree playwright Tomson Highway's brutal and comic mixed-form drama about "the rez" and the rape of Native cultures by Christianity, *Dry Lips Oughta Move to Kapuskasing*, was produced at the Royal Alexandria Theatre in Toronto. It was the first time that any Native play had been produced in a mainstream or commercial venue in Canada, let alone at one with the pedigree of the "Royal Alex." In 1997, Manitoban Cree Ian Ross's realist comedy *fareWel*, also about "the rez," about self-government, and about the dependencies produced by government subsi-dies, won the Governor-General's Award for Drama – the first work by a First Nations writer to have won the Award in any genre. Taken together, these events frame the 1990s as the period in which a viable contemporary First Nations drama emerged in Canada. This work includes: Ben Cardinal's *Generic Warriors and No Name Indians* (1994); Shirley Cheechoo's *Path with No Moccasins* (1991); Marie Clements's *Age of Iron* (1993), *Now Look What You Made Me Do* (1995), *Urban Tattoo* (1998), and *The Unnatural and Accidental Women* (2000); Greg Daniels's *Percy's Edge* (1995) and *Four Horses* (1998); Margo Kane's *Moonlodge* (1990) and *Confessions of an Indian Cowboy* (2001); Lenore Keeshig-Tobias's *Quest for Fire* (1990); Michael Lawrenchuk's *The Trial of Kicking Bear* (1994); John MacLeod's *Diary of a Crazy Boy* (1990); Vera Manuel's *Strength of Indian Women* (1992); Tina Mason's *Diva Ojibway* (1990); Monique Mojica, Jani Lauzon, and Michele St. John's *The Scrubbing Project* (2002); Daniel David Moses' *Coyote City* (1988), *Big Buck City* (1991), *The Indian Medicine Shows* (1996), *Brébeuf's Ghost* (1996), and *The Witch of Niagara* (1998); Teressa Nahanee's *Three Indian Women* (1989); Yvette Nolan's *Blade* (1990), *Job's Wife* (1992), *Video* (1992), *A Marginal Man* (1994), *Child* (1996), and *Annie May's Movement* (1998); Ian Ross's *The Gap* (2001); Sharon Shorty's *Trickster Visits the Old Folks Home* (1997); and Floyd Favel Starr's *Lady of Silences* (1992), *House of Sonya* (1997), and *Governor of the Dew* (1999). The best of these plays emerge from a contemporary lived experience that is at once hybrid, contemporary, and newly politicized. They go beyond revisionist content to the development of resistant new dramaturgical forms, and they make few attempts at a conciliatory interculturalism. A few examples will have to suffice.

Almighty Voice and His Wife, by Daniel David Moses (1991), reclaims a story that has been the subject of stories, poems, and plays by non-Native writers from Pierre Berton to Rudy Wiebe, including the play *Almighty Voice* by Len Peterson (1974), in which the title character is a tragic hero with familiar traces of noble savagery. Moses' version is a disjunctive two-part drama. The first act is a realistic, if lyrical, dramatization of the relationship between Almighty Voice and his wife, White Girl, moving through the stories of Almighty Voice's killing of a cow and of the mounties sent to track him down, and, finally, of the mounties' killing him in an outrageous mustering of troops that recalls the Oka crisis. Subtitled "Running with the Moon," the act is divided into nine scenes, framed by the changes of the moon. This lunar structure is suggestive – of the natural world, of course, but also, crucially, of "metamorphosis . . . transformation . . . possibility," which Moses has indicated are central to his way of thinking – and which are also reflected in his extensive use of shape-shifting puns and allusions.[21] The second act transforms the play itself into a different realm, as the ghost of Almighty Voice and an Interlocutor, in historically ironic *"white face"* (p. 53), stage the appropriation of his-story by a series of "other" voices, in the angry and ironic "Red and White Victoria Regina Spirit Revival Show." In the show's "Finale" (p. 95), Moses stages an appropriation of Aristotelian recognition, in which the Interlocutor is recognized by Almighty Voice as "*Ni-wikimakan*" – "my wife" (p. 96). Throughout the act, the Interlocutor has served as the white "master" (p. 55) – a position internalized by the appropriately named "White Girl" – for whose benefit "Indianness" is performed. In the final scene White Girl removes her whiteface make-up and lifts "*a baby-sized bundle*" to the audience "*as the spotlight drifts away to become a full moon in the night*" (p. 96–7). Ultimately, *Almighty Voice and His Wife* clears the ground of accumulated historical misrepresentations, destabilizes any claim to "authoritative" representations of the past, and provides tentative models for a reclamatory and transformational dramaturgy of Native historiography.

Monique Mojica's *Princess Pocahontas and the Blue Spots* and her radio play *Birdwoman and the Suffragettes* invoke historical modes, memories, and structures of meaning that are neither documentary nor mimetic, and that push further than does Moses the reconstructive use of transformational forms and of oral and performative conceptions of history and myth. These plays use a carnivalesque cacophony of generic materials, first to foreground the deconstruction of the western (here explicitly patriarchal) historical record as stabilizing inscription; and second to foreground the construction of histories conceived as transformative cultural memory. *Birdwoman and the Suffragettes* reclaims for Native women the story of "Sacajawea," "the trusty little Indian guide"[22] on the American Lewis and Clarke expedition in 1804–6, from the dubious honors being bestowed upon her by a cabal of caricatured suffragettes in 1905. Mojica reassembles fragments from the historical record, eschewing chronological order and avoiding the presentation of a simply correctionist account, to concern herself, rather, with a history of representations of Sacajawea, and an interrogation of the uses of history itself. Finally, history conceived as inscription and preservation, employed to honor, encage, and keep the dead dead, is set in contrast to history as orality and as memory employed in the service of enfranchisement and of keeping the ancestors alive. The suffragettes, in search of the "eternal womanly" ("Birdwoman," p. 83), appropriate the story of a Native sister, *naming* her, and listing those monuments, parks, and museums named after her. Meanwhile the subject of their history feels trapped. "If you remember me," she intones as she struggles to break from the bronze confines of a statue raised to commemorate her – "captured again" – "remember a child fighting to stay alive/ remember a slave girl gambled away/ remember a mother protecting her child/ remember a wife defying the whip/ remember an old one who loved her people/ remember I died at home on my land" (p. 84).

In *Princess Pocahontas* the spatial, temporal, national, and genealogical borders become fluid in a *performative* cultural history of mixed-race women in the Americas from contact to the present that serves the same destabilizing function as had orality and metatheatricality in *Birdwoman*. The play moves freely across the categories of history, fiction, and myth, "high" and popular culture; across material and political boundaries mapped on western representations of Turtle Island (North America); across the markers of historical periodization; across linguistic barriers; across typographical distinctions between prose and verse; and across the borders between performance genres, music, dance, drama, performance art, and stand-up. In performance even the borders between the characters are not always easy to discern, as Mojica seems to encompass all the roles. These are not clearly distinguished or demarcated in the published script, but they have historically and culturally shaped her as a mixed-race woman in precisely the way she is now theatrically constructed by them as a performer. Structurally, *Princess Pocahontas* is both challengingly disjunctive and ultimately visionary. Its organizing structure is explicitly based on "transformations" rather than scenes, invoking change rather than linear growth or development, and inciting Native women to "pick up their medicine" and "fashion [their] own gods out of [their] entrails" (*Princess Pocahontas*, p. 59). The play-ending "call to arms," sung in Spanish and English and danced to an Andean rhythm, emerges from a visionary structure that models change and demonstrates the strength of a Native nation residing in "the hearts of its women"(p. 60): powerful, fluid, hybrid, and transformational.

NOTES

1. Edward Haies, quoted in Richard Plant, "Drama in English," *The Oxford Companion to Canadian Theatre*, ed. Eugene Benson and L. W. Conolly (Toronto: Oxford University Press, 1989) p. 148.
2. Dates given throughout are where possible those of first production.
3. Sam Scribble, "Dolorsolatio: A Local Political Burlesque," *Canada's Lost Plays, Volume One: The Nineteenth Century*, ed. Anton Wagner and Richard Plant (Toronto: Canadian Theatre Review, 1978) p. 55.
4. Anton Wagner, introduction, *Canada's Lost Plays, Volume Two: Women Pioneers*, ed. Wagner and Richard Plant (Toronto: Canadian Theatre Review, 1979) p. 6.
5. Herman Voaden, *A Vision of Canada: Herman Voaden's Dramatic Works 1928–1945*, ed. Anton Wagner (Toronto: Simon, 1993) p. 137.
6. Tyrone Guthrie in *Renown at Stratford*, by Guthrie, Robertson Davies, and Grant MacDonald, special memorial edn. (1953; Toronto: Clarke, 1971) p. 28.
7. Carole Corbeil, interview with Michael Langham, "'It's Very Strange to Be Back,'" *Globe and Mail* [Toronto] 24 July 1982: p. E1.
8. Théâtre Passe Muraille, *The Farm Show* (Toronto: Coach House, 1976) p. 19.
9. Judith Thompson, *The Other Side of the Dark* (Toronto: Coach House, 1989).
10. John Mighton, *Body and Soul* (Toronto: Coach House, 1994) p. 16.

11. Thomas Nagel, quoted as an epigraph to John Mighton, *The Little Years* (Toronto: Playwrights Canada, 1995) p. 8.

12. Chris Johnson, "B-Movies beyond the Absurd," *Canadian Literature* 85 (1980): pp. 87–103; rev. version in *Essays on George F. Walker: Playing with Anxiety*, by Johnson (Winnipeg: Blizzard, 1999) pp. 41–60.

13. Jerry Wasserman, introduction, *The East End Plays, Part 1*, by George F. Walker (Vancouver: Talon, 1999) p. 7; Wasserman, introduction, *The East End Plays, Part 2*, by George F. Walker (Vancouver: Talon, 1999) p. 7.

14. Three of these – *Risk Everything*, *Problem Child*, and *Criminal Genius* – had received their world premieres earlier in 1997 at Theatre Off Park in New York.

15. George F. Walker, *Heaven* (Vancouver: Talon, 2000) p. 135.

16. George F. Walker, *Shared Anxiety: Selected Plays* (Toronto: Coach House, 1994).

17. Sky Gilbert, *Play Murder* (Winnipeg: Blizzard, 1995) p. 26.

18. Guillermo Verdecchia, *Fronteras Americanas* (Toronto: Coach House, 1993) pp. 78, 75.

19. Djanet Sears, "nOTES oF a cOLOURED gIRL: 32 sHORT rEASONS wHY i wRITE fOR tHE tHEATRE," introduction, *Harlem Duet*, by Sears (Winnipeg: Scirocco Drama, 1998) p. 14.

20. Sears, *Harlem Duet*, p. 73.

21. Daniel David Moses, in Hartmut Lutz, "Daniel David Moses," *Contemporary Challenges: Conversations with Canadian Native Authors* (Saskatoon: Fifth House, 1991) p. 158.

22. Monique Mojica, "Birdwoman and the Suffragettes," *Princess Pocahontas and the Blue Spots: Two Plays by Monique Mojica* (Toronto: Women's Press, 1991) p. 67.

6

Poetry

DAVID STAINES

A land without poetry

In *The Journals of Susanna Moodie* (1970), Margaret Atwood (1939–) reimagines Susanna Moodie, the nineteenth-century poet and novelist, who enters the "large darkness" that is Canada and fashions her life as a reluctant pioneer. Atwood's Moodie finds herself "a word / in a foreign language," an apt description of someone alien in her new environment and cut off irretrievably from her old environment of England. As she confronts her new home, she meets what she sees as an uncultured landscape awaiting transformation into a cultured world.

For the real Mrs. Moodie, who arrived from England in 1832, Canada was first and foremost a land without poetry. It was not until more than thirty years later that Edward Hartley Dewart (1828–1903) would publish the first anthology of Canadian poetry, *Selections from Canadian Poets* (1864), designed to "rescue from oblivion some of the floating pieces of Canadian authorship worthy of preservation in a more permanent form."[1] Casting a wide net that included most of the recognized poets of the period, including Susanna Moodie, he proclaimed that poets should be national heroes, though they would probably go unrecognized in such a young country as Canada: "if a Milton or a Shakspere . . . was to arise among us, it is far from certain that his merit would be recognized."[2] Canadians, he asserted, must be aware of the vitality and the significance of the poetic mind.

In his introductory essay Dewart also affirmed that a "national literature is an essential element in the formation of national character. It is not merely the record of a country's mental progress: it is the expression of its intellectual life, the bond of national unity, and the guide of national energy."[3] Although this sentiment uncritically equated history with story, a philosophy of literature that would be enshrined for several generations, his anthology did preserve the works of many writers, most of them of the genteel tradition Dewart favored. And throughout his book one can easily hear echoes of the Romantic and Victorian poets of England, of Wordsworth, Keats, and Byron, and of Tennyson and Browning. At this stage in a young land's history the colonial mentality militates against any direct confrontation with the nature of the new country.

But Dewart's anthology suggests that there was now a thriving if derivative poetry being written in Canada, and by "assembling the work of several dozen currently active poets, Dewart contributed to the heightened sense of cultural identity that was to accompany Confederation in 1867."[4] Thomas D'Arcy McGee (1825–68), the most persuasive spokesperson for Confederation, pointed out the path to a truly Canadian literature that very year:

> The books that are made elsewhere, even in England, are not always the best fitted for us; they do not always run on the same mental gauge, nor connect with our trains of thought; they do not take us up at the by-stages of cultivation at which we have arrived, and where we are emptied forth as on a barren, pathless, habitationless heath. They are books of another state of society, bearing traces of controversies, or directed against errors or evils which for us hardly exist, except in the pages of these exotic books…we do much need several other books calculated to our own meridian, and hitting home to our own society, either where it is sluggish or priggish, or wholly defective in its present style of culture.[5]

The post-Confederation poets and E. J. Pratt

For Archibald Lampman, Charles G. D. Roberts's *Orion* in 1880 provided the first glimpse of a Canadian poetry. Lampman had been

> under the depressing conviction that we were situated hopelessly on the outskirts of civilization where no literature or art could be…it was useless to expect that anything great could be done by any of our companions, still more useless to expect that we could do it ourselves. I sat up most of the night reading and re-reading *Orion* in a state of the wildest excitement, and when I went to bed I could not sleep. It seemed to me a wonderful thing that such a work could be done by a Canadian, by a young man, one of ourselves. It was like a voice from some new paradise of art.[6]

And it was in the last two decades of the nineteenth century that the first poets of the Canadian landscape wrote compelling verse.

There were four poets born in the 1860s who formed what Malcolm Ross terms "Poets of the Confederation":[7] Charles G. D. Roberts (1860–1943) and his cousin Bliss Carman (1861–1929), Archibald Lampman (1861–99), and Duncan Campbell Scott (1862–1947). They constitute a group more for literary classification than for any shared purpose, a group to which must be added the slightly older Isabella Valancy Crawford (1850–87) and W. W. Campbell (1858–1918). Roberts and Carman came from New Brunswick; Lampman, Scott, and Campbell settled in Ottawa; and Crawford's family settled in Toronto. These six poets give voice to the flowering of a distinctive Canadian poetry as it moves into the twentieth century.

As a poet, Roberts is attracted to particular areas of landscape, the tides, the rolling hills, and the Canadian backwoods, and this landscape is drastically altered by the seasons, the power of seasonal changes playing a primary role in his work. In such poems as "Tantramar Revisited" and "The Skater," the visual images combine to form the equivalent of an impressionistic painting. With a painter's eye he creates his own moods. He often takes subjects, not necessarily original but uniquely Canadian, and presents them with precise and unpretentious details:

> A high bare field, brown from the plough, and borne
> Aslant from sunset; amber wastes of sky
> Washing the ridge; a clamour of crows that fly
> In from the wide flats where the spent tides mourn
> To yon their rocking roosts in pines wind-torn;
> A line of grey snake-fence, that zigzags by
> A pond and cattle; from the homestead high
> The long deep summonings of the supper horn.
>
> ("The Potato Harvest")

Suggesting affinities with Wordsworth, Keats, and the early Tennyson, Roberts turned to nature for the inspiration of his poetry, and nature and its varied manifestations became his poems' focus.

In his poetry Roberts is the masterful Canadian heir of Wordsworth's pictorial art. But in his prose, especially in his many animal stories, he masters the Victorian as opposed to the Romantic vein, showing graphically the savagery and horror of nature. Thus he begins what will become a distinctive Canadian strain in poetry, the ambidextrous musings of major poets in prose as well as in poetry.

By far the most popular of these Confederation poets in his own time, Carman, like his cousin, was a nature poet, but where Roberts is precise and accurate, Carman is philosophical, exploring the transcendental potentials of the natural world. In "Low Tide on Grand Pré," for example, he describes a mystical experience through a series of romantic inner landscapes; without Roberts's sense of order, the poem chronicles lost love, grief at recollecting the past, and finally a life that can capture the past only through such grief. Only in the love lyrics of *Sappho* (1904) does he again capture the height of poetic achievement. At his best Carman is a lyrical impressionist whose sensual images re-create his jubilant feelings.

Whereas Roberts and Carman write of their Maritime worlds, Duncan Campbell Scott chooses lands much less cultivated and more primeval. By his choice of what he considered to be the wild and savage parts of the country, he brings Canadian poetry into a world where human beings are part of the landscape, where the landscape is distinctly Canadian, and where the form of the poem is a valiant attempt, as in "At the Cedars" or "The Forsaken," to be part of the story itself. Markedly different from the formal poetry of Roberts and Carman, Scott's verse moves into the realm of contemporary speech.

Isabella Valancy Crawford's "Malcolm's Katie" (1884), a long narrative in blank verse, chronicles a Tennysonian love threatened by an evil villain. Although widely uneven in its quality, the poem continues the tradition of narrative poems of substantial length, which reaches back to *The Rising Village* (1825) by Oliver Goldsmith (1794–1861) and extends down to the present day. And W. W. Campbell, though indebted to a variety of British and American poets and writing verse which reflects his natural settings and his religious idealism, is now best remembered for the weekly column "At the Mermaid Inn," written with Lampman and Scott for the Toronto *Globe* in 1892–3, in which they reflected on poetry, politics, and religion.

Of the six Confederation poets, Archibald Lampman is the most gifted and the most adventurous. In such early lyrics as "April," "Heat," and "In October" are detailed landscapes of a semicultivated nature somewhere between the urban and the primeval. In "The City of the End of Things," he paints a grim indictment of social desolation in an increasingly mechanistic universe. And in his posthumously published "At the Long Sault: May, 1660," he reimagines an incident from the past to enhance the stature of the poem's heroes. Lampman's early death in 1899 deprived Canada of a major poet who was already charting the literary map for future generations.

Writing with the wisdom of hindsight, E. J. Pratt (1882–1964) was able to crystallize the importance of these early poets:

> That Wordsworth, Keats, Tennyson, and Rossetti are traceable atmospherically in the work of this school means little more than that Aeschylus, Shakespeare, Milton, and Rousseau fertilized the thought of the first half of the nineteenth century. The relevant point is that in two decades following 1881, the English-speaking world was compelled to acknowledge for the first time the existence of a national consciousness making itself heard and felt through a Canadian literature. And for the first time adequately a nature poetry came into being. The claim is made for nature poetry only. The larger human currents, the

democratic visions, the creative impulses at work on myths and national origins are not so pronounced... [I]n the field, immense on its own right, of natural description and interpretation, the poets of this school have nothing to concede to the work of the English poets during the same period, and certainly nothing to the writers of New England over a period twice as long."[8]

Born and raised in the outports of Newfoundland, still a British colony, Pratt expanded the romantic limits of natural description, peopling his volume *Newfoundland Verse* (1923) with the sounds, characters, and animals of the Newfoundland seacoast. Later a professor of English at Victoria College in the University of Toronto, he wrote a series of long narrative poems that chart the world's tragedies, for example *The Titanic* (1935) and *Dunkirk* (1941), and documentaries on Canada's history, for example *Brébeuf and His Brethen* (1940) and *Towards the Last Spike* (1952). His reputation rests as Canada's mythologizer, giving voice to the images and myths that characterize his country. "When everybody was writing subtle and complex lyrics, Pratt developed a technique of straightforward narrative; when everybody was experimenting with free verse, Pratt was finding new possibilities in blank verse and octosyllabic couplets," wrote Northrop Frye (1912–91), Pratt's colleague and friend at Victoria College.[9]

The modernist poets

Already present in the poetry of Lampman, Scott, and Pratt is the employment of free verse and the use of imagist patterns. Although the rise of modern poetry took place at the end of the nineteenth century, the movement was freeing Canadian poetry in this early period from the trammels of end-rhyme. The movement to reshape and indeed to revolutionize poetry, to make poetry still more attuned to the speaking voice, crystallized in Montreal in the 1920s. From 8 October 1924 until 11 March 1925, A. J. M. Smith (1902–80) edited a Literary Supplement of the *McGill Daily*, which grew into the *McGill Fortnightly Review*, which ran from 21 November 1925 until 27 April 1927. What separated these reviews from earlier McGill magazines was the editor's originality and the promise of one of his editor-contributors, F. R. Scott (1899–1985). Together they made their magazine the center for the innovative spirit in poetry. Both men revolted against the Victorian conservatism they saw in contemporary poetry: "poetry does not permit the rejection of every aspect of the personality except intuition and sensibility. It must be written by the whole man. It is an intelligent activity, and it ought to compel the respect of the generality of intelligent men."[10]

The *McGill Fortnightly Review* attracted other young poets – Leo Kennedy (1907–2000) and A. M. Klein (1909–72) – and together they became the so-called Montreal group, dedicated to promoting the modernism of Canadian poetry.

Not a prolific poet, Smith maintained that 100 good poems represented the yield of any poet's life. In his four poetry collections he reprinted some poems and published a few new ones, always adhering to his belief that each poem is a carefully constructed object complete in itself. Revealing a detached coolness in his intellectual bearing, he commands a young poet to achieve the effect "of a hard thing done / Perfectly, as though without care" ("To a Young Poet"). In "The Lonely Land," his best-known poem, he views the Canadian landscape in its harsh reality:

> This is a beauty
> of dissonance,
> this resonance
> of stony strand,
> this smoky cry
> curled over a black pine

As a student in Edinburgh, Smith had become acquainted with H. J. C. Grierson's work on the seventeenth-century metaphysical poets, and the indissoluble union of the abstract and concrete in their poetry. Similarly, in "The Lonely Land," the words "beauty," "dissonance," and "resonance" lend universal meaning to the "stony strand," as does the synesthesia of a "smoky cry/ curled over a black pine." For Smith, the language of poetry, pure and direct, is akin to the language of Eliot, Pound, and other modernists.

F. R. Scott, a professor of constitutional law and civil rights, invoked satire as a way of indicting and mocking the literary establishment: "can / A day go by without new authors springing / To paint the native maple, and to plan / More ways to set the selfsame welkin ringing?" ("The Canadian Authors Meet"). Although he dismisses too easily the earlier Confederation poets, he practiced a social verse, closely linked to the political movements of his time, that denounced social injustices and championed social change and reform.

In 1936 Smith and Scott published *New Provinces*, a selection of poems by the Torontonians Pratt and Robert Finch (1900–95) and by the Montrealers Smith, Scott, Kennedy, and Klein. As Scott's preface acknowledges, "Equipped with a freer diction and more elastic forms, the modernists sought a content which would more vividly express the world about them."[11] This landmark collection had an effect similar to that of Wordsworth's 1798 preface to the *Lyrical Ballads*, arguing for, and exemplifying in its verse, the unadorned language of everyday speech. *New Provinces* solidified these poets as the Canadian modernists of their time.

Klein's contributions to *New Provinces*, a sequence of lyrics on Spinoza titled "Out of the Pulver and the Polished Lens" and the Eliot-like "Soirée of Velvel Kleinburger," stand out as major works of a superb poet. In these early poems, many of them later gathered in *Hath Not a Jew . . .* (1940), Klein celebrates the rich Jewish heritage of Montreal, frequently laughing at and with the world he understands well:

> In back-room dens of delicatessen stores,
> In curtained parlours of garrulous barber-shops,
> While the rest of the world most comfortably snores
> On mattresses, or on more fleshly props,
> My brother Velvel vigils in the night
> > ("Soirée of Velvel Kleinburger")

Using the highly textured and lofty language of formal poetry, Klein creates an affectionate mock epic, transforming the cramped quarters of a delicatessen into a fortress. This optimism gives way to the grim satire of *The Hitleriad* (1944), loosely based on Pope's *Dunciad*; his attack on Nazism and Hitler has moments of sheer brilliance in a work that cannot sustain its comic mode. *Poems* (1944) contains anguished psalms that reveal the poet's immediacy in dealing with evil. And in *The Rocking Chair and Other Poems* (1948), Klein, the spokesperson for Quebec, paints a full portrait of Quebec and Canadian society in a style that is direct, sympathetic, and at times ironical.

Later Klein wrote *The Second Scroll* (1951) – a novel that celebrates the innate human ability to self-renew, especially through language – and several short stories that were posthumously published. His poetry, however, is the brilliant realization of his all-encompassing vision: "there is a bold, full utterance and a fine profusion of imagery, depending on a buoyancy and force of temperament very rare in Canadian poetry, and rare, it is right to add, in the poetry of this age, wherever written."[12] Although he would spend his final years in a voluntarily mute state, his literary legacy will live on in generations of poets across the country.

In addition to these *New Provinces* poets, Smith also wanted to include Dorothy Livesay (1909–96), but Scott declined; he put off her inclusion to a planned second edition of the anthology, which never appeared. Born in Winnipeg, Livesay published her first poetry collection, *Green Pitcher* (1928), at the age of eighteen. Infused by the sights of poverty in the Depression era, she joined the Communist Party in the thirties and wrote poetry that attempted to combine the lessons of poetical craft with political ideas in such collections as *Day and Night* (1944) and *Poems for People* (1947).

Another politically motivated poet was Earle Birney (1904–95), a confirmed socialist, who wrote early poems that captured his harsh environment of British Columbia. In "David," for example, two young men climb mountains on the coast until an accident leaves David partly paralyzed and expecting his own death. A professor of medieval literature and creative writing at the University of British Columbia, Birney later expanded the language of his poetry, substituting space for regular punctuation and becoming a poet keenly interested in the visual dynamics of the printed page. This openness to experimentation parallels Livesay's later works which are much more open in style.

New Provinces upgraded the poetic consciousness of the country. In 1936, too, appeared the critical *The White Savannahs* by W. E. Collin (1893–1984) with its chapters on many of the poets already mentioned from a modernist perspective. And in the same year the *University of Toronto Quarterly* began an annual survey of Canadian letters with E. K. Brown (1905–51), the joint editor of the *Quarterly*, writing for the next fifteen years the surveys of poetry. Although poetry had a limited audience, it now met with an informed critical response.

The little magazines, which originated in Canada with the *McGill Fortnightly Review*, provide the milieu for new poetry in the forties. Alan Crawley (1887–1975), who founded *Contemporary Verse* in Vancouver in 1941, sought poetry which was "serious in thought and expression and contemporary in theme, treatment, and technique"; the magazine ran until 1952. *Preview*, which ran in Montreal from 1942 to 1945, noted the presence on its board of editors of F. R. Scott and P. K. Page (1916–). *First Statement*, which also ran in Montreal from 1942 to 1945, was the product of its editor John Sutherland (1919–56). In December 1945 *Preview* and *First Statement* merged to become *Northern Review*. Modeled on *Preview* and *First Statement*, the *Fiddlehead* was founded in 1945 at the University of New Brunswick under the direction of Alfred Bailey (1905–97) and Desmond Pacey (1917–75). While these magazines published poetry, they also encouraged "by the means available to them the development of a more serious criticism in Canada."[13]

P. K. Page found her voice in the company of the Montreal group, in particular her friends and colleagues A. M. Klein and F. R. Scott. Hers was already a more subtle version of the didactic and often declamatory style of those writers with whom she published in *Preview*. In *As Ten, as Twenty* (1946) and *The Metal and the Flower* (1954), the lyric poems as often have their origin in social observation as in romantic love. The two are memorably fused in her most concentrated early lyric, "As Ten, as Twenty," where, in four short quatrains, the poetry is at once political and intensely erotic:

> For we can live now, love:
> millions in us breathe,
> moving as we would move
> and qualifying death

The throb of monosyllabics is just varied enough in "millions," "moving," and "qualifying" to suggest a heartbeat accelerated by passion, and the long vowels of "breathe" and "move" mimic deep and leisurely exhalations of breath. Although the rhetoric echoes the biblical book of Acts, Shakespeare, and C. Day Lewis, the poem is triumphantly Page's own.

Exploring its own metaphors, her work then began to turn from what we perceive to how we perceive it. The new direction appears most plainly in *Evening Dance of the Grey Flies* (1981), where the poetry draws on contemplative discipline in which objects become pathways for perception. The meditative breakthrough enables her social voice to speak easily, now in a declarative note freed by experience and expressed in looser verse forms. These poetic tendencies govern successive volumes of new and collected poetry. Along with her solid achievement as a prose stylist in her novel *The Sun and the Moon* (1944) and several short stories and children's books, she has established herself firmly as a major poet who speaks with unforced authority to the experience of modernity with intelligence and sensitivity.

Phyllis Webb (1927–), born in Victoria and a graduate of the University of British Columbia, began writing as part of an off-campus group led by Earle Birney. Influenced by Page's poetry, she made her way to Montreal, where F. R. Scott introduced her to the Montreal writing scene of the fifties. Always open to influences, be they Page, Irving Layton (1912–), or the Black Mountain poets, she has shifted in her poetry from the rhetorical style of her early verse, for example "Marvell's Garden," to a restrained and starker approach in her minimalist later periods. Believing that the individual must embrace protective silence, she has striven to find a poetics supportive of woman's aesthetics. In her constant attempts to fashion and to refashion the simple elements of the line in poetry, she seeks "the wit of the syntax, the rhythm and speed of the fall, the drop, the assumption of a specific light, curved."[14]

Irving Layton published his early verse in *First Statement*, his first volume, *Here and Now*, appearing in 1945. In the five following decades he brought out almost a book a year, leaving it to later generations to separate the wheat from the chaff. "For me, a poet is one who explores new areas of sensibility," Layton asserts,[15] and influenced by his friend A. M. Klein he writes of his Jewish roots and his Montreal world in such sensitive lyrics as "Keine Lazarovitch 1870–1959" and in such lusty ones as "Berry Picking." But unlike Klein, he frequently sounds off at behaviors that prevent complete self-expression. Angry at people who fear themselves, their bodies, and their language, he wants his readers to assume responsibility for the pain of the world, and with this confrontation of themselves they can embrace the power of love.

A prominent later poet, Leonard Cohen (1934–) takes Klein and Layton as his forefathers in his first volume, *Let Us Compare Mythologies* (1956). As its title suggests, the book, a remarkable debut, brings together mythologies to assert the poet's seeking of his Jewish identity in a world where other forms of belief present different ways of organizing the individual's relationship to the world. Cohen went on to find other paths, his Jewishness no longer adequate to his needs, for fulfilling his quest for a full life. Often finding the erotic and the spiritual unified, he regards physical union as a means of spiritual purification. Despite his distinguished career as a novelist and later as a musician, his poetry best represents the journey of a soul that has gone from the American beat movement through the sensual world to the investigation of his own manifold experiences.

In the forties E. K. Brown's *On Canadian Poetry* (1943) proved to be the definitive account of the rise of the national poetic voice. And Northrop Frye began to write probing articles on the developing traditions in Canadian poetry. In 1950 he took over from Brown the section on Canadian poetry in the *University of Toronto Quarterly*, and for the next ten years his accounts continued Brown's patient but firm criticism. Frye's synthesis had a profound effect on poets from all regions of Canada. "The only 'influence' Frye had on those of us who wanted to be writers, and it was a considerable one, was to take us seriously," Atwood recalls. "In a society still largely provincial, where the practice of literature and the arts generally was regarded with a good deal of suspicion – immoral if not a frill – he made literature seem not only an honourable calling but a necessary one."[16]

George Johnston (1913–), who obtained his undergraduate degree from Victoria College, writes informed verse of lively wit with careful delineations of people in a small city like Ottawa; his poetry includes several translations of Icelandic sagas. A graduate also of Victoria College, Margaret Avison (1918–) pens verse in the manner of the seventeenth-century metaphysicals, affirming her personal and poetic dedication to Christianity. Another graduate of Victoria College, James Reaney (1926–), creates a world where the regional reveals the mythic; much of his poetry is rooted in the detailed life of Perth County, Ontario, where he was born, and this life discloses the realm of myth which is central to the formation of culture. And Jay Macpherson (1931–) came to Toronto for her graduate degrees; studying under Northrop Frye, she wrote *The Boatman* (1957), which rewrites mythological themes in colloquial idiom under the influence of Frye's mythic theories.

West Coast poetry and Al Purdy's landscape of Ontario

On the West Coast a new movement would revolutionize Canadian poetry in a manner similar to that of *New Provinces*. In the late 1950s, Warren Tallman (1921–94), a professor of English at the University of British Columbia, found himself drawn to the San Francisco poetry scene and to the American poet Robert Duncan. Inspired by this new generation of avant-garde writers, he helped bring Duncan to Vancouver twice for poetry readings: the first event took place in 1959 in a converted portion of Tallman's basement; the second was held in the spring of 1961 at the UBC Festival of the Contemporary Arts. After Duncan's second visit, George Bowering (1935–), Frank Davey (1940–), David Dawson (1942–), Lionel Kearns (1937–), Jamie Reid (1941–), and Fred Wah (1939–), all born and raised in British Columbia (with the exception of Wah, who was born in Saskatchewan but raised in British Columbia), formed a study group to discuss the work of such Black Mountain poets as Robert Creeley, Duncan, Denise Levertov, and Charles Olson. The group most noticeably embraced the poetics put forward by Olson in his 1951 essay "Projective Verse," especially the notion that poetry is chiefly an oral rather than a written form of expression.

In September 1961, Bowering, Davey, Dawson, Reid, and Wah launched a small magazine that would serve as a record of their Black Mountain explorations. Titled *Tish* (a rearranging of "shit"), the magazine was published between 1961 and 1969 and served as a counter-cultural response to the prevailing Central Canadian voices of poets. *Tish* successfully launched the writing careers of its editorial members, in particular Bowering, Davey, and Wah, who argued through their verse for a spoken energy that focused on the elemental aspects of life. Equally important was the magazine's influence on other poets including Margaret Atwood, Robert Kroetsch (1927–), Daphne Marlatt (1942–), and bpNichol (1944–88). In 1966 the *Tish* poets gained recognition as a national poetic movement when Raymond Souster (1921–) declared in his preface to *New Wave Canada* (1966) that the *Tish* group was the source of new poetical energy.[17] The group was the first Canadian wave in the postmodern tradition in Canadian poetry.

The most prolific member of the *Tish* group, Bowering, a professor of English at Simon Fraser University, has published more than thirty volumes of poetry, five novels, collections of short fiction, and many critical essays. His poetry champions the ideals of the Black Mountain school's spare style and its use of a flexible poetic line fashioned on the rhythms and cadences of colloquial speech:

> Words
> > coming together
> > > moving at one another
> > traction for the tongue
> > > Look at that! American
> > language shouting
> > > across the Potomac
> > > > ring coins over the river
> > open out western states
> > > – anywhere a man can
> > > > hear his voice
> > > > > ("For WCW")

Long sequences of poems or loosely unified long poems came to be Bowering's favorite form. His book-length *Kerrisdale Elegies* (1984) relocate Rainer Maria Rilke's *Duino Elegies* in contemporary suburban Vancouver. Although the theme is loss, as in many elegies, the poem finds the occasion to honor age by allowing the echoes of the original poem to offer a meditative counterpoint to the inevitability of mortality and the loss that permeates all of life.

Davey, a professor of English at the University of Western Ontario, began his writing career as a poet, trying to adapt Charles Olson's theories into a Canadian context and venturing into the long poem, his *King of Swords* (1972), for example, fashioning the medieval Arthurian legends to contemporary criticism. Moreover, as the founding editor of *Open Letter* (1965), a journal of experimental writing, criticism, and research, he has ventured into literary criticism, publishing many articles and books. And Wah, a professor of English at the University of Calgary, locates a perfect vehicle for his poetry in the Black Mountain poets' emphasis on simple syntax and organic literary forms. In *Loki is Buried at Smoky Creek* (1980) he works in spare imagistic style to write short poems about the events of everyday life, and in *Waiting for Saskatchewan* (1985) he locates personal history in concrete environments, showing how genealogy transcends place.

Through their teaching and, more importantly, through their creative work, these poets had a profound influence on Canadian poetry, revitalizing the language of poetry. And through their interdependent work (Bowering, for example, edited *Loki is Buried at Smoky Creek*; Wah and Davey edited

The Swift Current Anthology [1986]), they have maintained their goals and their influence.

A contributing editor of *Tish* from 1963 to 1965, Marlatt came to Canada from Australia and Malaysia in 1951. Much of her writing concerns itself with the desire to discover and belong to her new home, in her case the fishing community and the landscape of the Fraser River delta. In *Steveston* (1974) she creates a long line of poetry that suggests the river's movement, embracing the whole community in its seasonal diversity and its history: "I think of *Steveston* as actually a movement around, based on return. A cycle of poems, it moves around & keeps returning to the central interface of human lives with the river, picking up the threads (roads) that lead there. My image for it was a network, the ways in which all of the poems & all of a poem's parts, as all of us & where we live, are interconnected."[18] In 1980 Wah edited her *Selected Writing: New Work*. From the early 1980s Marlatt has increasingly identified with a feminist writing community, influenced in part by her reading of French feminist theory. In *Touch to My Tongue* (1984) she explores women's desires, their bodies, and their language, and in her two novels, *Ana Historic* (1988) and *Taken* (1996), she further expands on this theme. Investigating the fictional possibilities of autobiography in these works and in others, she probes constantly into the silences that disenfranchise women.

Meanwhile, back in Ontario, the *Tish* group met its parallel in the poetry of Al Purdy (1918–2000). In his first three books he wrote derivative verse that was fashioned on earlier models, including Roberts and Carman. But with the publication of *Poems for All the Annettes* (1962) he started to write his own distinctive verse, a loose, colloquial poetry that is unaffected and conversational in tone. From his regional base in Ameliasburgh, he composed poetry that captured the world around him:

> This is the country of our defeat
> > and yet
> > during the fall plowing a man
> > might stop and stand in the brown valley of the furrows
> > > and shade his eyes to watch for the same
> > > red patch mixed with gold
> > > that appears on the same
> > > spot in the hills
> > > year after year
> > > and grow old
> > plowing and plowing a ten-acre field until
> > the convolutions run parallel with his own brain –
> > > > ("The Country North of Belleville")

In the words of Michael Ondaatje (1943–), for "a person of my generation, Al Purdy's poems mapped and named the landscape of Ontario."[19] Wherever he traveled, whether to the Arctic, Russia, Japan, or the Galapagos Islands, Purdy took these regional experiences and made them his own, turning "them and himself into a representative voice of the multiple identity that is modern Canada. The voice celebrated a personal past and a range of futures."[20]

Contemporary poets

In *Double Persephone* (1961), her privately printed first volume of poetry, Atwood embarked on a literary career that embraces novels and short stories, literary criticism, and film writing in addition to her major work as a poet. In her poetry she often chooses individuals, usually alienated from their surroundings, and watches their distrust of the world around them, invoking their milieu as a place of shallow commercialism and consumerism. And this vision extends to her early assessment of human relationships, which are also victims of the disarrayed society around them. As her career develops, she embraces a more compassionate, less ironic vision of life.

In "Progressive Insanities of a Pioneer" (1968) Atwood paints a painful portrait of a man on the brink of despair in the "ordered absence" that was nineteenth-century Canada. Anticipating her reimagination of Susanna Moodie in *The Journals of Susanna Moodie*, the poem fashions the same details that prompt Atwood's Moodie to cry out, "I am a word / in a foreign language." *The Journals*, then, becomes her testimony to Canada, the country that is and the country that will be. In the end, Atwood's Moodie becomes a woman on a contemporary bus along St. Clair Avenue:

> I am the old woman
> sitting across from you on the bus,
> her shoulders drawn up like a shawl;
> out of her eyes come secret
> hatpins, destroying
> the walls, the ceiling
>
> Turn, look down:
> there is no city;
> this is the centre of a forest
>
> your place is empty
> ("A Bus along St Clair: December,"
> *The Journals*)

In this epic journey of one struggling pioneer Atwood re-creates a figure from Canadian history; like Purdy, she finds her world by digging through the present into the unexcavated regions of the past. *The Journals of Susanna Moodie*, a unified sequence of poems, transcends its creative time to become a landmark of the Canadian journey into its collective past.

In her poetry of the later seventies Atwood's subject matter expands, often embracing political themes that emerge out of her genuine concern with social injustices. *Two-Headed Poems* (1978), for example, takes its title from an impassioned series of poems about Canada's crisis as a "duet between two deaf singers." Her poems about love now bear scarcely a trace of the bitter irony of her earlier work. And in *Morning in the Burned House* (1995) an elegiac series of meditations on the death of her own father finds comfort and peace in human relationships.

Born in Sri Lanka and raised in England from the age of eleven, Michael Ondaatje came to Canada in 1962 to pursue his BA from the University of Toronto (1965) and his MA from the University of Western Ontario (1967). Although he has been an English professor, he prefers to devote his full attention to creativity. And his works suggest a breaking down of traditional boundaries between genres. In *The Dainty Monsters* (1967), his first book of poetry, Ondaatje writes lyric poetry from situations that are often autobiographical. But it is his third volume, *The Collected Works of Billy the Kid* (1970), that enunciates fully his remarkable talent. A transgeneric collage of poetry, fiction, and multimedia documents, the book chronicles the American outlaw and Pat Garrett's pursuit of him.

Some of the sixty-eight sections of the poem are lyrics, some are in prose, and others contain ballads, tall tales, excerpts from authentic memoirs, and photographs. Although the dates and settings are accurate, the book draws little of its power from historical fact, for Ondaatje invents many incidents: "I have edited, rephrased, and slightly reworked the originals. But the emotions belong to their authors."[21] And he plays with the possibilities of open-ended narrative, overtly challenging closed narratives. The book draws to a close with a photograph of a young Michael Ondaatje. In his more recent poetry he again returns to autobiography. *Secular Love* (1984), a book-length sequence, traces the dissolution of a marriage, the poet's own breakdown, and his recovery and return to a complete life through the love of another woman. And *Handwriting* (1998) returns to Sri Lanka to contemplate the rock paintings, buddhas, and books in a contemporary atmosphere of strife and bloodshed. Like Atwood, Ondaatje begins his writing career as a poet, then becomes a novelist, though he never abandons his poetic calling. The two writers dominate the poetic scene, one with her vision of early Canada, the other with his vision of the outlaw dream of America, and both maintain the autobiographical vein in their contemporary poetry.

Ondaatje's film *The Sons of Captain Poetry* (1970) captures the tremendous presence as a performing poet of his friend bpNichol. Born in Vancouver, Nichol attended the University of British Columbia, where he came under the influence of the visual experiments of Birney and of the *Tish* group. Unhappy with his own conventional lyrics, he began to write visual or concrete poetry. And although he moved in 1963 to Toronto, the West, and in particular the *Tish* group, continued to haunt his poetry.

A restless figure who did not want to stop and rewrite, Nichol does not have the unique ability to focus which is so manifest in Ondaatje's poetry. His multivolume and multisensory work *The Martyrology* – the first two books were published in 1972, and the ninth and final book was published in 1993, five years after his early death – follows the stories of fictional saints, fathers who abandon their sons or brothers searching for lost brothers, giving way towards the end to increasingly autobiographical books, the final volume confronting the imminence of the poet's own death. Rooted in Toronto, the work captures so much of Nichol's search for the proper word, and when he is at his most playful with language he finds the words, then contorts them, wrestling them into new meanings, new forms, and even new words.

Having grown up in the British Columbia interior, Patrick Lane (1939–) steadfastly clings to his Western Canadian roots. In his early poems the disadvantaged and the disenfranchised are seen in violent contexts; at the center is often a casual act of seemingly random self-destructiveness. Rooting his depictions in the experiences he has known, he investigates the male ethos, drawing moral conclusions about mankind's inhumanity and seeing some redemptive potential in the natural world. In *Poems New and Selected* (1978) he makes his observations of South American life a criticism of the self-obsessed Canadian preoccupations. *Old Mother* (1982) evinces a greater control of the poetic line as he looks at the violent patterns of human history. Purdy's colloquial poetry provides a major influence on Lane's poetic achievement.

In 1978 Lane began a relationship with Saskatchewan-born Lorna Crozier (1948–), which they celebrated in *No Longer Two People* (1979). In her first collection, *Inside Is the Sky* (1976), some themes of her poetry – the limitless prairie sky, the prairie landscape, and her own family – are already present; subsequent volumes explore sex and love, often under the guise of humor. *Inventing the Hawk* (1992) includes many poems on the death of her father, recalling the effects of alcoholism on her family. In *A Saving Grace: The Collected Poems of Mrs. Bentley* (1996) Crozier's feminist reinterpretation of the protagonist of the Sinclair Ross novel probes the silences in her diary. And *Apocrypha of Light* (2002) is a comic and often profound rewriting of biblical stories and themes.

Another Western figure who plays a major role in the poetic tradition is Robert Bringhurst (1946–). Born in Los Angeles of Canadian parents, he studied at the Massachusetts Institute of Technology and the University of Utah before taking his BA in comparative literature from Indiana University (1973) and his MFA in creative writing from the University of British Columbia (1975). A restlessly intellectual poet who is never sentimental or confessional, he broke away from the modernist techniques of Pound and Eliot to create his own unique way of regarding the world around him. Showing little support for the crass materialism of the present age, he captures the beauty of the past and the wisdom of the ages in austere poetry that is frequently rich with allusions. "I wanted – no matter how preposterous and impossible it might be – to learn all the words and grammars in the world," he affirms. "Poetry nevertheless precedes them all and can make its way, if it must, with the help of none."[22] Attuned deeply to the world's linguistic and poetic diversity, his work includes translations from writings in Arabic, French, Greek, Haida, Navajo, and Spanish. It is the importance Bringhurst places on the past that makes him a tireless researcher into Native American cultural history, seeking an understanding of these cultures and their oral literatures.

Towering over other Western poets is Robert Kroetsch, who turned to poetry in the midst of a distinguished career as novelist and critic. Beginning to write short lyrics in the early seventies, he fashions a complex archaeological metaphor out of autobiography, gathering up the fragments of his many stories to dig up his own being as a poet:

> This stone maul
> was found.
>
> In the field
> my grandfather
> thought
> was his
>
> my father
> thought was his
> . . .
> It is a stone
> old as the last
> Ice Age, the
> retreating/the
> recreating ice,
> the retreating

buffalo, the
retreating Indians
("Stone Hammer Poem")

Poetry becomes an ongoing set of field notes, signposts of where the poet has been. And this early poem turned out

> against my own anticipation, to be a prologue to a series of related poems ... I had in effect commenced a series of related poems that would in devious ways seek out the forms sufficient to the project (I leave it nameless) announced by Wordsworth and Whitman and rendered impossible by the history and thought and art of the twentieth century. Since the eloquence of failure may be the only eloquence remaining in this our time, I let these poems stand as the enunciation of how I came to a poet's silence. And I like to believe that the sequence of poems, announced in medias res as continuing, is, in its acceptance of its own impossibilities, completed.[23]

Increasingly intrigued with questions about form and structure in the long poem, he went on to publish nine sequential parts of *Completed Field Notes* (1989), where he creates his own poetics out of the Canadian prairies, challenging the centralized and centralizing idea of a unifyingly Canadian culture. He writes out of his place on the prairies, using autobiography to locate himself:

> *How do you grow a prairie town?*
> . . .
> *How do you grow a past*
> to live in

And in locating his context, he meets several writers of the Canadian tradition. There is Al Purdy, drinking in the revolving restaurant on top of the Chateau Lacombe. There are members of the *Tish* group, Bowering and Wah, their friends Ondaatje and bpNichol, and so many others.

In Kroetsch's poetry, there is always the intrusion of the locale, the omnipresence of field notes that consign the art to the soil of the prairies. When he lists the major achievements of western civilization, there are signposts that mark the presence of the local past:

> the absence of the Parthenon, not to mention the Cathédrale de Chartres
> the absence of psychiatrists
> the absence of sailing ships
> the absence of books, journals, daily newspapers and everything else but
>   the *Free Press Prairie Farmer*
> the absence of gallows (with apologies to Louis Riel)

In defining space and its absences, in marking out the landscapes that are filled with past stories waiting to be unraveled, Kroetsch creates poetry in the state of becoming, always aware of what can be and still is not.

It is impossible to posit prevailing poetic concepts that are equally applicable from sea even unto sea. A glance at some interesting poets of the present confirms the singular absence of defining characteristics.

In Ontario for example geographical transplants mix easily with native-born poets. Dionne Brand (1953–), originally from Trinidad, uses her poetry to present the alien experience of the immigrant in a supposedly tolerant new land; from her experience as a racial minority and as a lesbian, she writes cogently of immigrant dislocation. And George Elliott Clarke (1960–), originally from Nova Scotia, produces *Whylah Falls* (1990), a graphic account of an imagined Black community in Nova Scotia, using the rhythms of blues music with verse forms from the entire tradition of English literature. And then there are the poets born in Ontario: Steven Heighton (1961–) moves freely between prose and poetry, developing in his poetry a lyric voice that is unobtrusively eloquent; Christian Bök (1966–) experiments with sound and oral texts, making him a practitioner of radical poetry in the tradition of bpNichol; Stephanie Bolster (1969–) writes *White Stone: The Alice Poems* (1998), which considers the mythic and the actual figure of Alice Liddell Hargreaves, the model for Lewis Carroll's Alice in Wonderland.

In Montreal, Anne Carson (1950–), originally from Toronto and a classics professor at McGill University, re-creates the ancient worlds of her texts in thriving and vital new contexts. A devoted reader and scholar of the classics, she creates poems and prose works that challenge the assumptions of sexual roles and gender stereotypes. Sharing little with her Canadian predecessors and contemporaries, she looks back instead to the enduring and timeless power of the classics and draws inspiration too from such early modernists as Pound and Eliot.

And in Newfoundland, John Steffler (1947–), an Ontario-born transplant, writes of his adopted home in images that recall Pratt's early poetry. In a mingling of poetry and prose, *The Grey Islands* (1985) charts a newcomer's quest for solitude on an island off Newfoundland's coast. Steffler's only novel, *The Afterlife of George Cartwright* (1992), studies the complexities of European imperialism through the figure of the eighteenth-century soldier. Michael Crummey (1965–), who also published a work of fiction, *River Thieves* (2001), an account of the last known Beothuk, writes luminous poetry about nineteenth-century Newfoundland and Labrador and the worlds that still haunt the present.

More than 170 years after Susanna Moodie stepped onto Canadian soil, Canadian poetry is so variegated and so diverse, so resistant now to facile categorizations, that its richness and complexity become its salient traits. Atwood's Moodie lamented: "I am a word / in a foreign language." But that language was Canadian, and her lament is no longer applicable.

NOTES

1. Edward Hartley Dewart, *Selections from Canadian Poets* (Montreal: John Lovell, 1864) p. vii.
2. Dewart, *Selections from Canadian Poets*, p. xv.
3. Dewart, *Selections from Canadian Poets*, p. ix.
4. Carole Gerson and Gwendolyn Davies, eds., *Canadian Poetry from the Beginnings through the First World War* (Toronto: McClelland, 1994) p. 369.
5. Thomas D'Arcy McGee, quoted in "The Mental Outfit of the New Dominion," *Canadian Anthology*, ed. Carl F. Klinck and Reginald E. Watters, 3rd edn. (Toronto: Gage, 1974) p. 65.
6. Archibald Lampman, quoted in E. K. Brown, *On Canadian Poetry* (Toronto: Ryerson, 1943) pp. 91–2.
7. Malcolm Ross, *Poets of the Confederation* (Toronto: McClelland, 1960).
8. E. J. Pratt, "Canadian Poetry – Past and Present," *University of Toronto Quarterly* 8.1 (Oct. 1938): pp. 3–4.
9. Northrop Frye, ed., *The Collected Poems of E.J. Pratt* (Toronto: Macmillan, 1958) p. xxvi.
10. A. J. M. Smith, "Canadian Poetry – A Minority Report," *University of Toronto Quarterly* 8.2 (Jan. 1939): p. 138.
11. F. R. Scott, preface, *New Provinces* (Toronto: Macmillan, 1936) p. v.
12. E. K. Brown, "Letters in Canada: 1948," *University of Toronto Quarterly* 18.3 (April 1949): p. 256.
13. John Sutherland, "The Appendix to the Brief of the First Statement Press and *Northern Review* to the Royal Commission on the Arts," *Northern Review* 3.2 (Dec. 1949–Jan. 1950): p. 4.
14. Phyllis Webb, "On the Line," *Talking*, by Webb (Dunvegan: Quadrant, 1982) p. 66.
15. Irving Layton, foreword, *A Red Carpet for the Sun*, by Layton (Toronto: McClelland, 1959) n. pag.
16. Margaret Atwood, "Fifties Vic," *CEA Critic* 42.1 (Nov. 1979): p. 21.
17. Raymond Souster, "About This Book," preface, *New Wave Canada: The New Explosion in Canadian Poetry*, ed. Souster (Toronto: Contact, 1966) n. pag.
18. Daphne Marlatt, "Long as in Time? Steveston," *The Long Poem Anthology*, ed. Michael Ondaatje (Toronto: Coach House, 1979) p. 317.
19. Michael Ondaatje, foreword, *Beyond Remembering: The Collected Poems of Al Purdy*, ed. Purdy and Sam Solecki (Madeira Park: Harbour, 2000) p. 19.
20. W. H. New, *A History of Canadian Literature* (London: Macmillan, 1989) p. 240.
21. Michael Ondaatje, *The Collected Works of Billy the Kid* (Toronto: Anansi, 1970) p. 3.
22. Robert Bringhurst, *The Calling: Selected Poems 1970–1995* (Toronto: McClelland, 1995) p. 11.
23. Robert Kroetsch, author's note, *Completed Field Notes* (Toronto: McClelland, 1989) p. 269.

7
Fiction

MARTA DVORAK

Old World aesthetic codes in New World space

A loosely chronological overview of Canadian literary production reveals a pattern of development that is a constant in national literatures everywhere, albeit more visible in postcolonial societies, namely an initial period of imitation or emulation of metropolitan norms, then a configuration or shift towards assimilation, and finally – in a desire to forge a distinctive national culture – a reconfiguration or revaluation of that which had been considered marginal. Writers in Canada, like those in other settler societies such as Australia, New Zealand, or the United States, have had to raise questions about authenticity, namely the suitability of employing inherited or imported literary and artistic forms for a new environment and experience. Grounded in the socioeconomic, geopolitical space of eighteenth- and early nineteenth-century imperial relations, the earliest prose texts, generated by explorers, travelers, and settlers, were products of a British empire in economic and political expansion, manifest in the huge tides of emigration to Australia and then to British North America that occurred between 1805 and 1835.

Travel-writing, like essay writing, was avidly read by an intellectually curious English public geared towards the empirical, and partial to books dealing with geography, history, life writing, and social observation. The explosion of travel literature, memoir, and historical romance in this early colonial period was produced by a literate elite whose primary ideological identification was with the metropolitan center, which published and distributed their work. Many of these writers only resided temporarily in the colony. One notable example is the Englishwoman Frances Brooke, author of *The History of Emily Montague* (1769), a domestic romance written in the epistolary mode. Her novel is nevertheless considered to be the seminal work of Canadian English-language fiction, because it concerns itself with issues inescapable to the situation of British North America after the conquest of what is today Quebec, issues fundamental moreover to colonial/postcolonial literatures in general. Among them, we find the relations between the Native populations and the new settlers, the ambivalent relations of the latter with both the European imperial center and the more established Thirteen Colonies, and finally the friction of English/French relations that has haunted the country till the present day. Even the writer dubbed Canada's first native-born novelist, John Richardson, son of a British army officer, spent little time in Canada, moving instead from American military posts and colonies such as the West Indies to England, France, and Spain, where he fought as a mercenary. As a half-pay officer in London, he published his best-known historical romance, *Wacousta; or, The Prophecy: A Tale of the Canadas* (1832). Set in the Canadian wilderness, this account of the Indian uprisings, with its sensational descriptions of violence and savagery, targeted the European appetite for exoticist discourse, and the taste for the abnormal and monstrous that can be traced as a constant feature from the Jacobean revenge tragedy to the Gothic novel and Romanticism.

Central to the aesthetic codes of the Old World that were transplanted into the alien surroundings of New World space was the picaresque episodic mode adopted by Victorian writers of instalment fiction, which can be traced back to the Renaissance and its love of the labyrinthine. Adopted by the Romantics, shunned by the realist movement, and later rediscovered by postmodern writers also seeking to challenge balanced structures they deem to be mechanical, the loose, digressive style involves an arbitrary, nonhierarchical mixture of genres and a narrative technique of interwoven stories that reminds one of rhizomes – those rootless, tubular plants that send out horizontal, crisscrossing shoots at random.

Illustrative of early nineteenth-century travel-writing and immigrant writing are the hybrid texts in this picaresque, then baroque manner – published primarily for an English readership that considered the bush exotic – by Susanna Strickland Moodie and Catharine Parr Traill, two sisters belonging to the English gentry who emigrated to Canada in order to avoid dwindling economic and social circumstances. While that other frontier society – the newly emancipated United States – was beginning to produce a distinctive future-oriented literature rejecting the old order, upper-middle-class Canadian settlers like the Moodies were set on preserving their imported values based on family, education, property, and propriety. In the detailed reporting of landscape, customs, and language of *Roughing It in the Bush* (1852), set entirely in Canada, Moodie's writerly perspective is also predominantly that of her "dear, dear England."[1] The lofty, declamatory style is interpolated with transcriptions of the authentic speech of the writer's uneducated neighbors, in which the errors in pronunciation and grammar are emphasized the better to mock their pretensions to social equality. These interlocutors are notably often either "Yankees" or "late Loyalists," or Irish immigrants disinclined to acknowledge their former "betters." Interestingly, Moodie's writing nevertheless discloses a process of acculturation, in which new insights battle with old prejudices on issues such as work, class, and gender roles. Rooted in certain imported aesthetic models such as the novel of sensibility, Moodie's writing is moreover representative of the manner in which the sketch was developed in North America for purposes of humor and satire.

In satirical sketches written in the aftermath of the arrival in Nova Scotia of thousands of United Empire Loyalists, which were later collected to become the first Canadian bestseller, *The Clockmaker; or The Sayings and Doings of Samuel Slick of Slickville* (1836), Haliburton was the first fiction writer to use colloquial dialogue. Like Moodie and well before Twain (arguably drawing on the example of Anglo-Irish writers like Maria Edgeworth), he made astute use of regional dialects in these stories revolving round a brash Yankee pedlar. Intricate rhetorical devices were couched in the unpretentious language of the oral idiom, as in the following extended syllepsis concerning the Irish: "They are always in love or in liquor, or else in a row; they are the merriest shavers I ever seed."[2] Haliburton also developed the tall tale, that outlandish mode of storytelling that combines understatement and hyperbole, the ordinary and the extravagant, in a playful subversion of realism. His writing anticipates not only the outrageous stories of Twain and Leacock, but also the contemporary playful postmodern narratives of Robert Kroetsch.

The same fascination with social observation and history on the march can be detected in the popular historical romances of Rosanna Leprohon, an English Canadian woman married to a French Canadian and living in Montreal. Like Frances Brooke, Leprohon made use of the particular to describe the general, constructing a family history, notably in *Antoinette de Mirecourt* (1864), to stage the political and social turmoil surrounding the British conquest of New France. As Canada moved from the colonial period to post-Confederation, many writers of historical fiction continued to model themselves on European writers – notably Walter Scott, Ann Radcliffe, and Matthew Lewis – and went on representing historical events from the imperialist point of view. William Kirby's *The Golden Dog* (1877) and Gilbert Parker's *The Seats of the Mighty* (1896), both, like Brooke's novel, set in New France on the eve of the British Conquest, are but two examples. These novelists were among the few forging relationships between the two founding peoples which coexisted with little interaction within one state. Kirby's book, one of the few novels made available in translation to French-speaking Canadians, can be set in parallel with successful English translations such as that of Charles G. D. Roberts of *Les anciens Canadiens*, by Philippe Aubert de Gaspé. Alongside these texts viewing New World events from an Old World perspective, other writers were beginning to ground their work in the Canadian cultural matrix.

Emerging sense of national consciousness

It was not until 1931 that the British Parliament passed the Statute of Westminster recognizing the sovereignty of the dominions and renouncing its right to make laws for them, yet Sara Jeannette Duncan's novel of manners *The Imperialist* (1904) already timidly reflects Canada's emerging sense of national consciousness. Her only novel set in Canada, *The Imperialist* is arguably one of the first postcolonial works of fiction Canada can claim, in the sense that it partakes in a set of cultural values and representations that spill over the boundaries between national or even chronological categories. The novel, a social fresco revolving round the parallel love stories of a brother and sister, notably foregrounds the triangular turn-of-the-century tensions that existed between the young country, the former imperial center, and the already powerful United States, at a time when opinion was divided in Canada on matters of trade: a large part of the business class saw certain advantages in close economic ties with the United States, while the imperialists strived to establish a special trade agreement with England, whose free trade policy granted no preferential treatment to a loyal dominion devoid of the economies of scale of its dynamic neighbor. A prolific expatriate author as well as freelance correspondent, editorial writer, and columnist for major international newspapers, Duncan targeted the provincialism of the Canadian middle class with an acerbic wit reminiscent of Jane Austen or Edith Wharton, yet her deliberately digressive, intimate authorial voice is suffused with a celebratory sensuousness that anticipates Carol Shields. Writing in the genre of popular romance had not prevented Frances Brooke from dealing with serious political issues such as taxation and representation; similarly, the romantic novel allowed the cosmopolitan Duncan to construct a brilliant satire.

The novel criticizes the English sociopolitical system and sclerotic mindset, mocking institutions such as the House of Lords, the press, and an educational system deemed insufficiently secular, as well as a dearth of socioeconomic opportunity for the young. Lorne Murchison, a young lawyer who serves as authorial mouthpiece, points out the already dwindling economic prospects of an overpopulated England which cannot feed its own people. At the same time, Duncan systematically mocks Canadian provincialism, the tastes of a raw society that values size and ostentation.

The satire is often gentle, but at times also scathing, as in the ironic oxymoron labeling a Canadian businessman "an important non-entity."[3] Throughout the novel, the writer resorts to ironic devices like hyperbolic accumulation in order to ridicule the pretensions of a smug, parochial community:

> [Main Street's] appearance and demeanor would never have suggested that it was now the chief artery of a thriving manufacturing town, with a collegiate institute, eleven churches, two newspapers, and an asylum for the deaf and dumb, to say nothing of a fire department unsurpassed for organization and achievement in the Province of Ontario. (pp. 24–5)

In its views of the United States, as well, the novel cannot fail to appeal to contemporary sensibilities. Anticipating the debate surrounding the Free Trade Agreement and finally the North American Free Trade Agreement of the 1980s, Duncan's sympathetic protagonist urges his fellow citizens to actively resist American influence: "American enterprise, American capital, is taking rapid possession of our mines and our water-power, our oil areas and our timber limits" (p. 266). Yet the mention of a neighbor's "pretty feet in their American shoes" (p. 144) gleefully draws attention to the Canadian community's appetite for American goods. Again using oxymoron and antithesis, the young Canadian members of the learned professions or business class are described as "democrats who had never thrown off the monarch," with "less sophistication and polemic than their American counterparts, less stolid aggressiveness than their parallels in England," standing, in fact, for the development between the two: "they came of the new country but not of the new light" (p. 219). *The Imperialist* paves the way for Hugh MacLennan's subsequent didactic novels, *Two Solitudes* (1945), which explores the historical enmity between French and English-speaking Canadians, and *Each Man's Son* (1951), which records life in the mines of Cape Breton Island and is concerned primarily with national, and even regional, social and political issues. Duncan was a pathbreaker for intellectuals such as MacLennan, whose warnings against an economic, technological, and cultural takeover on the part of the United States (*The Watch That Ends the Night* [1959], *The Return of the Sphinx* [1967]) are to be considered against the backdrop of the Massey Commission's Report inciting the Canadian government to promote a national cultural production.

Literary realism

In spite of its playfully intrusive narratorial voice and digressive, episodic mode, and in spite of the idealism that underlies the corrective dimension of satirical writing, Duncan's style has often been classified under the category of literary realism. The leading figure of a narrower vein of realism that developed historically through the influence of Darwinism and positivism was Zola, who influenced not only his French but also his German counterparts. A multiple expatriate, Frederick Philip Grove – born in what is today Poland, and raised in Hamburg – began his writing career in Germany before emigrating to France, then the United States, and finally Canada, where he settled in the prairies of Manitoba and set out to represent the life of the pioneer immigrants arriving in unsettled territory and struggling with uncleared land and a hostile environment. His first novel in English, *Settlers of the Marsh* (1925), counted as one of the first works of prairie realism, was considered indecent and sold badly, and later novels such as *Our Daily Bread* (1928), *The Yoke of Life* (1930), and *Fruits of the Earth* (1933) – albeit with pastoral overtones – also depicted human failings and social flaws. As we can equally see from his essay "Realism in Literature," Grove apparently saw no contradiction in positing – as did the idealists – that his perception and representation of the world corresponded to an absolute, universal truth. In spite of a certain clumsiness in characterization and language, Grove won both critical and popular acclaim (the Lorne Pierce medal in 1934 and the Governor-General's Award in 1947).

The Canadian prairies have produced strong storytelling and innovative writing, ranging at the end of the twentieth century from Vanderhaeghe and Kroetsch to Aritha van Herk. Among the other earlier leading figures of the prairie novel were two writers very different in scope and approach: Sinclair Ross and W. O. Mitchell, both noteworthy short-story writers as well. Ross, a realist also concerned with social issues, has been likened to the French novelist François Mauriac, whom he admired. Ross is best known for his first novel *As for Me and My House* (1941). Unlike Grove's melodramatic writing, Ross's novel, set in the Dust Bowl of Saskatchewan during the drought and Depression, is a perfectly controlled representation of grey misery and despair. The focus on the domestic sphere, against the backdrop of a pitiless nature and equally implacable economic system, is all the more moving as it is quiet and understated. Later publications such as *Sawbones Memorial* (1974) took the shape of modernist interior monologue.

Also published in the forties was *Who Has Seen the Wind* (1947) by W. O. Mitchell, set in rural Alberta. The author of almost a dozen bestselling novels as well as being an essayist, fiction editor, author of popular radio and television scripts (notably the CBC series *Jake and the Kid*) and short stories, Mitchell, rather like Mark Twain, possesses a sensuous regional language that celebrates the land and its community. His effortless use of the oral idiom and its authentic imagery and power of invention – which he termed the "magic lies"[4] of folklore – as well as his control of structure and rhythm, and his ease in marrying the familiar with the incongruous, place him in line with the best comic writers. The idealism and sentimentality of Mitchell's work corresponded to the tastes of the forties and fifties, and then went out of fashion. Today, there has been a renewal of interest, along with a rediscovery of writers from other regions such as the Franco-Manitoban Gabrielle Roy and Nova Scotian Ernest Buckler.

Modernism

Mitchell's writing illustrates how literary realism was still the most powerful current in Canadian writing at a time when modernism was already at its height in Europe and the United States. It is always interesting to note a region's responses to major aesthetic currents, its artists' modes of conforming to such movements, transgressing them, or innovating within them. Modernism and its subsidiary tendencies such as surrealism and formalism notably came belatedly and sporadically to Canada. Writer and critic Robert Kroetsch has playfully remarked that Canadian writing evolved directly from Victorian to postmodern, and he is right to suggest that Morley Callaghan, the Canadian novelist and short-story writer often cited as briefly belonging to the expatriate circle of modernists in Paris, does not entirely conform to the common definitions of the term. Callaghan's writing (*Strange Fugitive* [1928] is his first novel) can aptly be described as realist, and does not partake in the innovative formal experiments of modernists such as James Joyce, Virginia Woolf, Gertrude Stein, or William Faulkner. Nor is it particularly self-reflexive or iconoclastic with respect to literary conventions concerning narrative voice, chronology, causality, or closure. Yet it does subscribe to the early modernist aesthetic of repetition, even monotony, of simple spoken English (such as Hemingway's), and it also reflects the interest in psychological activities that we find in pre-modernist and modernist writers such as Henry James and Scott Fitzgerald.

Other Canadian writers display different facets of modernist aesthetic practices, such as Mavis Gallant, Mordecai Richler, and A. M. Klein, as well as Elizabeth Smart (notably her meditative and plotless prose poem on illegitimate passion *By Grand Central Station I Sat Down and Wept* [1945]), Ernest Buckler, and Sheila Watson. Essayist, journalist, and scriptwriter as well as novelist, Richler was long the best-known Canadian writer on the English-speaking international scene. In the early texts (*The Acrobats* [1954] was his first novel) written during or soon after his brief

stay in Paris among other expatriate writers such as Mavis Gallant and
James Baldwin, or during his subsequent twenty years in England, some
critics detect the influences of American modernists such as Hemingway, Dos
Passos, or Fitzgerald, while others perceive the existential stances of Sartre or
Malraux. Many of his works, such as *The Apprenticeship of Duddy Kravitz*
(1959), represent with remarkable authenticity of voice as well as infectious
humor the experience of growing up in a working-class Jewish neighborhood
in Montreal, on the margins of both the powerful Anglo-Saxon Protestant
community which still controlled the affairs of the province, and the francophone Catholic community which was to take up the reins after the Quiet
Revolution and the founding of the Parti Québécois in the 1960s. From his
first article in the Canadian magazine *Maclean's* entitled "How I Became an
Unknown with My First Novel" (1958), on the impossibility of earning a
living as a writer in Canada, Richler established himself as the most caustic
satirist of his generation, evocative of Evelyn Waugh or the vitriolic French
novelist Céline. In books like *A Choice of Enemies* (1957), *The Incompara-
ble Atuk* (1963), or *Cocksure* (1968), he delighted in debunking the myths of
his time. His later novels, such as *Joshua Then and Now* (1980) or *Barney's
Version* (1997) dazzled readers with a dozen labyrinthine narrative lines interwoven with virtuosity, as well as with their vast cultural scope ranging
from literature to ice hockey. His irreverence outraged the middle-class Jewish community, as well as the larger Quebec community, which accused him
of presenting Quebec as a racist, tribal society.

Mavis Gallant, author of *Green Water, Green Sky* (1959) and *A Fairly
Good Time* (1970), also expatriated herself in order to earn her living as a
writer, but, unlike Richler, never went back to Canada. Settled in Paris since
the 1950s, she is recognized internationally as one of the best short-story
writers in the English language. The modernist mode of Gallant's texts –
which are multilayered, polygeneric, and open-ended constructions based
on clusters of images, points in time, memory, or perception – calls to mind
the pointillist technique of Katherine Mansfield at her best. Resonating in
the indirect modes of metaphor and irony, the language is always sharp
and clear. Gallant's fascination with formal effects, with the mechanisms
of language and those of the writing process itself is analogous with that
of British Columbian writer Sheila Watson, author of *The Double Hook*
(1959), judged to be the first truly modernist Canadian novel and often
compared to T. S. Eliot's *The Wasteland*. The writing, intensely preoccupied with language as visual sign and aural music, is dislocated – rather
like Gertrude Stein's – through a spatialized form which relies on such techniques as repetition, ellipsis, and nominal sentences, as well as a Faulknerian
privileging of image over discourse and inner vision over external reality.

Watson's biblical/mythological rhythms and allusions, recourse to foreign words, and lexical dislocations and word play – techniques that Joyce and Eliot were notoriously fond of – are equally to be found in *The Second Scroll* (1951), the only novel written by the poet A. M. Klein. Brought to Canada from the Ukraine as a child by orthodox Jewish parents, Klein grew up in the already cosmopolitan environment of Montreal, and his committed body of work stimulated other writers such as Matt Cohen, Mordecai Richler, and Leonard Cohen to write about the experiences of the Jewish community. Written after a trip to the newly created state of Israel, his novel traces the Jewish people's wanderings throughout Europe, North Africa, and Canada in search of a new homeland. In a manner that is reminiscent of Eliot and of the structural Homeric parallels of Joyce, Klein fuses oriental and western cultures, and draws on intricate literary and religious intertextuality, based mainly on the five books of the Old Testament termed the Pentateuch.

If the key notions governing modernist production are subjectivity and perception, as well as a preoccupation with the mechanisms of the creative process, then among its key literary figures is undeniably Ernest Buckler, whom Margaret Atwood called "one of the pathbreakers of the modern Canadian novel."[5] He studied at Dalhousie University and the University of Toronto alongside writers and thinkers such as Hugh MacLennan, Marshall McLuhan, Northrop Frye, and Harold Innis, who all elaborated theories on national culture, yet Buckler distanced himself from the movement yoking art to nationalistic purposes that was gathering momentum in the early 1950s. Although he had already produced countless short stories, radio plays, and essays in the 1940s, the elegiac first novel by this writer-farmer from Nova Scotia, *The Mountain and the Valley* (1952), was published alongside of Hemingway's *The Old Man and the Sea* and Steinbeck's *East of Eden*. A trained philosopher who grew up in a bookless society, Buckler was preoccupied by the manner in which reality manifests itself to our senses, and with the nature of Being itself. The writer's two novels (*The Cruelest Month* was published in 1963) and fictional memoir *Ox Bells and Fireflies* (1968) – a hybrid text blending autobiographical writing with contemplative prose poems, essays, anecdotes, portraits, and sketches – all disrupt readerly expectations of linearity and story. Yet readers find immensely satisfying his celebration of domesticity in an incantatory, metaphorical style that explores the relationship between words and things. They also find attractive his strong ethical vision, questioning the place of the individual within society, and exploring the social ties that bind the community together. Buckler's texts are in fact a crossroads between the old and the new, connecting Canadian literature to international modernism, yet paving the way for certain postmodern concerns. These range from epistemological preoccupations to an aesthetic grounded in literary and linguistic theory.

Postmodernism

Such overlapping disproves the notion that modernism has been neatly buried by postmodernism (to take the example of just one author, Helen Weinzweig's two novels, *Passing Ceremony* and *Basic Black with Pearls*, published in 1973 and 1980 respectively, are resolutely modernist). Postmodernism involves a continuation of modernism as well as a division from it. In a prolongation of modernist production, already characterized by discontinuity and fragmentation, postmodern writers interrogate notions of authority and conventions of constraint, their reassessment tending to value forms of diversity and plurality. Yet many postmoderns have distanced themselves from a certain hermeticism and the privileging of "high" art over popular culture characteristic of a large proportion of modernist work. This involves a renewed interest in narrative – the writer as storyteller – and a blending of the high literary tradition of print culture with the folk tales, tall tales, and local legends of popular oral culture. Their interrogation of the absolute or universal also involves a grounding of the artwork in the historical, social, and political society from which it emerges. This can account for that trademark of contemporary Canadian artistic production: the double discourse of irony that serves, as critics such as Linda Hutcheon have argued, to subvert the patterns and conventions of dominant culture from within. Simultaneously, in the light of the ground-breaking work of historians such as W. H. Carr, who have challenged the widely accepted notions of the objectivity and scientism of history, there has been a return to, and subversion of, historical fiction, life writing, and the *bildungsroman* (the latter nudged back towards its original eighteenth-century focus on the sociocultural forces that shape the protagonist, and with a further subversive element: women in central positions as narrators and as subjects). Since postmodern writers privilege the dynamics of reception, the presentation that follows will be loosely structured round some of the subsidiary tendencies of Canadian postmodernism, namely realism, magic realism, the neo-Gothic, fantasy or near-future fiction, historiographical fiction, and irony.

Many writers in the 1950s, as we have seen, still could not make a living from their fiction alone, or needed to go abroad in order to establish careers for themselves, in spite of institutions such as the Canadian Broadcasting Corporation or the National Film Board that had been set up during the 1930s to foster domestic cultural production. But the new mood of self-awareness and pride of the sixties and seventies, with the advent of

Centennial celebrations, the recent creation of the Canada Council for the Arts (1957), and the government's commitment to subsidize the arts nationwide, as well as a newly interested domestic readership, was accompanied by an astonishing frenzy of literary production by major writers such as Robertson Davies, Margaret Laurence, Margaret Atwood, Matt Cohen, Rudy Wiebe, Austin Clarke, Leonard Cohen, Michael Ondaatje, Timothy Findley, and Robert Kroetsch. These authors, albeit in different ways, were all aware of their responsibilities as writers, conscious of a cultural continuum, a heritage that dates back over 6,000 years.

This sense of mission coincides with an aesthetic mood that denies the existence of stable narratives. Generic instability is undeniably a fundamental characteristic of postmodern writing. Writers such as Atwood, Ondaatje, Leon Rooke, Carol Shields, and Aritha van Herk, to name but a few, have blended (auto)biography and fiction, novel and short story, prose and poetry, the linguistic and pictorial media, or even fiction, nonfiction, theory, and criticism (see van Herk, *Places Far from Ellesmere: A Geografictione* [1990], *In Visible Ink: Crypto-frictions* [1991], and *Mavericks* [2002]). Ondaatje's *Coming through Slaughter* (1976), the story of a legendary Black New Orleans jazz musician, Shields's *The Stone Diaries* (1993) and *Larry's Party* (1997), fictive explorations of the limits of (auto)biography; Leonard Cohen's provocative *Beautiful Losers* (1966); and Atwood's *The Blind Assassin* (2000) all contain intertexts from, or multiple allusions to, mass culture: comic books, advertising, pop songs, folk tales, formula fiction, or even recipes.

Contesting master narratives

The dominant mode of historiographical fiction that critics have identified effectively shatters the borders between history, biography, and story. The Canadian predilection for historical fiction previously alluded to was already manifest in the works of realist writers from the Atlantic provinces like Hugh MacLennan (*Barometer Rising* [1941]) and Thomas Raddall (*His Majesty's Yankees* [1942], *The Nymph and the Lamp* [1950]). In the period since the 1980s, Canada has witnessed an explosion in historical novels: George Bowering's *Burning Water* (1980), Jane Urquhart's *The Whirlpool* (1986) and *Away* (1993), Guy Vanderhaeghe's *The Englishman's Boy* and Margaret Atwood's *Alias Grace* (both 1996), or Richard Cumyn's *The Sojourn* and Frances Itani's *Deafening* (both 2003). Such publications often subvert traditional understandings of history and biography, reexamining and contesting the totalizing master narratives of our western culture, both ancient and modern. More often than not, these books reexamine historico-political events that have become New World myths, revolving around issues of territory, (de)possession, and appropriation, and interrogating the Eurocentric assumptions that have been offered and accepted as objective truth, or even as a given.

The ancient master narratives that are contested in such novels include the creation stories revolving round the Garden of Eden and Noah's Ark. Findley's *Not Wanted on the Voyage* (1984) blends historical and ahistorical writing, opening onto an indeterminate time-space inhabited by dragons migrating south and an authoritarian, Christianized Noah and his wife, preparing a banquet for a divine Guest and his retinue, terrified at the endless prohibitions regarding the menu. More recently, Thomas King's *Green Grass, Running Water* (1993) subverts western society's Judeo-Christian biblical heritage by blending it irreverently with homologous North American Native mythology. Parallel stories about the origins of the world are based alternately, in endless variations, on Genesis and the legend of First Woman, and, like the four Gospels of the New Testament, there are four interwoven stories. The manner in which the Lone Ranger, King's magical Native protagonist, parrots the Genesis story interrogates Eurocentric assumptions and suggests how white discourse has been imposed and superimposed upon Native culture.

Such interrogation is also found in the fiction centered on the twentieth century's world wars and Holocaust, the master narratives of our modern times. Alongside A.M. Klein's *The Second Scroll* (1951), already discussed, we can mention Findley's *The Wars* (1977), a ferocious chronicle of the destruction of a whole generation between 1914 and 1918, and his *Famous Last Words* (1981), which causes purely fictional characters to interact with historical figures such as Ezra Pound, Edward VII, Wallis Simpson, or Charles Lindbergh against a backdrop of pre-war fascism. There is also the Japanese Canadian perspective of World War II, with its accompanying evacuation and internment, unveiled by Joy Kogawa in the poetic, hauntingly devastating *Obasan* (1981). Dennis Bock's *The Ash Garden* (2001) stages the dropping of the atom bomb on Hiroshima through three intertwined narratives. We can also cite Leonard Cohen's "hagiography" of the Iroquois saint and martyr Kateri Tekakwitha in *Beautiful Losers* (1966), or Rudy Wiebe's fictional documentaries. In *The Temptations of Big Bear* (1973), Wiebe rewrites from the Native point of view the nineteenth-century white conquest of the West, as the Mounted Police, railroads, missionaries, government agents, and surveyors poured in and the buffalo died out. *The Scorched-Wood People* (1977) stages the resistance and rebellion of the Métis and their ambivalent leader Louis Riel. Wiebe's *A Discovery of Strangers* (1994) relates from the Native perspective Franklin's disastrous search for the Northwest Passage, and

Sweeter Than All the World (2001) casts a new gaze on both the Reformation and the Mennonite diaspora. Among other attempts to rewrite the past are notably Morley Callaghan's *A Time for Judas* (1983), Matt Cohen's *The Spanish Doctor* (1984), and Brian Moore's *Black Robe* (1985).

This development continues unabated in the twenty-first century, with Urquhart's *The Stone Carvers* and Sandra Birdsell's *The Russlander* (both 2001), and Austin Clarke's *The Polished Hoe* (2002). Among the writers who continue to question the nature of historical inquiry are Guy Vanderhaeghe, Wayne Johnston, and Katherine Govier. Prairie writer Vanderhaeghe, a trained historian, won the Governor-General's Award for *The Englishman's Boy* (1996), a historical novel interweaving a nineteenth-century massacre of Natives with the early twentieth-century Hollywood dream industry. His equally meticulously researched and magnificently written novel *The Last Crossing* (2002), set on the northwestern frontier in the 1870s, stages the encounter of the Blackfoot, the Northwest Mounted Police, and American whiskey traders, through the historical persona of a mixed-race scout. Wayne Johnston's novel *The Navigator of New York* (2002) relates the early twentieth-century race to the North Pole, focusing on an almost-forgotten rival of Robert Peary's. Johnston had already demonstrated that he had no qualms about invention in his controversial, artistically free biography of Newfoundland premier Joey Smallwood, *The Colony of Unrequited Dreams* (1998). Like Johnston, Katherine Govier emphasizes the artist's right to invent, pointing out that her historical protagonists are literary characters. Her novel *Creation* (2002) centers on a Labrador summer in the life of the painter Audubon.

Such fictional documentaries strive to show that values such as national ideals tend to be naturalized or accepted under the rubric of accuracy, and that such acceptance needs to be challenged. The writerly desire is almost militant in Atwood's *Alias Grace* (1996), or in Bowering's *Burning Water* (1980), which rewrites the story of George Vancouver in a contrapuntal manner that juxtaposes reminiscences of the "other George," the "realist novelist" himself,[6] with the deeds of the English navigator who first explored the Pacific coast of North America in the eighteenth century. Bowering inserts certain constructions containing powerful referential values that point to "real" life, setting the stage for an overlapping of subjectivity and objectivity, personal and national identity, verifiable historical figure and fictional persona, past event and present gaze, in effect self-reflexively fusing the reading and writing processes. The postmodern converging of autobiography, biography, documentary, and fiction within a single fictional space occurs as intensely, if not more so, in Ondaatje's *The English Patient* (1992) or *Running in the Family* (1982), in which the writer posits the equivalence between story and history, declaring that "[t]ruth disappears with history."[7] Like Wayne Johnston, whose fictional liberties with historical figures raised controversy, Ondaatje claims the artist's right to subsume public history by private memory and aesthetic considerations.

The realist tradition in contemporary writing

A large number of Canadian writers have continued to operate within the conventions of realism. As examples of this trend, critics cite authors such as Margaret Laurence (*The Stone Angel* [1964] was her first novel), one of the major figures of the literary revival of the 1960s and 1970s, and Robertson Davies. In spite of the novels he published in the 1950s and his significant contribution to drama in the 1940s and 1950s (notably the Salterton trilogy), it was not until the 1970s that Davies gained international recognition, particularly with his Deptford trilogy, *Fifth Business*, *The Manticore*, and *The World of Wonders*, which shifts from third-person narration to fictive autobiography or confession. Admired by American writers such as John Irving, and reminiscent of the French author Victor Hugo's splendid writing, the works are elegant, subtly ironic, and erudite, filled with fascinating discussions on subjects ranging from Jungian archetypes and Renaissance iconography to Rabelaisian carnival and female incontinence. Critics also point to the diverse forms of social realism of Jane Rule (the lesbian *Desert of the Heart* [1964]), of David Adams Richards (the naturalist depiction of the poor underclass of New Brunswick in *The Coming of Winter* [1974], *Mercy among the Children* [2000], and *River of the Brokenhearted* [2003]), and of Marian Engel, Carol Shields, or Austin Clarke. Clarke, who arrived in Toronto from Barbados to study economics and political science, worked as a journalist, industrial photographer, cultural attaché, director of Caribbean broadcasting in Barbados, and professor of Black Studies at numerous American colleges such as Yale. Although he published his first novels in the early sixties (*The Survivors of the Crossing* [1964] and *Amongst Thistles and Thorns* [1965]), it was his short-story collections and his Toronto trilogy (*The Meeting Point* [1967], *Storm of Fortune* [1971], and *The Bigger Light* [1975]) that established his literary reputation, with their stark depiction of immigration and exile, involving a faithful transcription of idiolect. Dubbed "one of the two or three most talented black writers in North America" by Norman Mailer, Clarke was awarded the prestigious Giller Prize for *The Polished Hoe* (2002).

Writers such as Laurence, Davies, Engel, Shields, and Clarke have been termed realists by many critics, whether their realism be of a domestic or of a political order. They nonetheless operate in a subtle, highly skilled manner that has more aptly been described as deceptive realism. They subvert the details of dailiness with unreliable narrators, shifting points of view, and a destabilizing manipulation of time so as to involve the reader in the construction of the text. Laurence's Manawaka cycle (four novels and a short-story collection), loose configurations of the *bildungsroman*, are suffused in this manner with the repressive Puritan spirit of prairie small towns and their Scots-Presbyterian founders, yet her book vibrates with empathy for those who had to forge a community in the face of hostile conditions. Using visual elements like film, typeface, and layout, Laurence captures the workings of consciousness and the acquisition of language. Richard Wright's *Clara Callan* (2001), and Bonnie Burnard's family saga *A Good House* (1999), with its deceptively simple writing and comforting domesticity, traces the landmarks of North American social evolution and revolution from never-locked kitchen doors and the birth of television to the growth of the suburbs, the rise of second-wave feminism and student protests, and finally to more contemporary questionings of gender roles and sexual orientation. The meticulous descriptions of pedestrian objects grounded in enumeration and sensual detail evoke Shields, or short-story writers Alice Munro and Bronwen Wallace.

Modes of the marvelous

Other writers functioning within the modes of the marvelous or mythopoeic have corroborated Stephen Slemon's observation that cultures situated at the fringes of mainstream literary traditions seem to generate works in the genre of magic realism.[8] As Nabokov's early short stories show, magic realism was already one expression of modernism and surrealism in the first half of the twentieth century, but it undeniably exploded in the 1960s in Latin America and the Caribbean, and is operative in other new literatures. A great deal of contemporary fiction produced in Canada draws on the coexistence of two opposing kinds of fictional worlds. A recent example is the Booker Prize-winning novel by Yann Martel, *Life of Pi* (2001), which enchanted the British jury with the fantastic fable of an adolescent boy from Bombay marooned in a lifeboat with only nonhuman fellow travelers, including a hungry Bengal tiger. More established authors such as Findley, Urquhart, Atwood, Leon Rooke (*The Magician in Love* [1981]), and Thomas King, for instance, have long had a strong predilection for fantasy, or for the extraordinary to emerge quietly out of the apparently ordinary. In her first novel, *The Edible Woman* (1969), Margaret Atwood shifts the narratorial voice from first person to third person to convey the alienation of her protagonist. In *Surfacing* (1972), the apparently realistic story explodes when the protagonist describes her boyfriend coming to join her in bed. Dream, visions, and the fantastic erupt and transform the banal in the disturbing sentence, "I feign sleep and he feels his way into the room, stealthy as moss, and unzips his human skin."[9]

With *Headhunter* (1993), Findley rewrites Conrad's famous novella, transposing it into urban Canada, with the opening sentence:

> On a winter's day, while a blizzard raged through the streets of Toronto, Lilah Kemp inadvertently set Kurtz free from page 92 of *Heart of Darkness*. Horror-stricken, she tried to force him back between the covers. The escape took place at the Metropolitan Toronto Reference Library, where Lilah Kemp sat reading beside the rock pool.[10]

A thriller with a strong neo-Gothic strain, on the fringes of near-future fiction such as Burgess's *A Clockwork Orange*, *Headhunter* features characters that are neither real nor imaginary, neither dead nor alive. In an apocalyptic mode, the author explores the boundaries between fact and fiction, and between reason and madness, particularly the self-destructive madness of a postindustrial society which sends its sons to die or to be devoured by discreet pedophiliac networks.

The neo-Gothic current is powerful in the contemporary Canadian artistic scene, including the plastic arts, performance art, body art, and cinema, which since the end of the 1960s have been interrogating gender roles, normality, and the relationship between the body and the subject. David Cronenberg's monstrous or mutant bodies epitomize the current of anglophone cinema working within the fantastic or grotesque modes. Similarly, neo-Gothic writing is perhaps best illustrated by Barbara Gowdy's phantasmagoric narratives peopled with monstrous characters exploring multiple forms of social deviance (notably *Mister Sandman*, or the story on necrophilia "We So Seldom Look on Love" that inspired Lynn Stopkewich's first long feature film, *Kissed*), or subversively staging an apocalyptic world of giant elephants (*The White Bone* [1998]).*The Romantic* (2003), a superbly written love story housing an epistemological investigation, is the first to move away from the modes of the quietly sinister or fantastic. We find powerful strains of the neo-Gothic in Findley's first novel as well, *The Last of the Crazy People* (1967), which slowly constructs the sinister atmosphere of a family destroyed by madness, in Susan Musgrave's surreal *The Charcoal Burners* (1980), Anne Michaels' *Fugitive Pieces* (1996), or Ann-Marie MacDonald's *Fall on Your Knees* (1996), as well as in works by Matt

Cohen and Audrey Thomas (not to mention the later texts by Munro) that are suffused with a dramatic, almost palpable undercurrent of oppression, terror or violence.

Near-future fiction with undercurrents of horror include MacLennan's *Voices in Time* (1980) and Atwood's *The Handmaid's Tale* (1985) and *Oryx and Crake* (2003). All three are set in the future after the devastation of civilization as we know it, and involve a reconstruction of the past (or the reader's present in the first two) through various documents such as tapes which have been discovered. MacLennan and Atwood – the former more overtly didactic than the latter – draw on a utopian/dystopian tradition which includes the prolific writer James de Mille (*A Strange Manuscript Found in a Copper Cylinder* [1888]), alongside writers such as H. G. Wells, William Morris, Huxley, and Orwell. They resort to the temporal and spatial defamiliarization of the genre to target the North American sociopolitical mechanisms and mindset of their contemporary readership.

Gentler, nonmilitant forms of magic realism are discernible in the works of Urquhart, who has been compared to the New Zealand filmmaker Jane Campion. Urquhart opens her first novel *The Whirlpool* (1986) with the scene of the poet Browning dying in Venice and dreaming of Shelley drowning. She then projects the reader into a story set in the watery zone of Niagara Falls, site of battles between Canada and the United States during the war of 1812, and border between the visible and the invisible. The novel is a surreal interrogation of the irrational, of language, and of writing. In *Changing Heaven* (1990), a Canadian academic goes to Yorkshire to write a book on the environment that generated the Gothic *Wuthering Heights*. She finds there the ghosts of Emily Brontë and of an aeronaut killed by her lover: a "real" love story weaves itself around a backdrop of voices from beyond the tomb. *Away* (1993), a family epic, begins in Ireland in 1840, with a young Irish woman haunted by a shipwrecked sailor who has died in her arms surrounded by floating cabbages and silver teapots. As well as being a story of migration and exile, it is also a story of metamorphosis, of Gaelic legends, and of enchantment.

The strongly connected mythopoeic mode is also a powerful contemporary current, for, as Findley has remarked, "a myth is not a lie, as such, but only the truth in larger shoes."[11] The mode, reminiscent of writers such as Faulkner, is grounded in the legend, folk tale, and tall tale. It allows postmodern writers such as David Arnason, of Icelandic origin (*The Pagan Wall* [1992]), to play formally with the limits of realism. It appears in the works of Native writers such as Thomas King and Tomson Highway (*Kiss of the Fur Queen* [1998]), but also in the novels of Jack Hodgins (particularly his first novel, *The*

Invention of the World [1977]) that are set mainly in the isolated rural and logging communities of Vancouver Island where old-timers told tales of the old days when men would steal a church with a tractor. Hodgins's writing contains the savory language that accompanies contingent experience ("You smell like a campfire that's been doused with horse's piss"[12]) or the hyperbolic, incongruous precision that is the cornerstone of the tall tale ("You'd think I was a one-legged killer with three glass eyes"[13]). Hodgins's tall-tale techniques that are the stuff of local legends – hundreds of thirty-pound salmon vying to crowd into a fisherman's boat, or the rebuilding of a hotel in one night – are to be found in the works of other Western writers such as Vanderhaeghe or Kroetsch. The combination of the fantastic and realist in Kroetsch's *What the Crow Said* (1978) anticipates the extravagant first chapter of Salman Rushdie's *The Satanic Verses* (1988) describing Gibreel's magic descent from a jumbo jet that has exploded in flight. Kroetsch's novel, in contrast, depicts a magical ascent and a descent that is only too natural. The protagonist Joe Lightning captures an eagle, but is overpowered, hangs on too long, and before he knows it, is looking down on the town of Big Indian.

A combination of laconic understatement with extravagant exaggeration is characteristic of a large part of postmodern Canadian writing, acknowledged by most critics as fundamentally ironic. With its Rabelaisian low style, Leonard Cohen's *Beautiful Losers* (1966) deflates inherited codes of decorum and high style, and creates a Canadian brand of farcical fantasy. Cohen's manner of dipping into colonial hagiography is notably irreverent. His narrator describes Jesuit missionaries proselytizing in New France, and depicts one priest sucking the toes of the saintly Iroquois virgin Kateri Tekakwitha, ostensibly to warm them, but with increasing onomatopoeic gusto ("Gobblegobblegobblewoggle. Slurp"), all the while that ironic parallels are being made with figures sacred to Christian mythos ("He was kneeling as Jesus had kneeled before a naked foot," and "Francis had done the same for lepers"), which are deflated even further through the bathetic use of anachronism: "his tongue going like a windshield wiper."[14] Inscribed in a long tradition of contestatory writing, the comic effects produced are similar to those produced by major satirical writers throughout the ages advocating inversions of values, such as Swift, Byron, Jarry, or Genet. At the core of the carnivalesque laughter is a bedrock of social criticism intended to challenge the dominant world-view with respect to religious institutions, political movements, or American corporate and popular culture generally. The criticism, foregrounding an axiological gap between Madison Avenue and the Canadian community, oscillates between frontal attack, designed to generate moral indignation, and playful parody, designed to produce detached amusement.

Demographic shifts

Leonard Cohen, poet and singer-composer as well as novelist, was born in Montreal into a Jewish family with roots in Lithuania, a family which gave Canada a chief rabbi as well as the founder of the *Jewish Times*, and which transmitted the legends and stories of Jewish culture. A large part of literature in Canada has long been generated by first-generation or second-generation immigrants coming to terms with displacement and relocation; however, in the final decades of the twentieth century, with one-fifth of the current Canadian population being foreign-born, the phenomenon is qualitatively different from that of preceding generations. Cohen, along with many authors already mentioned, is illustrative of the explosion in authorial voices from groups that have distanced themselves from the dominant Anglo-Saxon, then Germanic, as well as French, sociocultural communities[15] which, until the end of World War II, had almost exclusive access to publishing and distribution. The evolution of the literary scene reflects a radical demographic shift from 1867 (when ethnocultural groups other than English or French made up only eight percent of the population) to the beginning of the twenty-first century (when they account for one-third of the population, with a high proportion of Asians – almost half of the total immigration).[16] Marlyn's *Under the Ribs of Death* (1957) was among the first novels to give a voice to ethnocultural communities – in this case Central European – outside the mainstream. Entry to the canon was opened to writers of South Asian origin when Ondaatje won three Governor-General's Awards for poetry and fiction in the 1970s. When these writers are allophones (that is, authors speaking neither of the official languages) they sometimes continue to write in their mother tongue, and are subsequently translated. Josef Skvorecky, Nobel Prize nominee, novelist, and screenplay writer known for his work with the filmmaker Milos Forman, published *Dvorak in Love* originally in Czech after emigrating to Canada in 1968 and founding 68 Publishers, a publishing house targeting the Czech diaspora. He went on to win the Governor-General's Award in 1984 for *The Engineer of Human Souls*. Saad Elkadhem (*The Ulysses Trilogy* [1988]) continues to write in Arabic, his fiction appearing for the most part in bilingual editions. Other writers such as Ashok Mathur (*Loveruage* [1994]) learn to manipulate linguistic and textual codes with virtuosity. Mathur's "Thumbs, a poemnovel-in-progress," published in three extracts in the journal *Canadian Literature* in 1992,[17] deconstructs genre and syntax, playing with acoustical images and even punctuation and typographical conventions. Still others, such as Dionne Brand (*In Another Place, Not Here* [1996], *At the Full and Change of the Moon* [1999]), Marlene Nourbese Philip (*Looking for Livingstone: An Odyssey* of *Silence* [1991]), Ven Begamudré (*Van de Graaf Days* [1993]) or Cyril Dabydeen (*Dark Swirl* [1988]), are anglophone upon arrival. Through their schooling, still modeled on the standard British educational curriculum, they share many of the western cultural and literary markers of native-born Canadians of their generation. The cosmopolitan voices originate from all corners of the globe: Italy (Nino Ricci), the Caribbean (Dionne Brand, Austin Clarke, Neil Bissoondath, André Alexis), South East Asia (Ondaatje, Rohinton Mistry, Ven Begamudré, Shyam Selvadurai, Anita Rau Badami), China (Sky Lee, Wayson Choy, Evelyn Lau, Larissa Lai), or Japan (Joy Kogawa, Hiromi Goto, Kerri Sakamoto). Many, like M. G. Vassanji (*The Book of Secrets* [1994]) and Cyril Dabydeen, come from multiple diasporic backgrounds, brought up as Indians in predominantly African environments. Thomas King attributes the explosion of First Nations writing to the inspiration provided by the Pulitzer Prize awarded to Scott Momaday for *House Made of Dawn* in 1969. It was the first Pulitzer to be awarded to a Native author.

These texts, ranging from the elegiac to the ironic, are often largely or partially autobiographical, seeking to communicate personal, familial, or community experience as significant social event. They have contributed to the spectacular return of the self as subject and object of narration. The younger writers newly arrived on the literary scene often achieve acclaim with their first novel (Ricci's first novel, *Lives of the Saints* [1990], won the Governor-General's Award, Sakamoto's *The Electrical Field* won the 1999 Commonwealth Writers' Prize for Best First Book, and André Alexis's *Childhood* [1998] won the Chapters/Books in Canada First Novel Award). Many of them revolve round the dynamics of racial domination, economic and cultural dispossession, social fragmentation, and identity. Since a literature of resistance wishes to be accessible to a wide audience, the writing can be quite conventional. Yet many of the authors dip into their heritage, fracture conventional discourse, and develop dialect representation, offering an alternative to the stylistic and topical conventions of western literature. Among the fresh discursive strategies that can be isolated in the opening chapter of *Childhood* is enumeration, which Alexis uses paradoxically. The usual amplificatory function of the list – in this case the Trinidadian narrator-protagonist's only too repetitive timetable – actually foregrounds an existential paucity, even absence. Another example of imaginative intercultural voices is that of Peter Oliva, whose second novel, *The City of Yes* (1999), oscillating between Japan and Canada, stages a collision of cultures, languages, worlds, and perceptions of the world.

In one of the most urban societies in the world, where a majority of immigrants immediately gravitate to the cities of Toronto and Vancouver, a large part of Canadian fiction has surprisingly been set in the small town or rural area, with their accompanying symbolic resonances. It was only towards the end of the twentieth century that a strong movement of urban writing began to emerge, reflecting a brash energy and a new cosmopolitan sensibility. Douglas Coupland, Russell Smith, and Michael Turner have articulated urban landscape as a shifting site of cultural memory, in which a certain arbitrary randomness of space and proliferation of voices intertwine with rational territorial planning in narratives structured by atomization, which question the very cultural values they reflect.

Intercultural writers of multiple allegiances range from Janette Turner Hospital, who divides her time between Canada and Australia, to Nancy Huston. Hospital's pointillist writing blends classical western erudition (*Charades* [1989]) with the cultural mirages of the Australian outback: *Oyster* (1996) stages the collision of the world of Monet with a Dante-esque burning landscape. Operating within the same mode but in a manner reminiscent of bilingual writers such as Samuel Beckett or Romain Gary, Huston, who is an anglophone from Alberta living and writing in Paris, has chosen French as the language of writing. With exceptions such as *Plainsong* (1993), she has rewritten novels such as *The Goldberg Variations* (1980), *Instruments of Darkness* (1997), *The Mark of the Angel* (1999), and *Dolce Agonia* (2001) into English after they had previously been published in French. Moving from the affective sphere of the mother tongue to the cognitive sphere of a second language results in writing – like Beckett's – that is cerebral and detached, and marked by cultural, linguistic, and structural doubleness (the most striking example being the bilingual text *Limbes/Limbo, un hommage à Samuel Beckett* [2000]).

The work that has been discussed ranges from colonial writing that resists dislocation from a European culture (viewed as central), to contemporary writing that distances itself from international, national, or even local normative forms of production. On both sides of the spectrum, these texts underscore the composite nature of Canada's cultural heritage.

NOTES

1. Susanna Moodie, *Roughing It in the Bush* (1852; Toronto: McClelland, 1989) p. 73. This is an unabridged reprint of the "second edition with additions to the text."
2. Thomas C. Haliburton, *The Clockmaker, or The Sayings and Doings of Samuel Slick of Slickville* (1836; Toronto: McClelland, 1958) p. 69.
3. Sara Jeannette Duncan, *The Imperialist* (1904; Toronto: McClelland, 1990) p. 236.

4. Sheila Latham and David Latham, eds., preface, *Magic Lies: The Art of W. O. Mitchell* (Toronto: University of Toronto Press, 1997) p. ix.

5. Marta Dvorak, *Ernest Buckler: Rediscovery and Reassessment* (Waterloo: Wilfrid Laurier University Press, 2001) p. 2.

6. George Bowering, *Burning Water* (Toronto: General, 1980) p. 23.

7. Michael Ondaatje, *Running in the Family* (Toronto: McClelland, 1982) p. 53.

8. Stephen Slemon, "Magic Realism as Post-Colonial Discourse," *Canadian Literature* 116 (Spring 1988): pp. 9–24.

9. Margaret Atwood, *Surfacing* (1972; Toronto: General Paperbacks, 1989) p. 171.

10. Timothy Findley, *Headhunter* (Toronto: Harper, 1993) p. 3.

11. Timothy Findley, *Inside Memory: Pages from a Writer's Workbook* (Toronto: Harper, 1990) p. 191.

12. Jack Hodgins, *Broken Ground* (Toronto: McClelland, 1998) p. 12.

13. Jack Hodgins, *The Macken Charm* (Toronto: McClelland, 1995) p. 236.

14. Leonard Cohen, *Beautiful Losers* (1966; Toronto: McClelland, 1989) pp. 93 and 92 respectively.

15. The German community was the third largest ethnic group in Canada until 1986. See Donald Kerr and Deryck W. Holdsworth, eds., *Addressing the Twentieth Century 1891–1961* (Toronto: University of Toronto Press, 1990), vol. III of *Historical Atlas of Canada*, 3 vols., 1987–93, plates 4, 17, 59.

16. Statistics Canada reported that in 1996 over twenty-five percent of immigrants were from Hong Kong, China, Taiwan, and Vietnam, while over another twenty percent were from India, Sri Lanka, and the Philippines. See "A New Tide of Immigrants," *Maclean's* 17 Nov. 1997: p. 35. For a discussion of the 2001 Census, see Eva-Marie Kröller's introduction to this volume.

17. *Canadian Literature* 132 (Spring 1992): pp. 56–8.

8
Short fiction

ROBERT THACKER

Introduction

In May 1951 Robert Weaver, the person in charge of literary programming for the Canadian Broadcasting Corporation's national radio network, bought broadcast rights for a short story called "The Strangers." It had been written by a nineteen-year-old university student named Alice Laidlaw. After Laidlaw made some revisions, Weaver planned to broadcast it on 1 June on *Canadian Short Stories*, a fifteen-minute national program. But on 30 May he wired Laidlaw that "The Strangers" would not be broadcast as planned because the Massey Commission Report was to be released on the afternoon of 1 June; the story was broadcast later that year.[1]

Though anecdotal, this coincidental moment is an apt point of departure for a discussion of the Canadian short story in English. Throughout his long career at the CBC from 1948 through 1985, through a succession of programs the most prominent of which was *Anthology* (1953–85), Robert Weaver encouraged scores of writers to develop the form in Canada. More than this, with William Toye and others, he produced the *Tamarack Review* (1956–82), the leading Canadian literary magazine of its tumultuous times, and also edited a succession of influential short-story anthologies beginning with *Canadian Short Stories* (1960) through a *Fifth Series* volume in 1991. Alice Laidlaw, the young writer from whom Weaver bought "The Strangers" – the first story she had ever sold – went on to marry in 1951 and become Alice Munro; throughout the 1950s and into the 1960s, times of struggle and frustration for Munro as a writer, Weaver would remain her primary connection to a literary world. And that "The Strangers" was supplanted by the Massey Commission's report is an ironic juxtaposition – that report by that commission (actually named the Royal Commission on National Development in the Arts, Letters and Sciences) paved the way, through the various government-granting agencies that resulted from it, most notably the Canada Council, for a radical shift in the Canadian literary landscape from the late 1950s onward.[2]

The 1950s and 60s were difficult for Munro as a writer because although she found regular publication in such magazines as the *Canadian Forum*, *Queen's Quarterly*, *Chatelaine*, the *Tamarack Review*, and the *Montrealer*, and her reputation in Canada grew in consequence, book publication eluded her until 1968 when her first collection, *Dance of the Happy Shades*, appeared from Ryerson. Canadian publishers were uniformly hesitant – even skittish – over the publication of collections of short stories. In 1961, after reading in manuscript five Munro stories submitted on her behalf by Robert Weaver, McClelland and Stewart publisher Jack McClelland wrote Munro explaining his hesitancy over collections and encouraging a novel from her.[3] Even when the editors at Ryerson brought out Munro's first book – which won the Governor-General's Award for Fiction in English that year – they felt compelled to do so with a foreword by Hugh Garner, then a well-known writer of both novels and stories. And despite its glowing critical reception, *Dance of the Happy Shades* was not a commercial success; in 1972, four years after its publication, the publisher was still meeting orders from the first printing of 2,675 copies.

Yet with that book Munro's career changed. *Dance of the Happy Shades* was followed in 1971 by a novel, *Lives of Girls and Women* – a book that enjoyed some commercial success and also won a major prize – and, in 1974, by another story collection, *Something I've Been Meaning to Tell You*. In March 1977, the *New Yorker* published its first story by Munro, "Royal Beatings." Since then the *New Yorker* has published over forty Munro stories, stories that have been collected in her seven subsequent books and in her 1996 *Selected Stories*. Alice Munro is now unassailably Canada's leading short-story writer and, more than that, she is frequently cited as among the leading practitioners of the form in English.

But more than the facts of Munro's writing life, her career encapsulates the position of the short story in English in Canada – from first "publication" on CBC radio, through magazines (literary, academic quarterly, commercial), through hesitant book publication, to foreign publication (and so acclaim) in the *New Yorker* with US editions by Alfred A. Knopf, Munro's work embodies the Canadian short story. And by having the "publication" of the first story she sold supplanted by the Massey Commission Report in 1951, Munro has a connection to the most vexed issue in English Canadian intellectual life: how to ensure the success of literary and other artistic publication in English in a Canada that shares the continent with the United States. Before her, both Morley Callaghan and Mavis Gallant found reception for their stories in the

New Yorker, so an argument might well be made that, as a genre, the short story is more likely to find a home in foreign publication. Even so, and quite apart from the evident excellence of Munro's stories, her career encapsulates the Canadian short-story writer's position: taking a form that is both readily exportable and commercialized, one that has usually been deprecated to the advantage of longer narratives, one that shares the economic circumstances of writing in English in Canada generally, the Canadian short story has persisted and – since the 1970s led most evidently by the work of Gallant and, especially, Munro – prevailed. Without question, the Canadian short story in English has had a renaissance during the 1980s and 90s – there are now too many fine story writers to even name. Given this, what is offered here is less a naming than it is an argument as to how the present moment has come about.

Beginnings

It is sensible to say that Canada began almost concurrently with the published version of the short story as a consciously artistic form. Edgar Allan Poe's "The Philosophy of Composition" (1846), usually seen as the early critical essay key to the formation of the genre, appeared during the time when what was to become Canada was a group of loosely connected British colonies, when what literature there was existed in newspapers. Although short narratives existed before the 1830s – Indigenous creation myths and other oral tales told by Native peoples to one another – that decade saw the publication in Nova Scotia of Thomas Chandler Haliburton's *The Clockmaker* (1836). Sketches more than stories, these pieces pit Sam Slick – an itinerant Yankee clockmaker – against the Squire, a Nova Scotian, in a series of conversations detailing the times and topics of the day. Throughout, the attitudes and approaches of Nova Scotians are contrasted with the brash self-confidence of Americans who better succeed through their greater enterprise and wit. Put another way, Haliburton uses Slick to lampoon the characteristics of Nova Scotian, Englishman, and American alike. Haliburton's work influenced both Artemus Ward and Mark Twain although, as Canadian scholars often note, he is not given sufficient credit. As Gerald Lynch has argued in his book on the Canadian short-story cycle, *The One and the Many* (2001), Haliburton was "a colonial man" whose stories of Sam Slick testify "to a keen, not to say an anxious, awareness of his position on the margins of two great cultures."[4] Along with his argument that the short-story cycle is a characteristic Canadian form, Lynch points here to the critical position of Canadian writing in the nineteenth century: between

Great Britain and the United States, Canadian writing in English needed to conform with the practices found in one or the other place if publication was to be secured, an audience found.

Given this position, it is not altogether surprising that after Haliburton the two most prominent writers from mid-century Canada would be Catharine Parr Traill and Susanna Moodie, two sisters from a prominent English literary family – the Stricklands – who emigrated to Canada during the 1830s. Each had already published before coming to Canada, each used her experience in Canada as the basis for her subsequent writing, and each wrote works intended as guides for other immigrants from Britain, Traill's *The Backwoods of Canada* (1836), Moodie's *Roughing It in the Bush* (1852). At the same time as they were writing such practically intended works, the two sisters also found publication for poems and sketches in both Britain and the United States. For a short time, they were able to secure exposure in the *Literary Garland* (1838–51), a prominent though short-lived literary magazine published in Montreal.

The Strickland sisters have been the subject of extensive scholarship since the 1980s, deepening our understanding of both their work and their time.[5] Of the two, Susanna Moodie is the best known, and that is because the sketches that make up *Roughing It in the Bush* are both frequently and readily excerpted – two in particular, "A Visit to Grosse Isle" and "Brian, the Still-Hunter," are especially significant here. Though based on Moodie's own experience – the first an account of her family's arrival in Canada, the second of a neighborhood figure Mrs. Moodie came to know once they had settled near Lakefield, Ontario – these sketches have the effect of fiction. Moodie creates her narrative presence precisely, her characters vividly, and she manages in the narratives to be simultaneously humane, haughty over her superior English values, and detailed in her discriminations. That each of these sketches first appeared in magazines – "A Visit" in *Victoria Magazine* (1847), "Brian" in the *Literary Garland* (1847) – before inclusion (after being rewritten for a British audience) in Moodie's book is indicative of her ability, literary practice, and the circumstances of publishing short pieces in mid-century Canada. Like Haliburton's sketches in *The Clockmaker*, hers document the formation of a Canadian point of view, one in which an early subject was the differentiation between the cultural and political views of Canada, Great Britain, and the United States.

The cultural and historic importance of Canadian texts written and published before Confederation in 1867 – the change that created "Canada" as a country mainly independent from Great Britain, no longer a colony – is unquestionable. The literary quality of such texts, however, especially as they are seen as the precursors of later writers, is not only slim but necessarily so. Haliburton and Moodie are of interest in an overview of the Canadian short story because their work served, and still serves, to define the transformation that made literate colonials like Haliburton and literary English immigrants like Moodie Canadian. This is just the quality that drew Margaret Atwood to Moodie as a speaking persona in her *The Journals of Susanna Moodie* (1970) and, while arguably Atwood's Moodie is at some considerable distance from the biographical person, Moodie's vocal presence in Canada from 1832 until her death in 1885 is one crucial to any understanding of a Canadian point of view in nineteenth-century stories.[6]

Confederation through the turn of the century

Canada became a separate Dominion in 1867 through the Confederation of Canada (Quebec and Ontario), New Brunswick, and Nova Scotia (it maintained significant political connections to Britain until well into the twentieth century). Encouraged by this political change, a consciously Canadian group of writers emerged during the 1880s – for convenience these people, especially the poets, have often been called the Confederation group. However named, these writers took advantage of the growth in the magazine market in the United States during this era, and of the market for adventure stories on both sides of the Atlantic. Charles G. D. Roberts, Ernest Thompson Seton, and Edward William Thomson (who worked in Boston as an editor for *Youth's Companion*) availed themselves of such outlets as the *Atlantic*, *Century Magazine*, *Harper's Weekly*, the *North American Review*, and *Scribner's Monthly*. All wrote stories of romantic adventure: Roberts published animal stories, Seton tales of the woods, and Thomson aimed much of his work at the youth market. At this time too there was Gilbert Parker, who wrote stories of the far north (a place he never visited), New France, and Quebec. Parker's main publishing venue was Great Britain, although some of his books first appeared from US publishers and the stories of Métis, Mounties, Natives, and adventurers in his *Pierre and His People* (1892) first appeared in a New York newspaper. Yet, as W. H. New has argued in his book on the Canadian short story, "it seems fair to say that literary *influence* all went one way – North. Canadian writing in the United States was essentially an appeal to American taste for romantic tale and provincial stereotype."[7]

New is here pointing to an idea that was first (and probably still best) articulated by E. K. Brown in 1943 in *On Canadian Poetry*; there, he defines the predicament of the Canadian writer in English, and in commenting on two poets and a writer of short fiction, he offers a template for the issues confronting the short-story writer in particular:

> The serious Canadian writer has a choice among these modes of combining the pursuit of literature with success in keeping alive and fed. He may emigrate: that was the solution of Bliss Carman, and many have followed in his train. He may earn his living by some nonliterary pursuit; that was the solution of Archibald Lampman, and it has been widely followed. He may while continuing to reside in Canada become, economically at least, a member of another nation and civilization: that is the solution of Mr. Morley Callaghan.[8]

Brown's critique of Callaghan here is questionable yet, even so, his construction of the United States as proximate publishing venue for Canadian authors needs to be recognized and understood during the 1880s and since. For Canadian short-story writers, the US was a massive market for stories engaging its dominant styles and stereotypes. Along with Roberts, who wrote stories told from an animal's point of view (for example, "When Twilight Falls on the Stump Lots" [1902]), and Seton, who wrote about animals in the wild ("Lobo, the King of Currumpaw" [1894]), Pauline Johnson emerged in this period as a writer ("A Red Girl's Reasoning" [1893]) and performer asking audiences to rethink their attitudes towards Natives.[9] Taken together, the Canadian short-story writers of the late 1800s and early 1900s confirm the stereotypes that began – admittedly, as New argues, in American minds – with the Mounted Police in the 1870s: Canada as a wild, unsettled, harsh land populated by Natives, Mounties, adventurers, traders, trappers, and other such isolated types – a place of hardship, difficulty, and romance. Such stereotypes, which were taken up and transformed by the American film industry during the early twentieth century, remain alive today though they retain the limited intellectual power of advertising cliché.[10]

Scott, Leacock, and the press of modernism

Among the most popular Canadian writers to emerge around the turn of the century was Stephen Leacock, a McGill University professor of political science who began publishing books of humor in 1910 with *Literary Lapses*; another indicative volume of his is *Arcadian Adventures of the Idle Rich* (1914). Like adventure and animal stories by others, Leacock's sketches – *Sunshine Sketches of a Little Town* (1912) serving as the most significant example – were written for a popular non-Canadian audience, one encouraged to see itself as more sophisticated, more world-weary, than the charmingly naive citizens of Leacock's Mariposa, the mythical small town based on his longtime home, Orillia.

In creating Mariposa and using interconnected stories to do so, Leacock joined at a popular level what Gerald Lynch has described as an indicative English Canadian form: the short-story cycle. Beginning with D. C. Scott's *In the Village of Viger* (1896), Lynch cites Leacock's *Sunshine Sketches*, J. G. Sime's *Sister Women* (1919), F. P. Grove's *Over Prairie Trails* (1922), Emily Carr's *Klee Wyck* (1941), George Elliott's *The Kissing Man* (1962), and Munro's *Who Do You Think You Are?* (1978). The argument Lynch offers demonstrates convincingly that these Canadian writers have used the short-story cycle tellingly to create particular evocations of particular places. And like Scott and Leacock, most have done so with an eye to the re-creation of a small town.

But if Leacock's depiction of Mariposa is characterized by a gentle, ironic humor that accepts as it lampoons – a simple, sentimental attachment to the characters and their place which is nostalgic, serene – then Duncan Campbell Scott engages in incipient modernism as he characterizes Viger. The stories he offers in *In the Village of Viger*, especially "The Bobolink" and "Paul Farlotte," anticipate the stark loneliness of some of James Joyce's stories in *Dubliners* (1914) or, given the similar scope of Scott's volume, Sherwood Anderson's *Winesburg, Ohio* (1919), a much better-known book which Scott's seems to anticipate. For example, at the end of "The Bobolink," after Etienne and a little girl have let go a bobolink they have held in a cage, Scott writes:

> They stood there together for a moment, the old man gazing after the departed bird, the little girl setting her brown, sightless eyes on the invisible distance. Then, taking the empty cage, they went back to the cabin. From that day their friendship was not untinged by regret; some delicate mist of sorrow seemed to have blurred the glass of memory. Though he could not tell why, old Etienne that evening felt anew his loneliness, as he watched a long sunset of red and gold that lingered after the footsteps of an August day, and cast a great color into his silent cabin above the Blanche.[11]

Each story builds upon its predecessors to create a serene sense of life in Viger, corporately, but also by way of the separateness of each character. Viger is thus a village like Leacock's Mariposa, a representative town. As Frank O'Connor, the Irish short-story writer, once wrote, "there is in the short story at its most characteristic something we do not find in the novel – an intense awareness of human loneliness."[12] This very awareness characterizes the whole of *In the Village of Viger*, a text which both anticipates postwar modernism and lays the foundation for what Lynch calls the short-story cycle in English Canada.

The case of Morley Callaghan

Another modernist whom Scott anticipates is Ernest Hemingway, whose *In Our Time* (1924, 1925) has some of the same feel and who, among his circle in Paris in the 1920s, knew one Morley Callaghan, an aspiring writer from Toronto. Callaghan had worked on the *Toronto Star* with Hemingway and, through him, had met F. Scott Fitzgerald and James Joyce in France; the two Americans encouraged his writing and made Callaghan's case to publishers. Callaghan's *That Summer in Paris* (1963), a memoir occasioned in part by Hemingway's 1961 suicide, is among the most telling invocations of that time and that place. Yet Callaghan (1903–90), whose short stories appeared in the *New Yorker* and other American magazines, and who was later celebrated significantly as both writer of stories and novelist by Edmund Wilson in *O Canada* (1965), is now little known outside of Canada. He was, after all, a Canadian – and in ways vexed and difficult to define, that meant he was a North American of another sort, one something like, yet different from, Americans from the United States.

Such matters of identification and allegiance, of evaluation and audience, characterize any definition of Canadian writing in English. Owing to its historic dependence on American magazines as site of first publication, the case of the short story is especially problematic. Like Callaghan during the 1920s and 30s, or like Mavis Gallant during the 1950s and 60s, or like Alice Munro during the 1970s through the 90s, Canadian writers have always sought, and often found, foreign markets for their stories – and for most of the time that has meant US publication. D. C. Scott's *In the Village of Viger*, justly praised, was first published in Boston in 1896 and not in Canada until it appeared from Ryerson in 1945.

Callaghan is a central figure in these matters, and so deserves especial scrutiny here. As has already been seen, E. K. Brown wrote in 1943 that Callaghan was "a member of another nation and civilization" because, as Brown makes clear elsewhere in *On Canadian Poetry*, his fiction dealt too little with identifiably Canadian details. While such a charge was easy to make in the early 1940s, the matter is not so simple as Brown asserts. (Moreover, this is an ironic charge coming from Brown, since he was himself an expatriate from Canada for much of his life because of the professional allure of the United States, leaving to teach at Cornell and then the University of Chicago.) When writing in 1958 in the introduction to *Canadian Short Stories* (1960), Robert Weaver makes some important observations about Callaghan, saying that "It is because he has been for more than thirty years Canada's most distinguished novelist and short-story writer that Morley Callaghan is the only author represented in this book by two stories." Continuing, Weaver maintains that Callaghan "published abroad in the 1920's because there were almost no outlets in Canada for serious and experimental short fiction."[13]

Thus when Callaghan asserted a commitment to modernist style during the 1920s, his arguments and his own fiction addressed Canadian writing in market terms, those terms dictated by the proximity and extent of the American market. These reflected both conservative literary values and a disinterested native audience; writing in *Saturday Night* before his time in Paris, Callaghan pointedly critiqued Canadian conditions:

> the fact remains that there is no publication in the country interested in the publication of decent prose and poetry for its own sake, and until such a periodical appears, there will be no local expression in literature. It has often seemed to me that the trouble is mainly that we in Canada have no nationality, that the people, with the exception of two or three painters, have no feeling for the land.[14]

In so saying, Callaghan recognizes the postcolonial cultural position of English Canada: his reference to "decent prose and poetry" presupposes international critical standards then being articulated elsewhere while, by commenting on the "feeling for the land" (a reference to the Group of Seven landscape painters), he recognizes the need to focus on Canadian life itself.

The 1920s saw the arrival of the moderns and an attendant shift to a plain style so that several Canadians emerged who found publication in Canada, Europe, and the United States: in addition to Callaghan, there were Raymond Knister, William Murtha, and Graeme Taylor. Callaghan, reflecting these writers' view, pronounced on the generation of Canadian writers immediately preceding theirs, the writers of the 1910s and before, saying that they were "not interested in technique and had no identity. That is why they have always been regarded in the United States, where they attained some popularity, and where their books sold, as popular writers purely and simple."[15]

Callaghan published his stories predominantly in American magazines and, after 1929 and through the 1930s, when his collection *A Native Argosy* (1929) was published, his work was regularly included in the annual collections of "best American" stories. Callaghan's prose during these years is spare, laconic; his themes moralistic, Catholic; his settings vague, North American rather than Canadian. In an interview published earlier in 1928, also in *Saturday Night*, Callaghan argues for the need to "pull away from our colonial traditions," saying that "To reach our fullness we must let

America get us."[16] Similarly, in his essay on native prose Callaghan asserted that "The way lies through the acceptance of whatever speech we have in this country, and prose employing it will have the color, the raciness, the flesh and blood of the people of this section of the American continent. And because of the soil, we are American. Not United States, but American."[17]

Callaghan stands out as a short-story writer during the 1920s and 30s largely because he was able to assert his stories through *A Native Argosy* and, seven years later, with *Now That April's Here and Other Stories* (1936). The others who were publishing short fiction at the same time – Knister, Murtha, Frederick Philip Grove, Sinclair Ross, and Ethel Wilson, among others – appeared largely in periodicals. Collections of their stories in book form did not appear until the 1960s or later, if at all. Thus while Knister edited and published *Canadian Short Stories* in 1928 and foresaw in his introduction a new era in the form, in reality there were few publications in Canada that published short fiction and very little interest in story collections among publishers. Taking into account those periodicals active from the 1930s through the 50s, the list is not a long one: the *Canadian Forum*, *First Statement*, *Here and Now*, *Northern Review*, *Preview*, *Queen's Quarterly*, and the *Tamarack Review*.[18] Throughout, too, the CBC played a role. However seen, such paucity echoes the comments Callaghan made in 1928 and helps to account for his decision to publish in American outlets – a decision which also accounts for Brown's sniping at him in *On Canadian Poetry*.

In 1947, critic Desmond Pacey edited and published *A Book of Canadian Stories*; there, as he concludes his introduction, Pacey defines the relation between published stories and their Canadian audience in stark terms:

> But the chief inhibiting factor which has held back the growth of Canadian short stories has been the lack of a large and eager audience. This lack has expressed itself in the paucity, the virtual non-existence for almost a century, of magazines ready to print distinguished or experimental short stories. It is upon the Canadian people, and not upon the publishers or editors, that the responsibility must be placed. If there develops in Canada a reading public interested in serious short stories and ready to pay for them, publishers and editors will be found to print them and writers to write them.[19]

It was within such a literary landscape for the short story that Robert Weaver began working at the CBC and, a few years later in 1951, discovered the nineteen-year-old Alice Laidlaw, bought the first story she sold, "The Strangers," and eventually broadcast it once the Massey Commission had been reported on.

Transformation: The 1950s and 1960s

About ten years after Pacey's pronouncement, Robert Weaver introduced the first of his five solely edited volumes of Canadian stories from Oxford University Press – that introduction, and the four that were to follow, make interesting reading as snapshots of where the short story in Canada was, written by a man whose life's work itself focused upon that genre. Weaver, who has evidently decided to ignore both the Knister and Pacey anthologies, begins by claiming "that there is no tradition which an editor is required either to follow or explain away"; even so, he acknowledges that he "decided that there was not much point in venturing very far back into Canadian writing of the nineteenth century in a search for the short story" since he believes "few short stories of much literary consequence were published in Canada before the First World War."[20] Notwithstanding, Weaver includes four stories (of twenty-seven) published prior to the war with most of the balance – save those by Knister, Callaghan, Leo Kennedy, and Ross – from after World War II. Gallant and Munro appear here among the youngest writers included, Gallant through "The Legacy," a story from her first collection, *The Other Paris* (Boston, 1956), and Munro with "The Time of Death," the oldest story included in *Dance of the Happy Shades*. Among the other young writers included are Mordecai Richler and James Reaney, two figures destined to distinguish themselves largely through forms other than short fiction. Weaver also includes three French Canadian stories in translation, a noble attempt to bridge the Two Solitudes which he abandoned with the next anthology.

When *Canadian Short Stories: Second Series* appeared in 1968, Weaver included just twelve writers, whom he identifies with the 1950s and 60s, with seven of them – Hugh Garner, Gallant, Margaret Laurence, Richler, Hugh Hood, Munro, and Dave Godfrey – each represented by two stories. Again he notes that many of these writers first published some of these stories in American magazines and that this "reflects in part the notorious difficulty of finding enough markets for fiction in Canada." Despite this complaint, Weaver ends his introduction with a list of books, collections of Canadian short stories:

> A surprising number of impressive collections of stories by individual writers have been published in the last ten years. Books by writers in this anthology include *Morley Callaghan's Stories* (1959), Ethel Wilson's *Mrs. Golightly and the First Convention* (1961), Hugh Hood's *Flying a Red Kite* (1962), *Hugh Garner's Best Stories* (1963), Margaret Laurence's *The Tomorrow-Tamer* (1963), Mavis Gallant's *My Heart Is Broken* (1964), Dave Godfrey's *Death Goes Better with Coca-Cola* (1967), and Alice Munro's *Dance of the Happy Shades* (1968).

The appearance of these books shows the great interest there is in the modern Canadian short story. It also indicates the really substantial body of work that short-story writers in the postwar period have produced – and its quality.[21]

Clearly, as Weaver asserts, the stature of the short story in Canada had changed by the late 1960s, even if only in the number of short-story collections published. But it was more than that; the aid-to-publishing programs offered by the Canada Council – a government funding agency recommended and fostered by the Massey Commission – were beginning to have an effect on publishing in Canada. At the same time, the 1960s saw the rise of what might be called a more conscious Canadianism – a patriotism or nationalism born variously of that decade's social unrest, Canada's 1967 Centennial celebrations, the Vietnam War, the Quiet Revolution in Quebec, and the appearance as prime minister of Pierre Elliott Trudeau. Whatever the cause, as the 1960s closed, the audience for the short story that Pacey called for in 1947 was being born.

Mavis Gallant, Alice Munro, and the contemporary Canadian short story

In several ways, the respective careers of Mavis Gallant and Alice Munro seem to embody the shift in audience that characterized the transformation in the short story after 1970. As has been said, Munro's career dates from the 1950s, although arguably her prominence in Canada was not cemented until her work appeared in book form in the late 1960s and early 70s, and abroad not until the 1980s with her frequent appearance in the *New Yorker*. Gallant, on the other hand, after some initial publication in *Preview*, the *Northern Review*, and the newspaper magazine of Montreal *Standard*, began publishing in the *New Yorker* in 1951 and had published over seventy stories there before Munro's first appearance in its pages in 1977. Leaving Canada to live in Paris in 1950 has distanced Gallant from the Canadian literary culture, as has her infrequent Canadian publication. She is an expatriate writer, one whose great theme is living as a foreigner in another culture. Gallant's stories have a complex and controlled cerebral quality about them, and the author's relative distance from her characters is a point of continual scrutiny for her readers.

Together – and in some appropriate ways they are best taken together, as witnessed by the publication in 1996 of a *Selected Stories* from each author – Gallant and Munro's careers span the era from the 1950s to the present in ways that make the issues comprehensible. In 1951, a few months after Robert Weaver bought Munro's "The Strangers" for broadcast on the CBC, Gallant published her first story in the *New Yorker*. Throughout the 1950s, Gallant would publish over twenty more stories in that magazine plus others in *Esquire, Harper's Bazaar*, and other US outlets. Munro, meanwhile, had far fewer stories appear in Canadian outlets – *Mayfair*, the *Canadian Forum, Chatelaine, Queen's Quarterly*, the *Tamarack Review*. During the 1960s, Gallant kept up the same pace, almost all of her many stories appearing in the *New Yorker*, while Munro, for her part, published just eight stories in periodicals apart from her first book, *Dance of the Happy Shades*, which includes two stories that had not appeared in periodicals. With the Governor-General's Award for that book, however, and *Lives of Girls and Women* in 1971, Munro's reputation continued ascendant.

Another factor in these contexts was the work of John Metcalf, a fine writer of short stories in his own right and also an indefatigable editor of short-story anthologies. Given changes in audience and the rise of cultural nationalism, publishers saw a market for such books. Metcalf edited two such books at this time (both of which include Munro's work), *Sixteen by Twelve* (1970) and *The Narrative Voice* (1972). In addition, Penguin published a more broadly conceived volume edited by Mordecai Richler, who was then living in London, entitled *Canadian Writing Today* (a book dedicated to Morley Callaghan). While the latter volume was generically inclusive, Metcalf's books focused on the short story as a form and sought to bring Canada's best practitioners into classroom reading. Metcalf continued such work through the 1970s and 1980s and, more than any other single individual apart from Weaver, is responsible for shaping and promoting the short story in Canada.

From the 1970s on, the short story in Canada achieved what can only be called a renaissance; writers by the score emerged to publish distinguished story after story, collection after collection. This continued unabated through the end of the century. Speaking particularly, Munro's status as *the* significant presence in the landscape of the Canadian short story was reconfirmed in 1996 by the *New Yorker*: it closed its year with her "The Love of a Good Woman," a very long story (over seventy pages) that was later included among the O. Henry Prize stories for 1997 (à la Callaghan), and became the title story of Munro's 1998 collection. The *New Yorker* emphasized Munro's story as one of two featured in its double, end-of-year fiction issue, using its title as the basis for that issue's cover art.[22]

As Munro's 1996 story demonstrates at length, the short story has contributed significantly through the looming recent presence of Gallant and Munro as leading practitioners of the form, coupled with the ubiquitous presence of Margaret Atwood as the single most famous Canadian writing in the language. With three short-story collections of her own as well as myriad other publications in other genres, Atwood has shifted the Canadian bifurcation, seen in Callaghan previously as something negative, into a positive presence. And in this may be seen both accomplishment and a lingering colonialism since, arguably, part of Atwood's strength lies in her ability to caustically critique things from the United States – as a non-American herself she may be better able to see where North American culture is heading. Gallant and Munro, while their work may indeed appeal through something of the same detachment, have nevertheless confirmed the international stature of Canadian stories by just being in the *New Yorker* so often, and in other publications of the same ilk. The leading edge of a group of Canadian short-story writers living in a different "America," one born of some of the same history and some not the same, one buffeted by many of same cultural forces and some not the same, Gallant and Munro attest to the wider appeal of the Canadian point of view in their stories.

Beyond Callaghan and before and since Munro, there are numerous other authors of excellent stories to take up. Randomly, and leaving out many authors and stories that could have been mentioned, Sinclair Ross's "The Painted Door," one of his most affecting tales of the 1930s prairie dust-bowl Saskatchewan, has become a classic; it was collected in *The Lamp at Noon and Other Stories* (1968). The same may be said of Ethel Wilson's "Mrs. Golightly and the First Convention," Mordecai Richler's "Some Grist for Mervyn's Mill," Joyce Marshall's "The Old Woman," Margaret Laurence's *A Bird in the House* (1970), Alistair MacLeod's "As Birds Bring forth the Sun," anything by Mavis Gallant, Austin Clarke's "Leaving This Island Place," Rudy Wiebe's "Where Is the Voice Coming From" or "The Naming of Albert Johnson," Guy Vanderhaeghe's "The Watcher," Margaret Atwood's *Wilderness Tips* (1991), Neil Bissoondath's "Digging up the Mountains," Rohinton Mistry's "The Ghost of Firozsha Baag," and M. G. Vassanji's *Uhuru Street* (1992). The list goes on and on and on and has, in recent years, increased its pace – since 1983 some 600 collections by individual writers have appeared. To begin, an interested reader need only take up Michael Ondaatje's *From Ink Lake* (1990) or Margaret Atwood and Robert Weaver's *The New Oxford Book of Canadian Short Stories in English* (1995), the latter only the most recent in the succession of Canadian story anthologies from Oxford edited by Weaver.

To foreground the idiosyncratic nature of any such listing, let me mention other writers not already named, persons whose work deserves mention here and who might well have made the first naming. (Beyond all of these, there are many others still not named.) Thus lying beneath the very fact of over 600 collections of stories since 1983 (a fact far wider and deeper than one person can ever know, let alone detail) is a cultural heterogeneity in the Canadian short story since 1970 that far surpasses any attempt to summarize it. In many ways, too, this cultural variety in storytelling reflects the cultural variety in Canada itself – since the 1960s, especially, it has received immigrants from around the globe in addition to its historic ties to Europe and the United States.

Although I did not do so in my first pass, I might have cited Jack Hodgins or Hugh Hood or Norman Levine or Audrey Thomas or W. D. Valgardson among those who emerged in the 1960s and 70s. Or I could have noted Henry Kreisel, whose early novels were followed by *The Almost Meeting and Other Stories* (1981). Or I could have said something about Sandra Birdsell's first collection, *Night Travellers*, which became part of *Agassiz Stories* and was published in the United States as *Agassiz: A Novel in Stories* (or done something of the same for Edna Alford's stories, or Joan Clark's). Following the story cycle, I might have returned to George Elliott's *The Kissing Man* or looked at W. P. Kinsella's Native stories or his stories about baseball. I might have examined Thomas King's stories, or Carol Shields's, or Greg Hollingshead's, or Evelyn Lau's, or Newfoundlander Lisa Moore's. Moore's collection *Open* was a finalist for the 2002 Giller Prize for Canadian fiction. Yann Martel began with a collection of stories, *The Facts behind the Helsinki Roccamatios* (1993), but his latest book, *Life of Pi*, won Britain's Booker Prize in 2002. And Diane Schoemperlen's *Red Plaid Shirt: Stories New and Selected* (2002) was published to glowing reviews that seldom failed to mention Alice Munro's influence.

What these authors offer, finally, is less a characteristic Canadian style of the short story than it is each person's response to Callaghan's 1928 assertion that stories reflect "the flesh and blood of the people of this section of the North American continent." Thus, plumbing the lists just offered, there are stories set in Jewish Montreal, in urban Saskatoon, in rural Nova Scotia, in Vancouver, on Vancouver Island, in India, in northern Quebec, in Dieppe, on the prairies, and in small-town Ontario; meditations on history (Canadian, otherwise corporate, individual), mysteries set in summer camps, tales of emigration and immigration, and narratives of self-discovery; there are episodes of both conventional and unconventional being. For good or for ill, such stories reflect the Canadian point of view, a point of view that indeed is "American" in the larger generic sense that Callaghan meant when he said that Canadians should "let America get us": North American, yes, but emphatically *not* of the United States. Canadian. The *Canadian* short story.

NOTES

1. Robert Weaver, letters to Alice Laidlaw, 18 May 1951, 1 June 1951, Robert Weaver Papers, National Archives of Canada (MG 31 D 162).

2. See Paul Litt, *The Muses, the Masses, and the Massey Commission* (Toronto: University of Toronto Press, 1992).

3. Jack McClelland, letter to Alice Munro, 12 Oct. 1961, Alice Munro Fonds, University of Calgary (37.2.22.1).

4. Gerald Lynch, *The One and the Many: English-Canadian Short Story Cycles* (Toronto: University of Toronto Press, 2001) p. 9.

5. See, for example, Michael Peterman, *This Great Epoch of Our Lives: Susanna Moodie's* Roughing It in the Bush (Toronto: ECW Press, 1996).

6. Margaret Atwood, *The Journals of Susanna Moodie* (Toronto: Oxford University Press, 1970).

7. W. H. New, *Dreams of Speech and Violence: The Art of the Short Story in Canada and New Zealand* (Toronto: University of Toronto Press, 1987) p. 43.

8. E. K. Brown, *On Canadian Poetry* (1943; Ottawa: Tecumseh, 1977) p. 9.

9. In each case here I have cited the story reprinted in Misao Dean, ed. *Early Canadian Short Stories: Short Stories in English before World War I* (Ottawa: Tecumceh, 1999) as the most readily available text of pre-1914 Canadian short stories.

10. For a brief overview of the Mounted Police as an iconic entity, see Robert Thacker, "Canada's Mounted: The Evolution of a Legend," *Journal of Popular Culture* 14 (1980): pp. 298–312. See also Keith Walden, *Visions of Order: The Canadian Mountie in Symbol and Myth* (Toronto: Butterworth's, 1982).

11. Duncan Campbell Scott, *In the Village of Viger* (1896; Toronto: McClelland, 1996) p. 54. An interesting discussion of the evolution of this book's reputation may be found in John Metcalf, *What Is a Canadian Literature?* (Guelph: Red Kite, 1988).

12. Frank O'Connor, *The Lonely Voice: A Study of the Short Story* (1962; Cleveland: World, 1963) p. 19.

13. Robert Weaver, introduction, *Canadian Short Stories*, ed. Weaver (Toronto: Oxford University Press, 1960) pp. x–xi.

14. Morley Callaghan, "Looking at Native Prose," *Saturday Night* 1 Dec. 1928: p. 3.

15. Callaghan, "Looking at Native Prose."

16. Margaret Lawrence, interview with Morley Callaghan, *Saturday Night* 14 July 1928: p. 11.

17. Callaghan, "Looking at Native Prose."

18. Though focused on poetry, a useful study is Ken Norris, *The Little Magazine in Canada, 1925–80: Its Role in the Development of Modernism and Post-Modernism in Canadian Poetry* (Toronto: ECW, 1984).

19. Desmond Pacey, introduction, *A Book of Canadian Stories*, ed. Pacey (Toronto: Ryerson, 1947) p. xxxvi.

20. Weaver, ed., *Canadian Short Stories*, p. ix.

21. Robert Weaver, introduction, *Canadian Short Stories: Second Series*, ed. Weaver (Toronto: Oxford University Press, 1968) p. x.

22. Munro's prominence in any discussion of the Canadian short story is also borne out by the critical attention her work has received as well as by its ongoing

presence in the *New Yorker*. Notable among the critical studies are two books with the same title: E. D. Blodgett, *Alice Munro* (Boston: Twayne, 1988) and Coral Ann Howells, *Alice Munro* (Manchester: Manchester University Press, 1998); as well as Magdalene Redekop, *Mothers and Other Clowns: The Stories of Alice Munro* (London: Routledge, 1992). A recent collection of critical essays is Robert Thacker, ed., *The Rest of the Story: Critical Essays on Alice Munro* (Toronto: ECW, 1999).

9
Writing by women

CORAL ANN HOWELLS

Setting down her title[1]

This phrase, taken from a Canadian woman's novel written in the early 1970s, addresses the double issue of women's writing and its relationship to wider feminist questions of women's literary and political entitlement. It also marks a significant starting point for this chapter, which will focus on Canadian women's fiction in English since the late 1960s, the period when Canadian writing achieved high visibility at home and abroad. At the present time Margaret Atwood, Alice Munro, and Carol Shields, who all started publishing in the 1960s and 70s, are names that are synonymous with Canadian writing internationally. In addition, since the early 1990s a constellation of new women writers, including many from a wide range of ethnic and racial backgrounds, has enormously diversified Canada's literary image, and these women's novels and short stories feature in increasing numbers on international publishers' lists. Why should this be? What is so distinctive about these writers? And what factors have contributed to their popularity and visibility? This chapter will attempt to answer those questions by looking at the circumstances within which women have been writing in Canada since the 1960s (a period which includes changing social and cultural contexts as well as opportunities for publication) and, most importantly, by looking at the texts themselves. My emphasis will be on novels, though many of these writers work in other genres as well. This pattern of generic diversity is emblematically illustrated in the writing careers of the three women whom I have already mentioned: Atwood, who made her reputation as a poet before she became a novelist, is also a short-story writer, essayist, and cultural critic; Shields wrote novels, biographies, short stories, plays, and poems; only Alice Munro has achieved her formidable reputation on short-story writing alone, though she too produced one novel, *Lives of Girls and Women*, back in the early 1970s.

To begin with the question of why women's writing in Canada should have suddenly leapt to prominence since the 1970s, the answer would seem to lie in a confluence of factors, which might be summed up as the rise of Canadian cultural nationalism in the late 1960s and 70s, coinciding with the rise of North American second-wave feminism. New writing by women is located at the intersection of postcolonial and feminist perspectives, as women have sought to renegotiate their positions through the imaginative dimensions of creative writing, the most popular form of which has been the novel. Canada's postwar project of nation-building and its search for an independent identity coalescing around the 1967 Centennial year saw widespread changes on the cultural scene, as "culture" was appropriated as a vehicle for domestic and foreign policy. These political initiatives were accompanied by hugely increased funding for the arts at federal and provincial levels, and new structures were put in place to support Canadian writers and publishers. As Lynette Hunter remarked in her analysis of this phenomenon, "Where a nation is concerned to consolidate/ incorporate/ commodify a culture as part of an ideological project, it has to financially support the production and consumption of that culture."[2] Whatever criticisms might be made of such policies, and there have been many,[3] such state support fostered what has become known as the "Canadian Lit boom," a remarkable period which generated a new cultural self-consciousness and encouraged writers in formerly marginalized areas, such as women, multicultural communities, and Aboriginal peoples. Though government subsidies decreased significantly during the 1990s, these policies have ensured a flourishing literary culture as new writers' names continue to proliferate in the multinational publishing world.[4] Evident parallels could be drawn between an emerging narrative of postcolonial nationhood and women's struggles to emancipate themselves from traditions of patriarchal authority, famously spelled out by Margaret Atwood in *Power Politics* (1971) and further elaborated in *Surfacing* and *Survival: A Thematic Guide to Canadian Literature* (both published in 1972). This was the period when the reputations of Laurence, Atwood, and Munro were established, and these strong voices have paved the way for the reception of many women writers since, whose fiction shifts traditional emphases while continuing to reflect the cultural and ideological concerns which characterize contemporary multicultural Canada.[5]

A female literary tradition

Though the focus of this chapter is on the contemporary scene, we need to remember that nothing comes out of the blue and that these modern women are the inheritors of a long tradition of women's writing in Canada. The first Canadian novel in English was written by a woman: Frances Brooke's *The History of Emily Montague* (1769), an epistolary novel set in the newly acquired French colony of Quebec. Brooke's combination of sentimental plot and exotic location was immensely popular with late eighteenth-century readers and was translated into French and Dutch. In the nineteenth and early twentieth centuries a number of books by women were widely read in Britain and Canada, many of them written by British immigrants for readers back home. The two best known were Susanna Moodie and her sister Catharine Parr Traill, who wrote about the wilderness and pioneer settlement from a feminine perspective as wives and mothers. These narratives appealed to popular British constructions of Canada as an outpost of empire, a place of vast forests and sublime scenery, so enshrining women's wilderness experience in ways that have continued to influence contemporary writers, notably Laurence and Atwood. L. M. Montgomery's *Anne of Green Gables* (1908), together with the *Emily* trilogy of the 1920s, remains enduringly popular. These novels are pastoral idylls underpinned by sharp realistic insights into life in the Maritimes, though their chief appeal lies in their adolescent heroines. As Munro wrote in her afterword to *Emily of New Moon*, "There is so much going on behind, or beyond, the proper story. There's life spreading out behind the story – the book's life – and we see it out of the corner of the eye."[6] Sara Jeannette Duncan's *The Imperialist* (1904) offered a serious historical view of Canada's destiny in the drama of empire, cast as a romance set in small-town Ontario, but it was Mazo de la Roche's pulp romance *Jalna* (1927) and its fifteen sequels which ran till 1960 that caught the popular imagination, and by 1966 the series had sold 11 million copies, with translations in nine languages. Elizabeth Smart's *By Grand Central Station I Sat Down and Wept* (1945) is one of those rare novels which has achieved cult status, a combination of passionate love lyric and modernist prose fiction, in celebration of Smart's obsessive love affair with the English poet George Barker. These novels (except *The Imperialist*) were first published in either Britain or the United States; one significant difference with the later flowering is that the novels were published first in Canada, mainly by the Toronto firm of McClelland and Stewart, or by one of the small presses like Anansi. It is only recently with multinational publishing trends that novels are being published simultaneously in Canada and internationally.[7]

Shifts of emphasis

Canadian women writers of the late 1960s and the 1970s and 80s were very concerned, as was feminism at that time, with exposing the power politics of gender in heterosexual relations and with women's quests to discover their individual identities by finding their voices and reclaiming their rights over their own bodies. These are indeed the topics that are signaled in titles like Atwood's *The Edible Woman* (1969), Audrey Thomas's *Mrs Blood* (1970), or Munro's *Lives of Girls and Women* (1971). There was also a new emphasis on women's ambivalent relation to literary and cultural traditions and women writers' acknowledgment of their female literary inheritance, together with feminist revisions of Canadian cultural myths and official histories of settlement. Women were fighting their way out of silence via the fictional retailing of gossip and oral tales to project more dissident and authentic accounts of feminine emotional and psychological experience. A pervasive topic in the 1970s which suggests this new feminist self-consciousness and sense of entitlement is that of the woman writer: Munro's *Lives of Girls and Women* (1971), Laurence's *The Diviners* (1974), Atwood's *Lady Oracle* (1976), Shields's *Small Ceremonies* (1976), and Audrey Thomas's *Latakia* (1979) all have protagonists who are fiction writers, as women explore new dimensions of their creative powers. So, though there is a strong continuity between these women and their predecessors in the topics they choose to write about, there are also "shifts of emphasis that throw the storyline open to question,"[8] as women reshape their imaginative worlds. Yet such apparently radical dislocations left some things untouched: apart from Atwood's Toronto fictions and the cosmopolitan short stories of Mavis Gallant, who had been living in Paris since 1950, there was not much urban fiction by women yet, just as there was very little discussion of alternative sexualities. Jane Rule's lesbian romance *Desert of the Heart* (1964), set not in Canada but in Nevada, is a rare exception to this blanket of silence. A similar blankness occurs in relation to ethnicity and race, as published writers were dominantly white. Joy Kogawa's *Obasan* (1981) was the one notable exception here. In 1997–8 the federal government's Multiculturalism Department initiated its writing-and-publication program designed to support publications by minority writers; this program continues to be remarkably successful in bringing new writers to visibility.

However, significant changes were already under way in the 1970s and 80s in relation to demography, nationalist ideology, identity politics, and the First Nations cultural revival. Multiculturalism had existed as official government policy since 1971 and was codified in the 1988 Canadian Multiculturalism Act, which affirmed ethnic and racial diversity as a fundamental characteristic of Canadian society. As policy and social reality, multiculturalism has played a crucial role in radical refigurings of identity concepts which have been increasingly evident during the 1990s. Together with a new liberalism which included the representation of alternative sexualities as well as shifts from a rural small-town ethos to the urban, the cosmopolitan, and the global, there has been a historical movement away from Canada's white colonial inheritance to a redefinition of postcolonial contemporary Canadian identity and a remapping of the nation space.

In order to present the different stages in the development of contemporary Canadian women's fiction I have adopted a broadly chronological arrangement which I prefer to call a "generational" one, with an emphasis on literary mothers and their inheritors. Writers with long established careers do not easily fit into a grid marked out in decades, though this pattern is convenient to register when these women's voices were first heard. Laurence, Atwood, and Munro all received their first Governor-General's Awards in the 1960s: Laurence for her novel *A Jest of God* (1966), Atwood for her poetry collection *The Circle Game* in the same year, and Munro for her short-story collection *Dance of the Happy Shades* (1968), and then all of them received second Governor-General's Awards during the 1970s and 80s. Carol Shields on the other hand, whom I include in the 1960s and 70s section because her first novel was published in 1976, only achieved substantial success with her novels in the 1990s: "Arriving late, as always."[9] Indeed there are overlaps in time just as there are thematic continuities and a continuation of narrative experiments within the allusive framework of traditional genres, though negotiations over issues of identity have become increasingly complex as factors of race, sexuality, and hybridized and transcultural identities are highlighted by many of the new writers of the 1990s. These "daughters" are mapping fictional spaces for new versions of Canadian identity of which their "mothers" could not have been aware in the 1960s and 70s.

The new generation of the 1960s and 1970s

The generation of women who began publishing in the 1960s were mothers in more than the literary sense, just as they recognized themselves as daughters of foremothers who were Canadian, British, and American. White middle-class women, most of them followed traditional social patterns, married and had children before they or anyone else began to see them as writers. Alice Munro (who had sold her first story to the Canadian Broadcasting Corporation in 1951) is typical: "All through the 50s I was living in a dormitory suburb [in Vancouver], having babies, and it [writing] wasn't part of the accepted thing for a girl or a woman to do at that time either, but it never occurred to me that I should stop."[10] Munro's responses to the multiple pressures of domestic life and writing are evident in her comment to Graeme Gibson in the early 1970s: "I've read about myself, you know, Alice Munro has produced little, and I think it's a miracle that I've produced anything."[11] Shields, who had five children, was more optimistic about connections between motherhood and writing: "Having children woke me up, in a sense. I knew I had to pay attention. I wanted to pay attention. All my senses seemed sharpened, and I seemed capable of more. Like many a parent, I was astonished to discover how much love I was capable of feeling . . . In some way this revelation spilled over into writing."[12] Her first novel was published the week she turned forty. Atwood's career was the exception, for having won her first Governor-General's Award for poetry while still a graduate student, she had published three novels by the mid-1970s when her daughter was born. Such patterns of life experience affect women's careers just as they do their novels, which will be reflected in the different positions each of these novelists takes up as she explores "traditional cultural dependencies" in both a nationalist and a gendered sense.[13]

Margaret Laurence, the oldest of this group and often referred to as the "godmother" of contemporary Canadian women's writing, described her awareness of women's double colonized position as arising from her experiences as a wife and mother in colonial Africa in the 1950s. It was she who made explicit the analogy between the colonial mentality and women's condition in her 1978 essay, "Ivory Tower or Grassroots? The Novelist as Socio-Political Being."[14] Curiously it was Laurence's African experience which turned her into a prairie novelist, when having published four books about Africa on her return to Canada she produced *The Stone Angel* (1964), which was to become the first of her Manawaka cycle of novels over the next ten years. As George Woodcock noted: "The publication of *The Stone Angel* was hailed as marking the appearance of a new and original talent on the Canadian literary horizon, and rapidly made Laurence the most important novelist in that vitally formative period of Canadian writing – the late 1960s and early 1970s."[15]

The Manawaka cycle presents a history of the Canadian West in the feminine, as Manawaka is reinvented through the voices of five female narrators, covering the period from white pioneer settlement up to the 1970s, when most of the original families have died out or moved away. Beginning with 92-year-old Hagar Shipley in *The Stone Angel*, who is the daughter of one of the town's founding fathers, the cycle progresses through the 1960s *A Jest of God* (1966) and *The Fire-Dwellers* (1969), followed by *A Bird in the House* (1970), to end with *The Diviners* (1974). Here the narrator is a 47-year-old novelist and single mother, who tells her story from a location far from Manawaka, in Ontario (near Lakefield where Laurence herself lived, and Catharine Parr Traill before that). Clara Thomas demonstrated Laurence's realism,[16] though these novels are primarily experiments in the representation of female subjectivities as Laurence seeks the appropriate fictional form "through which the characters can breathe."[17] They rehearse the themes and narrative forms which contemporary women writers have continued to develop, as Laurence explores different versions of the confessional novel, moving from traditional realism crisscrossed with romance and fantasy in the earlier books to the fragmented modernist form of *The Diviners*. Laurence is always concerned with how women's autobiographical fictions can be made sufficiently expansive to contain wider social and political issues, and these novels problematize distinctions between personal and political, just as they insist on connections across the generic boundaries of fantasy and realism as modes of fictional discourse. Though her narrators are all of Scots Irish descent, Laurence moves beyond these limits to include the multi-ethnic inheritance of the prairie provinces, with their Ukrainian, German, and Icelandic settlers, along with stories of colonial dispossession in the tragic history of the Indigenous Métis. As a historical novelist, Laurence recognizes the ways that heritage is reinvented as it is passed down through generations, creating new myths to fit the new place: "Our task is not to reject the past but to assimilate it, to take the language and make it truly ours, to write out of our own familiar idiom and out of our deepest observations of our people and our place on this planet."[18]

Alice Munro's fictions are set mainly in her home territory, the rural communities and small towns of southwestern Ontario, in that quietly rolling countryside, "back where nothing seems to be happening, beyond the change of seasons."[19] Munro is Canada's greatest short-story writer, though her second book *Lives of Girls and Women* (1971) was published as a novel, a transgressive version of the *bildungsroman* where everything from the title onwards is pluralized and the different sections (less like chapters and more like short stories, each with its own title) enclose contradictory views within the same fictional space. *Lives* is the fictive autobiography of Del Jordan, a girl who grows up in the small town of Jubilee, Ontario, during the 1940s and 50s and who later becomes a writer, a fact revealed only in the final chapter. Del's story involves many other women's life stories as well – her mother's, her aunts', her girlfriends' – for though she is different from them in her aspirations, she is also like them the product of a small-town Canadian ethos.[20] Like Laurence, Munro is fascinated by local history and geography and the details of small-town life, though unlike Laurence she sees provincial ordinariness as only a surface layer covering over a darker secret world of scandal, violence, child abuse, and sudden startling deaths: "The part of the country I come from is absolutely Gothic. You can't get it all down."[21] This double vision, where realism is juxtaposed with fantasy and romance, is the distinctive quality of Munro's fiction, just as it characterizes Del's imagination: "People's lives in Jubilee, as elsewhere, were dull, simple, amazing, unfathomable, deep caves paved with kitchen linoleum."[22] It is Del's evolution as a writer which makes this such a ground-breaking text in the early 1970s. "Heirs of the Living Body" shows her rejecting the literary principles of her uncle's local-history record which focuses solely on men's public lives, while in "Epilogue: The Photographer" Del discovers the alternative kind of chronicle she wishes to construct as a woman writer, which spells out the territory of Munro's own fictions ever since: "And no list could hold what I wanted: every smell, pothole, pain, crack, delusion, held still and held together – radiant, everlasting."[23]

By the time Atwood won the Booker Prize for *The Blind Assassin* in 2000, she was an international literary celebrity who had collected numerous honorary degrees and awards, and her work has been translated into more than thirty languages. Her fiction features on school and university syllabuses worldwide, there is a thriving academic Atwood critical industry, and her publicity tours for every new book are sellouts around the world.[24] Singlehandedly, Atwood has established a high profile for Canadian writing generally and for Canadian women's writing in particular. It all began in the 1960s and 70s, when in a prodigious burst between 1969 and 1979 she published four novels, five poetry collections, one short-story collection, and her influential critical survey of Canadian literature.[25] Atwood's presence has continued to dominate the Canadian literary scene and her name will feature in every decade of my account, but it is the emergence of her voice as a female novelist at the heady time of Canadian cultural nationalism that I shall focus on here. She has always shown a genius for codifying and indeed for predicting popular cultural trends, and she has worked in a dazzling range of fictional genres, continuously experimenting across genre boundaries, exploring the political and ideological significance of such revisions: "What art does, it takes what society deals out and makes it visible, right? So you can see it."[26]

From the beginning Atwood's voice has been remarkably distinctive – witty, self-ironic, politically and morally engaged – as her female narrators have responded to what is actually going on in the world around them. Though her emphases have shifted over four decades, her major thematic preoccupations are recognizably there in her first four novels: gender politics and the representation of women's lives, their bodies, and their fantasies, questions of Canadian identity and Canada's international relations, human rights issues, environmental concerns. She is a Toronto-centered novelist who has cataloged the social history of her city from the nineteenth century to the present, just as she is very self-consciously a woman writer, and female artists figure prominently in her novels. *The Edible Woman*, hailed by the *Times* critic as the best first novel of 1969, heralded the beginning of second-wave feminist fiction in English, the territory charted by Betty Friedan in *The Feminine Mystique* (1963). It is the story of a young Toronto woman who suffers an identity crisis and a serious eating disorder as she approaches her marriage. Though the topic may be serious, Atwood presents it as social comedy bordering on the carnivalesque, to present a satirical exposure of women's condition of entrapment inside their bodies and social myths of femininity. *Lady Oracle* (1976) addresses a different kind of female dilemma, that of the sudden fame of a young woman writer who cannot tell her husband that she is now a popular Gothic novelist, and who escapes from Toronto to Italy by staging her own drowning in Lake Ontario, a plot as far-fetched as any in her fiction. This is a comic Gothic novel where the borders overlap between real life and Gothic romance, and at the end the storytelling heroine decides – wisely perhaps – to give up writing bodice rippers and turn to science fiction instead. Atwood does precisely that in *Life before Man* (1979) where a fantasy of dinosaurs and lost worlds drives a wedge through the realistic genre under which this novel masquerades. It was given accolades in the *New York Times Review* and the London *Times* critic praised it: "Life among the dinosaurs may have been simpler . . . But it cannot have been anything like as interesting."[27] Though never one of Atwood's most popular books, it signals new departures as her first multivoiced novel (including one male narrator), her first engagement with multicultural Toronto in the Ukrainian Canadian protagonist Lesje Litvak, and the wide historical dimensions of her imagination.

The most significant of Atwood's early novels was *Surfacing* (1972), published at the same time as *Survival*, and it quickly attained popular status as a "Canadian fable in which the current obsessions of Canadians become symbols in a drama of personal survival: nationalism, feminism, death, culture, art, nature, pollution."[28] American critics took notice of its ecological and feminist dimensions and British critics of its theme of psychological quest. Today we might be inclined to see its significance as the novelistic expression of English Canada's most popular cultural myth, as well as the record of a woman's quest to find "a dialect of her own" to speak of her Canadian identity in the feminine. All these features made *Surfacing* the paradigmatic Canadian feminist novel about wilderness, which influenced other novels like Marian Engel's *Bear* (1976) and Joan Barfoot's *Abra* (1978; also published as *Gaining Ground* in Great Britain). Since then, younger writers such as Gail Anderson-Dargatz and Eden Robinson have been revising this wilderness myth (see, for example, Anderson-Dargatz's novel *The Cure for Death by Lightning* [1996] and Robinson's *Monkey Beach* [2000]). The appeal of *Surfacing* lies in its combination of visionary quest with wilderness survival narrative, in a language which is often closer to poetry than to prose as Atwood charts one woman's regenerated sense of herself as human being in a distinctively Canadian space:

"This above all, to refuse to be a victim. Unless I can do that I can do nothing."[29]

Two other voices first heard in the 1970s were Carol Shields's with *Small Ceremonies* (1976) and *The Box Garden* (1977), and Aritha van Herk's with *Judith* (1978). Shields's novels belong to the genre of domestic fiction in the realistic tradition, though from the start there is the same emphasis on the importance of women's literary imagination as has been noted in so many of these novels. The protagonist of *Small Ceremonies*, wife of a Canadian academic and mother of two adolescent children, is writing a biography of Susanna Moodie and trying unsuccessfully to write a novel.[30] Yet that comfortable middle-class image is held up to scrutiny when Shields considers how women's imaginative needs may not be met within their daily lives:

> Judith Gill in *Small Ceremonies* talks about narrative hunger: why do we need stories? Her conclusion – and mine – is that our own lives are never quite enough for us. They're too busy, too dark, too narrow, too circumscribed, too bound by geography, by gender, by cultural history. It is through fiction that I've learned about the lives of women.[31]

It is this resistance to prescribed limits of social life and literary convention which signals Shields's more transgressive fictions of the 1990s. By contrast, van Herk's *Judith* is a far more aggressively feminist fiction which engages with the kind of revisionist myth-making that French theorist Hélène Cixous has proposed in "The Laugh of the Medusa." Judith, whose name has associations with the biblical Judith who decapitated Holofernes, is also a Circe figure, an isolated but charismatic young pig farmer. Van Herk's is a self-consciously prairie voice, belonging to the region of the West and "the region of woman," and this is the first of her novels of female empowerment: "Fiction's mandate is to explore the possibilities of the imagination, the possibilities of the world beyond its closure."[32]

Voices of the 1980s

Van Herk's restlessness and her ambitious project to expand the imaginative territory for feminist fiction sets the tone for women's novels in the 1980s, where suddenly "transgression" supplants "subversion" as the key motif. Many of these novels introduce topics new to fiction, such as women's exploration of alternative sexualities or issues of racial difference, frequently crossing national borders to move beyond Canadian locations, like Atwood's Caribbean novel *Bodily Harm* (1981) and *The Handmaid's Tale* (1985), the first of only two novels to date set in the United States. In *The Tent Peg* (1981) and *No Fixed Address* (1986) van Herk uses the geographical spaces of Western Canada and the Arctic North to figure out a new space for women in prairie fiction, taking them into unmapped territory outside the traditions of prairie realism into fantasy and myth, where "Landscape beckons escape; escapade."[33] *The Tent Peg* features a cross-dressing heroine, JL (with echoes of the biblical story of Jael and Sisera), who goes to the Arctic in this revisionist version of the western as a "Northern," while *No Fixed Address* represents a more spectacular transgression of gender stereotypes and generic borders, as its picaresque female hero Arachne Manteia (named after the Spiderwoman of Homeric myth) spins through rural Alberta and the Rockies in her vintage black Mercedes till finally she disappears off the map somewhere up in the Yukon. This is feminist frontier fiction, as Arachne pursues her romantic quest to map the inner territory of desire, leaving geography and realism behind. She is a nomadic subject, a fictive embodiment of Rosi Braidotti's theoretical formulation of a feminist politics of location, where nomadism is defined as "the intense desire to go on trespassing, transgressing."[34] Arachne's journey is the first stage in a feminist progress into forbidden territory which is amplified in van Herk's two texts of the 1990s: *Places Far from Ellesmere, a Geografictione: Explorations on Site* (1990) and *Restlessness* (1998), about a woman flirting with her hired assassin. There is something larger than life about these heroines, which is taken up by Susan Swan in *The Biggest Modern Woman in the World* (1983), a carnivalesque story about the Nova Scotian giantess Anna Swan, who becomes a circus performer.

Obasan (1981) might be described as a prairie novel, a female quest novel, or a historical fiction, but every one of these categories is skewed in Kogawa's case, for *Obasan* illustrates how "themes associated with traditional Canadian literature are radically recast in ethnic writing."[35] Writing as a Japanese Canadian, Kogawa with her first novel marks the entry of racial minority women's fiction into the Canadian mainstream, challenging traditional white definitions of Canadianness and official history by transgressing the barrier of a forty-year silence on the internment and dispersal of Japanese Canadians after Pearl Harbor. Told as a fictive autobiography of a young Sansei woman whose childhood memories go back to those terrible years, this is a story of one woman's longing and desire, politicized into the wider history of a persecuted racial minority. Here storytelling functions as the return of the repressed, signified in the absent women's ghost voices which are heard only in dreams. Yet this is a novel which betrays the deep divisions of much revisionist historical fiction in its double ending, where the narrative of female subjectivity is supplemented by harsh documentary realism in the form of a 1946 Memorandum condemning government policy on Japanese Canadians, reminding readers in 1981 that the past was not settled. (Only in 1988 were the survivors granted Redress by the Canadian government.)

Atwood adopts a similarly shocking shift back to the present with the ending of *The Handmaid's Tale*: "Are there any questions?" Her most popular novel belongs like *Obasan* to the genre of "herstory," a feminized revision of history. Yet it transgresses that generic classification by being also a dystopia told from the perspective of a Handmaid, marginalized by her sex in the American fundamentalist Republic of Gilead. Atwood's fable stages a scenario of catastrophe in the near future, though from another generic perspective it could be seen as one of her survival manuals, or even as an exploration of Canadian-American relations. Offred's tale records a woman's struggle to survive as a speaking subject and not simply as a "two-legged womb"[36] whose anonymous body is at the service of the state. Her storytelling is her most transgressive survival tactic, and her voice survives (recorded secretly on cassette tapes) to be heard 200 years later up in Denay, Nunavit in Arctic Canada when Gilead has fallen, making Offred the most important historian of the republic. As Atwood commented: "The writer retains three attributes that power-mad regimes cannot tolerate: a human imagination, in the many forms it may take; the power to communicate; and hope."[37] A similar impulse is demonstrated in feminist revisions of nineteenth-century history, such as Jane Urquhart's *The Whirlpool* (1986) and Daphne Marlatt's *Ana Historic* (1988). Marlatt's novel is particularly significant as a woman's version of history which centers on female relationships and the introduction of a lesbian perspective in its rereading of the lives of girls and women over three generations. The narrator's quest for freedom leads her beyond her marriage into new dimensions of female sexuality in her erotic relationship with a younger woman. Like Offred, the narrator here seeks to reclaim women's life stories erased by official history, just as she sees storytelling as a psychological necessity for women's survival.

New voices of the 1990s

In the 1990s there continued to be a flow of new fictions by established women writers, with major novels by Atwood and Shields, namely Atwood's *The Robber Bride* (1993) and *Alias Grace* (1996) and Shields's *The Stone Diaries* (1993) and *Larry's Party* (1997). However, what is most significant in this period is the sudden proliferation of novelists from previously marginalized minority groups, which has resulted in an unprecedented diversification of the Canadian literary scene as race and ethnicity, sexuality and nationality have all assumed new importance in the representation of identities in fiction. Those changes which reflect much wider cultural shifts in Canadian society (together with more hospitable policies towards "ethnic writing" by the big publishing houses) have meant that the old questions about national identity and what constitutes Canadian literature are being renegotiated, and even the questions themselves are under revision in the new era of multinationalism, multiculturalism, and globalization. It is within and against these large scale "isms" that women novelists have kept their readerships, precisely because their storytelling gives a human face and emotional particularity to the crises which characterize the present cultural climate in Canada as elsewhere.

Atwood has maintained her preeminent position and she is still, according to trendy Toronto novelist and newspaper columnist Russell Smith, "one of the hippest writers in Canada."[38] Her two novels of the 1990s, one about women's lives in Toronto in the early 1990s and the other about a double murder committed in mid-nineteenth-century colonial Canada on a farm just outside Toronto, belong to two very different genres – postmodern Gothic romance and historical fiction. *The Robber Bride* employs traditional Gothic motifs like dark doubles, shape-shifters, and magic mirrors, while it also chronicles Toronto's postwar social history with its unique mix of multiculturalism and racism. *Alias Grace* on the other hand challenges myths of white colonial innocence, as Atwood looks into "the mysterious, the buried, the forgotten, the discarded, the taboo,"[39] a programmatic sketch for much postcolonial historical fiction besides Atwood's own. In 1993 Carol Shields leapt to international fame with *The Stone Diaries*, winning both the Governor-General's Award in Canada and the American Pulitzer Prize, followed by the 1998 British Orange Prize for *Larry's Party* (1997). An American who came to Canada on her marriage, Shields never subscribed to cultural nationalist versions of Canadian identity and her novels cross national borders as easily as they cross genres and genders, moving between Winnipeg, Chicago, Toronto, and Florida. Indeed, she uses the genre of fictive biography to question the very notion of fixed identity, revealing instead the instabilities within her male and female subjects: "What is the story of a life? A chronicle of fact or a skilfully wrought impression?"[40] This questioning of generic boundaries which led Shields into what she described in *Small Ceremonies* as "that whorish field of biographical fiction"[41] goes back to her novels of the 1970s and 80s, with Judith Gill's doubts about her Susanna Moodie biography and the parodic literary detective fiction about a murdered woman poet in *Swann: A Mystery* (1987).

In *The Stone Diaries*, the autobiography of Daisy Goodwill, who was born in Manitoba in 1905 and died in Florida in the 1990s, Shields highlights the necessarily fictive dimension within life writing, reminding readers that in biography the crucial events of subjective inner lives frequently go unrecorded. While the novel sets up a reassuringly conventional frame with its family tree, clusters of family photographs, and chapters in chronological order marking Daisy's birth through the predictable phases of a middle-class woman's life: "Marriage," "Love," "Motherhood," "Work," "Sorrow," "Ease," "Illness and Decline" to "Death," Daisy's life story is anything but predictable just as she herself is anything but a reliable narrator. Orphaned from birth by a mother who did not even realize she was pregnant and who gave birth to Daisy on the kitchen floor just as she finished making a Malvern pudding (Shields with her passion for domestic detail includes the recipe), Daisy grows up with a terrifying sense of belonging to nobody and of self-erasure. Shields meets the narrative challenge of writing such a life through the ambiguously shifting perspectives which Daisy adopts in her storytelling:

> The long days of isolation, of silence, of boredom – all these pressed down on me, on young Daisy Goodwill and emptied her out. Her autobiography, if such a thing were imaginable, would be, if such a thing were ever to be written, an assemblage of dark voids and unbridgeable gaps. (pp. 75–6)

Daisy's autobiography becomes a multivoiced novel, where Daisy's version of her life is supplemented not only by other people's interpretations but by their life stories as well. However, Daisy is not crowded out of her own life as she had feared, for she manages to live "outside her story as well as inside" it (*Stone Diaries*, p. 123). Writing a woman's life within the spaces of domestic fiction, Shields transcends those limits by introducing dimensions beyond the ordinary. Just as in *The Republic of Love* (1992) she had disturbed the predictable genre of popular romance fiction by introducing the pagan folklore of mermaids and strange sea creatures, here she introduces other nonhuman mysteries relating to biology and paleobotany via the dual motifs of flowers and stones from which she draws an analogy between the impossibility of knowing anyone's subjective life and the intricacies of the life sciences. Every systematic account is likely to be frustrated because "the variables are too many" and something is bound to be overlooked, just as at Daisy's funeral her coffin is covered in pansies whereas "Someone should have thought of daisies" (pp. 293, 361).

With *Larry's Party* Shields shifts the gender of her biographical subject as she explores the question, "What's it like being a man these days?"[42] Again she uses a conventional grid that marks twenty years in Larry Weller's life between the ages of twenty-six and forty-six (1977–97), only to overturn the reader's expectations by mapping his interior life through the spatial figure of a maze. There are maze designs at the head of every chapter as Larry's life story is constructed like a labyrinth. These intricate designs satisfy Larry's own "narrative hunger" and represent his way of living outside his story as well as inside it, but there are also evident analogies between mazemaker and novelist as creative artists, both working within established traditions with everyday materials while searching, through the power of art, to cross over from realism into imagination and desire. Shields's border-crossing protagonists prefigure the kind of mobile, multiple identities which become such a distinctive feature with younger writers in the 1990s.

This is the period when Canadian women's fiction becomes insistently pluralized, as a new generation produced their first novels (though many of them had already published short-story collections, poems, and plays with small independent presses), laying down new coordinates for mapping identities by highlighting issues of race, ethnicity, and alternative sexualities. These "Unbecoming Daughters,"[43] many of whose mothers and grandmothers did not come from Canada, continue the tradition of women's revisions of history though frequently from the position of being "others" in Canadian society, and the stories they tell are stories of diaspora, immigrancy, racial and cultural hybridity, and transculturalism.

Sky Lee's *Disappearing Moon Cafe* (1990) signals the decade in which this new multicultural fiction assumes prominence, especially around the mid 1990s. As a third-generation Chinese Canadian, Sky Lee writes out of a visible minority whose history, like that of the Japanese in Canada, has been marked by white racial prejudice, counterpointed by their own exclusionary heritage cultures. *Disappearing Moon Cafe* is a matrilinear saga, a revisionist history of Chinese diasporic experience in British Columbia told by the greatgranddaughter of a Chinese immigrant bride who arrived back in the 1890s. It is the story of women's survival as the narrator thinks back through her mothers, "a lineage of women with passion and fierceness in their veins. In each of their woman-hating worlds, each did what she could."[44] As icons of heritage cultures, matriarchal figures may be demonized as they are here,[45] or idealized as they are in Hiromi Goto's *Chorus of Mushrooms* (1994). Here again it is the Canadian-born granddaughter who tells the story of three generations of Japanese Canadian women living in Alberta. However, Goto's novel, with its generic border crossings between fantasy and realism as she reimagines the grandmother's storytelling voice long after the old woman has disappeared, is less like Lee's epic of a dynasty and more closely resembles the postmodern prairie fiction of van Herk, told from a racialized perspective. Goto's carnivalesque element is lacking in Kerri Sakamoto's *The Electrical Field* (1998). Following in the tradition of *Obasan*, Sakamoto writes a serious historical and political novel about the psychological legacy of internment where anger, paralysis, and shame find their tragic expression in betrayal, murder, and domestic violence. The dominating image in this fraught autobiographical novel is the wasteland, figured by the Electrical Field where the main protagonists circle around each other in a strange drama of attraction and repulsion. Writing in the next generation, Sakamoto insists that history has to be acknowledged in order to move beyond it, and this novel is less about reconciliation than an exorcism of ghosts.

By a curious logic of history the Canadian identity question so dear to the cultural nationalists is still the central question in the new wave of multicultural novels, though questions of identity have become more complicated. The old question "Where is here?" is transformed into "Where am I?" or "Who am I?" as the daughters' searches for location, identity, and origins are driven by their awareness of slippage from origins, motherlands, mother cultures, and mother languages. These novels represent women's negotiations across memory and imagination for, as Shani Mootoo remarked, it's all an act of "forgetting and remembering and inventing."[46] 1996 was the year when the new wave peaked, with new multicultural novels being published by the big international presses, symptomatic of the shift in Canadian fiction away from national to international focus and marketing. These novels may be representative of a trend, yet these writers speak from a wide variety of individual perspectives. While Mootoo and Dionne Brand are both immigrant lesbian writers from Trinidad whose fiction might be classified as belonging to the new Caribbean Canadian literature in English, their racial and cultural heritages are completely different: Brand is Afro-Caribbean and Mootoo is Indo-Caribbean, and while Brand locates herself within a black feminist tradition, Mootoo's emphasis is on cultural hybridity. Such politics of location have consequences in their fiction: Mootoo's *Cereus Blooms at Night* (1996), though set entirely on a fictive Caribbean island, positions itself in between the Caribbean and Canada through its characters' desire for escape from their colonial past to a new postcolonial future, and its focus is on liminal identities in relation to sex and race through a liminal fictional form close to magic realism. Brand's *In Another Place, Not Here* (1996) focuses on dislocation, as its title suggests with its binary oppositions between geographical, cultural, and linguistic locations, in a narrative divided between the voices of two black immigrant female protagonists: "Go home, this is not a place for us."[47] Brand's frequent use of Caribbean demotic speech is an act of resistance to the dominance of the white culture and its language by voices from the margins, as she reveals the hidden subtexts of multiculturalism with their complex interactions between immigrant aspirations, systemic racism, and the tragic effects of isolation on visible minority women.[48] *At the Full and Change of the Moon* (1999) carries this exploration of dislocated nomadic subjects back to slave history and its late-twentieth-century consequences.

The split narrative represented by women's conversations across temporal and spatial boundaries which is a common trope in much diasporic fiction is the structuring principle in Anita Rau Badami's *Tamarind Mem* (1996), where a daughter studying in Calgary writes back to her mother in Madras and in the process writes the memoir of her life as a child in the postcolonial India of the 1960s. This novel, like Shauna Singh Baldwin's *What the Body Remembers* (1999), is significant as a version of the new transnational Canadian fiction written about places and histories outside Canada, a reminder of the multiple cultural affiliations contained within Canadian national identities. In *The Hero's Walk* (2000) Badami reverses the image of immigrancy when the orphaned daughter of a young South Asian woman and her white Canadian husband is brought to India for the first time to live with her grandparents in their sprawling old house in a small seaside town outside Madras. Here the traumatic experience of foreignness is transposed: the little girl wants to go home to Vancouver while for her Indian family Vancouver is just somewhere else, in "that America-Canada place."[49] Though there is a kind of homecoming at the end for this "half-foreign granddaughter," the novel raises serious questions about homes lost and found, as it does about the bewilderment experienced by transcultural/transnational subjects.

The immigrant consciousness and the experiences of white ethnic-minority subjects are important topics in several of these novels, which despite their differences in fictional representation may be grouped together around the question of home. Anne Michaels's *Fugitive Pieces* (1996), a Canadian Holocaust fiction, is a story about fugitives and exiles as the title suggests, with a fuguelike structure which holds two male narrators' voices – one a Holocaust survivor and the other a Canadian-born son of Jewish refugees – in counterpoint. The same themes are repeated with variations, each bringing a homecoming to Canada one step closer. This poetic novel is a meditation on maps, journeys, and lost things which, like Ondaatje's *The English Patient* (1992), locates Canada in a truly international context through the personal histories of its main narrators. Janice Kulyk Keefer's *The Green Library* (1996) constructs a shifting balance between homecomings and psychic dislocations in postwar Ukrainian Canadian experience in her multivoiced novel which negotiates border crossings between past and present, Toronto and Kiev, as Keefer explores the meanings of that "kaleidoscopic term, ethnicity."[50] With *Fall on Your Knees* (1996), set on Cape Breton Island, Ann-Marie MacDonald combines crucial identity issues related to ethnicity, race, and sexuality in a strongly regional historical novel, for this is Maritime Gothic, full of monsters, disasters, and terrible family secrets. Told as a dynastic narrative involving two Cape Breton families – one Scottish and the other Lebanese – it traces their fortunes from the beginning of the twentieth century up to the 1960s when the last two family members meet, not in Cape Breton but in New York. This is family history told from a feminine perspective, where it is the daughters who revise the myths of their white father so as to incorporate their silenced Lebanese mother, in a full recognition of their multiracial inheritance.

2000 and since

Looking at fiction by women since 2000 is like looking into a swirl of crosscurrents: new historical novels like Atwood's *The Blind Assassin* (2000) and Urquhart's *The Stone Carvers* (2001), Badami's transcultural novel, and Shields's angry protest novel against women's throttled lives in *Unless* (2002). Set firmly in the first year of the twenty-first century, this novel marks a series of new departures for Shields with its dramatic dislocations in the plot of middle-class family life, its explicit concern with feminist politics, and its emphasis on the pleasures and the necessity of fiction writing as a strategy of survival. This story is told by a novelist, Reta Winters, whose eldest daughter Norah has suddenly become a dropout, sitting silently on a Toronto street corner wearing a cardboard sign with the word GOODNESS on it hanging around her neck. As a novel with trauma at its center, it exhibits a complex rhythm, alternating between retrospection and engagement with the immediate present of domestic routine, female friendships, and writing "where the rhythm of typing-and-thinking" maintains "a semblance of on-going life" (p. 109), all held in precarious balance against parental anguish and bewilderment at Norah's behavior. The odd chapter titles like "Nevertheless," "Meanwhile," and "Not Yet" (and of course *Unless*) are integral to the structure, being "little chips of grammar" which hold the isolated contingent events of life in relationship until the narrative is resolved within the conventions of comedy, providing a momentary balance through fictive artifice: "The uncertainty principle; did anyone ever believe otherwise?" (p. 318).

Beside these established voices, new voices are emerging who speak neither from the center nor from immigrant positions, but from other socially marginalized groups – an Aboriginal community in British Columbia, economically deprived communities in the Maritimes, and a small black community in southwestern Ontario, which is perhaps the most underrepresented group in Canadian fiction. Many of the protagonists here are alienated teenagers struggling to figure out who they are and how to survive: "It's a stupid, embarrassing life," as one of them comments.[51] These novels are embedded in local contexts and to that extent are related to the tradition of regional and small-town fiction, but with different emphases. Eden Robinson's *Monkey Beach* (2000), set in Kitamaat and the surrounding forests of British Columbia, is a contemporary Aboriginal version of a wilderness quest combined with the growing-up novel, where a Haisla adolescent girl seeks to bridge the cultural gap between Native and white cultures in her own hybridized situation. Her narrative with its border blur between realism, fantasy, and vision is closer to Lee Maracle's *Ravensong* (1993) than to anything in white Canadian regional fiction. From the other side of Canada, Lynn Coady's Cape Breton novels *Strange Heaven* (1998) and *Saints of Big Harbour* (2002), like Donna Morrissey's Newfoundland novels *Kit's Law* (1999) and *Downhill Chance* (2002), mix social criticism with adolescent angst in novelistic language that "recreates the opulence that is the contemporary vocabulary and syntax of Atlantic Canada."[52] Lori Lansen's *Rush Home Road* (2002) offers a more sentimentalized version of small-town fiction from the unusual narrative perspective of an old black Canadian woman who adopts a young mixed-race girl abandoned by her white trailer-trash mother. This is "heritage fiction" in the guise of a story about mothers and daughters, as Lansen traces the history of nineteenth-century black settlement around Chatham near Lake Erie, which was at the terminus of the Underground Railroad for fugitive and freed slaves from the United States.

It seems appropriate to end this chapter with a novel which positions itself on the threshold between the twentieth and the twenty-first centuries: *The Blind Assassin*, published at the beginning of the new millennium and told by a voice from beyond the grave. Atwood's narrator is an old woman writing her memoir in 1999 as a legacy for her granddaughter who is away traveling in India, and who will not read it till after her grandmother is dead. As private confession and public memorial, this Gothic narrative is concerned with questions of inheritance in its double dimensions of family and national history, told from a dissident feminine perspective which discredits traditional master narratives, so that the question of inheritance becomes a questioning of inheritance and of the legitimacy of heritage myths: "Since Laura is no longer who you thought she was, you're no longer who you think you are, either... You're free to reinvent yourself at will."[53] Like her duplicitous old narrator's tale, Atwood's storytelling holds out possibilities of escape from the imprisonment of the past, opening up new spaces for women to write their identities while in the process remapping the boundaries of what constitutes Canadian fiction.

NOTES

1. Margaret Laurence, *The Diviners* (1974; Toronto: McClelland, 1984) p. 453.
2. Lynette Hunter, *Outsider Notes: Feminist Approaches to Nation State Ideology, Writers/Readers and Publishing* (Vancouver: Talon, 1996) p. 17.

3. See Robert Wright, *Hip and Trivial: Youth Culture, Book Publishing, and the Greying of Canadian Nationalism* (Toronto: Canadian Scholars' Press, 2001) p. 18.

4. See Donna Pennee, "Culture as Security: Canadian Foreign Policy and International Relations from the Cold War to the Market Wars," *International Journal of Canadian Studies* 20 (Autumn 1999): pp. 191–213.

5. My focus on fiction in English inevitably occludes Quebec women's writing and the francophone dimensions of Canadian culture and nationalism.

6. Alice Munro, afterword, *Emily of New Moon*, by L. M. Montgomery (1923; Toronto: McClelland, 1989) p. 360.

7. On the "merger mania" see Wright, *Hip and Trivial*, pp. 45–8, and for a critical assessment of its effects on Canadian writing, see Stephen Henighan, *When Words Deny the World* (Erin: Porcupine's Quill, 2002) pp. 91–107 and 133–56.

8. Alice Munro, *Lives of Girls and Women* (1971; Harmondsworth: Penguin, 1984) p. 177.

9. Carol Shields, *Unless* (Toronto: Random, 2002) p. 270.

10. Harold Horwood, interview with Alice Munro, *The Art of Alice Munro: Saying the Unsayable*, ed. J. Miller (Waterloo: University of Waterloo Press, 1984) pp. 123–35.

11. Graeme Gibson, interview with Alice Munro, *Eleven Canadian Novelists. Interviewed by Graeme Gibson* (1972; Toronto: Anansi, 1973) pp. 236–64.

12. Mark Honigsbaum, "The Goddess of Small Things: The *Guardian* Profile," *Guardian* 23 May 1998: pp. 6–7.

13. The phrase is taken from Robert Kroetsch, "Death Is a Happy Ending," *Canadian Novelists and the Novel*, ed. D. Daymond and L. Monkman (Ottawa: Borealis, 1981) pp. 244–51.

14. Margaret Laurence, "Ivory Tower or Grassroots? The Novelist as Socio-Political Being," *Canadian Novelists and the Novel*, ed. Daymond and Monkman, pp. 251–9.

15. George Woodcock, *Introducing Margaret Laurence's* The Stone Angel: *A Reader's Guide* (Toronto: ECW Press, 1989) p. 67. For a recent reassessment of Laurence, see David Staines, ed., *Margaret Laurence: Critical Reflections* (Ottawa: University of Ottawa Press, 2001).

16. Clara Thomas, *The Manawaka World of Margaret Laurence* (Toronto: McClelland, 1976) pp. 173–87.

17. Margaret Laurence, "Gadgetry or Growing: Form and Voice in the Novel," *A Place to Stand On: Essays by and about Margaret Laurence*, ed. George Woodcock (Edmonton: NeWest, 1983) pp. 80–9.

18. Laurence, "Ivory Tower or Grassroots?," p. 255.

19. Alice Munro, "What Do You Want to Know For?," *Writing Away: The PEN Canadian Travel Anthology*, ed. Constance Rooke (Toronto: McClelland, 1994) pp. 203–20.

20. For the evolution of *Lives*, see J. R. (Tim) Struthers, "The Real Material: An Interview with Alice Munro," *Probable Fictions: Alice Munro's Narrative Acts*, ed. Louis K. MacKendrick (Toronto: ECW Press, 1983) pp. 5–36.

21. Gibson, interview with Alice Munro, *Eleven Canadian Novelists*, p. 248.

22. Munro, *Lives*, p. 248.

23. Munro, *Lives*, p. 249. See Barbara Godard's classic essay, "Heirs of the Living Body: Alice Munro and the Question of a Female Aesthetic," *The Art of Alice Munro*, ed. Miller, pp. 43–71.

24. For an account of Atwood's achievements, see Reingard M. Nischik, ed., *Margaret Atwood: Works and Impact* (New York: Camden House, 2000), which won the Atwood Society Prize for Best Book in 2001.

25. See Rosemary Sullivan, *The Red Shoes: Margaret Atwood, Starting Out* (Toronto: Harper, 1998) and Nathalie Cooke, *Margaret Atwood: A Biography* (Toronto: ECW Press, 1998).

26. Margaret Atwood, *Bodily Harm* (1981; London: Virago, 1983) p. 208.

27. Philip Howard, review of *Life before Man* by Atwood, *The Times* 14 March 1980: p. 14.

28. Kildare Dobbs, "Canadian's Second Novel Even Better Than Her First," *Toronto Star* 12 Sept. 1972: p. 31.

29. Margaret Atwood, *Surfacing* (1972; London: Virago, 1991) p. 185.

30. Shields had just finished an MA on Susanna Moodie at the University of Ottawa, which was published in 1977 as *Susanna Moodie: Voice and Vision*.

31. Marjorie Anderson, interview with Carol Shields, *Prairie Fire* 16.1 (Spring 1995): pp. 139–50.

32. D. Jones, interview with Aritha van Herk, *SPAN* 25 (1987): pp. 1–15.

33. Aritha van Herk, "Women Writers and the Prairie: Spies in an Indifferent Landscape," *A Frozen Tongue*, by van Herk (Sydney: Dangaroo, 1992) pp. 139–51.

34. Rosi Braidotti, *Nomadic Subjects: Embodiment and Sexual Difference in Feminist Theory* (New York: Columbia University Press, 1994) p. 36.

35. Jonathan Kertzer, *Worrying the Nation: Imagining a National Literature in English Canada* (Toronto: University of Toronto Press, 1998) p. 123.

36. Margaret Atwood, *The Handmaid's Tale* (London: Vintage, 1996) p. 146.

37. Margaret Atwood, *Second Words: Selected Critical Prose* (Toronto: Anansi, 1982) p. 397.

38. Wright, *Hip and Trivial*, p. 153.

39. Margaret Atwood, *In Search of Alias Grace* (Ottawa: University of Ottawa Press, 1997) p. 19.

40. Carol Shields, *The Stone Diaries* (1993; London: Fourth Estate, 1994) p. 340.

41. Carol Shields, *Small Ceremonies* (London: Fourth Estate, 1995) p. 53.

42. Carol Shields, *Larry's Party* (London: Fourth Estate, 1997) p. 315.

43. See Shirley Chew and Anne Rutherford, eds., *Unbecoming Daughters of the Empire* (Sydney: Dangaroo, 1993).

44. Sky Lee, *Disappearing Moon Cafe* (Vancouver: Douglas and McIntyre, 1990) p. 145.

45. See Mari Peepre, "Resistance and the Demon Mother in Diaspora Literature: Sky Lee and Denise Chong Speak Back to the Mother/land," *International Journal of Canadian Studies* 18 (Autumn 1998): pp. 79–92.

46. Shani Mootoo, *Out on Main Street* (Vancouver: Press Gang, 1993) p. 66.

47. Dionne Brand, *In Another Place, Not Here* (1996; London: Women's Press, 1997) p. 230.

48. See Peter Dickinson, *Here Is Queer: Nationalisms, Sexualities and the Literature of Canada* (Toronto: University of Toronto Press, 1999) pp. 156–72.

49. Anita Rau Badami, *The Hero's Walk* (Toronto: Knopf, 2000) p. 226.

50. Janice Kulyk Keefer, "Personal and Public Records," *Tricks with a Glass: Writing Ethnicity in Canada*, ed. R. G. Davis and R. Baena (Amsterdam: Rodopi, 2000) pp. 1–18.

51. Lynn Coady, *Saints of Big Harbour* (London: Cape, 2002) p. 6.

52. Lesley Choyce, introduction, *Atlantica: Stories from the Maritimes and Newfoundland*, by Choyce (Fredericton: Goose Lane, 2001) p. 9.

53. Margaret Atwood, *The Blind Assassin* (2000; London: Virago, 2001) p. 627.

10

Life writing

SUSANNA EGAN AND GABRIELE HELMS[1]

The last quarter of the twentieth century has been a profoundly autobiographical age with the personal narrative providing an important lens both on to history and on to the contemporary world. Narratives, productions, and performances of identity have begun to permeate and transform Canadian culture in every medium. Furthermore, personal narratives no longer depend on speakers belonging to dominant social groups but emerge with pride from minority positions, cultivate the value of undervalued experiences, and risk distinctly intimate subject matter. Because the personal is also expressed as political, recent life writing contributes explicitly to changing cultures and to changing understanding of personal, communal, even national identities. In short, quite apart from the range and quality of life-writing production in Canada since the 1970s, and the rich archives that contribute to Canadian history, life writing is now recognized as preeminent among the genres in which the evolving character and concerns of the nation have been and continue to be written.

Life-writing practices in Canada, as elsewhere in the western world, have traditionally been associated with the written word, in particular with the genres of memoir, autobiography, diary, biography, letters, and travel-writing. The term "life writing" suggests the broad continuum of life-writing discourses that range from writing about the self (autobiography) to writing about another (biography), acknowledging that writing about the self and writing about someone else are not as distinct from each other as they used to be. Contemporary writers of autobiography and biography tend to be self-reflexive and to situate their stories in well-developed contexts of family and community. Such multiple perspectives complicate and enrich the generic possibilities of life-writing practices. While this essay, for practical reasons, will focus on prose narratives in English that are self-identified as life writing, have been published, and are therefore widely accessible, it must acknowledge the multiple genres in which life writing is now available. Apart from the collaborative work or the family memoir, now very popular in print, life writing is also common in the quilt or collage or art installation, the film, the drama, or the website, and the oral performance familiar in nonliterate cultures. These varieties of life-writing production necessarily extend the range of what life writing can say and mean and the effects it can have.

Such contemporary explorations seem key to the articulation of distinctly Canadian identities and will therefore provide the focus for this chapter. The "now" of writing necessarily inflects the "then" to be considered, helping, perhaps, to explain how life-writing work in Canada has become so influential in the construction and interpretation of Canadian culture. Above all, contemporary writers address a Canadian audience; even when they consider themselves in transit or as belonging in more than one place, they challenge their fellow Canadians to engage in self-identification. While this development is surely one feature of historical evolution, it is also central to the role that life writing currently plays in Canada.

Life writing came to Canada with European explorers and settlers and has, like their descendants, contributed to the evolution of distinctly Canadian cultures. However, the early French explorers, such as Jacques Cartier and Samuel de Champlain, and the French missionaries who produced logs and journals that charted their courses and chronicled important daily events were all contributing to European history. One of the best known of these texts is *Relations des Jésuites*, reports the Jesuit priests sent from Quebec to Paris, 1632–73, where they were then published (first translated and published in seventy-three volumes as *The Jesuit Relations* between 1896 and 1901). Land explorers, such as Henry Kelsey, Anthony Henday, Samuel Hearne, Alexander Henry, Alexander Mackenzie, David Thompson, and John Franklin, and the English captains James Cook and George Vancouver were also prolific. Since their main purpose was documentation, their logs, reports, journals, diaries, and letters provide rich sources of information about the Canadian landscape and the First Nations they encountered, but also about their authors' personalities and expectations.

While exploration reports define Canada as part of a French or British empire, Confederation sparked the publication of collections that archive Canadian lives defined by their value to the emerging nation. Henry J. Morgan, one of the founders of the nationalist Canada First Movement, produced with his *Sketches of Celebrated Canadians* (1862) the first collection of biographical sketches in Canada. Morgan's *Bibliotheca Canadensis* (1867) provided short accounts of pre-Confederation writers. His *The Canadian Women and Men of the Time* (1898) is noteworthy because, although he devotes only three percent of the total number of entries to women, he acknowledges in his selection and sketches of these women that they had major interests and/or careers outside the home. This volume was later incorporated into the first version of *The Canadian Who's Who* in 1910. George Rose's *A Cyclopedia of Canadian Biography* (1886–8) and W. Cochrane's *The Canadian Album: Men of Canada or Success by Example* (1891–6) further attest to a strong interest in professional and political lives that were to form a solid historical foundation for a new nation; these lives (of men) were to act either as a mirror of existing accomplishments or as a claim to the possibilities available to all men. Similar purposes inform the multivolume biographies in the early twentieth century, such as the twenty volumes of *Makers of Canada* (1903–8), the thirty-two volumes of *Chronicles of Canada* (1914–16), and the eleven volumes of Lorne Pierce's *Makers of Canadian Literature* appearing between 1923 and 1926. The many volumes of the *Dictionary of Canadian Biography* (begun in 1966) remain the most comprehensive of their kind in Canada.

In their early manifestations these works document exemplary lives that model specific values (Eurocentric, colonial, largely masculine). What happens, then, when the former colony brings its constitution home, redefines European immigrants? Life writing changes – as it reflects such historical developments but also as it imagines new possibilities for further change. Not surprisingly, late-twentieth-century Canadian life writing reflects these changes, extending and reshaping earlier models of Canadian identity. Often its postmodern attitudes and habits of irony that undermine heroic examples seem to challenge the very possibility of writing about the self and the other. Self-representation that lacks master narratives becomes problematic, provisional, and temporary. Social values that shift from a hierarchical to a situational model for the production of life writing introduce new opportunities for narrative and provoke unpredictable responses in readers. Despite or because of these developments, readers still identify keenly with life writing. Sales figures for life writing reflect its popularity. Prestigious literary prizes, such as the University of British Columbia's Medal for Canadian Biography (by or about a Canadian, since 1952), the Governor-General's Award for non-fiction (since 1936), and the Charles Taylor Prize for literary non-fiction (since 2000) attest to the public recognition that life writing informs contemporary cultures. Scholarly attention to life writing in disciplines well beyond literature (such as medicine, education, history, or social work) brings it into college and university curricula. Given such pervasive interest and attention, the questions now must be what contributions more recent works can make, what readers they assume as audience, and what Canada they create.

Immigration

Indigenous peoples in Canada have claimed life-writing practices for their own uses only since the 1970s. As a result, life writing since the late seventeenth century has very largely represented the experience of people who came from elsewhere. Much of the content of contemporary life writing therefore in many cases derives from pre-Canadian experience, but this does not seem to prejudice publication, promotion, and reception of the work. Rather, the "cleft-/tongue" of the immigrant voice, to borrow Roy Kiyooka's phrase,[2] appreciative but without patriotic fervor, and speaking as much from elsewhere as from here, contributes quite distinctively to Canadian culture. In *Notes from the Hyena's Belly* (2000), Nega Mezlekia situates his story in Ethiopia, merely pointing to new beginnings in Canada at the end, as does Cecil Foster writing about Barbados in *Island Wings* (1998). Michael David Kwan, in *Things That Must Not Be Forgotten* (2000), situates his story exclusively in China. Such apparently remote life writing plays an important role in the entirely conscious, deliberate construction of identities that explore the meaning of "Canadian." One title by Dionne Brand could describe a vast body of literature that combines the exploration of personal belonging with literal presence in Canada: *A Map to the Door of No Return: Notes to Belonging* (2001).

Here, Canada does not provide the setting for immigrant stories, but it provides the audience. In some cases, immigrants' stories would not be interesting in their country of origin; in others they would not even be possible. For example, Ken Wiwa can analyze his relations with his father and with Nigeria (*In the Shadow of a Saint* [2000]) in Canada in ways that he could not in Nigeria. Other immigrants may winkle secrets from their primary contexts and expose them safely for a Canadian readership (as with Roy Kiyooka's *Mothertalk: Life Stories of Mary Kiyoshi Kiyooka*, edited by Daphne Marlatt [1997], Janice Kulyk Keefer's *Honey and Ashes* [1998], Myrna Kostash's *The Doomed Bridegroom* [1998], Lisa Appignanesi's *Losing the Dead* [1999], Eric Wright's *Always Give a Penny to a Blind Man* [1999], or Anna Porter's *The Storyteller* [2000]). In the case of Kiyooka's *Mothertalk*, the story of the immigrant to Canada would not be as relevant to a Japanese reader.

Immigrant Canadian writers are in fact quite deliberate and explicit about importing foreign wares with the implications that their contribution is "exotic" and that producing their story for their new audience helps to locate them, and the personal narratives collected in *Passages: Welcome Home to Canada* (2002), with authors ranging from Ying Chen and Dany Laferrière to Shyam Selvadurai and Moses Znaimer, bear ample testimony to the complications involved. Life writing translates foreign experience into claims on a homegrown culture. For example, Porter subtitles *The Storyteller* (2000), her narrative of herself and her grandfather, *A Memoir of Hungary*. Similarly, Rachel Manley, in *Drumblair* (1996) and *Slipstream* (2000), writes a political history of Jamaica in terms of the history of her own family, drawing on the distance and the audience that Canada provides. And Austin Clarke, in *Pig Tails 'n Breadfruit* (1999), uses the subtitle *A Barbadian Memoir*. Whereas Clarke's *Growing Up Stupid under the Union Jack* (1980) may have evoked for many Canadians as well as for Barbadians the complex relations of colonized to colonizer, *Pig Tails* brings Barbadian English into a Toronto kitchen to demonstrate both the narrator's own transplantation and that of his reader. Because, in Henry Kreisel's words, "only intimate knowledge can confer authority upon the imagination,"[3] these immigrant writers create Canada out of their earliest and most intense sources of knowledge.

For early immigrants, too, these sources of knowledge were their place of origin, but they did not import these stories to the New World. Rather, they wrote about their lives in the New World for their familiar audience at home. Susanna Moodie, Catharine Parr Traill, and Anne Langton all wrote letters home, introducing their relatives to the wonders and the oddities of their lives here, eking out their incomes with publications that romanticized their hardships. Where Moodie sounds a note of warning, Traill gives practical advice to prospective immigrants. Like Georgina Binnie-Clark in the early years of the twentieth century, Moodie and Traill were part of the commodification of Canada, their personal experiences becoming an early Canadian export. Their lives, of course, have become part of the mythology of Canada, but only in retrospect, long after they had ceased to figure largely in England. Their lives are part, too, of conventional wisdom about the Canadian landscape and climate as large and hostile for the isolated human figure (though Traill's enthusiastic botanical studies provide some intimacy).

The promise that Canada first seemed to offer proved disappointing, not necessarily to these early pioneers and founders of young communities but to their successors who hoped for more sophisticated opportunities than the new country could provide. Kreisel, enthusiastically exploring the Canadian literary scene in the early 1940s, wanting to know, as he puts it, "what songs [Canadians] sang and what stories they told" (*Another Country*, p. 110), found that the Canadians he consulted had no sense of a homegrown culture but thought themselves a young nation that had not yet produced anything significant. Whereas many causes have clearly contributed to improving Canadian self-perception and international recognition since Kreisel's arrival during World War II, no small part of that development is likely due to autobiographical work that has articulated not just a literature but a self-reflexive literature that can and must position the writer in relation to time, place, and opportunity. It seems fair to think of Frederick Philip Grove's *In Search of Myself* (1946) and John Glassco's *Memoirs of Montparnasse* (1970) as the onetime classics of Canadian life writing not simply for their literary merit or the problems associated with them but also for their sense of alienation from and their disparagement of Canada as a land of cultural opportunity.

Towards the end of the twentieth century, Asian Canadian literature began to transform older Eurocentric perceptions of Canada. Canadians of European ancestry were quick to control the significant Asian immigration to the West Coast during the Gold Rush with discriminatory legislation. Memoirs of Asian immigrants have only emerged, therefore, since the descendants of the earliest immigrants have been able to take their place among other Canadians. Apart from their political value, these works have also contributed to the country's imagination of the Pacific Rim and Canadian connectedness to Asia. Denise Chong's memoir *The Concubine's Children* (1995) is one carefully researched and deeply moving account of three generations of Chinese immigration. In *Paper Shadows: A Chinatown Childhood* (1999), Wayson Choy explores both the secrets of his own background and the Chinatown culture of his childhood. In *Diamond Grill* (1996), the poet and critic Fred Wah, born in Canada, traces his Chinese ancestry through three generations of migration, settlement, and culture. Postwar activism on the part of Canadians of Japanese ancestry, protesting the Canadian government's appropriation of their goods and internment of their communities, led also to an outpouring of Japanese Canadian work in film, drama, poetry, visual arts, fiction, and formal autobiography and biography. Roy Kiyooka's work is among the most varied both for his personal generic explorations and for his remarkable narrative of three generations of his family in *Mothertalk*.

Place

Belonging derives from place, community, and historical continuity and evolves for immigrants only as they develop new roots. Ironically, belonging in Canada has had almost more to do with the land and the history of particular regions than with the relatively new and consistently unstable concept of Canada as a whole. The geographical features of place, from climate to political and economic opportunity, have obviously played a significant part in the division of Canada into distinctive regions, contributing to the ways in which writers conceive of space and thus to the ways in which they identify themselves in it.

The North, as the chapter on exploration and travel illustrates, has dominated the very idea of Canada from the earliest times of European settlement, but to the travelers' tales we must add the more recent narratives of Native autobiographers.[4] As with the Indigenous peoples further south, Native northerners have also created their own versions of North, to some degree in response to being misconstrued from outside. Living among the whites, or *qallunaat*, in Ottawa, Minnie Aodla Freeman seems to be responding to Flaherty's title *My Eskimo Friends* with her title *Life among the Qallunaat* (1978). Others who establish a distinctly northern perspective include Germaine Arnaktauyok Markoosie, *Harpoon of the Hunter* (1970); John Tetso, *Trapping Is My Life* (1970); Tom Boulanger, *An Indian Remembers* (1971); Peter Pitseolak, *People from Our Side* (1975); and Anthony Apakark Thrasher, *Thrasher... Skid Row Eskimo* (1976). With the celebration of Nunavut Day on 1 April 1999, northerners claimed their region as emerging from homegrown narratives of identity.

Immigrants to Canada have written regional narratives from the earliest times. They have written, too, about the cultural communities that regions have produced. Autobiographical works by Moodie and Traill are foundational for Lower Canada, in particular the lands just north of Lake Ontario. Binnie-Clark did not merely settle in Saskatchewan in 1905 and set herself up against considerable odds as a single woman farmer. Her *Wheat and Woman*, first published in 1914, was designed to persuade others of the wonders of prairie farming. The prairies are also central to Laura Salverson's experience, narrated in her prize-winning *Confessions of an Immigrant's Daughter* (1939), of being an Icelander in Winnipeg. As with Fredelle Bruser Maynard and, later, Don Gillmor, the narrative is permeated by the mid-west, what Maynard calls "that free wild perilous world."[5] Salverson's friend Nellie McClung, who lived in Winnipeg as well as Edmonton, produced highly political works that represent her feminist activism from her prairie roots, *Clearing in the West* (1935) being the best known. Susan Allison (*A Pioneer Gentlewoman in British Columbia* [1976/1991]) traces her migrations over many years (1860–94) from England to New Westminster at the mouth of the Fraser River and then across the mountains into the Okanagan valley, identifying in the process members of the pioneer community whose names have become part of the geography of British Columbia. Emily Carr, in painting as in personal stories and journals, has been a powerful explorer and creator of the Canadian West Coast, from small-town European Victoria to the deep forests and ancient coastal villages of the Indigenous peoples.

Where early immigrants had pioneer stories to tell and identified themselves as the narrators of the new places in which they settled, later life writing inserts itself into the increasingly complicated history of Canada as interpreter and critic. *Baltimore's Mansion*, Wayne Johnston's memoir of his father (1999), evokes a passionately pre-Confederation Newfoundland. His family's history on the Avalon Peninsula makes even Newfoundland look like part of the continental land mass. David Macfarlane, in *The Danger Tree* (1991), writes a family history of the Goodyears of Newfoundland, focusing on the impact of World War I on the local community. Helen Buss subtitles her *Memoirs from Away: A New Found Land Girlhood* (1999), and Warren Cariou calls his *Lake of the Prairies: A Story of Belonging* (2002). Clive Doucet, living and working in Ottawa, traveled to New Brunswick in order to evoke his own childhood in Nova Scotia as an Acadian without a home-land (*Notes from Exile: On Being Acadian* [1999]). Don Gillmor's search for "origins" and "home" in *The Desire of Every Living Thing* (1999) traces his family's life in Scotland but then centers on the prairies and the early years of the city of Winnipeg. For content, for location, as for a haunting sense in each text of dis-content and dis-location, these works are thoroughly, in-disputably Canadian; they also express a desire for origins and for ethnic belonging.

Family memoir – generations

Increasingly, as ordinary people have seized the tools available for self-representation, they have seen themselves as members of families and com-munities and have embedded themselves in their generational relationships. Where writers might traditionally have declared their lineage or included memories of grandparents, parents, uncles, and aunts, they would still have perceived their own individuality as the reason for writing. Since the 1970s, however, inspired by women's writing, Indigenous narratives, and immigrant narratives, autobiographers and biographers have identified themselves as part of a web of relations without which their own story would be incom-plete. Mary Kiyooka, Appignanesi, Kulyk Keefer, Porter, Michael Ignatieff, Johnston, Macfarlane, and Chong are just a few who have written family memoirs. Remembering their forebears, these authors instruct their chil-dren and, by inserting their extended relationships into the history of their times and places, combine the autobiographical and biographical. Fredelle Bruser Maynard is an interesting case in point. *Raisins and Almonds* (1972) is a gently romanticized collection of stories about her Jewish family in Saskatchewan, creating impressions that she radically revised with *The Tree of Life* sixteen years later (1988). Her daughter, Joyce Maynard, then brought out her own memoir (*At Home in the World* [1998]), in which she re-visits and revises her parents' lives in order to illustrate their damaging effect on her own. Clearly, family memoir can also disconnect relationships.

First Nations

Métis scholar Deanna Reder takes issue with Arnold Krupat's suggestion that Indigenous American life writing is the ground where two cultures meet, the textual equivalent of the frontier.[6] Preferring to identify a more reciprocal relation between immigrant and Native cultures, Reder suggests "fireweed" as a more useful metaphor in Canada. A hardy perennial, fireweed spreads rapidly wherever the ground has been scarred by fire or other disasters. Her suggestion is persuasive because of the blossoming of personal works in Indigenous communities across Canada since the 1970s. This is the resurgence that Tomson Highway describes as predicted by the shamans who foresaw the coming of white people, the near-destruction of Native people, and the return of Native power seven generations after Columbus.[7] Taking many forms, from individual testimony, to collections of personal stories, to collections of essays, to poetry, drama, history, commentary, criticism, and interviews (such as Janet Silman's *Enough Is Enough* [1987]), and very often including community stories, ancient legends, and tales of the land, life-writing practices have given Native writers and activists the means to articulate their own sense of their identity and a platform for redress of systemic injustice.

Despite their use of English and of narrative tropes borrowed from white cultures, these works resist white dominance more effectively than their nineteenth-century predecessors could. Where George Copway wrote in 1850 about having "but recently been brought out of a wild and savage state,"[8] Jeannette Armstrong finds herself "answering back . . . saying 'That's not true! Indian people don't see things that way; we see it this way.' "[9] Not surprisingly, therefore, the Report of the Royal Commission on Aboriginal Peoples, published in 1996, relied heavily on Indigenous life writing in order to make sense of the residential school experience. Similarly, the Supreme Court's decision in favor of Aboriginal title in the *Delgamuukw* case in 1997 rested on life stories. Life stories also quite deliberately contribute to Native healing. For example, in *Stolen from Our Embrace* (1997), Suzanne Fournier and Ernie Crey present personal stories of suffering and of healing arrived at by traditional methods. Across Canada, First Nations, Innu, and Métis have articulated their particular experiences as individuals and as communities and have made themselves heard. In the words of the editorial in a special issue of *Canadian Literature* (1990), "Native Writers and Canadian Writing," white readers are "Learning to Listen."[10]

Maria Campbell's *Halfbreed* (1973) was an immediate bestseller and marks a significant turning point for Native life writing. In the same year, a

Cree woman, Jane Willis, published *Geniesh: An Indian Girlhood*, about her residential school experience. Lee Maracle's *Bobbi Lee, Indian Rebel* (1975) was inspired in part by the leadership of Howard Adams, a Métis scholar who taught her to think beyond the shame of white stereotyping. Adams's *Prison of Grass*, also published in 1975 (revised in 1989), included his personal story with a call to Native pride, suggesting that Native people would create their own solutions. Basil H. Johnston in particular with *Ojibway Heritage* (1976) and *Indian School Days* (1988), Shirley Sterling with *My Name Is Seepeetza* (1992), Rita Joe with *The Song of Rita Joe* (1996), and Drew Hayden Taylor with *Funny, You Don't Look Like One: Observations from a Blue-Eyed Ojibway* (1996) address a large readership with individual stories.

Although many Native writers have been adopting dominant cultural modes in order to reach a wide public, collaborative production between white and Native remains problematic, seeming to replay the history of relations between Native informant and white anthropologist. Lenore Keeshig-Tobias has scathingly described white academics as merely stepping into the shoes of the missionaries and the Indian agents in their power to determine the Native story.[11] However, Maracle, even as she identifies her initial collaboration on *Bobbi Lee* with Donald Barnett as a disaster that he had never intended, also ascribes to him the inspiration for her to take command of her own voice. Collaboration is an issue because it raises serious questions about who ultimately controls or even owns the story. *The Book of Jessica* (1989) by Linda Griffiths and Maria Campbell provides one intense example of such a dispute, initial communication between the two women becoming contentious when a written contract threatens Campbell and her own life story with a fixed and subordinate role. The book that prefaces the play, in which Griffiths played Campbell, spells out in narrative and transcribed dialogues the bitter struggle of this collaboration between white and Métis and between oral and literary traditions. With more apparent harmony, but with seriously problematic imbalances of power, the white novelist Rudy Wiebe has collaborated with Yvonne Johnson on *Stolen Life: The Journey of a Cree Woman* (1998). Using tapes and interviews and thousands of pages of Johnson's own writing, Wiebe constructs a redemptive narrative for Johnson who has been sentenced to life in prison for her part in a brutal murder. Whereas his intervention is friendly, the effect is by no means that of an equal collaboration, the Native woman emerging quite distinctly as the construction of the white author.

Working within the discourses of anthropology, Julie Cruikshank with *Life Lived Like a Story* (1990), Flora Beardy and Robert Coutts with *Voices from Hudson Bay* (1996), and Nancy Wachowich with *Saqiyuq* (1999) produce texts that attend more closely to the subjectivity of their participants. In her introduction, Cruikshank contrasts her initial assumptions with those of the three Native Elders from the Yukon to show that their assumptions were different. Whereas she wanted to know about the impact of change and development on their lives, they understood their lives in terms of kinship and landscape and shaped their narratives to include mythological tales, songs, and long lists of personal and place-names. Nearly ten years later, Wachowich seems to work on more common ground with three generations of Innu women, but questions about editorial process and ultimate control remain. Notably, Campbell and Armstrong, identifying themselves as outsiders, resisted an invitation to write Innu lives. The most successful collaborations seem to be those in which Native people work together for productions that address both the white readership and their own communities. Emma Minde's *Their Example Showed Me the Way* (1997) and Alice Ahenakew's *They Knew Both Sides of Medicine* (2000) have involved only Native participants and have been published in English and Cree. Other writers involved in multiple tellings include Margaret Blackman, Beverly Hungry Wolf, and Pitseolak.[12]

Despite continuing economic and political difficulties, this seventh generation since Columbus that the shamans predicted seems to have regained a cultural high ground initially lost when immigrants overwhelmed oral cultures with the orthodoxies of the printed word. Oral narratives remain the possession of particular people and communities, still serve their ancient cultural purposes, and are still performed for those purposes and, on occasion, for white communities. Wendy Wickwire's transcription of Harry Robinson's stories (*Write It on Your Heart* [1989]) provides one example of printed text functioning as oral narrative in that it needs to be read aloud. However, the earliest Indigenous peoples to produce personal narratives in print were necessarily acculturated into both print and English as the tools of a foreign culture that they then addressed. Further, both print and English came to them by way of missionaries and the Bible, thus ensuring that the personal stories of Natives were conversion stories addressed to the invader. They took many forms – diaries, histories, letters, sermons, reports, autobiographies, and travelogues (Petrone, *Native Literature*, p. 35) – and served to raise funds and extend missions as well as to present "the Indian" for European audiences. George Copway was among the earliest and most distinguished of these autobiographers, publishing *Recollections of a Forest Life* in London in 1850. Others providing personal stories for the most part in sermons and letters include Peter Jones (1802–56), George Henry, who published his European travels in the late 1840s, and Peter Jacobs, with a journal published in 1858.

Trauma – national, communal, and personal

Because Canadian participation on the battlefields of Europe became significant for the articulation of Canadian identity, it is no surprise that personal stories of war should figure prominently in Canadian literature, surely covering every campaign in every part of Europe and beyond. The range of writers is as various as the participants of war – chaplains, reporters, airmen, officers, doctors, nurses, prisoners – and the form as various too, including letters, diaries, logs, photographs and documents, collections of memories, and personal narratives. Mary Peate, for example, with *Girl in a Sloppy Joe Sweater* (1988) presents the home front during World War II. Fred Cederberg's *The Long Road Home* (1984) makes clear in its subtitle (*The Autobiography of a Canadian Soldier in Italy in World War II*) the very specific nature of war narratives. Under the wonderful title *Boys, Bombs and Brussels Sprouts: A Knees-Up, Wheels-Up Chronicle of WWII* (1981), J. Douglas Harvey presents the personal history of Canada's only bomber force, No. 6 Group. George G. Blackburn's three extensive memoirs, *The Guns of Normandy* (1995), *The Guns of Victory* (1996), and *Where the Hell Are the Guns?* (1997) use a second-person narrator rather than the usual first person, implicating the reader in graphic and detailed memory. Among the most literary and well known of these war narratives is Farley Mowat's *And No Birds Sang* (1979). Extending personal narrative with line drawings and with paintings, Charles Fraser Comfort recounts his experience as an artist at the front in *Artist at War* (1956/1995) and Maxwell Bates his time as a prisoner behind enemy lines in *A Wilderness of Days* (1978). Such war memoirs record military life, battle strategies, intense suffering, and heroic action. They speak to nationalist generations of veterans for whom they form part of the historical record.

For the incomplete or recurring traumas of personal experience, life writing, in Canada as elsewhere, is paramount. Jewish community centers and archives across the country serve as repositories and even publishers of personal stories of the Holocaust, or Shoah. Among the earliest Canadian publications are Jack Kuper's *Child of the Holocaust* (1967) and Chava Kwinta's *I'm Still Living*, in translation from the Hebrew (1974). In 1981, Anita Mayer published *One Who Came Back*, and Eva Brewster's *Vanished in Darkness: An Auschwitz Memoir* (1984) was revised and expanded to appear in 1994 as *Progeny of Light/Vanished in Darkness*. In each case of personal witness to the Nazi death camps, the writer claims the urgent need to educate future generations in the history of this period and in the dangers of hatred and discrimination. Production of these texts becomes more urgent as Holocaust survivors reach old age. Ibolya Szalai Grossman's *An Ordinary*

Woman in Extraordinary Times (1990) and Elisabeth Raab's *And Peace Never Came* (1997) both come to uneasy rest in Canada. Similarly, *Bialystok to Birkenau* (2000) is another example of a late and painful Canadian narrative, told by Michel Mielnicki to John Munro. Despite the personal material and narratives of appalling experience, these personal stories seem secondary to their witness to collective trauma. Their work is political rather than therapeutic. Brewster, for example, explains that she began writing in response to signs of neo-Nazism in Alberta and became active as an educator and spokesperson when Ernst Zündel and Jim Keegstra were identified in Alberta as Holocaust deniers.

Several Canadian writers suffered internment camps not in Europe but, of a rather different order, in Canada itself. They were Canadian immigrants of Japanese descent removed from the West Coast and interned after the bombing of Pearl Harbor in December 1941. Takeo Nakano had arrived in Canada in 1920. His divided allegiances and resistance to systemic discrimination against people of Japanese descent led to his internment at Angler, just north of Lake Superior. His diaries from this period and his tanka poetry were published as *Within the Barbed Wire Fence* (1980), first in Japanese and then in English. The Nisei, or second-generation, experience is expressed by Muriel Kitigawa in her "Letters to Wes" and to other friends, and writings on the Japanese Canadian relocations, collected and edited by Roy Miki under the title *This Is My Own* (1985). Identifying a whole community, they contributed to the climate of change in which, for example, the Canadian government could apologize to its citizens of Japanese descent in 1988. Kreisel's experience of internment in Canada began in Europe rather than Asia; fleeing Austria for England in 1938, Kreisel was deported as an enemy alien to holding camps in Canada, temporarily at least sharing quarters with German prisoners of war. He kept his records of that time in English, determined to master his new language and the cultures it opened to him. Kreisel's early diaries, letters, photographs, and documents, of fiction and interview, and later commentary and analysis of the European and Jewish experience of immigration, provide a rich sense of work in process.

Writings about illness, disability, and personal trauma are a more recent phenomenon. They, too, come out of intense personal suffering and create communities of recognition. In many cases, these texts seem to begin as what Suzette Henke has called "scriptotherapy," a writing cure in which the victim takes control of the story that has been silenced by medical bureaucracies or by societal taboos.[13] Because this phenomenon of the 1990s has become extremely popular, it has seemed to legitimize the whole syndrome of suffering, endanger happier species of narrative with "victim envy," and lead to something of a backlash against "victim" literature. It is, nonetheless, important for a number of reasons.

As a phenomenon, narratives of illness, disability, and trauma have given voice to marginalized experiences and raised awareness in medical communities about the danger of substituting patient for person or health problem for the whole human situation. With *The Wounded Storyteller: Body, Illness, and Ethics* (1995), Arthur Frank uses his own experience of cancer to identify the commonly used narrative tropes of illness. In *The Perfection of Hope: A Soul Transformed by Illness* (1997), Elizabeth Simpson examines the role and even the value of illness (lung cancer) in her life as do Wayne Tefs and Suzanne Giroux when they chronicle their experiences with carcinoid cancer in *Rollercoaster* (2002) and breast cancer in *A Chance for Life* (2001) respectively. Although these writers carefully detail their diagnosis and treatment, they are equally concerned with the need to create a new sense of self; sometimes the writing process contributes to this re-creation. While Giroux told her story to a professional writer, Bonnie Sherr Klein collaborated with Persimmon Blackbridge in *Slow Dance: A Story of Stroke, Love and Disability* (1997) to orchestrate her own voice and those of family members, friends, and health professionals, an approach that conveys some of the social and psychological complexity of her experience. These auto/biographical narratives are testaments to the spirit of the survivor, suggesting that even the most difficult illness can be managed, if not cured.

Further, life writing lifted taboos that have shamed generations into silence. With *How Linda Died* (2002), for example, Frank Davey presents his wife's terminal illness, narrating her decline and its toll on the family. Miriam Toews tells of her father's mental illness and suicide in *Swing Low* (2000), but she does so by assuming her father's first-person perspective, thus continuing the kind of writing she did for him in hospital which he could read to himself later when he forgot why he was there. With such works, illness becomes an open secret, creating public confidence that narrative remains possible, that meaning is available, and that disease, disability, and death itself are open for discussion.

Incest and childhood trauma remain particularly problematic, but autobiographical practices since the 1980s have done more immediately perceptible work in this area than in almost any other. Claire Martin's autobiographies first appeared in French in 1965 (*Dans un gant de fer*) and 1966 (*La joue droite*, for which she received the Governor-General's Award, curiously enough, in the fiction category); they were then combined into one English volume, *In an Iron Glove* (1968). Her books significantly pre-date the now relatively frequent practice of writing about domestic abuse. Charlotte Vale Allen's *Daddy's Girl* appeared in 1980 and *My Father's House: A Memoir of*

Incest and of Healing by Sylvia Fraser in 1987. Where Allen tells a painful story of family dysfunction and sexual abuse in traditional narrative form, Fraser creates two personae, one in italics, to navigate the labyrinth of memory and trauma. Elly Danica's *Don't: A Woman's Word* (1988) is more raw and direct than earlier texts, and many readers have confirmed that they identify with it. Given that autobiographers take personal risks when they confine their narratives to crisis, Danica's sequel provides an unusual but important opportunity for the text to move ahead with the life; *Beyond Don't: Dreaming past the Dark* appeared in 1996. Liza Potvin, in *White Lies (For My Mother)* (1992), addressing her mother and replicating the white lies by using white spaces on the page, demonstrates with Fraser and Danica the original strategies often required by untellable stories for which no models exist. The shortcomings of the process notwithstanding, Wiebe and Johnson's *Stolen Life* (1998) depends on collaboration to convey just how deep the damage of child abuse may be and how necessary its narration.

Gay and lesbian life writing

Contemporary life writing recognizes that sexuality plays a crucial role in identities. Following the gay liberation movement of the 1960s and 70s, gay and lesbian life writing has increasingly challenged the expectations of North American heterosexist society. Early examples include the personal writings of expatriate Patrick Anderson, *Snake Wine* (1955), *Search Me* (1957), and *The Character Ball: Chapters of an Autobiography* (1963), and John Glassco's *Memoirs of Montparnasse* (1970), describing his time in Paris. Glassco's book was immediately praised as one of the finest Canadian autobiographies. However, when it was discovered that most of the book had been written in the 1960s and not, as Glassco says in *Memoirs*, while he was in hospital in 1932–3, its claims to authenticity were questioned.[14]

To explore homoerotic desire, writers have extended traditional forms of life writing to accommodate their own life experiences. Stan Persky's "meditations" combine elements of memoir, travelogue, and philosophy in *Buddy's* (1989), *Then We Take Berlin* (1995), and the innovative *Autobiography of a Tattoo* (1997). Daphne Marlatt's work may be best known for her explicit engagement with questions of sexual identity and her challenges to generic forms to explore these questions. From her travelogues/journals of the 1970s, *Zócalo* (1977) and *Month of Hungry Ghosts* (1976), to her journal/poem *How Hug a Stone* (1983) and the collaborative *Double Negative*, in which she and Betsy Warland contemplate the parallels between the theft of Aboriginal lands in Australia and the limitations on space for lesbians, Marlatt relentlessly explores how gender, sexuality, race, and class inform cultural experiences and our sense of history, and how language can liberate or oppress us in the process. In her collection of critical essays, spanning fifteen years, *Readings from the Labyrinth* (1998), she provides autobiographical contexts for each piece by including journal entries and letters from the time of their writing, an approach that keeps alive the exploratory spirit of her earlier work.

Collections of essays are the medium of choice for a number of writers, such as Jane Rule in *A Hot-Eyed Moderate* (1985) and journalist Michael Rowe in *Looking for Brothers* (1999), who contemplate, among other things, what it means to be a gay/lesbian writer in Canada, how cultural representations interact with their self-representations, or the ways society continues to stigmatize homosexual relations. For Dionne Brand in *Bread out of Stone* (1994) and *A Map to the Door of No Return* (2001), and Beth Brant in *Writing as Witness* (1994), racism and homophobia go hand in hand, and their insistence on struggle and resistance is informed by the complexities of their own identities as Black and Mohawk lesbians respectively. A similar concern, albeit not in essay format, characterizes the memoir *Thunder through My Veins* (1999) by Métis writer Gregory Scofield who focuses on his childhood years, describing his sense of displacement and loss before he could later accept himself as a gay Métis man with a promising future as a writer.

What it means to be a writer is also central in *Elsa: I Come with My Songs* (1986) by Elsa Gidlow, whose career began in Montreal before she left for the United States; in the award-winning *Inside Memory: Pages from a Writer's Workbook* (1990) by Timothy Findley; and in Marianne Brandis's *Finding Words: A Writer's Memoir* (2000). Brandis revisits her whole life to understand her identities as an immigrant, a daughter, a single woman who discovered her lesbianism in mid-life, and a writer and teacher who has just turned sixty. Painter and writer Mary Meigs also explores different aspects of her life, but does so in separate volumes of autobiography, an approach that Helen Buss has described as developing "serial selves":[15] *Lily Briscoe: A Self-Portrait* (1981), best known for its depiction of Meigs's emergence from the closet and her relationship with Marie-Claire Blais, *The Medusa Head* (1983), *The Box Closet* (1987), *In the Company of Strangers* (1991), and *The Time Being* (1997).

One of the most controversial narratives of recent years has been Elspeth Cameron's *No Previous Experience: A Memoir of Love and Change* (1997). Cameron, biographer of Birney, Hugh MacLennan, and Irving Layton, zeroes in on the breakdown of her marriage and her coming-out as a lesbian. *No Previous Experience* has been publicly challenged by some of the people portrayed in its pages, and it raised important ethical questions about, for instance, the effect of her disclosures on her children. Similar coming-out stories became popular in North American anthologies in the 1990s. They typically include some Canadian writers and feature a range of genres, such as Frances Rooney's *Our Lives: Lesbian Personal Writings* (1991), Betsy Warland's *InVersions: Writings by Dykes, Queers & Lesbians* (1991), and Makeda Silvera's *Piece of My Heart: A Lesbian of Colour Anthology* (1991). Some anthologies focus on experiences of homophobia (Mona Oikawa et al., *Resist: Essays against a Homophobic Culture* [1994]), survivors of childhood sexual abuse (Queer Press Collective's *Loving in Fear* [1991]), disability (Shelley Tremain's *Pushing the Limits* [1996]), or Asian culture (Song Cho's *Rice* [1998]).

The sexuality and sexual politics of public figures have their own market appeal. Carole Pope's *Anti Diva* (2000) continues the provocative style she and her band Rough Trade became known for. Sky Gilbert's *Ejaculations from the Charm Factory* (2000) covers the years when he was artistic director of Buddies in Bad Times Theatre in Toronto. Jim Egan may be best known for his, and his partner Jack Nesbit's, Supreme Court challenge to the exclusion of same-sex couples from pension benefits, but in *Challenging the Conspiracy of Silence: My Life as a Canadian Gay Activist* (1998), Donald McLeod presents an oral history of Egan's whole life. Kevin Bourassa and Joe Varnell's *Just Married: Gay Marriage and the Expansion of Human Rights* (2002) focuses on their fight to become the first gay couple to receive a city-issued marriage license in 2001. David Reimer became a celebrity of sorts after John Colapinto published *As Nature Made Him: The Boy Who Was Raised as a Girl* (2000), once again sparking fierce discussions about whether gender differences are the result of biology or social conditioning. Whereas sexuality is important to identity and to social experience, these texts illustrate the recent tendency to focus less on a life-so-far and rather more on a single issue that is central to the narrator's experience of him/herself.

Literary autobiography and biography

The lives of writers have always sparked the public's curiosity – to learn about the man or woman behind the books. Many prominent writers themselves published autobiographical works during their lifetime (some more than one), reflecting on their careers, the writing of a particular book, their lives beyond their careers, or the historical and cultural contexts of their lives. Few have attempted to map out the full trajectory of their lives as did Hugh Garner (1973) and Margaret Laurence, who organized her chapters around mothers and motherhood (1989). More commonly, writers have limited their focus, for instance to a single year, such as Morley Callaghan's summer in Paris in 1929 (1963), and the year that Clarke Blaise and Bharati Mukherjee spent in India (*Days and Nights in Calcutta* [1977]). Or they refer to their childhood and young adulthood (Stephen Leacock [1946], Earle Birney [1980], Al Purdy [1983], Adele Wiseman [1987]). Dorothy Livesay's serial autobiographical explorations began with her childhood years (1973, expanded edn. 1988) and moved on to the 1930s (1977), only to revisit these periods of her life and then take her readers forward to the mid-1960s in *Journey with My Selves* (1991). Similarly, George Woodcock produced serial life writing (1983, 1987, 1994) and wrote extensively on the lives of other people. While these books always include some reflections on the autobiographer's writing career, Robert Kroetsch (1995) explicitly limits his selection of essays, talks, and poems to speak to his writing life, not his personal life. Similarly, Birney's *Spreading Time* (1980) documents his early development as reader and writer, lamenting, for example, the absence at the time of Canadian literature on Canadian curricula and providing important details about literary contexts, but unwilling to reveal the "more colourful Birney" that many readers had expected to find in revelations about his private life.[16] One of the most (in)famous of Canadian literary autobiographies must be Frederick Philip Grove's *In Search of Myself* (1946). When D. O. Spettigue tried to verify some of Grove's biographical details in the late 1960s, he discovered that Grove was actually Felix Paul Greve, a German writer, and that his description of his childhood in Europe and his early American years was largely fictionalized.[17] Biographical scholarship on Grove did not end with this discovery, however. Richard Cavell analyzes the "normatizing" effects of some of this scholarship in terms of Grove's sexuality and nationality, and thus draws attention to the critical process through which lives are constructed.[18]

While the retrospective autobiography and memoir are usually written with an audience and publication in mind, the publication of private documents (diaries, journals, letters, and notebooks) tends to be the result of scholarly interest and usually becomes possible only after the author's death. Often considered "artless" representations of the writers' selves, these genres promise access to their (more or less) undistorted personalities. Rather than being literary works in their own right though, such texts, whose secrecy or limited audience is one of their defining characteristics (a characteristic possibly challenged as these genres move from the printed text to web-based media), gain value precisely because they may reveal the unknown and thus can enhance readers', and especially critics', understanding of a writer and his/her "true works of art." The selected journals of Lucy Maud Montgomery (ed. Mary Rubio [1985]), the private writings of Elizabeth Smart (ed. Alice van Wart [1986] and Christina Burridge [1987]), as well as the unpublished autobiographical writings of A. M. Klein (ed. Zailig Pollock and Usher Caplan [1994]) may suffice as examples here. Letters, in spite of their air of naturalness, may contain a more deliberate self-representation on the part of the writer, who anticipates the addressee's reception. For this reason, collections of letters can reveal much about specific relationships (as does Laurence's correspondence with Purdy, published by John Lennox in 1993, and with Wiseman, published by Lennox and Ruth Panofsky in 1997); they can also provide extensive sociohistorical contexts as do the letters of Moodie, edited by Carl Ballstadt in 1985. Exactly because of their relationality, letters can also map out a writer's social network and highlight the ways in which writers adapt their self-representations to their readers, as becomes evident, for instance, in the letters of Malcolm Lowry (ed. Sherrill Grace [1995/96]).

Some writers have published selected journals or letters during their lifetime, however. Kiyooka's *Transcanada Letters* (1975), for instance, presents a unique collection of notes, photographs, letters, poetry, reflections on art, and so on, giving the reader a good sense of his movements between the mid-1960s and 1974 and demonstrating the extent to which he saw every aspect of his life as relational. Kroetsch's *The Crow Journals* (1980), on the other hand, has a much more limited focus; it is a journal he kept while working on the novel *What the Crow Said* (1978). Equally limited in scope is Evelyn Lau's *Runaway* (1989), which includes her diary of the two years she spent on the streets as a teenager; it depicts her struggle with drugs and prostitution, but also her desire to become a writer.

A significant number of Canadian scholars have published two or more literary biographies during their careers. They include Clara Thomas, Betty Keller, Marian Fowler, Elspeth Cameron, Sandra Djwa, James King, Rosemary Sullivan, Lorraine McMullen, and Ira Nadel. Moreover, the Canadian Biography series published by ECW Press has devoted over half of its titles to Canadian writers. A comprehensive list of writers who have been the subject of biography would be extensive;[19] some have even attracted biographers more than once.[20] 1998, for example, saw the publication of two biographies on Margaret Atwood. While Sullivan and Cooke obviously cover some of the same material, they show how two biographies can never be the same. Both books follow chronology, but Sullivan's *The Red Shoes*, which she calls a "not-biography" for its lack of nostalgia and retrospection,[21] ends in the late 1970s, focusing on Atwood's creative life (as a woman) and situating her within a context of Canadian social, political, and literary culture. Nathalie Cooke's approach in her unauthorized biography is more personal and narrowly defined although she covers an extra twenty years. No Canadian, however, has received more attention than Emily Carr, whose careers as writer and painter have led to biographies by Maria Tippett (1979), Paula Blanchard (1987), Doris Shadboldt (1979, 1990), Kate Braid (2000), and Susan Crean (2001). Comparing these multiple accounts of a single artist may suggest the impossibility of the biographical project, or signal the importance of perspective and contexts in constructing a life.

Controversy always leads to public interest, which is no less true for the Canadian literary canon. Pauline Johnson (Betty Keller [1981], Carole Gerson and Veronica Strong-Boag [2000], Charlotte Gray [2002]) and Grey Owl (Lovat Dickson [1973], Donald Smith [1990], Jane Billinghurst [1999]) have repeatedly been the subject of biographies to (re)assess their lives and works in light of their mixed and faked heritage respectively. At times controversy can also follow the publication of a biography when information revealed remains contentious or seems inappropriate. This is what happened when James King (1997), for example, contextualized Laurence's suicide by providing an extensive account of her struggles, including her alcoholism. In his memoir of Sinclair Ross (*As for Me and My Body* [1997]) written after Ross's death, Keath Fraser presents a biographical reading of *As for Me and My House* based on conversations in which Ross had revealed to Fraser that he was homosexual.

Many of the biographies since the 1980s have been devoted to women writers, without doubt because of the feminist movement and the advent of feminist theory in literary studies. From McMullen's work on Frances Brooke (1983) and Fowler's on Sara Jeannette Duncan (1983), to Sullivan's on Elizabeth Smart (1991) and Gwendolyn McEwen (1995), and Elizabeth McNeill Galvin's on Isabella Valancy Crawford (1994), women biographers in particular have chosen female subjects, asserting their importance in Canadian literary history. These scholars have significantly expanded the canon of women writers, primarily by (re)discovering the work of nineteenth-century writers, such as Anna Jameson, Agnes Maule Machar, Elizabeth Simcoe, and others, in addition to the well-established life stories of Moodie and Traill. McMullen's *Re(Dis)covering Our Foremothers* was the ground-breaking collection of essays to "look at Canadian women writers in the nineteenth century and point to the need to recover those once known but now forgotten and to discover those never publicly known whose diaries, letters, and autobiographical writings are – or should be – a valued part of Canadian tradition."[22] The fifteen biographical essays collected by Cameron and Janice Dickin in *Great Dames* (1997) address a long tradition in which biography was limited to extraordinary white men and their public lives. Instead, the collection introduces ordinary Canadian women and in the process takes on conventional techniques of biography which seem inappropriate given the lack of archival material, the frequently personal relationships between contributors and subjects, and the relational lives of these women. Often this kind of scholarly work takes place in archives where researchers unearth private writings (for example, diaries and letters) and public documents to reestablish records of women's lives, in the process revaluing, for example, the diary form, long considered feminine and therefore inferior.[23] Jean Barman's *Constance Lindsay Skinner: Writing on the Frontier* (2002) and *Sojourning Sisters: The Lives and Letters of Jessie and Annie McQueen* (2002), as well as Kathryn Carter's *The Small Details of Life* (2002), an anthology of diary excerpts by twenty Canadian women between 1830 and 1996, are the result of such archival work.

Popular life writing

Canada, like many other countries of the western world, has a long-standing tradition of autobiographies and biographies by or about people of public renown. Always, everywhere, one can find the lives of entertainers, stars of sport and popular culture, and politicians. Works that often create hero figures, such as those on Wayne Gretzky, Paul Tracy, Terry Fox, k.d. lang, and Joyce Wieland, for example, or memoirs by Céline Dion, Rita MacNeil, Pamela Wallin, Jan Wong, Karen Kain, and Michael J. Fox, assume a fan club and create a mythic persona who is, after all, one of the people. These texts typically promise to reveal the story of the celebrity's rise to fame or a private self previously hidden from public view. Such life writing represents and contributes to Canadian culture by virtue of its eclectic nature and its homegrown success. Economic success, in fact, is the driving force of biographies and autobiographies by and about the Canadian business world (for example, Conrad Black, Jimmy Pattison, the Bronfmans, the Eatons, and the Molsons). By focusing on the development of character and a strong sense of place, Donald Creighton's biography of John A. Macdonald (1952, 1955), Canada's first Prime Minister, set the stage for the ever-popular stories of politicians. Pierre Berton and Peter C. Newman, in particular, have contributed numerous volumes of popular biography to the Canadian market, including Berton's autobiographical narratives (1993, 1995).

New forms of life writing

In addition to the broad range of life-writing practices, the innovative nature of much Canadian work deserves special attention. If generic features are contextual constructs rather than components of an abstract, synchronic system, if genres, in other words, are ways of seeing and conceptualizing the world, then formal innovations are not only inseparable from the "content" of the life story, but can also tell us about the Canadian cultural contexts from which they emerge and in which they will operate. In fact, such challenges to generic conventions can be important means of resistance and social change. Michael Ondaatje's *Running in the Family* (1982) is an excellent example of a text that resists easy generic categorization. It includes stories, poems, sketches, and photographs in its fictionalized portrait of Ondaatje's family in Sri Lanka. Ondaatje challenges unproblematic self-referentiality as he plays with the roles of author, narrator, writer, and reader. In the acknowledgments at the end of the text, Ondaatje refers to the two trips to Sri Lanka which led to the writing of the book, but then "confess[es] that the book is not a history but a portrait or 'gesture'."[24]

There is no shortage of new generic terms in contemporary writing: George Bowering's "biotext" in *Errata* (1988) (further developed by Fred Wah in *Diamond Grill*), Aritha van Herk's "crypto-frictions" in *In Visible Ink* (1991), Daphne Marlatt's "fictionalysis" in "Self-Representation and Fictionalysis" (1990), and Linda Griffiths and Maria Campbell's "theatrical transformation" in *The Book of Jessica* (1989). The new generic labels signal difference and a reconceptualization of life-writing conventions, often focusing explicitly on the curious relationship between living a life and telling or writing one. Resistance to generic expectations and claims to referentiality and transparency lead Bowering in *A Magpie Life* (2001) and Wah in *Diamond Grill* (1996) to explore new forms for life writing. Robert Kroetsch's first sentence in his acknowledgments for *A Likely Story* (1995) captures this spirit: "This is (not) an autobiography."[25] Scholars, too, have examined the conventions of the genres they write in. In the Canadian context, Helen M. Buss has used the term "autocritography" to describe the self-conscious writing of critics who provide autobiographical information about the conditions that have shaped their professional interests.[26]

Collections of personal essays explore new ways of self-representation by bringing together conventions of life writing and the essay. The personal essay as a window on an individual's culture can highlight the interdependence of self and contexts, but a collection of personal essays can also trace changes in those relationships. While the collection of essays as a form of life writing is not new in literature, its self-consciousness in recent writing sets it apart as different. For example, a collection can examine the evolving essay form itself, quite possibly, in Fred Wah's words, undercutting "the hegemony of such forms."[27] Whether writers explicitly reflect on their own unease with the essay form or the problem of rereading essays from a later perspective (Wah in *Faking It*, Marlatt in *Readings from the Labyrinth* [1998], and Diana Brandt in *Dancing Naked* [1996]), whether they insist on the importance of writing as a social act (Roy Miki in *Broken Entries* [1998]), or attempt to think outside of the constraints of generic conventions by speaking instead of "recollections" and "notes" (Dionne Brand in *Bread out of Stone* [1994] and *A Map to the Door of No Return* [2001]), they all explore questions of identity and positioning in innovative ways through the autobiographical and biographical practice of the personal essay.

Looking back – thinking forward

Not surprisingly, Canadian academics have been slower to recognize new directions than autobiographers and biographers have been to produce them. They have also come to life-writing studies more than two decades after their European and American colleagues – a delay that reflects both the relative isolation of Canadian literature after World War II and uncertainty about a Canadian focus for Canadian scholarship. Nonetheless, the academic history of this field in Canada maps a gradual evolution from the celebration of distinctive literary works ("The Art of Autobiography," *Canadian Literature* 80 [Autumn 1981]) to probing recognition of the multiple roles that life writing plays in this culture. In 1990, Shirley Neuman published a massive chapter on "Life-Writing" in *The Literary History of Canada* (vol. IV) edited by W. H. New, and, in 1991, a collection of essays entitled *Autobiography and Questions of Gender*. Notably, for the date, this collection dealt not with women but with gender as a category of identity, introducing into Canadian scholarship the notion that life writing made more diverse contributions to Canadian culture than had been imagined. Neuman's work led to a groundswell in conferences, articles, collections of essays, and monographs dedicated to life writing in Canada. By 1996, she had fertile ground for the suggestion "that Canadian autobiography is . . . not what we have taken it to be, and that it is many more things than we have taken it to be."[28] The collection of essays in the spring 2002 issue of *Canadian Literature*, which was dedicated to "Auto/biography," certainly demonstrates wide recognition of the range and relevance of life-writing studies in Canada. Similarly, the *Encyclopedia of Literature in Canada* (2002), edited by W. H. New, includes several discrete entries on autobiographical and biographical genres in Canada and the unique cultural work that these genres perform. Further, the Wilfrid Laurier Life Writing Series, under the general editorship of Marlene Kadar, marks a serious commitment to the archiving and the production of life writing in Canada.

Notably, none of this work has attempted to define or even suggest a life-writing "canon." Perhaps delayed attention to life writing in Canada has produced this significant benefit; neither scholarship nor publishing is restricted in its understanding of what life writing can be or is afraid of new beginnings. In 2003, it is possible to say that Canadians from all walks of life and from all regions of the country, and the scholars who analyze, teach, and promote their work, are increasingly engaged in the life-writing enterprise. The retrospective undertaken here from the present circumstances of so much life-writing activity may well point not just to the "then" of the past but also to the "then" that is to come.

NOTES

1. We would like to thank Manuela Costantino, Peter Dickinson, Janice Fiamengo, Sherrill E. Grace, W. H. New, Deanna Reder, and Penny van Toorn for answering our questions, providing information and suggestions, and reading sections of this chapter.
2. Roy Kiyooka, "home is a throng-of-voices," *Pacific Windows: Collected Poems of Roy K. Kiyooka*, ed. Roy Miki (Vancouver: Talon, 1997) p. 177.
3. Henry Kreisel, *Another Country: Writing by and about Henry Kreisel*, ed. Shirley Neuman (Edmonton: NeWest, 1985) p. 134.
4. See Sherrill E. Grace, *The Idea of North* (Montreal: McGill-Queen's University Press, 2001).
5. Fredelle Bruser Maynard, *Raisins and Almonds* (1972; Don Mills: PaperJacks, 1973) p. 13.
6. Deanna Reder, "Stories of Destruction and Renewal: Images of Fireweed in Autobiographical Fiction by Shirley Sterling and Tomson Highway," *Creating Community: A Roundtable on Canadian Aboriginal Literature*, ed. Renate Eigenbrod and Jo-Ann Episkenew (Penticton: Theytus and Bearpaw, 2002) p. 277.
7. Penny Petrone, *Native Literature in Canada: From the Oral Tradition to the Present* (Don Mills: Oxford University Press, 1990) p. 162.
8. Quoted in Petrone, *Native Literature*, p. 200.
9. Jeannette Armstrong, "Writing from a Native Women's Perspective," *In the Feminine: Women and Words / Les femmes et les mots*, ed. Ann Dybikowski et al. (Edmonton: Longspoon, 1985) p. 55.
10. W. H. New, "Learning to Listen," "Native Writers and Canadian Writing," special issue of *Canadian Literature* 124/125 (Spring/Summer 1990): p. 4.
11. Lenore Keeshig-Tobias, "The Magic of Others," *Language in Her Eye*, ed. Libby Scheier et al. (Toronto: Coach House, 1990) pp. 173–7.
12. See Sophie McCall, "'A Life Has Only One Author': Twice-Told Aboriginal Life Narratives," *Canadian Literature* 172 (2002): pp. 70–90.
13. See Suzette Henke, *Shattered Subjects: Trauma and Testimony in Women's Life Writing* (New York: St. Martin's Press, 1998).
14. See Michael Gnarowki's useful introduction in the second edition of Glassco's book, *Memoirs of Montparnasse* (1970; Oxford: Oxford University Press, 1995).
15. Helen M. Buss, "Serial Selves: Mary Meigs's Autobiographical Texts," paper presented at the Centre for Research in Women's Studies and Gender Relations, University of British Columbia, 28 Feb. 2001.
16. Elspeth Cameron attributes this phrase to Al Purdy in her biography, *Earle Birney: A Life* (Toronto: Viking, 1994) p. 552.

17. Douglas O. Spettigue, *FPG: The European Years* (Ottawa: Oberon, 1973).

18. Richard Cavell, "Felix Paul Greve, the Eulenburg Scandal, and Frederick Philip Grove," *Essays on Canadian Writing* 62 (1998): pp. 12–45.

19. They include Earle Birney, Leonard Cohen, A. M. Klein, Margaret Laurence, Stephen Leacock, Dorothy Livesay, Hugh MacLennan, Alice Munro, Alden Nowlan, and F. R. Scott.

20. For example, Robertson Davies (Michael Peterman [1986], Judith Skelton Grant [1994]), Malcolm Lowry (Douglas Day [1973], Gordon Bowker [1993]), E. J. Pratt (Sandra Djwa [1974], David Pitt [1984, 1987]), and Lucy Maud Montgomery (F. W. P. Bolger [1974], Mollie Gillen [1975], Mary Rubio and Elizabeth Waterston [1994]).

21. Rosemary Sullivan, *The Red Shoes: Margaret Atwood Starting Out* (Toronto: Harper, 1998) p. 2.

22. Lorraine McMullen, ed., *Re(Dis)covering Our Foremothers: Nineteenth-Century Canadian Women Writers* (Ottawa: University of Ottawa Press, 1990) p. 1. See also Helen M. Buss, *Mapping Our Selves: Canadian Women's Autobiography in English* (Montreal: McGill-Queen's University Press, 1993).

23. In Helen Buss and Marlene Kadar, eds., *Working in Women's Archives: Researching Women's Private Literature and Archival Documents* (Waterloo: Wilfrid Laurier University Press, 2001), Canadian scholars discuss archival research on women's lives and challenge the neutrality of such archives, introducing a range of Canadian women in the process.

24. Michael Ondaatje, *Running in the Family* (Toronto: McClelland, 1982) p. 206.

25. Robert Kroetsch, *A Likely Story: The Writing Life* (Red Deer: Red Deer College Press, 1995) p. 217.

26. For an example, see Helen M. Buss, *Repossessing the World: Reading Memoirs by Contemporary Women* (Waterloo: Wilfrid Laurier University Press, 2002).

27. Fred Wah, *Faking It* (Edmonton: NeWest, 2000) p. 1.

28. Shirley Neuman, ed. "Reading Canadian Autobiography," special issue of *Essays on Canadian Writing* 60 (1996): p. 6.

I I

Regionalism and urbanism

JANICE FIAMENGO

Imagined geographies

Canada's vast distances, natural barriers, diverse patterns of settlement, and locally specific histories have led many commentators to see regionalism as a defining feature of Canadian culture. George Woodcock articulated a widely held view when he asserted that Canadian literary traditions have always been fundamentally regional, developing differently in different parts of the country.[1] In the preface to *The Bush Garden* (1971), Northrop Frye stressed the importance of regions to the creative imagination, arguing that an imagination conditioned by prairie stretching to the horizon would develop differently from one shaped by the huge mountains and trees of British Columbia or by the churning sea around Newfoundland.[2] According to these influential literary critics, the experience of living in a vast country of strikingly different landscapes has inevitably led Canadian writers to assert a primary imaginative allegiance to specific regions rather than to the whole country.

Yet what might seem an undeniable and uncontentious theory of Canadian literature has had a complex history and continues to inspire debate. Regional has often been a pejorative label with connotations of limitation and triviality, as for example when E. K. Brown argued that regionalist writing stressed the "superficial" over the "universal."[3] During periods of heightened nationalism, regionalism has been regarded as a negative force of fragmentation. On the other hand, in the post-1988 era of free trade, when national and cultural distinctions are threatened by globalization, the insistence on difference and specificity has acquired a new value in Canada. The current political climate favoring de-centralization has combined with a general waning of faith in national narratives to make regional particularity an attractive focus of critical interest. This chapter considers the various roles that place and region have played in English Canadian literature.

In the simplest definition, regional literature portrays regional experience, using "the details of real-world geography" to assert the value of the particular.[4] Regionalism examines the impact of a distinctive terrain, topography, and climate upon the people who experience them, sometimes suggesting quasi-mystical explanations for the force of geography. One form of regionalism (usually called formal regionalism) privileges geographical location over all other aspects of identity, suggesting that the fact of living in a certain place has a force greater than family history, gender, or political affiliation in shaping identity. Contemporary literary scholars usually extend the meaning of region to include not only geography but also social, historical, economic, and cultural dynamics, casting a broad net over the experience of place and acknowledging differences within regions.[5] Many critics use place and region interchangeably while others insist that not all places are regions, emphasizing relative poverty and political powerlessness as distinguishing characteristics of regions. Jeanette Lynes and Herb Wyile see regions as "distinctive and traditionally subordinate" and suggest that an oppositional, or at least a de-centered, stance is a defining feature of the regional writer.[6] The vocabulary of heartland (dominant region) and hinterland (subordinate region) reflects this focus on unequal relations of power. Recently, critics such as W. H. New have begun to use region as a metaphor for social or psychological marginality, but such use, as David Jordan warns, risks emptying the term of meaning altogether.[7] The majority of critics maintain some focus on real-world geography, however problematically defined it may be.

What counts as a regional text depends on the definition one applies. In *Barometer Rising* (1941), Hugh MacLennan makes the city of Halifax a central focus, describing its topography and culture in detail. Yet this is not usually considered a regional novel because MacLennan presents Halifax as representative of the yet unborn Canadian nation struggling to emerge from thralldom to Europe. Susanna Moodie, writing of the Hamilton Township in *Roughing It in the Bush* (1852), is in one sense regional in her concern with the geography, peculiar local customs, ethnic character, and puzzling cultural idioms of bush life in a particular region. Yet because she directed her sketches to all immigrants contemplating the Canadian backwoods, she writes of region but not as a regional writer. The same might be said of many Ontario writers in a province that, as W. J. Keith has observed, "sees itself as a centre – or even, perhaps, *the* centre."[8] However, some Ontario writers do identify with a particular region, as Alice Munro does with the poorer, rural stretches of southwestern Ontario. As W. H. New notes, region often depends not only on place but also on "idiom or 'accent' of perspective."[9]

As the above discussion suggests, regionalism is complicated by its relation to ideas of the nation. Canadians in general – and scholars of Canadian culture in particular – have often relied on geography to define Canadianness, emphasizing wilderness, intense cold, snow, vast expanses, and rugged topography. Certain regions – above all the Algonquin region of Ontario depicted in Group of Seven paintings, but also the Rocky Mountains and prairie grasslands – have been made to stand for the essential Canadian experience, while more temperate regions, such as southern British Columbia, or those with topography on a smaller scale, such as Prince Edward Island, are more rarely made representative. In Margaret Atwood's *Surfacing* (1972), regional particularity serves a nationalist vision, with the northern Quebec bush symbolizing a Canadian space not yet infected by the disease spreading up from the south. In *Baltimore's Mansion* (1999), by contrast, Wayne Johnston declares Newfoundland's geographical and cultural difference from (the rest of) Canada, emphasizing its literal and metaphorical position on the margin of the nation. Ursula Kelly claims that the designation regional almost always indicates insignificance,[10] though such was not the case when the Governor-General's Award Jury gave the fiction prize to Gloria Sawai's *A Song for Nettie Johnson* (2001) and described it as "a profoundly light-filled collection of short stories set on the Prairies."[11] That regional *does* often signify parochial is evident from an item in the *Guardian* from September 2002, praising Canada for moving away from regional fiction, described as "generally a bit depressing," and instead embracing "a new wave that is more urban, more male, and more engaged with the wider world."[12] Nonetheless, the relationship between region and nation has never been simple, as is demonstrated by the long-standing centrality of prairie writing in the Canadian national canon.[13]

Not surprisingly, questions of particularity and emphasis arise in defining a regional text. One of the most significant regional novels in Canada is Sinclair Ross's *As for Me and My House* (1941), widely assumed to describe a small town in Saskatchewan. Both Margaret Laurence and Robert Kroetsch have acknowledged Ross as a literary forefather who proved one could write out of one's particular place. In fact, the novel never locates the fictional town of Horizon in any province, state, or even country, probably so as not to alienate a potential American readership. Ross's decision, understandable given the economic realities of Canadian publishing at the time, does not invalidate the place of the novel in the Canadian prairie canon, but it does complicate a clear identification between text and locale. A book more recently inducted into the prairie canon is Maria Campbell's autobiography *Halfbreed* (1973), which describes growing up in northern Saskatchewan; Campbell's sense of connection to place and people is strong, but her subject is not relationship to place per se; it is the Indian and Métis struggle for self-respect and self-determination. Identity, in her text, is more a matter of race, culture, social experience, and political affiliation than it is of region. A question of emphasis also complicates the definition of a novel such as Richard B. Wright's *Clara Callan* (2001), which moves between small-town Ontario and New York City, thus balancing the regional with the metropolitan.

Sometimes the regional designation depends, as in the case of Al Purdy, on a myriad of assumptions about a writer's orientation to place, canonical stature, and cultural context. A prolific writer with a long career, Purdy in collections such as *The Cariboo Horses* (1965), *North of Summer* (1967), and *In Search of Owen Roblin* (1974) gives poetic articulation to Canadian places and histories. He demonstrates a special attachment to the Ontario countryside near Ameliasburg. In the frequently anthologized "The Country North of Belleville" (1965), Purdy describes the muted beauty and harsh conditions of rural Ontario. The very title marks the poet's sense of his place as remote from centers of power and affluence: it is a northern place of rocky soil and scrub brush, full of abandoned farms and evidence of defeat; those who left and have returned "must enquire the way / of strangers." Purdy's use of place-names throughout the poem defines a known place and also suggests a need to conjure a lost connection. The sense of identity both affirmed and mourned through local reference is quite typical of regional writing – but does this make Purdy a regional writer? Purdy set poems in nearly every region of the country as well as many outside of Canada. A number of critics have referred to him as the quintessential Canadian poet, even "the last Canadian poet."[14] Is he both regional and national?

For many critics, regional is both too limiting and too broad a term to be used with assurance. It is limiting because it implies that the writer does not speak to larger national and universal issues and that the work is mainly of referential rather than aesthetic interest. At the same time, it is too broad because it cannot clearly distinguish between texts set in a particular region and regional texts (and perhaps such a distinction is impossible). Therefore, most critics use the term, as I do here, with the understanding that its meanings are unstable and that, as a category, it is rarely absolute or exclusive.

To create further difficulties, the boundaries of regions are notoriously hazy and their defining features far from uniform. Regions are thought to be natural entities, distinguished by a dominant geographical feature and an associated industry or way of life: we think, for example, of the Atlantic region's geographic and economic links with the sea; the North's frigid climate and associations with adventure and death; the Prairies' vast open spaces; and British Columbia's sublime geography of mountains and forest at the western edge of the country. But such generalizations do not stand up to scrutiny. The prairie is not all flat grassland; it includes rolling parkland, foothills, northern bush, and marshlands – a great diversity. British Columbia contains many strikingly distinct subregions west of the Rockies, including the fruit orchards of the Okanagan and the lush farmland of the Fraser Valley. Prince Edward Island has little in common culturally, economically, or geographically with the other Maritime subregions with which it is grouped, such as Cape Breton or the Miramichi region of New Brunswick. Looked at closely, most regions break up into micro-regions (and most writers portray micro-regions). Moreover, regions often overlap when literary critics try to place specific texts. Is Howard O'Hagan's *Tay John* (1939), set in the Rocky Mountains, a novel of the North or of the West – or both? Michael Ondaatje has defined it as a "western"[15] novel while Sherrill Grace calls it "the urnorthern novel."[16] North in general is a region with a decidedly "protean capacity,"[17] often extending well down into temperate land in southerners' representations (though the boundaries of North are changing as northerners begin to represent their region from the inside). Regional borders and fictional affiliations are not easy to delineate.

The abiding assumption that regions are rural or small-town in character also fails to withstand investigation. Given the demographic reality that the vast majority of Canadians live in large urban areas, it can be argued that distinctive urban spaces constitute important regions in themselves, amenable to the same sort of investigation that rural areas have traditionally received. The problems of definition continue: if the most important dynamic in modern Canada is that between urban and rural, then how does one define the urban? Does Regina count? Moncton? Urban – not to mention suburban – is also relative, a function of perspective and political context.

Moreover, investigation of a region reveals ethnic and gender disparities, economic and social asymmetries that further complicate ideas of regional identity. Frank Davey argues, in fact, that regions are political constructs that function to smooth over differences and create the effect of a natural and homogeneous entity where none exists.[18] Davey also cautions that, contrary to the assumption that regions are sites of political contestation, regional identities are often deeply conservative, effacing alternative forms of identity. Other critics, such as Lisa Chalykoff, have objected to the outmoded geographical determinism implied by regionalism, which assumes that specific landscapes determine particular imaginative responses rather than themselves being constructed by stories, myths, tourism, and political discourse. Recognition of these various conceptual problems need not block investigation of regionalism; rather, it may shift attention to the way that regions are created in language. Chalykoff has recently argued that regions are best understood as social spaces rather than purely geographic or imaginative ones.[19]

This chapter cannot survey all of the Canadian writers who have written out of or about particular places. Instead, it discusses a selection of writers, arranged in roughly chronological order, whose work highlights some of the ongoing issues and debates associated with region as a critical category. Emphasis is placed on the various literary forms that authors have used to articulate their place as well as on the diverse ways writers have conceived of the formative role of place in identity. I focus on texts in which place is not merely a vividly realized setting (as in Elizabeth Hay's *A Student of Weather* [2000] and *Garbo Laughs* [2003]) but a central subject in its own right. However, I define place quite loosely to include any distinct locale presented as existing in vital relationship with an individual or community.

Literary places

Representations of place are never merely neutral depictions of the real, much as – or especially when – they may lay claim to a transparent referentiality. They are always to some extent political, a form of (linguistic and imaginative) land claim. From the earliest literary representations of colonial topography, in poems such as Thomas Cary's *Abram's Plains* (1789), which links the field where General Wolfe died with freedom and prosperity for French Canadians under benevolent British rule, the regional is inseparable from the political. Much landscape poetry of the late eighteenth and nineteenth centuries was written for a local audience and intended to inspire pride of place through detailed enumeration of geographical features and local industry – though celebration was not the objective in J. Mackay's *Quebec Hill* (1797), which focuses on the negative aspects of Quebec climate and topography. Oliver Goldsmith's *The Rising Village* (1825; rev. 1834) provides a history of the development of agriculture, an allegory of settlement, and an overview of contemporary social concerns in its topographical description of a Nova Scotian village. Charles Sangster used a boat trip down the St. Lawrence and up the Saguenay Rivers to structure his observations of water and shore scenery in *The St. Lawrence and the Saguenay* (1856). Despite their detailed emphasis on local features, these long poems are perhaps too rigidly tied to European literary conventions and poetic diction to be successful examples of regional poetry.

More successful in capturing the texture of a specific place from a local perspective is Thomas Haliburton, whose use of the sketch form for satiric purposes in *The Clockmaker* (1836) enabled him to combine shrewd observation of local conditions with comic caricature, witty aphorism, and canny advice on how Nova Scotians could overcome an economic downturn. An influence on Haliburton was Thomas McCulloch, who also wrote didactic sketches about lazy Nova Scotians needing a lesson in thrift and industry in *Letters of Mephibosheth Stepsure*, serialized from 1821 to 1823 and later published as *The Stepsure Letters* (1862). McCulloch's community portraits were so vividly local that a number of readers were delighted or chagrined to recognize themselves and their neighbors in the text. Freed of the need to impose an ideal order on experience, satirical sketches could create memorable regional portraits.

Later in the nineteenth century, poets of the post-Confederation period, influenced by the Romantic and Victorian poets in England and America, turned to nature both to observe details of landscape and to find emotional and spiritual sustenance. Often considered the first regional masterpiece, Charles G. D. Roberts's "Tantramar Revisited" (1886) is a topographical poem of return in which the speaker contemplates a landscape known intimately in boyhood, the Tantramar River district of New Brunswick. Form and content complement one another as Roberts uses syntactical repetition and elegiac hexameter to suggest through rhythm and sound the spatial distances of the Tantramar marshes. The poem's attention to the colors and textures of hills, fields, and villages, the detailed description of fishing activity associated with the region, and the mood of regret and loss all indicate Roberts's interest in the emotional significance of place and his desire to convey the particular sensibility produced in him by the Tantramar.

In E. J. Pratt's early lyric poetry, human beings are not only influenced by the land but seem to become an extension of it. Especially in *Newfoundland Verse* (1923), Pratt wrote of the harsh challenges facing seafaring communities and the way that sea, wind, and rock pervade Newfoundland being. In the title poem, "Newfoundland Verse," the tides of the sea even "run / Within the sluices of men's hearts."[20] In *The Witches' Brew* (1925), elements of tall tale, rhyming ballad, and mock epic carry the flavor of Newfoundland folk songs. While his later dramatic narratives are clearly nationalist attempts to portray the spirit of the whole country, these earlier short lyrics pay homage to Pratt's first country, the pre-Confederation colony of Newfoundland.

In fiction, an important subgenre of regional literature that has received relatively little critical attention, probably because of its association with popular or juvenile work, is local-color fiction. Bestselling authors Ralph Connor, Nellie McClung, and L. M. Montgomery wrote local-color novels – also known as regional idylls – which presented an idealized small place, usually remote, rural, or frontier, and stressed its connection to character development, spiritual fulfillment, and community cohesion. Connor (Charles W. Gordon) was internationally read and beloved for his frontier adventure tales promoting muscular Christianity and the Northwest Mounted Police. In *The Man from Glengarry* (1901), the work of clearing the bush of Glengarry

County in eastern Ontario produces the heroic virtues necessary to civilize the country. In *Sowing Seeds in Danny* (1908), McClung creates stories of Christian conversion on the prairie to envision a new form of democratic citizenship developing in the ethnic mix and mutual hard work of settlement. In Montgomery's *Anne of Green Gables* (1908), a spunky orphan girl's imaginative response to the trees, ponds, and flowers of beautiful Avonlea, Prince Edward Island, opens the hearts of the conventional but caring residents. With *Sunshine Sketches of a Little Town* (1912), Stephen Leacock may be included in this group, though irony and implied criticism play a large role along with affection in his complex portrait of Mariposa, a small town in Ontario.

   The last two authors deserve particular attention because of their influence on subsequent generations of writers and readers. Montgomery is cited as an important model by Alice Munro, Margaret Atwood, and Jane Urquhart while Hugh Hood and Robertson Davies have expressed a debt to Leacock. Furthermore, *Anne of Green Gables* initiated a tourist migration to Montgomery's home town of Cavendish that continues to fuel the island economy. The visitors' belief in a one-to-one correspondence between the actual place and its fictional representation speaks to the power of Montgomery's evocation, though one might argue that her romantic descriptions of pastoral nature turned a real place into a generalized consumer commodity attractive to Swedes, Poles, and Japanese. Given that Montgomery set *Anne* in the early 1880s and continued to write about communities insulated from electricity and the automobile, nostalgia was a strong component of her regional appeal. Nostalgia combines with satire in Leacock's *Sunshine Sketches*, which portrays a human but ineffectual community, by turns lovable and deplorable. The naive narrator exposes the innocence but also the narrowness, vanity, and hypocrisy of the small-town residents; ultimately, however, Leacock's portrait suggests an enduring affection and sees Mariposa as a possible bulwark against the community-destroying materialism of the twentieth century. In these local-color texts, small towns and villages are intimately associated with kindness, authenticity, and Christian love.

   In contrast to the critical neglect of the regional idyll, the realism developed by prairie writers from the 1920s onwards has generated a mini-industry of scholarly books and articles. Critics such as Edward McCourt (*The Canadian West in Fiction* [1949, rev. 1970]), Henry Kreisel ("The Prairie: A State of Mind" [1968]), Laurie Ricou (*Vertical Man/Horizontal World* [1973]), and Dick Harrison (*Unnamed Country* [1977]) have seen in the work of Frederick Philip Grove, Martha Ostenso, Robert Stead, Sinclair Ross, and W. O. Mitchell a regional literature that captured, in Kreisel's words, the prairie as a "state of mind." In these works, the prairie is the central subject both as an awesome physical fact and a site of metaphysical reflection. Recurrent images are the rippling expanse of prairie grass, the distant horizon, the wind by turns melancholy or relentless, the silence of snow. It is a spare but all-absorbing landscape, an image of bare essentials, expansive and isolating. In Grove's *Over Prairie Trails* (1922), a series of autobiographical sketches describing journeys Grove made between home and the village where he taught school, the prairie is a harsh testing ground against which the narrator's self-reliance wins a tenuous victory. Particularities of the prairie environment and weather are rendered with precise scientific detail and care amounting to reverence. But in most of Grove's fiction, such as *Settlers of the Marsh* (1925) and *Fruits of the Earth* (1933), the implacable and harsh environment defeats human efforts at self-assertion, illuminating Grove's tragic vision.

A similar perspective characterizes Ostenso's *Wild Geese* (1925), in which the winds that sweep across the prairie emphasize both the vulnerability of human communities and their extraordinary persistence. Caleb Gare's obsession with dominating the land is figured as a mutually destructive clash of titans. In *Grain* (1926), Robert Stead's experience growing up on a Manitoba farm enabled him to record its day-to-day operations of harvesting and threshing in greater detail than either Grove or Ostenso. Stead too sought symbols for the impact of the land on the mind, finding in the furrows of wheat fields an ironic symbol for the protagonist's subordination of self to farm work. In Ross's narrative of the Depression in *As for Me and My House*, the prairie expanse confronts the diarist Mrs. Bentley with the possibility of her own nothingness in an indifferent universe. For the boy growing up on the prairies in Mitchell's *Who Has Seen the Wind* (1947), the Saskatchewan prairie is not an indifferent environment but an elemental Book of Nature, its seasons leading the boy to contemplate eternity, the divine, and the meaning of existence. In its seeming assertion of itself as an implacable and majestic presence, the prairie for these novelists demanded extended meditations on how a land might imprint itself on human consciousness. Despite the significant differences in their conceptions, these five writers were at one in identifying the prairie as an absolute reality prior to and quite apart from cultural and linguistic impositions.

Alison Calder has objected that such depictions of the prairie and their reification in criticism have become clichés, masking the diversity of prairie landscapes and communities with a prescriptive uniformity: the prairie must always be oppressive, life-denying, and harsh.[21] Calder argues that critics have tended to overlook the fact that these novels are fictional rather than documentary representations. These are important criticisms although a sympathetic reading of the primary texts and the criticism reveals an awareness of the relationship between landscape and metaphor. Nonetheless, Calder's assessment of the overemphasis on realism and on the erasure of social conflict and alternative aesthetic visions has been widely taken up, and recent criticism, such as Deborah Keahey's *Making It Home* (1998), has focused on stylistic experimentation and social conflict in prairie writing.

Experimental regionalism

Heirs to Grove and Ross who take prairie regionalism in new directions are Margaret Laurence and Robert Kroetsch. For Laurence, the prairie is a socially mediated experience rather than a physical fact while for Kroetsch it is primarily accessible through narrative and myth. In her five-volume fiction cycle consisting of *The Stone Angel* (1964), *A Jest of God* (1966), *The Fire-Dwellers* (1969), *A Bird in the House* (1970), and *The Diviners* (1974), Laurence experiments with nonlinear, fragmented form and narrative polyphony, creating in the fictional Manitoba town of Manawaka a distinctive setting rife with class and race conflict. Laurence mines Manawaka landmarks to create powerful metaphors for the town's entrenched social divisions (the Tonnerre shack in the valley; the Logan house on Hill Street; the imposing Brick House of Vanessa's grandparents) and psychological complexion (the blind stone angel in the cemetery; the Nuisance Grounds as repository of the town's unconscious; the Japonica Funeral Home as carnivalesque site of truth). Because of this attention to social complexity, the Manawaka cycle is often seen as a culmination of prairie regionalism.

Kroetsch approaches the Alberta landscape with machismo and bawdy irreverence. In such works as *The Words of My Roaring* (1966), *The Studhorse Man* (1969), and *Gone Indian* (1973), which Kroetsch called his Out West triptych, he parodies regional stereotypes while also forging a distinctive prairie poetic using an allusive and playful postmodern mode in which the real and the surreal commingle. *The Words of My Roaring*, for example, draws extensively on Alberta history of the 1930s, using recognizable historical situations and characters – such as the alienation of Western Canada, radical prairie populism, the Depression and the Dust Bowl, Bible Bill Aberhart, founder of the Social Credit Party (here named John George Applecart) – to transform prairie realism by emphasizing its mythic dimensions. In later novels, Kroetsch's interest in European myth broadens to include Aboriginal Trickster stories. The mythological allusions proliferate such that although the local references are Western Canadian – with emphasis on such prairie symbols as the horse and the buffalo – there are so many mythic intertexts that no single reading of prairie identity is possible. Radical indeterminacy complicates Kroetsch's portrayal of this particular subregion of northern bush forest, muskeg, and lakes, making Kroetsch an example of postmodern regionalism in which anti-referentiality and suspicion of grand narratives are paradoxically combined with a strong commitment to place.

Discussion of Kroetsch's postmodernism raises the large question of how various nonmimetic literary forms can articulate regions. Sheila Watson's *The Double Hook* (1959) is a good example of a stylistically innovative work that is often considered regional. Watson herself has denied that she intended to write a regional novel; and certainly, if one defines regionalism strictly in terms of accuracy of description, this brief poetic work of fiction does not present anything near a mimetic portrait of the British Columbian Cariboo region out of which it was written. Elements of the Cariboo landscape are present: the dry land, the parched creek bed, the prickly pear scrub cactus, the low surrounding hills; instead of aiming for referentiality, however, Watson indicates imagistically the impact of place, speaking of a region by turning all of its referential details into highly charged symbols.

Moving regionalism in the direction of magic realism is Jack Hodgins, a British Columbian writer associated with Vancouver Island, especially the Comox Valley and Nanaimo. Hodgins's work, which blends realistic detail with elements of the fabulous, raises again the internal diversity of regional labels, for although both Watson and Hodgins write from west of the Rockies, the specific environments they portray are markedly different. Hodgins presents an island community of loggers, beach-combers, and fishermen living at the western edge of the country and on the margin of approved convention. In *The Invention of the World* (1977), Hodgins balances and occasionally blurs legendary and documentary modes, describing an oversized island geography of giant trees, ferocious rainfall, and rugged mountains appropriate to the scenes of carnivalesque laughter, shouting, drinking, and copulating that fill its pages. The extravagant concluding scene, in which a wedding becomes a mass brawl as participants hurl food and demolish the hall with chain saws, combines elements of epic and folk tale to convey the exuberance with which Hodgins represents his up-island community.

Less radical in his narrative experimentation but fully engaged with representation as a literary problem, Ernest Buckler focused on the Annapolis Valley of Nova Scotia in *The Mountain and the Valley* (1952), conveying the small rural community he had known as a child. Although Buckler is often referred to as a regional realist, his preoccupation with language suggests a strong debt to international modernism. Alice Munro is similarly fascinated by the texture of lived experience and the impossibility of accurate representation. In stories and story cycles rich with detail about the run-down houses, ramshackle yards, piles of junk, and ill-maintained fields of poor districts in southwestern Ontario, Munro's use of the catalog and her unusual combinations of adjectives indicate her interest both in a form of photographic realism and in the way that language derails representation to become its own subject.

While writers such as Buckler and Munro implicitly valorize peripheral rural places as worthy of literary investigation, the radical social critic and poet Milton Acorn creates a more directly political regionalism in which his place becomes a site of opposition to central Canadian hegemony. Acorn lived for the first thirty years of his life in Prince Edward Island, and much of his work declares his sense of himself as an Islander, developing both a critique of its provincialism and also a celebration of its natural beauty, history of class struggle, and potential for community solidarity. *The Island Means Minago* (1975) focuses almost exclusively on Prince Edward Island with poems of regional description, observations of working people, and investigations into local history, especially the struggle by tenant workers against absentee landlords. Beginning with a manifesto-like preface in which Acorn exhorts islanders to know their history, the book combines poems, fictional dialogue, and passages of explanatory prose to create a mythic sense of "a fierce people's struggle against landlords"[22] and to oppose the assumption that small, peripheral communities are expendable and exploitable.

Locating resistance at the level of the sentence itself is the poet Daphne Marlatt, whose dedication to breaking down expectations about syntax, line breaks, and image patterns coexists with a strong regional commitment. Marlatt's radical focus on word etymology, sound, and rhythm have meant that she is rarely grouped with other regional writers, yet two of her books, *Vancouver Poems* (1972) and *Steveston* (1974), announce their association with place. For both works, she conducted extensive research, in the first case into Vancouver newspaper archives and Northwest Coast Native myth in order to create a poetic archaeology of the city; in the second, into the local history around a fish cannery in Steveston, a small town on the Fraser River. Although Marlatt's focus is on place, she leads the reader not to images of place but to place experiences, taking the reader inside a perceiving consciousness in the moment-by-moment flux of sense impressions, memories, and associations, representing place as a highly personal and phenomenologically complex place-in-process.

The persistence of realism

While forms of experimental regionalism have flourished in the 1960s and 70s, for a majority of regional writers working since 1970, some form of referential realism has remained a dominant mode, often with excursions into fable, legend, magic realism, and the Gothic. A particularly fertile site of such work has been Canada's East Coast, perhaps because of its strong identity as a region fighting for economic self-sufficiency and social survival. In novels combining regional focus with moral fable and tragedy, David Adams Richards writes about rural men displaced by economic and social change in the Miramichi area of New Brunswick. In his Miramichi trilogy *Nights below Station Street* (1988), *Evening Snow Will Bring Such Peace* (1990), and *For Those Who Hunt the Wounded Down* (1993), the displaced Acadians and poor Irish who make up the community have been hit hard by the devaluing of manual labor, the loss of resource-based industries, and a feminist culture of recrimination against uneducated men. Much of the descriptive writing is both referential and symbolic, stressing those aspects of the landscape – the desolation, neglect, decay, and barren splendor – that apply also to the economically struggling, occasionally beautiful, and socially dispossessed characters. Even for his villains, in a novel such as *Mercy among the Children* (2000), Richards has a certain empathy, showing how their viciousness is part courage, a reckless defiance of the "pointless and mediocre lives" to which they are sentenced by class and region.[23]

Class and region are a less bitter focus in Alistair MacLeod's admired short fiction and award-winning novel *No Great Mischief* (1999). The place that inspires MacLeod's reflections on families, tradition, work, and tribal affiliation is primarily a Cape Breton peopled by the descendants of Scottish immigrants who have lived for generations mainly as fishermen and miners. In *The Lost Salt Gift of Blood* (1976), the presence of the mines cut into the green hills is a reminder of a history of hard, often deadly, work while Scottish ballads link these Cape Islanders to their Gaelic roots. Recurring concerns are the bonds that shore up economically fragile communities struggling to hold on to old ways of life. Equally, the stories are about the loss of these bonds when children leave in search of employment. In "The Vastness of the Dark," a boy leaving Cape Breton for the first time realizes his connection with his family only in the moment of going away. In these stories, characters carry their home place with them as both a burden and a precious inheritance.

In the later work of Wayne Johnston, particularly *Baltimore's Mansion* (1999), comedy shades into elegy to portray Newfoundlanders trying to maintain cultural integrity and independence in the face of economic deprivation, the declining fishery, depopulation, and absorption into mainstream Canada. *Baltimore's Mansion*, a generic hybrid claiming to be nonfiction while resorting to all the techniques of fiction, is about the hold that the land has over people. Exploring how the vote on Confederation divided a father and son, *Baltimore's Mansion* is both a lament for the old Newfoundland and an ironic commentary on the absurdity of anti-Confederate passion, in which insistence on a pure and everlasting resistance to Canada is shown to be self-defeating. Balancing skillfully between tragedy and wild humor, Johnston chooses scenes to illuminate the tension between an idealized past and a compromised present, and to indicate the emotional complexities of a regional psyche ripe with "inferiority complexes, delusions of grandeur, savage irony, impotent malice, unwarranted optimism, entirely justified despair, tall tales, [and] pipe dreams."[24] In blending the personal with the historical, Johnston aims to be representative while making clear that his story is only one of many versions of Newfoundland.

This concern for the loss of a way of life connected to the land has also inspired strong regional writing on the prairies. Although Sharon Butala is best known for her nonfiction works about the discovery of a nature-inspired spirituality, her fiction, which blends regional realism with myth and fantasy, is arguably of greater interest. In *The Fourth Archangel* (1992), dream, vision, and reality interpenetrate for the large cast of characters struggling to save their small town of Ordeal, Saskatchewan at the end of the millennium. Other towns in the area are named Remorse, Solitude, and Crisis, and all are suffering from a seven-year drought, massive crop failure, exploitation of the environment, the rise of agri-business, and the withdrawal of health services. Apocalyptic experiences are rampant: a schoolteacher has visions of massive storms and herds of skinned buffalo stampeding while a young girl has stigmata. In a surprisingly unsentimental lament for the end of the family farm, the novel condemns human greed while recognizing both that there is no permanence in the world and that life on the prairie will endure in some form.

That magic realism continues to have a special association with British Columbia is suggested in the acclaim generated by Gail Anderson-Dargatz's first novel, *The Cure for Death by Lightning* (1996). In this story about a girl's coming-of-age during World War II in the interior of British Columbia, the dailiness of life in a rural community – the items for sale at the general store, techniques for milking cows, paper-making and baking recipes – are a source of lavish textual attention. Side by side with this documentary commitment is a strong Gothic insistence on the bizarre and the supernatural. In its interest in Coyote stories, strong evocation of a remote rural community, and its matter-of-fact intermingling of the beautiful and the perverse, the novel has been compared to Watson's *The Double Hook*, though its extravagant style is very different from Watson's spare and cadenced prose.

Even more strongly touched by elements of Gothic – especially the evocation of a sinister, hidden past from which has developed a pervasive cycle of violence – and presenting a luminous portrait of the remote coastal region of Kitamaat Village in northern British Columbia is Eden Robinson's *Monkey*

Beach (2000). Part coming-of-age story, part supernatural mystery peopled by Raven, B'gwus (Sasquatch), a spirit guide, and the ghosts of ancestors, the novel makes the rain forests, mists, mountains, and rivers of the north Pacific coast a formidable presence alongside its history of the Haisla people and the community's present-day struggle with the legacy of colonialism. A number of critics, including Jennifer Andrews,[25] have used the term Native Gothic as a generic term for the novel, suggesting that the meeting ground of regionalism and Gothic continues to be productive for writers seeking to claim and contest a long-standing Canadian tradition of mythologizing small communities.

The small community has been an equally important focus in Canadian dramatic literature, with regional theatre groups making a profound impact in the 1970s and 80s. In particular, Théâtre Passe Muraille, a Toronto-based theatre company, and various local affiliations have enabled actors and producers to delve into local history to create what has sometimes been called dramatic journalism. *The Farm Show*, first produced in 1972, is a notable example of Passe Muraille's characteristic collective method and local commitment. Similar collectives such as 25th Street House Theatre in Saskatoon created documentary plays that sprang from and spoke to the cultural and economic concerns of Saskatchewan. One of the best known is *Paper Wheat*, a history of agrarian politics in the province, which premiered in 1977 under the direction of Andy Tahn. It was both intensely local and national in its documentary and mythic interest in ordinary people working together to overcome obstacles. In Newfoundland, the Mummers Troupe, established in 1972 in St. John's, dedicated itself to speaking to and for Newfoundlanders regarding their issues, especially threats to outport communities. In 1978, the Mummers took the controversial *They Club Seals Don't They?* on a cross-Canada tour to counter animal rights protests against sealing. In creating collaborative plays based on regional experience, the collective theatres took regional representation in a significant new direction.

Individual playwrights have also worked with regional subjects. One of the best known is James Reaney, who turned to playwriting after establishing a career as a poet. Reaney's best-known group of plays is his multimedia Donnelly trilogy, *Sticks and Stones* (1974), *The St. Nicholas Hotel* (1976), and *Handcuffs* (1977), based on the history of an Irish immigrant family, five of whom were murdered in Biddulph township near Lucan, Ontario. The story had intrigued Reaney since he was a child because it captured something essential about the world of nineteenth-century "souwesto," the small-town and farming area of southwestern Ontario with which Reaney identified. English-born Michael Cook, who immigrated to St. John's in 1966, found in Newfoundland the linguistic exuberance and cultural richness that his training in the English and Irish theatrical traditions had taught him to appreciate. In his plays, Cook uses naturalistic detail to evoke Newfoundland culture (the seal hunt, the gutting of codfish, the life-threatening storms) and focuses on the sound of Newfoundland speech. Especially in *Jacob's Wake* (1975), Cook achieves a balance of black humor and pathos, using realism and surrealism to portray one family's disintegration as well as the threatened collapse of a culture.

Urban literature

In the work of Richards, MacLeod, Johnston, Butala, Robinson, Reaney, and Cook, the power of the local is embodied in a small, economically and politically subordinate rural community or town. The implicit or explicit thrust of much regional writing is against "central" Canadian places: Toronto, Montreal, Ottawa, Vancouver, the urban centers of culture and political power. And yet the experience of living in a large city, as many Canadian writers have demonstrated, is not necessarily an experience of power and centrality. Cities themselves have centers and peripheries, have local and oppositional cultures; indeed, urban living can involve both deep intimacy with a specific place and a profound awareness of disempowerment.

From the beginnings, urban texts have addressed the particularities of city geography and the psychology of distinct neighborhoods. As did many rural and small-town fictions, early urban texts often featured cities affected by the Depression. Gabrielle Roy's *Bonheur d'occasion* (1945) drew attention to the urban slum as a Canadian literary setting and has been consistently popular with anglophone readers since its translation in 1947 (as *The Tin Flute*). Portraying Montreal's Saint-Henri district, the novel indicts government and the Catholic Church for colluding in human misery. In *Cabbagetown* (1950; rev. 1968), Hugh Garner presents a sympathetic but unidealized portrait of the working-class WASP enclave of downtown Toronto during the interwar years. Vancouver is brought to literary life in Ethel Wilson's *The Innocent Traveller* (1949) and *The Equations of Love* (1952). Wilson's Vancouver is not only the city of mountains, forest, and sea, but also a working city with an active CPR dock, a handkerchief and notions shop on Commercial Drive, a plant nursery in Burnaby, and a gambling den in Shanghai Alley off Pender Street, all very particular urban spaces where her characters seek work, endure humiliations, put in time, and plan escapes.

Also interested in the working life of a city, with an even stronger focus on class and ethnic topography, Mordecai Richler in *The Apprenticeship of Duddy Kravitz* (1959) highlights Montreal's St. Urbain Street Jewish ghetto in the era following World War II, focusing on the difficult temptations facing a poor boy scrambling to succeed in an exploitative world. Richler is attentive to the physical layout of his working-class neighborhood, which, as he also makes clear in *The Street* (1969), a series of autobiographical sketches, registers ethnic difference and minuscule distinctions in income-level. He pays attention to the precise locations of tenement buildings, shops, and institutional structures, especially in the memorable scene from *The Apprenticeship* in which the Fletcher's Cadets march through the streets. Richler also creates the sound and psychology of the neighborhood through the use of Yiddish-inflected idioms in his characters' speech, especially in Max's mythic tale of the Boy Wonder. In Adele Wiseman's *Crackpot* (1974), an urban ghetto reveals in microcosm the social problems and potential of Canadian urban life. Although the city is not named, *Crackpot* presents a recognizable Winnipeg with its working-class immigrant district in the North End, the City Hall on Main Street with its (ironically deployed) motto of Commerce, Prudence, and Industry, and the violent suppression of the Winnipeg General Strike; the city also becomes a powerful symbolic backdrop for the protagonist's perilous moral journey.

Concerned more broadly with a city's development over time, Margaret Atwood's *Cat's Eye* (1988), in which a woman artist returns to Toronto for a gallery retrospective of her work and confronts the past she has disowned, is also a detailed retrospective of Toronto, focusing on its transformation from a provincial backwater to an affluent, multicultural metropolis with ethnic restaurants, art galleries, and trendy boutiques – as well as a subterranean landscape of ravines and buried memories. Equally committed to recording Toronto in various moods and conditions, Raymond Souster's imagistic and understated poems, in collections such as *A Local Pride* (1962) and *It Takes All Kinds* (1986), are often named for specific Toronto streets and parks; over the years he has recorded the many changes Toronto has undergone. Souster's Toronto is often drab and sordid but also shot through with opportunities for wonder. Michael Ondaatje creates a historical portrait of Toronto in *In the Skin of a Lion* (1987), emphasizing the contribution made by immigrant workers – the Finns, Poles, Macedonians – whose hard labor built the city's bridges and tunnels and operated its abattoirs and tanneries. In his narrative of union battles and workers' misery, Ondaatje suggests the many unofficial histories that underpin a seemingly known place. Learning of a union organizer's death, Patrick Lewis has a typically Canadian, and regional, experience when he realizes that although "[h]e had lived in this country all of his life," he knew it less fully than those immigrants who live in its shadows.[26]

In recent urban fiction and poetry, two narratives of city life seem to dominate: one explores how the bourgeois dream of consumer affluence and cultural vitality becomes a nightmare of overconsumption, shallow trendiness, and middle-class despair; the other explores the city from the perspective of those for whom the bourgeois dream has never been achievable. Both narratives have produced some trenchant critiques of contemporary Canadian realities in the past decade. In the former category is Russell Smith's *Noise* (1998), a portrait of contemporary Toronto life from the perspective of a young restaurant and culture critic and also a manifesto on Canadian culture, which Smith sees as caught between its rural and small-town past and its faceless, global present. Although many Canadians still imagine Canada in terms of rural or small-town experience, regional fictions no longer represent most Canadians' lives, as symbolized in *Noise* by the fact that Ludwig Boben, the prairie writer whom James interviews, has not been able to write anything in twenty-five years and is featured in *Glitter*, a New York magazine, only because his association with northernness fits a momentary cultural trend. Urban Canadians have yet to accept their own cities as places where original culture is produced and meaningful experiences occur, and thus Torontonians are caught in feverish imitation of New York, culturally dependent and self-absorbed but not self-aware. As James explains to his girlfriend of the moment, "It used to be that you could get a lot of recognition by writing about Canada, as long as it was about small towns and nature" but now you have to write about "the Holocaust or something."[27] With what seems a dismissive reference to Anne Michaels's *Fugitive Pieces* (1996), Smith signals his own local allegiance and implies that Canadians need to confront the particularity of their urban environments.

In *All the Anxious Girls on Earth* (1999), a collection of insistently topical short stories mainly focused on Vancouver, Zsuzsi Gartner uses caricature and bathos to expose the anxiety behind Vancouver affluence. Gartner lampoons the smugness of Vancouverites, mocks Canadian wilderness mythologies, and loads her stories with references to Vancouver's trendy shops and alternative lifestyles. Especially in "City of My Dreams," Gartner diagnoses Vancouver's pervasive malaise, describing it as a city of "aggressive mellowness" whose inhabitants have replaced God with fashionable forms of exercise, environmental activism, New Age spirituality, and socially approved consumption; yet, underneath the conviction that the right soap can confer holiness is an abiding fear of meaninglessness and collapse. In this focus on the dread of some unnamed disaster, Gartner demonstrates her literary affiliation with Douglas Coupland, who in *Girlfriend in a Coma* (1998) describes Vancouver as the place where West Coast utopian ideology and the still breathtaking beauty of the coastal rain forest meet the materialism and environmental mess of the urban millennium. In *Girlfriend in a Coma*, Vancouver is literally the city of the last chance as six friends are given the opportunity to bring the world back from global apocalypse only if they work ceaselessly to revise their relationship to their community and place.

Timothy Taylor's *Stanley Park* (2001) is not only a deftly realist/surrealist regional novel but also a novel about regionalism. Jeremy, a chef and restaurant owner, wants to create an experience of food intimately linked to place. He considers himself a Blood cook, having divided the restaurant world into Bloods and Crips. Bloods are "linked to 'local' by the inheritance or adoption of a culture, linked to a particular manner and place of being."[28] Crips, in opposition, are "post-national" and prefer inventive food with no consideration for culinary tradition. The meaning of globalization is presented in the demonic figure of Dante Beale, who runs a Starbucks-style coffee chain (called Inferno Coffee, no less!) and eventually takes over Jeremy's restaurant, turning it into a slick Crip venture. The novel is a gastronomic allegory about the costs of globalization and the human need to forge and maintain connections with one's place.

Bare survival rather than resistance to globalization occupies the city residents in Dionne Brand's *Thirsty* (2002), a portrait of Toronto in a series of linked narrative poems. Toronto is not named until halfway through the poem, but its identity is clear from early references to street names and neighborhoods. The poem traces the disintegrating life of a mentally disturbed man who is eventually shot by Toronto police and also explores the speaker's own yearning for peace and fulfillment in the city, looking with fierce pity at "the brittle, gnawed life" offered to so many inhabitants.[29] The speaker hates the city's ugliness but finds it, above all else, a microcosm of the human, a repository of despair and desire, and occasionally of beauty. Observing the banter in a fish market between Portuguese merchants and querulous Jamaican women, Brand is momentarily soothed and comforted. At the cross-street of Yonge and Bloor, she recognizes that what compels her is the city's insistent, undeniable longing.

The vitality of urban struggle is celebrated no less ambiguously in Michael Turner's *Kingsway* (1995), a collection of linked poems addressing Kingsway Street, the sinuous thoroughfare that winds from downtown Vancouver through various commercial and business districts out to the suburbs. Turner uses minimal punctuation and nonstandard syntax to present Kingsway as a sometimes chaotic meeting point where individual lives, cultures, classes, professions, and world-views are brought into contact; it becomes a microcosm for Vancouver's difficult and not fully achieved – but nonetheless vital – diversity. Although Gregory Scofield does not name Vancouver in his *Native Canadiana: Songs from the Urban Rez* (1996), references to the "100 Block" (of East Hastings) and the fact that Scofield has worked with street youth in Vancouver identify the downtown eastside as the gritty locus of tenuous survival and walking despair in these poems about urban displacement. The poems provide powerful testimony of Vancouver as the place where many Native youths from Western Canada seek some kind of freedom and find too often instead a hell of addiction, disease, violence, and death.

Recent regional writing

Writers as diverse as Richler, Gartner, and Brand all insist that cities, districts, and neighborhoods, as much as small towns or rural areas, have power to engage the literary imagination, shape identity, and provoke political resistance. Yet while the city has become an increasingly important focus for late twentieth- and early twenty-first-century Canadian writers, rural and small-town life remain at the center of innovative regional writing. Increasingly, writers are opening regions to multicultural and international influences, exploring how experiences of place change radically according to one's social position and racial heritage; the formally inventive and pluralistic texts of George Elliott Clarke and Fred Wah oppose attempts to create definitive or totalizing representations. In *Whylah Falls* (1990), Clarke creates a mythic community of the 1930s to give voice to the African Loyalist heritage of Black Nova Scotia and its central, if neglected, place in Maritimes history. Combining poetry with prose passages as well as photographs and fictionalized newspaper articles, the narrator attempts to capture the many voices necessary to a full epic portrait of Nova Scotia. In Clarke's vision, the one particular place must encompass the otherness of migration, translation, and dislocation.

In *Diamond Grill* (1996), a collection of prose poems examining cultural inheritance and regional memory, Fred Wah launches a challenge to traditional understandings of region. Wah uses a fragmented form – 132 short pieces – to document a fragmented relationship to place. Calling the work a bio-text or partly fictionalized memoir, Wah makes it clear that the place anchoring his diverse personal memories – the Diamond Grill restaurant in Nelson, BC – is shot through with memories and stories of other places, including earlier cafés in Swift Current and Trail, faraway China where his father and aunt were sent as children, and the Detention Hospital in Victoria, BC, where his father was held upon his return to Canada. In Wah's narrative, the Nelson café becomes a space of cultural negotiation in which the challenge is to hold the tension between multiple ethnicities so as not to lose difference. Connections to place, the text suggests, are always tenuous and contingent, needing to be creatively forged and continually renegotiated.

Questions of place in Canadian literature continue to engage critics at the turn of the millennium, not least because of the publication of a significant cluster of acclaimed Canadian works with no direct connection to Canadian places, including Michael Ondaatje's *The English Patient* (1992), Barbara Gowdy's *The White Bone* (1998), and Rohinton Mistry's *Family Matters* (2002). That the novels were widely praised can be read as evidence of Canadian cultural maturity or as a worrying sign of what Stephen Henighan calls a free trade mentality and corresponding loss of confidence in Canadian realities.[30] It seems too early, however, to declare the end of regional literature. Writers are moving away from assumptions of a natural connection between place and identity, yet the desire to record Canadian places remains evident. These places, however, reflect Canadians' increasingly diverse circumstances: as Asian Canadian families move back and forth between Hong Kong and Vancouver; as Muslim and Jewish Canadians experience the repercussions of global terrorism; and as First Nations people organize for cultural autonomy, relationships to place continue to change. Although predicting the future of regional writing is impossible, it is likely that we will see a continued recognition that places are at once a fact of geography and a social and literary construction, and an increasing interest in how mythologies of place illuminate, acknowledge, and perhaps even work to bridge the differences between people sharing the land.

NOTES

1. George Woodcock, *Northern Spring: The Flowering of Canadian Literature* (Vancouver: Douglas and McIntyre, 1987) p. 21.
2. Northrop Frye, *The Bush Garden* (Toronto: Anansi, 1971) pp. i–ii.
3. E. K. Brown, *Responses and Evaluations: Essays on Canada*, ed. David Staines (1943; Toronto: McClelland, 1977) p. 21.
4. David M. Jordan, *New World Regionalism: Literature in the Americas* (Toronto: University of Toronto Press, 1994) p. 7.
5. For a discussion of formal regionalism, see R. Douglas Francis, "Regionalism, W. L. Morton, and the Writing of Western Canadian History, 1870–1885," *American Review of Canadian Studies* (Winter 2001): pp. 569–88. Francis uses the term mythic regionalism for approaches emphasizing regions as linguistic constructs and postmodern regionalism for approaches emphasizing multiplicity and conflict.
6. Jeanette Lynes and Herb Wyile, "Regionalism: Reconstruction or Deconstruction?," *Diverse Landscapes: Re-Reading Place across Cultures in Contemporary Canadian Writing*, ed. Karin Beeler and Dee Horne (Prince George: University of Northern British Columbia Press, 1996) p. 26.
7. Jordan, *New World Regionalism*, p. 9.
8. W. J. Keith, *Literary Images of Ontario* (Toronto: University of Toronto Press, 1992) p. 14.
9. W. H. New, *Land Sliding: Imagining Space, Presence, and Power in Canadian Writing* (Toronto: University of Toronto Press, 1997) p. 117.

10. Ursula Kelly, *Marketing Place: Cultural Politics, Regionalism and Reading* (Halifax: Fernwood, 1993) pp. 30–1.
11. Gloria Sawai, *A Song for Nettie Johnson* (Regina: Coteau, 2001), back-cover blurb.
12. Aida Edemariam, "Us? Boring? Ha!," *Guardian* 27 Sept. 2002: n. pag., online, *Guardian Unlimited*, Internet.
13. Laurie Ricou, "Region, Regionalism," *Encyclopedia of Literature in Canada*, ed. W. H. New (Toronto: University of Toronto Press, 2002) p. 952.
14. Sam Solecki, *The Last Canadian Poet: An Essay on Al Purdy* (Toronto: University of Toronto Press, 1999).
15. Michael Ondaatje, afterword, *Tay John*, by Howard O'Hagan (Toronto: McClelland, 1989) p. 265.
16. Sherrill E. Grace, *Canada and the Idea of North* (Montreal: McGill-Queen's University Press, 2001) p. 171.
17. Grace, *Canada and the Idea of North*, p. 51.
18. Frank Davey, "Toward the Ends of Regionalism," *A Sense of Place: Re-Evaluating Regionalism in Canadian and American Writing*, ed. Christian Riegel and Herb Wyile (Edmonton: University of Alberta Press, 1997) pp. 8–12.
19. Lisa Chalykoff, "Overcoming the Two Solitudes of Canadian Literary Regionalism," *Studies in Canadian Literature* 23.1 (1998): pp. 160–77.
20. E. J. Pratt, *Newfoundland Verse* (Toronto: Ryerson, 1923) p. 87.
21. Alison Calder, "Reassessing Prairie Realism," *A Sense of Place*, ed. Riegel and Wyile, pp. 51–2.
22. Milton Acorn, *The Island Means Minago* (Toronto: NC Press, 1975) p. 9.
23. David Adams Richards, *Mercy Among the Children* (Toronto: Doubleday, 2000) p. 200.
24. Wayne Johnston, *Baltimore's Mansion: A Memoir* (Toronto: Random House, 1999) p. 123.
25. Jennifer Andrews, "Native Canadian Gothic Refigured: Reading Eden Robinson's *Monkey Beach*," *Essays on Canadian Writing* 73 (Spring 2001): pp. 1–24.
26. Michael Ondaatje, *In the Skin of a Lion* (Toronto: Random House, 1987) p. 157.
27. Russell Smith, *Noise* (Erin: Porcupine's Quill, 1998) p. 135.
28. Timothy Taylor, *Stanley Park* (Toronto: Knopf, 2001) p. 23.
29. Dionne Brand, *Thirsty* (Toronto: McClelland, 2002) p. 1.
30. Stephen Henighan, *When Words Deny the World: The Reshaping of Canadian Writing* (Erin: Porcupine's Quill, 2002).

12

Canadian literary criticism and the idea of a national literature

MAGDALENE REDEKOP

Narratives of community

Although the idea of a national essence has long been recognized as a fiction, national literatures continue to be set apart in university curriculums, and the nation, a concept blithely dismissed by many literary scholars, remains an international political reality. Indeed, Benedict Anderson has termed nation the "most universally legitimate value in the political life of our time."[1] The connection between the story of a nation and the stories written by its citizens may be highly problematic, but connection there undeniably is. History provides frightening examples of what happens when nationalism reduces people to a totalitarian mass, but it behooves the literary critic to remember also that it is not nationalism but rather the power of transnational corporations that today threatens to homogenize global mass culture. It is not hard to see why some version of the idea of a national literature lies intransigently, albeit often silently, at the heart of many of the hotly debated theoretical issues of the day. Any effort to pin down the concept, however, is destined to be an exercise in futility, and this will not be my aim here. On the contrary, I will argue that if a nation has a vital literary tradition, the national literature is like a conversation in progress, not like a fixed and static monument. In the preface to *Home Truths* (1981), Mavis Gallant makes the bold claim that her stories are Canadian simply because she is Canadian. Aunt Emily, in Joy Kogawa's *Obasan* (1981), similarly claims that if a Canadian citizen tells the story of Momotaro, then it becomes a Canadian story. Issues of appropriation of voice aside, the argument has a certain inevitable logic and makes a good starting point when teaching a course in Canadian literature. At its best, Canadian literature is characterized by a readiness to change with its authors and readers. This kind of resilient strength is nowhere more evident than in a willingness to laugh at the impossibility of fixed solutions.

Comedy, I will argue, has a special place in Canada that is hard to separate from the Canadian idea of a national literature, although this fact is seldom noted by literary critics. A catalog of comic writers is testimony to this connection: T. C. Haliburton, Thomas McCulloch, Antonine Maillet, Paul Hiebert, L. M. Montgomery, Robert Kroetsch, Jack Hodgins, Stephen Leacock, Robertson Davies, Mordecai Richler, Margaret Atwood, Thomas King, Terry Griggs, and many more. Perhaps comedy and absurdity are inevitable ingredients in contemporary theories that purport to contain a national literature. Certainly any constructed nationalist fictions are readily falsified by the reality of material conditions in a country as pluralistic as Canada, and it is surely no wonder that Canadians have, in Frye's words, "a highly developed sense of irony."[2] Like the grain elevators on a flat prairie horizon, anything made by human hands stands out in a sparsely populated country and does so, furthermore, with a certain air of absurdity. Canadian literatures, both written and oral, constitute a collective repudiation of Herder's model of a *Geistesgeschichte* as the one story of one nation told in one language. Anderson defines a nation as an "[i]magined political community" (*Imagined Communities*, p. 13). Adapting Anderson, Robert Lecker writes that "Canada is nothing less than a dramatic narrative about community. The strongest expressions of this community will be those that recreate the country by imagining it anew."[3] Lecker sees it as the role of the critic to explain that the idea of Canada is constructed and that everyone can participate in the process. My aim in this essay is consistent with Lecker's view. To emphasize the constructed nature of terms like "nation" is to see the literary critic as a participant in the process of imagining communities.

Historical contexts

Many critics credit postmodernism with the power to expose the constructed nature of positions traditionally seen as natural or universal. I am grateful for insights provided by theorists of the postmodern (preeminent among these being Canada's Linda Hutcheon, author of *The Canadian Postmodern* [1988] and *Splitting Images: Contemporary Canadian Ironies* [1991]) and I will be building on those insights here. At the same time, however, I want to counter the myth of progress in literary criticism and argue for a reconsideration of earlier historical contexts. A useful exercise is to isolate the place where the idea of a national literature intersects with the idea of a literary period. Thus the poetry of Margaret Atwood issues a radical challenge to Emerson's romantic image of the male poet as a "transparent eyeball" who is all and sees all. If you should happen to be sitting across from the poet in an Atwood poem, her eyes would more likely be shooting knitting needles at you. Such a doubling back, as Hutcheon has made clear, is itself a feature of postmodernism. What is true of architecture (that the old is installed inside the new) is true also of the structure of a nation, and a view of nation as a conscious construction, as a look at the ideas of George Grant, Marshall McLuhan, and Northrop Frye will illustrate, has informed Canadian writing since the sixties. In *Technology and Empire*, Grant argued that "[t]echnique is ourselves [and] comes forth from and is sustained in our vision of ourselves as creative freedom,"[4] while Frye (according to Mandel) envisioned society as "a series of conventions, a form of art" that offers "the possibility of ritual and therefore of grace."[5]

The wise critic, conscious of the multiplicity of ethnicities and regions in Canada, does well to keep open the possibility of grace. In a collection of essays entitled *Literary Pluralities*, edited by Christl Verduyn (1998), pluralism is cited repeatedly as an antidote to claims that there is a single Canadian identity. During the brief vogue for thematic criticism following 1967, such claims were often implied, but who would now dare to venture such generalizations? Conspicuous differences between American and Canadian historical contexts do exist and these were often cited in criticism inspired by the patriotism of the Centennial decade. Works such as poet Al Purdy's *The New Romans* (1968) and Robin Matthews and James A. Steele's *The Struggle for Canadian Universities* (1969) passionately advocated cultural autonomy for Canada. Although there are some sustained comparative studies (see, for example, Camille La Bossière, ed., *Context North America: Canadian/U.S. Literary Relations* [1994]), critics have been increasingly reluctant to make any appeal to these differences in interpretation of literary texts. When they are noted at all, differences are often phrased as negatives: Canada had no Declaration of Independence, no Civil War, no period of Transcendentalism.

The distinctive positive aspects of Canadian history do periodically come up for discussion. In the wake of the Centennial, numerous translations and several government-sponsored studies were published (for example, Ronald Sutherland's *Second Image* [1971] and *The New Hero* [1977] as well as Clément Moisan's *L'âge de la littérature canadienne* [1969]). With some exceptions, however (as in the work of Sylvia Söderlind, Winfried Siemerling, and Marie Vautier), comparative work in anglophone and francophone writing has not been sustained, despite the fact that there is a call for such studies from communities who have to contend with their own issues of multilingualism in general and English-French bilingualism in particular. Work in Canadian Black studies for example currently takes place either in English or in French, but leading critics like George Elliott Clarke have urged that they be brought together. More notable than the issue of language is the abiding fascination that the North has exercised on the Canadian imagination, as literary critics such as Sherrill Grace (*Canada and the Idea of North*

[2001]) and Renée Hulan (*Northern Experience and the Myths of Canadian Culture* [2002]) have illustrated. In *Strange Things: The Malevolent North in Canadian Literature* (1995), Margaret Atwood's comedic approach to the topic may be read as a Canadian muting of strident American individualism. Similar ideas are explored by Wallace Stegner in *Wolf Willow* (1962), a novel that takes place on the border between Canada and the United States. Distance from American individualism is also passionately affirmed in seminal texts such as George Grant's *Lament for a Nation: The Defeat of Canadian Nationalism* (1965) and Dennis Lee's acclaimed essay "Cadence, Country, Silence: Writing in a Colonial Space" (1973).

Changes in demographics have tended to blur distinctions between Canadian and American culture, but these historic differences will not go away and will shape the literatures whether or not literary critics write about them. It is not surprising, however, that they have found it difficult to do so, given the camouflage effect of vocabularies that appear to be shared but differ at a deep level. Liberalism and multiculturalism, for example, are terms used in both countries but they do not have the same history and have different meanings in contemporary usage. What is beyond debate is the radical difference in power between the two countries. Pierre Elliot Trudeau once likened Canada to a mouse sleeping next to an elephant. Robert Kroetsch suggests that Canadians "survive by being skilful shape-changers . . . by working with a low level of self-definition and national definition."[6] How this power difference relates to ideas about national literatures is not clear. Certain it is, however, that misperceptions multiply between the two countries and that mostly friendly laughter is a frequent response in Canada – all the more so when the southern giant does not notice the existence of Canada. Invisibility is a useful condition for tricksters. Humor is deeply embedded in cultural context and it is paradoxically at moments when a mixed readership concedes that it cannot reach anything resembling mutual understanding that irrepressible laughter breaks up – and at least temporarily creates – a community of readers. Paul Quarrington's divided communities in *Home Game* (1983) offer an example: the circus freaks and the religious fanatics are linked not only by the fact that they play the very American game of baseball (so changed that it is no longer American) but also by the laughter of the community of readers.

Rethinking the contexts of Canadian criticism

Comedy, on one level, is an abdication by the theorist, but the vexing issues remain before us when the laughter dies down. To focus specifically on Canadian literary criticism is to make it hard to evade those questions that arise as a result of locating a literary text in a particular space and time. The question in any nation is how to negotiate the relationship between the texts written and the contexts within which they are written. In his introduction to an influential collection of essays, *Contexts of Canadian Criticism* (1971), Eli Mandel isolated three such contexts: environmentalism, formalism, and literary tradition. I will use Mandel's tripartite division to organize my own reflections here because it offers perspectives on questions about national literature that have refused to go away. Mandel was writing at a time when the Laurendeau-Dunton Commission on Bilingualism and Biculturalism, with its supplementary investigation of "The Cultural Contribution of the Other Ethnic Groups," had made it clear that the meaning of "Canadian" was up for revision. His description of the embarrassed evasiveness of the critics still has an uncanny accuracy. He points to a "precarious, mannered control that marks out the 'Canadian' part of the critic," and describes it as "marked by the struggle to avoid talking about national identity or local politics as much as by desire to find distinctive national characteristics" (p. 22). The more things change, the more they stay the same. Herschel Hardin's claim that Canadians paradoxically express nationalism by rejecting nationalism still seems reflected in the nervousness about the subject that characterizes the debate in Canada.[7]

In *New Contexts of Canadian Criticism* (1997), a collection of essays that signals its continuity with Mandel's earlier volume, Ajay Heble expresses an urgent "need to move beyond a nationalist critical methodology" in favor of a transnational traffic between cultures.[8] Although I am not convinced that nationalist longings can be so easily rejected, I agree with Heble that the workings of power in regard to the construction of national identity must be interrogated. Responsible readers must identify and challenge the ideologies that determine what parts of the vertical mosaic[9] are at the bottom of the pyramid. The way to do so, in my view, is to make ourselves increasingly conscious of the conventions that condition our readings. Russell Brown notes that the idea of a "code" is a "revealing concept to bring to our discussions of a culturally defined body of literature" because it helps in the formulation of new questions. "Is there a cultural code we learn as Canadian readers?" he asks. "If so, what are the messages that are being sent between author and reader?"[10] Such questions offer useful substance when critics become involved in the heated debates surrounding identity politics.

Like other settler colonies, Canada is bound to experience resistance to efforts to construct a group identity based on linguistic, racial, or religious homogeneity. Group loyalties will out, as separatist movements demonstrate, and the postcolonial emphasis on culture as hybridized captures the dilemma.

Tomson Highway, Dionne Brand, Hiromi Goto, Rohinton Mistry, George Elliott Clarke, and numerous other writers have explored often highly resistant versions of belonging and home. The titles of Arun Mukherjee's *Towards an Aesthetic of Opposition: Essays on Literature, Criticism and Cultural Imperialism* (1988) and *Oppositional Aesthetics: Readings from a Hyphenated Space* (1994), a revision of the former, articulate challenges to conciliatory visions of Canada, and she and others do so in texts that blur the distinction between autobiographical and critical writing. Aboriginal writers like Lenore Keeshig-Tobias and Lee Maracle resist the theories of postcolonial critics and collaborators as yet another effort to deprive them of their own voice. The sheer multiplication of these voices makes it increasingly difficult to sustain separatist identities based on race – a welcome development to those who, like Edward Said, believe that "all cultures are involved in one another; none is single and pure, all are hybrid, heterogeneous."[11] Enoch Padolsky has argued that the Canadian perception of race is predominantly of mixed races, differing from the United States, where the racial system, because of the history of slavery, is fundamentally biracial.[12] Instead of the horror of miscegenation, Tamara Palmer Seiler envisions a situation in which hybridity is embodied in the person of a particular "'mixed-blood' writer who explodes stereotypes and mediates across cultural spaces."[13] The possibility is modified, however, by writers such as Thomas King who is claimed as a Native writer despite being in fact of mixed race.

Appeals to the category of race are always deeply troubling. More important than the actual blood content of any writers in Canada, surely, is the mixture of stories and the ongoing dialogue between various texts. Identity politics tends to produce an anti-formalist criticism, but the history of Canadian literary criticism demonstrates that it is not possible to reject a convention without first making it visible and recognizing it as a convention. Ajay Heble cites E. J. Pratt's poem, *Towards the Last Spike* (1952), suggesting that Pratt left the Chinese laborers out of the poem "because he was concerned to present Canada as a unified and autonomous entity." Heble then refers to F. R. Scott's response to Pratt, in "All the Spikes but the Last" (1957), as a poem that points to "the unsustainability of such a construction" ("New Contexts of Canadian Criticism," p. 88) by drawing attention to the existence of the Chinese. More significant to me than the final interpretation of either of these poems is the existence of the dialogue between them and the exposure of cultural codes.

A more recent contribution to the same dialogue serves to illustrate this point. Sky Lee's *Disappearing Moon Cafe* (1990) begins with a prologue narration describing a search for the bones of the very chinese (the lower case is deliberate) laborers left out of Pratt's poems. Wong Gwei Chang, the young man sent on the bone-searching expedition, is startled by the appearance of a living creature who seems like a spirit of the landscape: "She was an Indian girl, dressed in coarse brown clothing that made her invisible in the forest." But the invisibility and the stereotypical oneness with nature are belied by the high visibility of the scene *as* scene and by the steamy romanticism that appears in the prologue like a conscious cliché, as histrionic as any Hollywood film. She calls him a "chinaman" and he calls her a "wild injun," but she speaks Chinese and becomes his guide, "as if the barren wasteland around him had magically opened and allowed him admittance."[14]

Reader responses to this scene will vary widely, depending on various factors. Gender and race are probably less important here than the reader's skill in "*cultural* listening" (Heble, "New Contexts of Canadian Criticism," p. 86). The reader who has read the poem by Pratt and the poem by Scott will be at an obvious advantage, and awareness of the cultural codes being mocked allows the reader to enjoy both the ironic distance from the cliché and the pleasure of reading a romance. It could be argued that those stories are most powerfully Canadian that can somehow resonate with the plurality of voices and stories, evoking the layers upon layers of yet to be discovered revised history.

Canadian literatures and geography

By locating her romantic scene in the Canadian wilderness and peopling it with a "chinaman" and a "wild injun," Sky Lee touched a chord that resonates in Canadian history. Geography is the first of Mandel's three contexts and it appears to be predominant in this opening scene. Lee goes on, however, to write a revisionist history of Western Canada that challenges the environmental determinism that looms large in our literary criticism. In doing so, she contributes to a dialogue about Canadian literary history. In 1928, A. J. M. Smith described Canadian poetry as "altogether too self-conscious of its environment, of its position in space, and scarcely conscious at all of its position in time."[15] The trouble with Canada, as Prime Minister William Lyon Mackenzie King put it in a speech to the House of Commons on 18 June 1936, is that we have too much geography and not enough history.[16] Earle Birney may have been thinking of King's famous comment when (in 1962) he ended his poem "Can. Lit." with the often-quoted line: "It's only by our lack of ghosts we're haunted."[17] Perhaps Birney did not yet know (what King's belatedly released diaries revealed) that King's political decisions were influenced by communications with the spirit of his dead mother. From our postcolonial vantage point, Birney's lament, in any case, seems a dated expression of colonial mentality. A lack of ghosts? Try telling that to Sky Lee after you have read about Wong Gwei Chang's search for bones in the forests of British Columbia. Try telling that to Eden Robinson, author of *Monkey Beach* (2000), or to Rohinton Mistry, author of "The Ghost of Firozsha Baag" (1987). Unforeseen spectres roam through the Canadian geography and continually revise our way of reading place in Canadian literature.

Surely it is fortunate, given the magnitude of the challenge posed by such an enormous and ancient land to the collective national imagination, that no less a critic than Northrop Frye should happen to be a citizen of the country. Surely so powerful an imagination could counter the tendency to environmental determinism – could set out to build Jerusalem on the Great Canadian Shield. Frye appeared, however, to abdicate that role in 1965, with his forceful account of the "tone of deep terror in regard to nature" that he heard in Canadian poetry. This "terror of the soul" he saw as a response to the fact that "the vast unconsciousness of nature" is "an unanswerable denial" of the "human and moral values" that the mind must cling to "if it is to preserve its integrity or even its sanity." As a response to this bleak vision, he offered instead the now famous image of the "garrison mentality" – a "closely knit and beleaguered society" of settlers, in which there is absolute certainty about "moral and social values." Constructed as a defense against the terror of meaninglessness, the "garrison mentality" creates another "real terror": "something anti-cultural comes into Canadian life, a dominating herd-mind in which nothing original can grow" and which spells "the death of communication and dialogue."[18]

In the fledgling world of Canadian literary criticism, Frye's ironic construct acted as a provocation – almost as if he were daring writers to prove him wrong or offering a negative model of a national literature: how not to imagine a Canadian literature. Frye's metaphor is partly responsible for the fact that John Richardson's Gothic novel *Wacousta* (1832) was elevated to national icon by critics and writers as diverse as John Moss, Robin Matthews, and Gaile MacGregor. The creative response most true to Frye's irony appears in the work of E. J. Pratt, a poet who was Frye's colleague and close personal friend. In his long narrative poem "The Titanic," Pratt posits the ship as a garrison of sorts – an allegedly unsinkable ship that sinks when confronted with the reality of northern geography. Like Frye's theory, the poem is a test of the environmental determinism that dominates early Canadian literary criticism. Designed as a kind of parody of *The Odyssey*, "The Titanic" tests the very idea of a national literature. In Homer, each ordeal confronted by the epic hero is an occasion for confronting the values of the nation; the departure/return pattern leads to a concluding homecoming that not only affirms those values but provides an occasion for telling the story of male heroism. In stark contrast, the voyage of the ship produced by Harland & Wolff is no match for the iceberg, that "grey shape with the paleolithic face" whose origins are invisible. Human values of kindness and unselfishness, while diminished, are nevertheless affirmed by Pratt, and the structure of the poem (unlike that of the ship) supports those values. So basic are those human values, that by no stretch of the imagination could they be called inherently Canadian, but it is tempting to argue that what is Canadian about Pratt's version of the tragedy is the strong commitment to the human need to construct something out of the disaster.

"The Titanic" features prominently in Atwood's *Survival: A Thematic Guide to Canadian Literature* (1972). If Frye's "garrison mentality" was an example of how not to imagine a Canadian literature, Atwood's book offered pages of illustrations of the kinds of "victim positions" resulting from such environmental determinism. So sinister and overwhelming is the threat of the hostile environment that the writer's ability to shape literary forms – in the works of Atwood, Pratt, Frye, and many other writers – is like the tool of survival seen by McLuhan as a "counter-environment."

Canadian literatures and the limits of form

Not all the criticism written during the heady nationalist years after 1967 was as entertaining as *Survival*, but much of it was similarly dominated by geography and the tendency was to employ sweeping themes to paper over the huge cracks in Canadian unity. Essays and books such as Warren Tallman's "Wolf in the Snow" (in *Canadian Literature* 5 and 6 [Summer and Fall 1960]) and D. G. Jones's *Butterfly on Rock: A Study of Themes and Images in Canadian Literature* (1970) eventually provoked a backlash against the nationalist demands for Canadian content. Frank Davey's lecture "Surviving the Paraphrase" (1974, published in a book with the same title in 1983) initiated an appeal to form over content. Barry Cameron and Michael Dixon published a collection of essays entitled *Minus Canadian: Penultimate Essays on Literature* (1977), calling for a rejection of thematic focus and more critical attention to issues of literary form. There was and is considerable embarrassment in Canada about the thematic stage. Relief was evident as the critical practice moved, with the times, into the more sophisticated area of postmodernist theory. In the literature itself, however, theme and form work in tandem even in texts that pre-date postmodernism. Earle Birney's "Bushed," written in 1952, reads like a gloss on Frye's vision of a landscape of horror, but Birney chooses verbs that emphasize conscious construction. In the poem, a solitary figure speaks out from inside a land-scape that gradually turns horrific, and the poem ends with the speaker waiting "for the great flint to come singing into his heart" – usually read as proof of the insanity for which the word "bushed" is a Canadian synonym. The word "singing" paradoxically affirms the existence of the poem itself as song – a conscious construction that flies in the face of the random indif-ference of nature. The tone of Birney's poem captures what Frye saw as the counterforce to the self-destructive tendencies of the "garrison mentality," something he described as a "creative paranoia, a unifying power that works towards life and the fulfillment of desire instead of towards death."[19] Frye obviously viewed these violently contrasting forces as part of his vision of "Culture as Interpenetration" – the title of his essay. In the criticism written after the thematic period, however, other critics tended to treat forms as if they were somehow neutral and free of cultural bias. More recent criticism is by no means free of such an assumption, but critics tend to take up differing stances in response. Frank Davey's later work, for example, seems to view any appeal to referentiality as anathema. Arun Mukherjee, conversely, seems tempted to reject the very idea of form. Such debates can, with some effort, be situated within the historical context of early Canadian literary criticism. The terms may change (formalism may, for example, appear as a kind of romanticism), but the binaries remain recognizable and astonishingly repeti-tive. Again and again some idea of form keeps smashing up against some idea of reality. A sustained interrogation of realism marks every nook and cranny of the Canadian literary tradition. It is "real life" (a phrase that resonates through the fiction of Alice Munro) that necessitates constant revision of codes and conventions.

In the literary criticism of the 1920s we can observe the roots of this on-going process and the ways it relates to developing ideas about a national literature. In 1928, for example, motivated by a call for greater cultural au-tonomy in Canadian letters, A. J. M. Smith, modernist poet and influential publisher of anthologies of Canadian verse, perceived a conflict between the "cosmopolitan tradition" and the "native tradition" of Canadian poetry. Smith saw the poets of the native tradition – the Post-Confederation Poets among them – as concentrating on the unique and the local in Canadian life, whereas the poets of the cosmopolitan tradition tried to rise above colo-nialism by writing about universal issues.[20] Challenged by John Sutherland who insisted that cosmopolitanism was an evasion of homegrown traditions, Smith revised his views to highlight a contrast between "literary colonial-ism," which he saw as a kind of romanticism, and "literary nationalism," to him a form of realism. Romanticism, for Smith's purposes, was "an escape from reality." Realism, however, avoided the "abstract and the grandiose" and concentrated "on the sympathetic insight upon the familiar and the local."[21]

Canadian literatures and the idea of a literary period

The third of Mandel's categories is the most incomplete and the least clear. He begins the essay by promising that his third category will be concerned with "patterns of literary development" and will seek to "define literary tradition or whatever may be discussed as distinctive in national literature" (introduction to *Contexts of Canadian Criticism*, p. 4). No such discussion materializes, however, and Mandel returns instead, as if drawn by an irresistible magnetic force, to a version of environmental determinism. "But perhaps what prevails, after all," he concludes, "is what we would on all grounds – theoretical, logical, historical, cultural, political, social – want to reject: the image with which we began" (pp. 23–4). This is followed by a long quotation from Atwood that underlines the image of Canadians as slightly demented invaders of an alien land: "We are all immigrants to this place even if we were born here: the country is too big for anyone to inhabit completely, and in parts unknown to us we move in fear, exiles and invaders."[22] This, he concludes, may be bad criticism but it is all we have.

Developments in Canadian literary criticism have filled in the blank left by Eli Mandel in his third category. Glenn Willmott (*Unreal Country: Modernity in the Canadian Novel in English* [2002]), Lynda Jessup (*Antimodernism and Artistic Experience: Policing the Boundaries of Modernity* [2001]), and Ian Mackay (*The Quest of the Folk: Antimodernism and Cultural Selection in Twentieth-Century Nova Scotia* [1994]) are only three of the critics who have published work on literary periodization. Were Eli Mandel now more than one of our friendliest ghosts, I believe he would himself revise his third category and break out of the closed circle, prompted by his emphasis on the importance of immigrants who people his land. Janice Kulyk Keefer describes where we are now as a time when a Canadian writer can write about "Bombay, Sri Lanka, Trinidad . . . and still be intensely Canadian."[23] Keefer, herself of Ukrainian origin, isolates the "act of bridge-building" as a crucial feature of the idea of Canadian national literature and situates the writer on a swaying bridge balancing between cultures: "It's the writer's being situated on the bridge between cultures, and thus free to turn her or his gaze in any direction, to critique, to defend, to redress wrongs – not just in the adopted but in the home culture as well – that makes him or her Canadian" (Keefer, "The Sacredness of Bridges," p. 105).

That's a tall order and rather an earnest project but there are any number of other Canadian writers who would be quick to play fast and loose with that swaying bridge, noting how it unsettles the linear constructs of literary history. Thomas King's mock creation myth, "One Good Story, That One," demolishes, in a few hilarious pages, any fixed notion of origins that might be lingering in our perception of the Canadian past. The narrator tells his story into the recording device of anthropologists who do not recognize their own preconceived European codes and therefore cannot see how those codes are being distorted. At the end of the story, there are a lot of coyote tracks on the floor, but no clear sense of direction or origin.

There is a delicious irony in the fact that Canada's dubious ontological status has found a reflection in other literatures of the postcolonial world and given Canada an international presence. The openness to new constructions, the provisional nature of those constructions, the ironic play that affirms a mutual humanity: all these are part of what makes Canada a nation that welcomes creative invasion.

NOTES

1. Benedict Anderson, *Imagined Communities: Reflections on the Origin and Spread of Nationalism* (London: Verso, 1983) p. 12.
2. Northrop Frye, conclusion, *Literary History of Canada: Canadian Literature in English*, ed. Carl F. Klinck, 2nd edn., vol. III (1965; Toronto: University of Toronto Press, 1976) p. 319.
3. Robert Lecker, *Making It Real: The Canonization of English-Canadian Literature* (Toronto: Anansi, 1995) p. 10.
4. George Grant, *Technology and Empire: Perspectives on North America* (Toronto: Anansi, 1969) p. 137.
5. Eli Mandel, introduction, *Contexts of Canadian Criticism*, ed. Mandel (Chicago: University of Chicago Press, 1971) p. 20.
6. Robert Kroetsch, *The Lovely Treachery of Words: Essays Selected and New* (Toronto: Oxford University Press, 1989) pp. 27–8.
7. Herschel Hardin, *A Nation Unaware: The Canadian Economic Culture* (Vancouver: J. J. Douglas, 1974) p. 26.
8. Ajay Heble, "New Contexts of Canadian Criticism: Democracy, Counterpoint, Responsibility," *New Contexts of Canadian Criticism*, ed. Heble, Donna Palmateer Pennee, and J. R. (Tim) Struthers (Peterborough: Broadview, 1997) p. 79.
9. See John Porter, *The Vertical Mosaic: An Analysis of Social Class and Power in Canada* (Toronto: University of Toronto Press, 1965).
10. Russell Brown, "Critic, Culture, Text: Beyond Thematics," *Essays on Canadian Writing* 11 (1978): p. 180.
11. Edward Said, *Culture and Imperialism* (New York: Knopf, 1993) p. xxvi.
12. See Enoch Padolsky, "Ethnicity and Race," *Literary Pluralities*, ed. Christl Verduyn (Peterborough: Broadview, 1998) pp. 22–4.
13. Tamara Palmer Seiler, "Multi-Vocality and National Literature," *Literary Pluralities*, ed. Verduyn, p. 62.

14. Sky Lee, *Disappearing Moon Cafe* (Vancouver: Douglas and McIntyre, 1990) pp. 3–5.

15. A. J. M. Smith, "Wanted: Canadian Criticism," *Canadian Forum* 8 (April 1928), quoted in Louis Dudek and Michael Gnarowski, eds., *The Making of Modern Poetry in Canada: Essential Articles on Contemporary Canadian Poetry in English* (Toronto: Ryerson, 1967) p. 33.

16. William Lyon Mackenzie King, in John Robert Colombo, *Colombo's All-Time Great Canadian Quotations* (Toronto: Stoddart, 1994) p. 126.

17. Earle Birney, "Can. Lit.," 1962, *The New Oxford Book of Canadian Verse in English*, ed. Margaret Atwood (Toronto: Oxford University Press, 1982) p. 116.

18. Northrop Frye, conclusion, *Literary History of Canada: Canadian Literature in English*, ed. Carl F. Klinck (1965; 1st edn. reprinted with corrections, Toronto: University of Toronto Press, 1966) pp. 830–1.

19. Northrop Frye, "Culture as Interpenetration," *Divisions on a Ground: Essays on Canadian Culture*, ed. James Polk (Toronto: Anansi, 1982) pp. 22–3.

20. See Philip Kokotailo, "Native and Cosmopolitan: A. J. M. Smith's Tradition of English-Canadian Poetry," *American Review of Canadian Studies* 20.1 (Spring 1990): pp. 31–40.

21. A. J. M. Smith, "Colonialism and Nationalism in Canadian Poetry before Confederation," *Canadian Historical Association Reports* (1944): p. 74, quoted in Philip Kokotailo, "The Bishop and His Deacon: Smith vs. Sutherland Reconsidered," *Journal of Canadian Studies* 27.2 (Summer 1992): p. 67.

22. Margaret Atwood, *The Journals of Susanna Moodie* (Toronto: Oxford University Press, 1970) p. 62.

23. Janice Kulyk Keefer, "'The Sacredness of Bridges': Writing Immigrant Experience," *Literary Pluralities*, ed. Verduyn, p. 105.

FURTHER READING

Reference works

Historical and general

Cook, Ramsay, et al., eds. *Dictionary of Canadian Biography*. 13 vols. as of 2003. Toronto: University of Toronto Press, 1966–.

Gough, Barry M. *Historical Dictionary of Canada*. Lanham: Scarecrow, 1999.

Green, Rayna, with Melanie Fernandez. *The Encyclopedia of the First Peoples of North America*. Toronto: Douglas and McIntyre, 1999.

Hayes, Derek. *Historical Atlas of Canada: A Thousand Years of Canada's History in Maps*. Vancouver: Douglas and McIntyre, 2002.

Hoxie, Frederick. *Encyclopedia of North American Indians*. Boston: Houghton, 1996.

Marsh, James H., ed. *The Canadian Encyclopedia*. 1985. 2nd edn. 4 vols. Edmonton: Hurtig, 1988. (Online version: <http://www.thecanadianencyclopedia.com>).

Matthews, Geoffrey, cartographer/designer, and R. Cole Harris et al., eds. *Historical Atlas of Canada*. 3 vols. Toronto: University of Toronto Press, 1987–93.

Bibliographies

Bond, Mary E., comp. and ed., and Martine M. Caron, comp. *Canadian Reference Sources: An Annotated Bibliography/Ouvrages de références canadiens: une bibliographie annotée*. Vancouver: University of British Columbia Press, 1996.

Early Canadiana Online. Canadian Institute for Historical Microreproductions in partnership with the National Library of Canada. <http://www.canadiana. org>.

Ingles, Ernie, comp. and ed. *Bibliography of Canadian Bibliographies*. 1960. 3rd edn. Toronto: University of Toronto Press, 1994.

Watters, Reginald E. *A Checklist of Canadian Literature and Background Materials, 1628–1950*. 1959. 2nd edn., rev. and enl. Toronto: University of Toronto Press, 1972.

Literary companions and encyclopedias

Benson, Eugene, and L. W. Conolly, eds. *The Oxford Companion to Canadian Theatre*. Toronto: Oxford University Press, 1989.

—, eds. *Encyclopedia of Post-Colonial Literatures in English.* 2 vols. London: Routledge, 1994.

Benson, Eugene, and William Toye, eds. *The Oxford Companion to Canadian Literature.* 1983. 2nd edn. Toronto: Oxford University Press, 1997.

Brydon, Diana, ed. *Postcolonialism: Critical Concepts in Literary and Cultural Studies.* 5 vols. London: Routledge, 2000.

Canadian Authors and Their Works. 24 vols. Downsview: ECW Press, 1983–91.

Lemire, Maurice, ed. *Dictionnaire des oeuvres littéraires du Québec.* 5 vols. Montreal: Fides, 1978–94. Vol. VI: Gilles Dorion, ed., 1995. Vol. VII: Aurélien Boivin, ed., 2003.

MacSkimming, Roy. *The Perilous Trade: Publishing Canada's Writers.* Toronto: McClelland & Stewart, 2003.

Makaryk, Irene, ed. *Encyclopedia of Contemporary Literary Theory: Approaches, Scholars, Terms.* Toronto: University of Toronto Press, 1993.

New, W. H., ed., *Dictionary of Literary Biography.* Vols. LIII (*Canadian Writers since 1960*, first series), LX (*Canadian Writers since 1960*, second series), LXVIII (*Canadian Writers, 1920–1959*, first series), LXXXVIII (*Canadian Writers, 1920–1959*, second series), XCII (*Canadian Writers, 1890–1920*), XCIX (*Canadian Writers before 1890*). Detroit: Gale/Bruccoli Clark, 1986–90.

—, ed. *Encyclopedia of Literature in Canada.* Toronto: University of Toronto Press, 2002.

Sage, Lorna, ed. *Women's Writing in English.* Cambridge: Cambridge University Press, 1999.

Literary histories

Blodgett, Edward D. *Five-Part Invention: A History of Literary History in Canada.* Toronto: University of Toronto Press, 2003.

Klinck, Carl F., ed. *Literary History of Canada: Canadian Literature in English.* 1965. 2nd edn. 3 vols. Toronto: University of Toronto Press, 1976. Vol. IV: W. H. New, ed. Toronto: University of Toronto Press, 1990.

New, W. H. *A History of Canadian Literature.* London: Macmillan, 1989.

Towards a History of the Literary Institution in Canada/Vers une histoire de l'institution littéraire au Canada (E. D. Blodgett and A. G. Purdy, eds., *Prefaces and Literary Manifestoes*; I. S. MacLaren and C. Potvin, eds., *Questions of Funding, Publishing and Distribution*; C. Potvin and J. Williamson, eds., *Women's Writing and the Literary Institution*; Joseph Pivato, ed., *Literatures of Lesser Diffusion*; E. D. Blodgett and A. G. Purdy, eds., *Problems of Literary Reception*; I. S. MacLaren and C. Potvin, eds., *Literary Genres*). Edmonton: The Research Institute for Comparative Literature, University of Alberta, 1988–92.

General and cultural histories

Berger, Carl. *The Sense of Power: Studies in the Ideas of Canadian Imperialism 1867–1914.* Toronto: University of Toronto Press, 1970.

Bouchard, Gérard. *Genèse des nations et cultures du Nouveau Monde: essai d'histoire comparée.* Montreal: Boréal, 2000.

Finlay, J. L., and D. N. Sprague. *The Structure of Canadian History.* 1979. 6th edn. Scarborough: Prentice, 2000.

Friesen, Gerald. *Citizens and Nation: An Essay on History, Communication and Canada*. Toronto: University of Toronto Press, 2000.

Litt, Paul. *The Muses, the Masses, and the Massey Commission*. Toronto: University of Toronto Press, 1992.

Morton, Desmond. *A Short History of Canada*. 1983. 5th edn. Toronto: McClelland, 2001.

Parker, George L. *The Beginnings of the Book Trade in Canada*. Toronto: University of Toronto Press, 1985.

Tippett, Maria. *Making Culture: English-Canadian Institutions and the Arts before the Massey Commission*. Toronto: University of Toronto Press, 1990.

Studies of particular interest

Aboriginal writing

Armstrong, Jeannette, ed. *Looking at the Words of Our People: First Nations Analysis of Literature*. Penticton: Theytus, 1993.

Brant, Beth. *Writing as Witness*. Toronto: Women's Press, 1994.

Campbell, Maria, ed. *Give Back: First Nations Perspectives on Cultural Practice*. North Vancouver: Gallerie, 1992.

Hoy, Helen. *How Should I Read These? Native Women Writers in Canada*. Toronto: University of Toronto Press, 2001.

King, Thomas, Cheryl Calver, and Helen Hoy, eds. *The Native in Literature*. Montreal: ECW Press, 1987.

LaRocque, Emma. "Here Are Our Voices – Who Will Hear?" Preface. *Writing the Circle: Native Women of Western Canada*. Comp. and ed. Jeanne Perreault and Sylvia Vance. Edmonton: NeWest, 1990. pp. xv–xxx.

Lutz, Hartmut, ed. *Contemporary Challenges: Conversations with Canadian Native Authors*. Saskatoon: Fifth House, 1991.

Petrone, Penny. *Native Literature in Canada: From the Oral Tradition to the Present*. Toronto: Oxford University Press, 1990.

Francophone writing

Beaudoin, Réjean, and André Lamontagne, eds. "Francophone/Anglophone," special issue of *Canadian Literature* 175 (Winter 2002).

Chassay, Jean-François. "La Littérature québécoise sous le regard de l'autre," special issue of *Voix et Images* 24.3 (Spring 1999).

Green, Mary Jean. *Women and Narrative Identity: Rewriting the Quebec National Text*. Montreal: McGill-Queen's University Press, 2001.

Lemire, Maurice, ed. *La vie littéraire au Québec*. Vols. I, II, IV. Sainte-Foy: Presses de l'Université Laval, 1991, 1992, 1999. Vol. III: Lemire with Denis Saint-Jacques, eds. Sainte-Foy: Presses de l'Université Laval, 1996.

Moisan, Clément, and Renate Hildebrand. *Ces étrangers du dedans: une histoire de l'écriture migrante au Québec (1937–1997)*. Quebec: Nota Bene, 2001.

Purdy, Anthony. *A Certain Difficulty of Being: Essays on the Quebec Novel*. Montreal: McGill-Queen's University Press, 1990.

Shek, Ben-Zion. *French-Canadian & Québécois Novels*. Toronto: Oxford University Press, 1991.

Shouldice, Larry, ed. and trans. *Contemporary Quebec Criticism*. Toronto: University of Toronto Press, 1979.

Warwick, Jack. *The Long Journey: Literary Themes of French Canada*. University of Toronto Romance Series. 12. Toronto: University of Toronto Press, 1968.

Exploration and travel

MacLaren, Ian. "Exploration/Travel Literature and the Evolution of the Author." *International Journal of Canadian Studies* 6 (Spring 1992): 39–68.

Rajotte, Pierre, with Anne-Marie Carle, and François Couture. *Le récit de voyage au XIXe siècle: aux frontières du littéraire*. Montreal: Triptyque, 1997.

Ruggles, Richard. *The Hudson's Bay Company and Two Centuries of Mapping, 1670–1870*. Montreal: McGill-Queen's University Press, 1991.

Van Kirk, Sylvia. *Many Tender Lies: Women in Fur Trade Society in Western Canada, 1670–1870*. Winnipeg: Watson, 1980.

Warkentin, Germaine. *Canadian Exploration Literature: An Anthology*. Toronto: Oxford University Press, 1993.

Warkentin, John. *The Western Interior of Canada: A Record of Geographical Discovery*. Toronto: McClelland, 1964.

Nature-writing

Berger, Carl. *Science, God and Nature in Victorian Canada*. Toronto: University of Toronto Press, 1983.

Grady, W. Introduction. *Treasures of the Place: Three Centuries of Nature Writing in Canada*. Ed. Grady. Vancouver: Douglas and McIntyre, 1992. pp. 1–10.

Maclulich, T. D. "Reading the Land: The Wilderness Tradition in Canadian Letters." *Journal of Canadian Studies* 20.2 (Summer 1985): pp. 29–44.

New, W. H. *Land Sliding: Imagining Space, Presence, and Power in Canadian Writing*. Toronto: University of Toronto Press, 1997.

Raglon, Rebecca, and Marion Scholtmeijer. "Canadian Environmental Writing." *The Literature of Nature: An International Sourcebook*. Ed. Patrick D. Murphy. Chicago: Fitzroy Dearborn, 1998. pp. 130–9.

Ricou, Laurie. *The Arbutus/Madrone Files: Reading the Pacific Northwest*. Edmonton: NeWest, 2002.

Drama

Bessai, Diane. *Playwrights of Collective Creation*. Toronto: Simon, 1992.

Brask, Per, ed. *Contemporary Issues in Canadian Drama*. Winnipeg: Blizzard, 1995.

Filewod, Alan. *Collective Encounters: Documentary Theatre in English Canada*. Toronto: University of Toronto Press, 1987.

Glaap, Albert-Reiner, with Rolf Althof, eds. *On-Stage and Off-Stage: English Canadian Drama in Discourse*. St. John's: Breakwater, 1996.

Guthrie, Tyrone, Robertson Davies, and Grant MacDonald. *Renown at Stratford*. 1953. Memorial edn. Toronto: Clarke, 1971.

Johnson, Chris. "B-Movies beyond the Absurd." *Canadian Literature* 85 (Summer 1980): pp. 87–103.

—. *Essays on George F. Walker: Playing with Anxiety*. Winnipeg: Blizzard, 1999.

Knowles, Ric. *The Theatre of Form and the Production of Meaning: Contemporary Canadian Dramaturgies*. Toronto: ECW Press, 1999.

Maufort, Marc, and Franca Bellarsi, eds. *Siting the Other: Re-Visions of Marginality in Australian and English-Canadian Drama*. Brussels: PIE-Peter Lang, 2001.

Rubin, Don, ed. *Canadian Theatre History: Selected Readings*. Toronto: Copp, 1996.

Walker, Craig Stewart. *The Buried Astrolabe: Canadian Dramatic Imagination and Western Tradition*. Montreal: McGill-Queen's University Press, 2001.

Wallace, Robert. *Producing Marginality: Theatre and Criticism in Canada*. Saskatoon: Fifth House, 1990.

Poetry

Bentley, D. M. R. *Mimic Fires: Accounts of Early Long Poems on Canada*. Montreal: McGill-Queen's University Press, 1994.

Brown, E. K. *On Canadian Poetry*. 1943. Rev. edn. Toronto: McClelland, 1977.

—. *Responses and Evaluations: Essays on Canada*. Ed. David Staines. Toronto: McClelland, 1977.

Dudek, Louis, and Michael Gnarowski, eds. *The Making of Modern Poetry in Canada: Essential Articles on Contemporary Canadian Poetry in English*. Toronto: Ryerson, 1967.

Glickman, Susan. *The Picturesque and the Sublime: A Poetics of the Canadian Landscape*. Montreal: McGill-Queen's University Press, 1998.

Higgins, Iain, ed. "Contemporary Poetics," special issue of *Canadian Literature* 155 (Winter 1997).

Livesay, Dorothy. "The Documentary Poem: A Canadian Genre." *Contexts of Canadian Criticism*. Ed. Eli Mandel. Chicago: University of Chicago Press, 1971 pp. 267–81.

Mackay, Don. *Vis-à-vis: Fieldnotes on Poetry and Wilderness*. Wolfville: Gaspereau, 2001.

McNeilly, Kevin, ed. "Women & Poetry," special issue of *Canadian Literature* 166 (Autumn 2000).

Ondaatje, Michael, ed. *The Long Poem Anthology*. Toronto: Coach House, 1979.

Trehearne, Brian. *Aestheticism and the Canadian Modernists: Aspects of a Poetic Influence*. Kingston: McGill-Queen's University Press, 1989.

—. *The Montreal Forties: Modernist Poetry in Translation*. Toronto: University of Toronto Press, 1999.

Fiction and short fiction

Davey, Frank. *Post-National Arguments: The Politics of the Anglophone-Canadian Novel since 1967*. Toronto: University of Toronto Press, 1993.

Dean, Misao, ed. *Early Canadian Short Stories: Short Stories in English before World War I*. Ottawa: Tecumseh, 1999.

Gadpaille, Michelle. *The Canadian Short Story*. Toronto: Oxford University Press, 1988.

Hutcheon, Linda. *The Canadian Postmodern: A Study of Contemporary English-Canadian Fiction*. Toronto: Oxford University Press, 1988.

Kertzer, Jonathan. *Worrying the Nation: Imagining a National Literature in English Canada*. Toronto: University of Toronto Press, 1998.

King, Thomas, ed. *All My Relations: An Anthology of Contemporary Canadian Native Fiction.* Toronto: McClelland, 1990.

Lynch, Gerald. *The One and the Many: English-Canadian Short Story Cycles.* Toronto: University of Toronto Press, 2001.

New, W. H. *Dreams of Speech and Violence: The Art of the Short Story in Canada and New Zealand.* Toronto: University of Toronto Press, 1987.

Rooke, Constance. *Fear of the Open Heart: Essays on Contemporary Canadian Writing.* Toronto: Coach House, 1989.

Vauthier, Simone. *Reverberations: Explorations in the Canadian Short Story.* Concord: Anansi, 1993.

Vautier, Marie. *New World Myth: Postmodernism and Postcolonialism in Canadian Fiction.* Montreal: McGill-Queen's University Press, 1998.

Women writers

Atwood, Margaret. *Strange Things: The Malevolent North in Canadian Literature.* Oxford: Clarendon, 1995.

—. *Negotiating with the Dead: A Writer on Writing.* Cambridge: Cambridge University Press, 2002.

Gerson, Carole. *Canada's Early Women Writers: Texts in English to 1859.* Ottawa: Canadian Research Institute for the Advancement of Women, 1994.

Hoy, Helen. *How Should I Read These? Native Women Writers in Canada.* Toronto: University of Toronto Press, 2001.

Irvine, Lorna. *Sub/Version: Canadian Fictions by Women.* Toronto: ECW Press, 1986.

Much, Rita, ed. *Women on the Canadian Stage: The Legacy of Hrotsvit.* Winnipeg: Blizzard, 1992.

Mukherjee, Arun. *Postcolonialism: My Living.* Toronto: TSAR, 1998.

Neuman, Shirley, and Smaro Kamboureli, eds. *A Mazing Space: Writing Canadian, Women Writing.* Edmonton: Longspoon/NeWest, 1987.

Rimstead, Roxanne. *Remnants of a Nation: On Poverty Narratives by Women.* Toronto: University of Toronto Press, 2001.

Scheier, Libby, Sarah Sheard, and Eleanor Wachtel, eds. *Language in Her Eye: Writing and Gender.* Toronto: Coach House, 1990.

Shields, Carol, and Marjorie Anderson, eds. *Dropped Threads: What We Aren't Told.* Toronto: Vintage Canada, 2001.

Smart, Patricia. *Writing in the Father's House: The Emergence of the Feminine in the Quebec Literary Tradition.* Toronto: University of Toronto Press, 1991. Trans. of *Ecrire dans la maison du père: l'émergence du féminine dans la tradition littéraire du Québec.* Montreal: Québec/Amérique, 1988.

Zimmerman, Cynthia. *Playwriting Women: Female Voices in English Canada.* Toronto: Simon, 1994.

Life writing

Buss, Helen M. *Mapping Our Selves: Canadian Women's Autobiography in English.* Montreal: McGill-Queen's University Press, 1993.

Egan, Susanna. *Mirror Talk: Genres of Crisis in Contemporary Autobiography.* Chapel Hill: University of North Carolina Press, 1999.

Egan, Susanna, and Gabriele Helms, eds. "Autobiography and Changing Identities," special issue of *biography* 24.2 (2001).

—, eds. "Auto/biography," special issue of *Canadian Literature* 172 (Spring 2002).

Kadar, Marlene, ed. *Essays on Life Writing: From Genre to Critical Practice*. Toronto: University of Toronto Press, 1992.

Neuman, Shirley, ed. "Reading Canadian Autobiography," special issue of *Essays on Canadian Writing* 60 (1996).

Regionalism and urbanism

Beeler, Karin, and Dee Horne, eds. *Diverse Landscapes: Re-Reading Place across Cultures in Contemporary Canadian Writing*. Prince George: University of Northern British Columbia Press, 1996.

Jordan, David M. *New World Regionalism: Literature in the Americas*. Toronto: University of Toronto Press, 1994.

Keith, W. J. *Canadian Literature in English*. London: Longman, 1985.

Riegel, Christian, and Herb Wyile, eds. *A Sense of Place: Re-Evaluating Regionalism in Canadian and American Writing*. Edmonton: University of Alberta Press, 1997.

Multiculturalism

Bissoondath, Neil. *Selling Illusions: The Cult of Multiculturalism in Canada*. 1994. Rev. edn. Toronto: Penguin, 2002.

Hutcheon, Linda, and Marion Richmond, eds. *Other Solitudes: Canadian Multicultural Fictions*. Toronto: Oxford University Press, 1990.

Kamboureli, Smaro, ed. *Making a Difference: Canadian Multicultural Literature*. Toronto: Oxford University Press, 1996.

—. *Scandalous Bodies: Diasporic Literature in English Canada*. Toronto: Oxford University Press, 1999.

Siemerling, Winfried. *Writing Ethnicity: Cross-Cultural Consciousness in Canadian and Québécois Literature*. Toronto: ECW Press, 1996.

Literary criticism

Allard, Jacques. *Traverses de la critique littéraire au Québec*. Montreal: Boréal, 1991.

Atwood, Margaret. *Second Words: Selected Critical Prose*. Toronto: Anansi, 1982.

Ballstadt, Carl, ed. *The Search for English-Canadian Literature: An Anthology of Critical Articles from the Nineteenth and Early Twentieth Centuries*. Toronto: University of Toronto Press, 1975.

Brydon, Diana, ed. "Testing the Limits: Postcolonial Theories and Canadian Literature," special issue of *Essays on Canadian Writing* 56 (1995).

Clarke, George Elliott. *Odysseys Home: Mapping African-Canadian Literature*. Toronto: University of Toronto Press, 2002.

Davey, Frank. "Canadian Theory and Criticism: English." *The Johns Hopkins Guide to Literary Theory and Criticism*. Ed. Michael Groden and Martin Kreiswirth. Baltimore: Johns Hopkins University Press, 1994. pp. 131–4.

Daymond, Douglas, and Leslie Monkman, eds. *Towards a Canadian Literature: Essays, Editorials, Manifestoes*. Ottawa: Tecumseh, 1984.

Dickinson, Peter. *Here Is Queer: Nationalisms, Sexualities, and the Literature of Canada.* Toronto: University of Toronto Press, 1999.

Frye, Northrop. *The Bush Garden: Essays on the Canadian Imagination.* Toronto: Anansi, 1971.

Gerson, Carole. *A Purer Taste: The Writing and Reading of Fiction in English in Nineteenth-Century Canada.* Toronto: University of Toronto Press, 1989.

Heble, Ajay, Donna Palmateer Pennee, and J. R. (Tim) Struthers, eds. *New Contexts of Canadian Criticism.* Peterborough: Broadview, 1997.

Hutcheon, Linda. *Narcissistic Narrative: The Metafictional Paradox.* 1980. London: Methuen, 1984.

Moss, Laura, ed. *Is Canada Postcolonial? Unsettling Canadian Literature.* Waterloo: Wilfrid Laurier University Press, 2003.

Purdy, Anthony. "Canadian Literature and Criticism: French." *The Johns Hopkins Guide to Literary Theory and Criticism.* Ed. Michael Groden and Martin Kreiswirth. Baltimore: Johns Hopkins University Press, 1994, pp. 134–8.

Robert, Lucie. *L'institution du littéraire au Québec.* Quebec: Presses de l'Université Laval, 1989.

Simon, Sherry, and Paul St.-Pierre, eds. *Changing the Terms: Translating in the Postcolonial Era.* Ottawa: University of Ottawa Press, 2000.

Verduyn, Christl, ed. *Literary Pluralities.* Peterborough: Broadview, 1998.

Journals and magazines

American Review of Canadian Studies (1973–); <http://www.acsus.org>

British Journal of Canadian Studies (1986–); <http://www.canadian-studies.net>

Canadian Ethnic Studies/Etudes Ethniques au Canada (1969–); <http://www.ss.ucalgary.ca/ces/>

Canadian Journal of Native Studies/Revue Canadienne des Etudes Autochtones (1981–); <http://www.brandonu.ca/Library/CJNS/>

Canadian Literature (1959–); <http://www.canlit.ca>

Canadian Poetry (1977–); <http://www.arts.uwo.ca/canpoetry/>

Canadian Theatre Review (1974–); <http://www.utpjournals.com>

Essays in Theatre / Etudes Théâtrales (1982–)

Essays on Canadian Writing (1974–); <http://www.ecw.ca>

Etudes Littéraires (1968–); <http://www.fl.ulaval.ca/lit/et-litt/>

International Journal of Canadian Studies / Revue Internationale d'Études Canadiennes (1990–); <http://www.iccs-ciec.ca>

Journal of Canadian Poetry (1978–81; 1984–); <http://www.borealispress.com>

Journal of Canadian Studies/ Revue d'Etudes Canadiennes (1966–); <http://www.trentu.ca/jcs/>

Lettres Québécoises (1976–)

Studies in Canadian Literature (1976–); <http://www.lib.unb.ca/Texts/SCL/>

The En'owkin Journal of First North American Peoples (1990–)

Theatre Research in Canada / Recherches Théâtrales au Canada (1980–); <http://www.lib.unb.ca/Texts/TRIC/>

Voix et Images (1967–); <http://www.er.uqam.ca/nobel/vimages/>

Zeitschrift für Kanada-Studien (1981–); <http://www.kanada-studien.de>

CAMBRIDGE COMPANIONS TO LITERATURE